To Amy + Andy

I hope that you enjoy reading through my book - Thanks -

Michael

THE HISTORY OF TRANSPORTATION IN NEW JERSEY

From Indian Trails to High Speed Rails

By

Michael E. Ferlise

This book is a work of non-fiction. Names and places have been changed to protect the privacy of all individuals. The events and situations are true.

ISBN: 1-4033-7450-3 (e-book)
ISBN: 1-4033-7451-1 (Paperback)

Library of Congress Control Number: 2002095174

This book is printed on acid free paper.

Printed in the United States of America
Bloomington, IN

1stBooks - rev. 11/14/03

For Michelle, Ivy, and Holly

INTRODUCTION

To begin with, I am not a professional writer, nor have I ever worked for any railroad. I'm simply a 31 year old New Jersey State Parole Officer who loves history and enjoys writing as a hobby. I grew up in Union County's New Providence where I was exposed to Conrail, Amtrak, and NJ Transit through my father who is still a conductor for NJT. I graduated from New Providence High School in 1989 after which I attended Kean College (now a university) in nearby Union Township. I graduated from Kean in 1994, and became a NJ State Parole Officer in May of 1997. I am assigned to a caseload that covers Union County and work out of Elizabeth. I got married in 1999 and moved out to Basking Ridge in Somerset County.

I have noticed that when people outside of New Jersey think of the Garden State it's usually the Turnpike that comes to mind first. Our state is more than just highways, oil refineries, and industries. Our state is one of mountains, lakes, rivers, and parks. You can swim at the Jersey Shore, gamble in Atlantic City, ski in the mountains, or canoe on the Delaware River. From High Point to Cape May there are hundreds of points of historical interest. Much of this gets lost to the rest of the U.S. as we're between New York City and Philadelphia. This also applies to Garden State residents though who have either a New York or Philadelphia orientation. We listen to their radio stations, watch their T.V. news shows, and root for their teams. It's no wonder many of the residents in N.J. have a bit of an identity crisis.

Nearly everyone in the country is aware of the Apache Indians, yet most N.J. residents can't even name the native inhabitants who used to live here. Every child can talk a little about George Washington and Valley Forge or Yorktown, but at the same time can't discuss Morristown or Middlebrook. Yet Washington spent more time in Somerset County during the Revolutionary War than anywhere else. Our state today with all of its place names still has a heavy influence from the Lenape, Dutch, and English. A lifelong Newark resident probably can't say what Newark or Essex means while someone 3,000 miles away in England can. Thousands of people here probably can't even say where the New Jersey in N.J. Transit even comes from. With this book I have decided to change that by including as much information as possible. I started off with a "place name" book on the state, but noticed that almost every town or city had something that involved transportation in one form or another.

I intended to begin this book around the 1820's with the Morris Canal, but began to work backwards. I had to include steam boats, stage vehicles, and even the Lenape with their footpaths our modern roads still follow. If you mention the Lenape though, the Dutch and English settlers who followed must be included. The old Lenape paths were made into wider roads for stage wagons while canoes gave way to sail ferries.

The second chapter on N.J. and its importance in the American Revolution was longer than I first planned. With the patriotism after September 11, 2001, I was inspired to add a little more. Washington's simple retreat down Route 27 and the ensuing Battle of Trenton literally changed the history of the world. For context, I also included other events of this time outside of New Jersey.

The third chapter reflects a change from sail or rope ferries on the Hudson and Delaware Rivers to steam powered ferries. People now traveled across New Jersey between New York City and Philadelphia on comfortable stagecoaches. The roads across the state were slightly improved, but now these "turnpikes" required tolls. In order to move more goods across the state, the canal idea came to the forefront in the form of the Morris and Essex Canal.

In the fourth chapter I focused on N.J.'s early railroads, but included those in other states like New York or Pennsylvania because they later came into New Jersey. I also mentioned our second canal aka the Delaware and Raritan Canal which began to bring goods across the state. NJ Transit can trace its roots back to this time with the M & E, New Jersey, Camden and Amboy, or Elizabethtown and Somerville Railroads. With more railroads as competition there were fewer stagecoaches while turnpikes went out of business.

In the fifth chapter, the railroad names become more recognizable with the Central, Lackawanna, Erie, and Pennsylvania Railroads. Their steam locomotives that once burned wood now ran on coal which became "king" everywhere. The two N.J. canals still brought coal eastward, but their use declined due to the railroads in the state. In Jersey City alone there were three large railroad terminals on the Hudson River. The Central had theirs at Communipaw (Liberty State Park), the Erie built theirs at Pavonia, while the PRR brought its passengers to Exchange Place. NJT commuters who ride into Hoboken are well aware of the Lackawanna Terminal here still in use today.

With the next chapter, the H & M (today's PATH) starts bringing passengers underneath the Hudson River between N.J. and Manhattan. Trolleys officially put old stagecoaches to rest although with petroleum came motor vehicles. The PRR soon had electric locomotives as did the Lackawanna. Along with cars, trucks, and buses came bridges, tunnels, and highways. This chapter goes into World War II where the railroads that cut across the New Jersey were at their peak.

The final chapter picks up after World War II as motor vehicles, planes, and other problems led to a decline in both ferries and trolleys. Railroads began to lose money and the CNJ, Erie, NYC, and PRR abandoned their Hudson River terminals in N.J. To save themselves some of these roads merged into newer ones like the Penn Central (PRR and NY Central) or the Erie-Lackawanna. Eventually these all go bankrupt and Amtrak, Conrail, and NJ Transit take over things in N.J. There is even a rebirth in ferries on the Hudson River although the events of September 11th put a damper on everything. This final chapter follows local events up until August of 2003.

I'd like to thank my entire family including my friends, neighbors, and co-workers. A special thank you also goes out to both the New Providence and Cranford Historical Societies. I would also like to extend a special thanks to 1st Books Library for getting this book published. A thank you goes out to N.J. Transit as well as to Bill Bilarczyk for the Penn Central Items. A sincere thank you to Chris Chirone for all his time and work on the cover.

CHAPTER ONE

The Lenape, Dutch, and English
In Early New Jersey

There were several places where I could have started this book from and decided on the Lenape Indians. New Jersey's first inhabitants were here somewhere between 6,000 and 10,000 years ago. Some sources say they came from Canada in search of a warmer climate while others point to an origin from across the Mississippi River. The name "Lenape" has several translations to "Original People," "Our Men," "Men of the Same Nation," and "Male of Our Kind." In N.J. there were three main sub-tribes with the Minsi to the north, the Unalatchtigo in the south, and the Unami in between. Each had its own sachem or chief and was further divided into several sub-tribes under other minor chiefs. They called New Jersey "Scheyichbi" which meant "Land Along the Water." For food, the Lenape spent their time hunting, fishing, gathering, and farming. They grew maize, squash, beans, pumpkins, and even tobacco. In addition to cultivated vegetables, the Lenape foraged for herbs, nuts, roots, and berries. The woods here were filled with animals like deer, beavers, foxes, raccoons, and even bears which were used for food as well as clothing.

The Lenape had an extensive series of footpaths which were used to walk around the area. Many of our modern roads we drive along today still follow these paths and include but are not limited to, Routes 10, 22, 27, 29, 31, 202, and 206. The Minisink Trail for instance started on the Delaware River in Sussex County and ran past Lake Hopatcong to Dover, down to Morristown, through Chatham (Main St.) and into Short Hills. From here a portion followed the Rahway River through Cranford, Westfield, Metuchen, New Brunswick, and Matawan to the ocean. Of course, there were other branches of the Minisink Trail with a path from Whippany to Newark. Another portion ran from the Short Hills out to the Somerset Hills. Still another trail ran from the Short Hills to Elizabeth where it continued down through Linden, Rahway, Woodbridge, and further south where it ran to the Atlantic Ocean.

When New Jersey residents think of rivers, the Hudson, Delaware, Hackensack, Passaic, Raritan, and Manasquan come to mind as a start. Credit for the first form of water transportation in New Jersey goes to the Lenape who used birch bark and dugout canoes to travel our state's rivers and lakes. Their dugout canoes made from entire elm and oak trees were large enough for several dozen Lenape.

Today in modern New Jersey a lot of the names we use are European versions which were derived directly from the Lenape's words for these areas. The Lenape didn't write or have an alphabet and over time their place names were "Americanized." I have included a small list of some of these for the reader although the spellings and meanings are not completely 100% accurate.

ABSEGAMI "Little Sea Water"
ACQUACKANOCK "Place in the Rapid Stream Where the Nets are Set"
ASSUNPINK "A Rocky Place That Is Watery"
AWIEHAWKEN, AWIEHAKEN, WIEHACKEN which was a stream's name which became Weehawken.
COMMUNIPAW "Landing Place From the Side of the River"
HACKENSACK "Stream that Unites With Another On Level Ground"
HOBOCAN HACKING "Land of the Tobacco Pipe" which changed to Hoboquin and Hoboken.
HO HO KUS "Tall Cedars" or "Cleft in the Rocks"
HOPATCONG "Honey Water of Many Coves"

KITTATINY "Chief Town"
LACKAWANICK, LACKAWANECK, LACKAWANNUCK, LACKAWANNY, and LACKAWANNA "Stream That Forks" or "The Forks of a Stream"
LELATAN "Forked River" This Lenape name later became Raritan.
LOPATCONG "Winter Water Place for Deer"
MAGAGKAMACK "Pumpkin Field" This area is known today as Port Jervis.
MAHWAH "Beautiful"
MANAHAWKIN "Good Corn Land"
MANALAPAN "Good Country Producing Good Bread"
MANATASQUAWHAN "Stream of the Island for Squaws"
MUSCONETCONG "Big Bass" or "Big Pike"
OMPAGE "Large Level Ground" Evolved to Emboyle, Amboyle, and Ambo into Amboy.
PARSIPPONG "Place Where the Stream or River Moves Through the Valley" or PARSIPPANY
PASSAIC, FISHAWACK, PISHAWACK, PASAWICKE, PASSAYA, PASAYACK, PISHAWACK, PESIAK, PESAICK… "Peace" or Place (or Valley) Where the Land (or River) Splits'.
PAUPOCK "Quail" This name was later changed to today's Peapack.
PEQUANNOC or PEQUANNOCK "Cleared Ground"
PICATINNY "Peak With Broken Rocks or Cliffs"
RAHWACK Rahway is derived from this Lenape Chief's name.
ROCKAWACK or ROCKAWAY "Running out of a Deep Gorge" or "Sandy place"
SECAUCUS "Land Where the Snake Hides"
SISQUEHANNA "Muddy River"
SUCCASUNNA "Black Stone"
TOTAWA "Heavy Falling Weight of Waters"
WACH UNKS or WATCHUNG "High Hills"
WIPPANONG "Place of the Willows"

I thought it was nice to include this list as railroaders thousands of years later still use names like Hoboken, Communipaw, Lackawanna, Hackensack, or Raritan. An interesting side note is that the Lenape Indians are sometimes referred to as the Delaware Indians. This actually is not a Lenape name as it honors Thomas West from England, the Third Baron De La Warr. Lord Delaware (1577-1618) prior to his death was appointed the Royal Governor of Virginia. The state, New Jersey's longest river, the D & R Canal, and the D L & W Railroad all honor Lord Delaware.

In 1497 Giovanni Caboto or John Cabot left England with patent letters that King Henry VII gave him to discover new lands in his name. On his second attempt across the uncharted Atlantic Ocean, Cabot reached New Jersey's coast and claimed it for England. He was followed by Giovanni de Verrazano who anchored off Sandy Hook in 1524. He was sent across the Atlantic Ocean by King Francis I of France and in turn named the area New France.

In April of 1609, an Englishman named Henry Hudson in the employ of the Dutch East Indian Company left Holland on his third attempt to find a "Northwest Passage" to Asia. In August, he reached Virginia's coast and sailed to the north. He ventured into the Delaware

Bay, saw what he named the South River and turned around. He continued up the coast and anchored off Sandy Hook. He made contact with the Lenape, but relations soon turned bad and John Coleman died with an arrow in his throat. He explored what he named the North River (today's Hudson) for a few weeks after which he returned to Europe before December. By 1614 the Dutch had an outpost set up on Lower Manhattan Island to trade furs with the Lenape. In 1621 the Dutch West Indian Company was chartered to get things going in the New World. In 1626 Peter Minuit bought Manhattan Island from Chief Tammanend for 60 guilders or $24.00. There were a few hundred residents in New Amsterdam within several years. In the rest of the New Netherlands colony across Hudson's River though there were only a few people if that. To get people to settle across from New Amsterdam a patroon system was set up by the Dutch West Indian Company. With this, large parcels of land were given to people who in turn had to settle a certain amount of people within several years. Michiel Pauw obtained land from the Lenape which they called Hobocan Hacking along with Ahismus to the south (Jersey City). Pauw didn't come over in person, but this area of N.J. started off with his name in the form of Pavonia. Pavo was Latin for Pauw and Pauw was Dutch for peacock. So Pavonia translated to "Land of the Peacock." He failed to settle 50 people in 4 years and the land returned to the Company.

To get around Hudson's River, the Dutch used skiffs and sloops which were like rowboats that could be sailed if there was a breeze. Periaugas were larger with a mast at both ends so it could travel in either direction. Both ends were rounded and the steering was done with a large oar. Early periaugas carried cattle, sheep, barrels of goods, and passengers. They weren't large enough for the two and four wheeled carts the Dutch used on land. In N.J., the Dutch introduced horses and oxen who hauled the carts. The Dutch followed the Lenape's paths which then became cart paths. In the 1640's Dutch settlers from Esopus (Kingston, N.Y.) followed a trail into the Kittatinny Mountains. In the Delaware Water Gap area they found a spot where the Lenape gathered copper from the ground. After the Dutch realized this they started the first copper mine in the U.S. To get the copper ore from the Pahaquarry Copper Mine to Esopus, the Dutch built the first major length road in all of North America. The copper ore was hauled over the Old Mine Road (through modern Warren and Sussex Counties) in carts pulled by oxen for the 140 mile trip to Esopus. From here it was floated down Hudson's River to Manhattan for shipment to Holland. They could have used the Delaware or South River, but didn't think to try it.

Relations with the Lenape soon turned sour though and Pavonia was destroyed in two separate wars in the 1640's and 50's. Peace followed and settlers were once again at Pavonia. As per Director Peter Stuyvesant, the residents had to place their dwellings within a stockade. The Village of Bergen built on "the heights" above Communipaw Bay was New Jersey's first town. New Jersey's first organized government, school, and church were in this little hamlet named after the Dutch word for hill. It was built in Jersey City where Bergen Square stands today. When the Lenape left the walls around the village were torn down.

With all the small watercraft on the waters around the area, it wasn't until 1661 that the first commercial ferry service started on the Hudson River. Jensen's Ferry ran from Communipaw Bay to New Amsterdam with large periaugas. Back then though the land where Liberty State Park is did not exist. Prior to this area being filled in later by the CRRNJ, Communipaw Bay or Cove was located here. The original shoreline was about a mile inland where Phillip Drive is in Jersey City.

In March of 1664, King Charles Ii of England gave his brother James the Duke of York all the land between the Connecticut and Delaware Rivers. The Dutch were here, but the English claim was based on John Cabot's 1497 voyage. The Duke of York appointed Colonel Richard Nicholls as his deputy and sent him across the Atlantic Ocean to New Amsterdam. In June of 1664 as Nicholls was out at sea, James gave his land to two friends Lord John Berkeley and Sir George Carteret. As Carteret was from the Isle of Jersey, they named the area Nova Caesarea or New Jersey. A distant relative of Sir George named Phillip Carteret was appointed governor and sent across the Atlantic Ocean.

In September of 1664, Colonel Nicholls arrived outside of New Amsterdam with four ships. He forced the Dutch Governor, Peter Stuyvesant to surrender New Amsterdam which he renamed New York in honor of James. James's Scottish title was "Duke of Albany" which led to the land to the west of New York being named New Albania. Colonel Nicholls was approached by several people from what was then The Long Island who wanted to settle in this New Albania. The settlers purchased the land along what they called Achter Kull from where Newark Bay is at the mouth of the Passaic River to the Raritan River. The tract of land purchased from the Lenape ran from the Raritan to the Passaic and 34 miles inland. This settlement first called Achter Kull consisted of all modern Union County with some of Essex, Middlesex, Morris, and Somerset. Governor Phillip Carteret arrived in mid-1665. He renamed the settlement Elizabethtown in honor of Sir George's wife Elizabeth. This was New Jersey's second settlement, but the first English speaking one. Elizabethtown was New Jersey's first capital as well as the place where both church and school were held in English.

The next year Puritans from Connecticut purchased a tract of land above Elizabethtown from the Lenape. This parcel ran from the Passaic River towards the Watchung Mountains. First called New Milford, the name was later changed to Newark Town as their religious leader back in Connecticut was from Newark On Trent in England. Afterwards, other towns followed like Woodbridge, Piscataway, Middletown, and Shrewsbury. As the 1670's got underway, early sail ferries were leaving Elizabethtown Point where Elizabeth Avenue ends for New York via the Kill Van Kull.

To the southwest a small group of Quakers from England settled on the Delaware River in 1677. The next year more Quakers came from Yorkshire to this settlement named Burlington for an English village. Lord John Berkeley's half of New Jersey was soon sold to John Fenwick. He bought it for a Quaker named Edward Byllynge with credit problems. The matter went to arbitration under William Penn. Fenwick named the area he bought Salem after the Hebrew work Shalom for peace. Penn ruled that Fenwick could keep only 10% while Byllynge got the other 90%. With Byllynge's debt problem this land was held in trust under William Penn and other Quakers.

Sir George Carteret still had his half of New Jersey to the northeast which resulted in problems with the Quakers. New Jersey was then split into two colonies of east and west. The 1676 boundary ran from Little Egg Harbor above Atlantic City to the Delaware Water Gap area. Anyway Sir George Carteret died in 1681 which led to East New Jersey being put up for auction. Modern Ocean, Monmouth, Middlesex, Union, Essex, Hudson, Passaic, Bergen, and some of Somerset Counties were purchased by William Penn and twenty-three other "proprietors." In the mid 1680's the Earl of Perth bought into East New Jersey. He then allowed several hundred persecuted Scots to immigrate to East New Jersey. They settled above the mouth of the Raritan River at Amboy Point. By 1686 Perth Amboy was the new capital of East New Jersey. Down in West New Jersey the capital was Burlington. To facilitate communication between the two capitals, some old Lenape footpaths were widened. In the late 1860's, John Inian lived in modern New Brunswick which then was called Prigmore's Swamp. He started a ferry across the Raritan River here as the area became known as Inian's Ferry. On the Delaware River, Henry Baker, who lived in Pennsylvania where Makefield Township is, also had a ferry. Early ferries like these consisted of two dugout canoes with planks across them for passengers or a horse which were poled across the water. To get between the two capitals, the Upper Road could be taken from Inian's Ferry through Stony Brook (Princeton) to where Trenton is. The second way was via the Lower Road between South Amboy to Burlington via Cranbury. In the 1680's William Royden had a license for a ferry between New Jersey and Philadelphia. William Cooper purchased this ferry which gave the area where modern Camden is the name of Cooper's Ferry.

Due to problems over land rights and property claims between the proprietors and settlers, New Jersey became a single English royal colony. While there was a royal governor the assembly still alternated between Perth Amboy and Burlington.

In 1711, Samuel Bayard purchased Weehawken, Hobocan, and other tracts in what was then old Bergen County. He operated an informal ferry between Weehawken and New York City.

At around the same time, but on the Delaware River, Thomas Yeardley also started a ferry between Pennsylvania and New Jersey. He inherited the land from his uncle William where the Borough of Yardley is today. In order to handle the increased traffic, the ferry boats used on the Delaware River were now larger. These scows were flatboats with hinged ends that could be lowered like ramps. With the ends lowered a couple of horses or oxen with a wagonload of hay, barrels, or other goods simply walked onto the scow. These flatboats were about 20 feet long and 10 feet wide. At both shores of the Delaware River was a tree made into a post with a slack rope draped in between. The scow also had a rope which ran to a sliding metal ring on the line above. This helped the person who poled the scow across the Delaware as he no longer had to battle the current.

An interesting side note is that at this time Burlington County included modern Burlington, Hunterdon, Morris, Sussex, Warren, and some of Mercer. I'm sure that many settlers complained about the long journey to the town of Burlington which was the county seat.

By 1711, settlers from Elizabethtown had traveled down the Lenape trails to Succasunna or "Place of the Black Stone." The Lenape gave this area the name because these black stones were everywhere on the ground. The settlers realized these rocks were actually iron ore. While it could simply be picked up from the ground, they started iron mines to extract more from below ground. Furnaces made from stones about thirty feet high were built near hillsides. For fuel, a large number of trees were cut down and burnt to create charcoal. The furnace was somewhat like a large chimney. The iron ore and charcoal was dumped through the opening at the top. The furnace was fired with the heat increased by one or more bellows powered by waterwheels in a nearby stream. When the temperature got hot enough the iron ore melted. The actual iron is heavier that the other components and worked its way to the bottom while the waste floated on top. The molten iron was drained from the furnace where it ran into molds. From here the iron went to the local forge where it was heated once again. It was pounded with hammers until it ended up in the shape of long curved bars. At the forge, the iron was also worked into a variety of tools and other implements. From

Succasunna the curved bars left on horseback where they were taken to Newark or Elizabethtown. Here they were either turned into tools or shipped over to New York.

In 1713 Hunterdon County left Burlington and also took modern Morris, Sussex, and Warren.

In 1719 a New York merchant named Arent Schuyler purchased a tract of land in what was then called New Barbadoes Neck. Today this is East Newark, Harrison, Kearny, Lyndhurst, North Arlington, and some of Rutherford. Schuyler's plot of land was where Arlington and North Arlington are today. A slave found some copper on the property which led Schuyler to start a copper mine just above Arlington Cemetery.

As the 1720's started, the iron industry in the Succasunna area in what was then Hunterdon County had increased. In modern Dover for instance, then named "Old Tye," John Jackson had an iron mine and a forge. Along with the iron furnace and forge came sawmills, grist mills, cider mills, blacksmith shops, and stores. As more and more houses were built small towns developed around the local iron industry.

During the 1720's the old Queen's Highway named in honor of England's Queen Anne was widened and improved. Of course with King George I on the throne since 1714 it was now referred to as The King's Highway. It ran from Bergen Town above Communipaw Bay to the south via modern Bergen Avenue. It continued south through Minkakwa (Greenville), into Pamrapo (Bayonne between the 50's and 30's), down along the Newark Bay to Bergen Point on the Kill Van Kull. After a ferry ride, the next section started in Elizabethtown on the Arthur Kill where Elizabethtown Avenue ends. From here it ran across The Broad Street in Elizabethtown and followed The Old Dutch Road. Today this section follows St. George's Avenue through Linden and Rahway. In Woodbridge it went southwest along Route 27 into New Brunswick via Inian's Ferry. Once across the Raritan River it went through Kingston, Prince Town, and into Trent's Town on the Delaware River. Trent's Town was named in honor of William Trent. He was a wealthy merchant from Philadelphia who owned a large amount of land in the area. Trent, who died in 1724 was also New Jersey's first Chief Justice. His son James started a ferry across the Delaware to take advantage of the increased traffic on the King's Highway. The origin of the road goes back to the Lenape who used it to walk between the Delaware River and the Arthur Kill.

During the 1720's on the Pennsylvania side of the Delaware River John Wells started a ferry service. Back then New Hope in Pennsylvania was referred to as Well's Ferry. Up the Delaware River a bit, but on the New Jersey side, John Reading also had a ferry. On the other side of New Jersey there was a ferry service to Staten Island via the Arthur Kill. Peter Tremley had a ferry from the family property of Tremley point in modern Linden. There was another ferry between Bergen Point and Elizabethtown via the Kill Van Kull.

In the early 1730's Solomon Smith and James Moon started the first public transportation service in the United States to run on a regular basis They had a couple of stage wagons that ran once a week between Perth Amboy and Burlington. By this time in modern Lambertville, Emanuel Coryell established a ferry across the Delaware River. His ferry was opposite from Well's Ferry in Pennsylvania.

Back in 1733, England's King George II granted a charter for the Pavonia Ferry Company to operate on the Hudson River between New Jersey and New York City. One of the drawbacks to New Jersey's larger counties was the long walk or ride to county seat to conduct business. In 1739 Morris County was created from Hunterdon and included Sussex and Warren. At the same time of course Morris Town became the county seat. Ever since the 1700's started both New York and New Jersey shared the same royal governor. New Jersey though finally had its own when Royal Governor Lewis Morris was appointed in 1738. With more settlers from Newark and Elizabethtown moving out west to this area, the old Lenape Minisink Trail was widened. By now, small groups of settlers lived in the Spring Fields, Minisink Crossing (Chatham), and Watnong Plains (Morris Plains). People lived in an area called "Turkey" due to all the wild birds where New Providence, Summit, and Berkeley Heights are today. On the other side of what was then Essex County other Elizabethtown settlers followed a Lenape trail into the fields to the west. This trail was where North and South Avenues are today through Cranford and Westfield. The West Fields were a large area that included all or some of Clark, Fanwood, Scotch Plains, Garwood, Rahway, Cranford, Mountainside, Westfield, and Piscataway. They met with other Scottish settlers from Perth Amboy who had already followed a Lenape trail up to the Plain Fields and Scot's Plain below the Watchung Mountains. These people in turn ventured on another trail through a gap in the Watchungs (Somerset Street) to the Watchung and Warren Township area. They were in turn joined by people from Turkey (New Providence) who followed the Passaic River to here. This is just one area of New Jersey that was developed as residents followed the same system of trails created by the Lenape.

Princeton University, as we know it, started back in 1746 when the College of New Jersey was chartered and classes began in Elizabethtown. By 1748 the College of New Jersey had moved with its eight students to Newark. In 1750 though the trustees wanted a bond of £1,000, ten cleared acres, and 200 wooded acres to which Newark, Elizabethtown, and New Brunswick didn't respond. Princeton did which resulted in the College of New Jersey relocating to there in the mid 1750's. Nassau Hall, where classed were held at the time was the largest building in America.

By this time in Pennsylvania, near Easton, Robert Durham had an iron furnace. In order to get his iron down the Delaware River to Philadelphia, the so named Durham boats were used. They were made from wood and some were nearly seventy feet long and eight feet wide. They were poled, rowed with twenty foot long oars, and steered with a large rudder. Iron was brought down to Philadelphia and food along with other supplies were brought back up.

In Bordentown, Joseph Borden started some stage wagon runs on the New York City to Philadelphia route. These early stage wagons were just farm wagons with small sides that had curved hoops over the top covered with canvas. Stage wagons like these in New Jersey were nothing like the stagecoaches that came later. There were several wooden planks inside which served as seats. Two or three passengers could sit on each of these uncushioned seats that had no seatbacks. These wagons had no springs or suspension and were pulled by either two or four horses. While there were roads in New Jersey none of them were paved yet. These dirt roads were covered with holes, rocks, roots, and even downed trees. During the winter they would have been frozen and rutted. When everything was dry the passengers got covered with dirt and dust. After it rained the roads turned to nothing but mud. In the summertime heat the stage wagons were swarmed by mosquitoes. Besides the elements there were also accidents. A driver might have lost control while going downhill, a wheel might fall off, a horse could break loose, and that was just a start. Stage wagons going too fast could run off the road and crash into trees, streams, or ditches. They sometimes overturned, crashed into other wagons, and even ran into pedestrians and animals.

A farmer in New Jersey at the time traveled on either a farm horse or his own wagon. A wealthy person rode across the area on one of probably several Arabian style horses. Someone with little or no money simply walked around New Jersey. The freight of the day was moved in large Conestoga wagons. Conestogas were similar to the wagons the pioneers later used to go out west. With wheels that were six feet in diameter, they were pulled by four or six horses. With the horses attached the total length might have been nearly sixty feet which led to new larger ferries on the Delaware River.

On the Hudson River prior to this time there were always informal ferries between New Jersey and New York. I'm sure that there were dozens of people who owned watercraft that were used to ferry goods and people across the Hudson. England's King George II did grant a charter to Stephen Bayard for a ferry from Weehawken to New York City. In New Jersey, the ferry landing was near to where the Amtrak tunnels run under Weehawken. From Weehawken, Bayard's periaugas ran to the area of Manhattan where Vesey Street is.

In the early 1760's, a formal ferry started from Paulus Hook Island to New York City. At the time Paulus Hook was located just below today's Exchange Place in Jersey City. It was separated from what was then Harsimus Island (the Grove Street area) by a tidal marsh. Paulus Hook's outline was roughly Hudson, Essex, Van Vorst, and Montgomery Streets. From here, Cornelius Van Vorst had some flatboats he used to carry wagons and horses while several small boats ferried people back and forth. He also built a small wooden bridge to Harsimus Island where Newark Avenue is today.

Down on the Delaware River, John Coryell assumed control over Well's Ferry on the Pennsylvania side. The ferry landings on both sides of the Delaware River (Lambertville and New Hope) were called Coryell's Ferry.

During 1764 in New Jersey, The York Road opened up for vehicles like stage wagons. This east to west road that ran between Elizabethtown and Philadelphia via Coryell's Ferry (Lambertville) is known today as The Old York Road. It ran from Elizabethtown (Elizabeth Avenue) to the Westfields pretty much via Route 28. In Scotch Plains it ran past the tavern at Park Avenue and Front Street where it continued through Plainfield, Bound Brook, and Bridgewater where Somerville is. From here it ran to Readington, Centerville, Three Bridges, and Reaville via Route 613. It continued through Larison's Corner in modern East Amwell Township and into Ringoes down modern Route 179. After Mount Airy the portion in New Jersey ended at Coryell's Ferry where it continued through Pennsylvania to Philadelphia.

To prevent accidents amongst the ships coming and going past Sandy Hook, a lighthouse was constructed here 1764. The lighthouse at Sandy Hook is the oldest operating one in the entire United States as we speak.

In the meantime on the Arthur Kill, the Blazing Star Ferry opened between Woodbridge and Staten Island where Modern Travis is. People could now cross the Hudson from Lower Manhattan to Paulus Hook Island via Van Vorst's Ferry. From here they took a stage wagon to Bergen Town (Bergen Square) and down south through modern Bayonne to Bergen Point. After a ferry was used to cross to Staten Island (Port Richmond), a stage wagon would have run through Staten Island and used the Blazing Star Ferry to cross to Woodbridge. From here, passengers went on to New Brunswick, over the Raritan River through Princeton and on to Trenton. After taking the Trenton Ferry across the Delaware River, the two day trip to Philadelphia was almost complete. This wasn't a fast trip though as a nighttime stay at a tavern halfway in New Jersey was needed.

As New Brunswick became more prominent on this New York City to Philadelphia "corridor", it's no surprise that a new college here was chartered in 1766. Rutgers University started on the Raritan River here as a Dutch Reformed school named Queens College.

For Newark residents though there was no direct land route to the Hudson River. The N.J. Legislature then allowed for a road which provided Newarkers access to the Paulus Hook Ferry. Modern Ferry Street still follows this same route to the Passaic River. Thomas Brown had a ferry across the Passaic where Routes 1 and 9 cross the lower part of Kearny. Brown's Ferry was again taken in order to cross the Hackensack River after which a road (Communipaw Avenue) was taken to Paulus Hook. Up above Brown's Ferry, John Schuyler built a road from his copper mine down to the Hackensack River where NJ Transit's tracks cross enroute to Hoboken. Schuyler established Douw's Ferry in order to cross the Hackensack River. This "Schuyler's Road" is basically the Belleville Turnpike with some Newark Turnpike.

I'd like to go back to 1763 for a moment when the Treaty of Paris ended the French and Indian War. While they had beaten the French, England was left with a national debt of £133,000,000 with a high interest rate. This resulted in the passage of The Stamp Act of 1765 which imposed a small tax on almanacs, dice, bonds, diplomas, deeds, legal documents, newspapers, playing cards, and so on. While it led to the Stamp Act Riots in Boston, in New Jersey during September of 1765 John Parker published his "Constitutional Courant." While it only had a run of one issue, I'm sure that copies of New Jersey's first newspaper went up and down The King's Highway. It had a viewpoint that criticized England's Parliament as did others from Philadelphia and New York City that were carried through New Jersey. It's important, to remember that back then there was no telephone, telegraphs, televisions, or an internet. Any news of the day had to be carried by hand. With New York City on one side and Philadelphia on the other, New Jersey became an important thoroughfare across which news was carried. When The Stamp Act was repealed in England, the word first reached New York City in April of 1766. To spread the word to the other colonies, the good news went to New Jersey on a ferryboat where it made its way towards Philadelphia.

In England 3,000 miles away though, a cabinet member named Charles Townsend had what he thought was a good idea. The Townsend Revenue Act of 1767 imposed an import duty on glass, lead, paper, paint, and tea. Townsend felt that while Americans were opposed to a direct tax they wouldn't mind a duty on imported items. To collect these duties and to catch smugglers, the American Board of Customs Commissioners was created. Commissioners appointed in England came to Boston which was selected as their headquarters.

In 1768, John Hancock's sloop "Liberty" entered Boston Harbor with some goods that included Madeira wine. The wine was quickly unloaded into Hancock's warehouse to avoid a duty while customs inspectors were locked below deck. The next day these officials seized the "Liberty" and began to tow it towards a nearby British ship. An angry mob appeared that soon began to throw various items at the inspectors who ran for their lives. Problems like this led to customs collectors in Boston requesting the protection of British troops who arrived in September of 1768. On March 5, 1770, a British sentry was on guard duty outside of Boston's Custom's House. A small mob began to verbally abuse the lone sentry, but soon began to throw rocks, ice, snowballs, and oyster shells. A dozen British soldiers came to his aid to help disperse the unruly mob. Objects continued to be thrown at the soldiers until a

British musket was discharged by accident. This first shot was followed by others after which there were five deaths. On the same day as the Boston Massacre, the Townsend Acts were being repealed in England. The tea duty remained as it was the only one that made money.

In New Jersey, the local mail was carried to a town on horseback or sometimes by stage wagon. There could be a problem however if you lived in an area that had no name of its own. This was the case with a small community located halfway between Elizabethtown and Morristown. People here received their mail addressed as "…at the Passaic River." With such an address, the mail was often delivered dozens of miles away to other spots along the Passaic River. This led to a town meeting in late 1773 when the area was officially named Chatham to solve the problem. Chatham's name honored William Pitt, the Earl of Chatham who spoke up for the American Colonies in the English Parliament. Chatham was derived from the two Anglo Saxon words chete and ham for cottage and village.

As the 1770's got underway in New Jersey there were more stage wagon routes. From Paulus Hook, stage wagons ran to Morristown via Springfield, Bergen County, and towards Philadelphia. With the intense competition for riders came improvements in comfort. Some wagons by now were enclosed with hardtops and had cushioned seats with seatbacks and even curtains. The wagons of old were starting to resemble stagecoaches. With an increase in stage traffic across from Trenton in modern Morrisville, Pennsylvania, Patrick Colvin started a ferry to New Jersey. Colvin's "Blazing Star" ran across the Delaware in the same area where Northeast Corridor trains travel today.

Back in England during 1773 there was about 17,000,000 pounds of tea in warehouses. The Tea Act of 1773 allowed English tea to go across the Atlantic where it was now cheaper than smuggled Dutch tea. In America the old Townsend import duty remained where to buy the cheaper English tea was the same as giving in to the tax. By December of 1773 there were about 350 chests of tea on three ships in Boston Harbor. On the night of December 16, 1773, 200 Son's of Liberty dressed as Mohawk Indians marched to Griffin's Wharf where they dumped 342 tea chests into Boston Harbor. After the Boston Tea Party, Boston's Committee of Correspondence drew up a report on the event. To get the news to New York City and Philadelphia they chose Paul Revere who left on a horse. Revere made it to New York with the word of the Boston Tea Party on December 20th. He took the Paulus Hook Ferry to New Jersey where he rode through Newark and Elizabethtown on his way to Philadelphia. All the way through he yelled the news about the tea on the road to Philadelphia. Revere returned through New Jersey several days later on his 700 mile round trip that took eleven days.

In order to get information across the Atlantic Ocean to England 3,000 miles away it often took more than a month by ship. On January 19, 1774, a copy of the Boston Evening Post reference to the Boston Tea Party arrived in England. The English press and King George III ignored it as an American exaggeration. It was soon followed by other British dispatches that confirmed the event and labeled Samuel Adams and John Hancock as the head trouble-makers. In response, The Boston Port Bill was passed which closed off Boston's harbor as of June 1, 1774. It was to remain in effect until all the money lost in the Boston Tea Party was paid for. On leave in England, British General Thomas Gage met with King George III. He departed with instructions to arrest John Hancock and Samuel Adams. In May, when the Boston Port Bill reached Massachusetts, Paul Revere was sent on a second ride to New York City and Philadelphia. He crossed the Hudson on the Paulus Hook Ferry

11

on May 18, 1774 enroute to Philadelphia. He returned having drummed up support for Boston so the residents there wouldn't starve when the port closed in June. If England was trying to isolate Massachusetts from the other colonies, it made a mistake as it only drew them closer together. In order to do something about the situation in Massachusetts, The First Continental Congress was set to meet in Philadelphia at Carpenter's Hall in September of 1774. Samuel Adams and his cousin John Adams took the Paulus Hook Ferry across the Hudson. They rode in an elegant coach complete with red wheels and footmen. The other delegates from New England and New York State traveled to Philadelphia via New Jersey's ferries and highways. While the delegates met during September and October, back in Boston Military Governor Gage had prohibited town meetings. Paul Revere was sent on his third trip across New Jersey to Philadelphia during which he crossed via the Paulus Hook Ferry on September 15th. He returned a few days later through New Jersey with the newly adopted Suffolk Resolutions on his way back to Massachusetts. A short time later General Gage refused to allow the Massachusetts Colonial Assembly to convene. They met anyway and created a new Massachusetts Provincial Congress. John Hancock then sent Paul Revere to Philadelphia again for his fourth ride. He crossed on the Paulus Hook Ferry to New Jersey on October 20th. Revere later returned through New Jersey as did the delegates from New York and New England who headed home from Philadelphia.

In 1774 at Hoboken, Hermanus Talman obtained a charter for the Horsimus Ferry which ran between Southern Hoboken and Manhattan. By 1775, William Bayard also had a sail ferry from Hoboken to Vesey Street in Lower Manhattan.

CHAPTER TWO

New Jersey
The Crossroads of a Revolution

This second chapter on New Jersey and the American Revolution was going to be short, but I decided to lengthen it with all the patriotism after September 11th. When N.J. and the Revolutionary War are mentioned together, the Battles of Trenton, Princeton, and Monmouth are always mentioned, but seldom is anything else. During the conflict Washington spent more time in Somerset County than anywhere else. Everyone across the U.S. knows about Valley Forge in Pennsylvania, but not the encampments in Morristown or Middlebrook. Hopefully I can change that with this chapter.

By April of 1775, General Gage in Boston heard the Americans had some arms and ammunition stockpiled 16 miles away at Concord. Gage also learned that John Hancock and Sam Adams were 11 miles away at Lexington and about to leave for the Second Continental Congress. On the way to Concord, British troops could first arrest these two "troublemakers." On the night of April 18, 1775, Gage ordered about 800 redcoats out from Boston and on to Lexington and Concord. Dr. Joseph Warren had already sent out a few riders to alert the countryside including Paul Revere. By dawn, the British reached Lexington Common where about 70 militiamen were standing. The locals began to disperse as a shot rang out from somewhere. The redcoats opened fire and charged with bayonets. The British had one soldier with a small leg wound while 8 Americans were killed and 9 wounded. The redcoats headed off to Concord though without Hancock and Adams who already departed.

The redcoats reached Concord around 8 a.m., and began to search for the patriot's 3 cannon and other supplies. About 100 troops were sent to secure the North Bridge above the town. With these redcoats around the bridge, some 400 militiamen stood nearby watching from a ridge. Back in Concord the British set fire to 3 gun carriages along with some tools. When the 400 militiamen above the North Bridge saw the smoke from the fires, they thought that the British were burning the town. They marched down to the bridge after which shots were exchanged. There were casualties on both sides as the redcoats fled back to the town. Soon after the 800 British soldiers set off on their 16 mile march back to Boston. All along the road back though were thousands of militiamen from miles around. The Americans fired shots from behind walls, trees, rocks, fences, and buildings into the retreating redcoats. The British were only saved in Lexington when a 1,000 man relief column with two cannon arrived from Boston. The redcoats were hounded with lead until they reached Boston's outskirts with 73 dead and 200 other casualties. In comparison the Americans had 93 casualties among which were 49 dead. That day Israel Bissell left Lexington enroute to Philadelphia with news of the event. He reached New York City four days later after which he crossed to New Jersey via the Paulus Hook Ferry. On his way to Philadelphia he spread the news of Lexington and Concord to patriots and loyalists alike. Bissell was soon followed by the delegates from New England and New York like John and Samuel Adams, John Hancock, John Jay, and Robert R. Livingston. These founding fathers also used the Paulus Hook Ferry on their way enroute to the Second Continental Congress in Philadelphia.

As the Second Continental Congress convened on May 10, 1775, Ethan Allen and Benedict Arnold captured Fort Ticonderoga on Lake Champlain, and in several days two smaller British posts nearby. In the process these Americans managed to capture about 180 cannon from the British. Down in Boston General Gage and his 4,000 redcoats were pretty much under the watchful eye of about 15,000 New England militiamen who were camped nearby. Gage got some relief as 1,100 more redcoats arrived along with Generals Henry Clinton, William Howe, and John Burgoyne.

Since the Second Continental Congress began, one of the delegates from Virginia always showed up dressed in his colonel's uniform. Colonel George Washington, with his experience in the Virginia Militia, was unanimously chosen to lead the American army around Boston on June 15, 1775.

Outside of Boston and across the Charles River was the Charlestown peninsula on which were Bunker and Breed's Hills. On the night of June 16th a small group of Americans began digging fortifications on Breed's Hill. On the morning of the 17th the British in Boston awoke to see American fortifications where there were none the day before. General Gage felt the Americans wouldn't stand up to a frontal assault by his redcoats so this is the method he chose. General Howe was to lead the 1,550 British soldiers up Breed's Hill. The Americans waited until the redcoats were several yards away when they opened fire. Several hundred British soldiers fell either dead or wounded as the rest retreated down Breed's Hill. They came back up a second time where hundreds more fell followed by another retreat. The Americans were nearly out of powder as the British came back up a third time. This time the Americans fell back and retreated down the other side of Breed's Hill. One of the Americans killed was Dr. Joseph Warren who stayed behind so others could escape. In New Jersey both Warren County and Warren Township are named after him. While the Americans took about 440 casualties, the British suffered 1,054 causalities out of the 2,200 redcoats who took part in the Battle of Bunker Hill.

On June 23rd America's first commander in chief left Philadelphia with Major Generals Charles Lee and Phillip Schuyler. They crossed into New Jersey and spent the night at New Brunswick. The next morning they rode up to Newark and on to Hoboken. The Hoboken Ferry was used instead of the Paulus Hook Ferry as the British ship "Asia" was nearby. They crossed over to Manhattan after which Washington reached Cambridge on July 2nd. He assumed command of his army the following day.

What Washington found though was an army of 16,000 men who were unfit, untrained, and unfed. There was no shelter, blankets, and hardly any powder.

By July, Gage's reports on Bunker Hill's 50% casualties reached England where he was made the scapegoat. Back in Boston neither Gage or Washington made any major moves. As September of 1775 ended Gage received letters from England that instructed him to return which he did in October. He didn't return back and General William Howe took over command. Gage had a connection to New Jersey as he married the daughter of a wealthy landowner in Morris County named Peter Kemble (as in Mount Kemble).

Washington remembered the numerous large guns that were 300+ miles away at Fort Ticonderoga. He appointed Henry Knox as his Colonel Commandant of Artillery who then left for Fort Ticonderoga. As 1775 ended Benedict Arnold and General Richard Montgomery launched an attack against the walled City of Quebec on December 31, 1775. The attack went bad as Arnold was wounded and General Montgomery was killed. As per the story, an aide named Aaron Burr carried Montgomery away in a hail of British lead. Burr was born in Newark where his father Aaron Burr Sr. was the President of the College of New Jersey. The Burr family left Newark in 1756 when the small college moved down to Princeton. Burr went on to become U.S. Vice-President under Thomas Jefferson after the 1800 election. Burr had a duel with Alexander Hamilton in Weehawken on July 11, 1804 during which Hamilton was mortally wounded.

15

As 1776 started, Washington had about 8,000 men in his camp outside of Boston. Henry Knox was dragging his cannons across New York State with four, six, an even eight oxen. Knox's heavy guns arrived by February of 1776 which set another plan into motion. Washington realized that he could put the British in a bad position if he could sneak Ticonderoga's big guns onto the nearby hills. Since the ground was frozen, fortifications were out of the question. The Americans simply built fortifications in advance. These dirt filled barrels and bundles of hay were carried up to Dorchester Heights on the night of March 4th by 3,000 men. The British were surprised in the morning to see Dorchester Heights fortified. The British ships wouldn't be able to hit that far up so an assault had to be mounted. As the redcoats were about to attack a three day long hurricane blew in. In the meantime the Americans were able to get their guns on Nook's Hill even closer to Boston. It was a bluff that the British bought as there wasn't enough powder to bombard Boston with the guns. The British evacuated Boston on March 17th and left for Nova Scotia.

In New York City, Major General Charles Lee was in command, but he soon departed for the Carolinas. In anticipation of a British attack on New York, Washington quickly left Boston and rode down. In April of 1776 he had about 8,300 men who were fit for duty.

Across the Delaware in Philadelphia on June 7th, Richard Henry Lee introduced legislation in the Second Continental Congress for independence. Lee's resolution stated that "These united colonies are, and of right ought to be free and independent states..." Not all the delegates were for independence yet so the vote was put off until early July. A five man committee that consisted of John Adams (Mass), Roger Sherman (Conn), Robert R. Livingston (NY), Ben Franklin (Penn), and Thomas Jefferson (VA) was put together to draw up the Declaration. The members deferred to Jefferson who went straight to work.

Down off of South Carolina, General Henry Clinton met up with another small fleet under Admiral Sir Peter Parker. Charleston was located eight miles inland and separated from the Atlantic Ocean by a harbor. James's and Sullivan's Islands were located at the mouth of this harbor. The Americans built a fort on Sullivan's Island which General lee thought was worthless. The British ships opened fire on the small fort under the command of William Moultrie. It was made with palmetto logs in which the British cannonballs only lodged. The fort stood up and soon returned fire. In the confusion two British ships collided while the frigate "Actaeon" was set afire. Admiral Parker's ship was hit and his pants were actually blown off. The British never reached Charleston due to Moultrie's heroics and set sail back towards New York. Charles Lee also left Charleston for New York City as the "hero" who saved Charleston.

On July 2, 1776 in Philadelphia, the independence resolution was voted on and passed. On July 4th the Congress officially approved the Declaration of Independence. Up in New Jersey at Elizabethtown Point, Captain Daniel Neill had two small cannons set up. At midnight on the 4th when a British ship sailed by, Neill's two guns opened up, and set the ship on fire with casualties. Since the Declaration had just been approved these were the first shots "in anger" fired by the new United States of America. On July 5th some continental land agents purchased land in N.J. down where Billingsport is. A fort was going to be built here on the first land bought by the new U.S.A. Back in June N.J.'s Royal Governor William Franklin (Ben Franklin's son) was arrested, imprisoned, and deported up to Connecticut.

By August the largest fleet of British troops to ever leave England was slowly being assembled in New York Harbor, the Arthur Kill, and the Kill Van Kull. To deal with the Americans the British had about 32,000 troops, 10,000 sailors, and about 450 ships. These numbers also included Hessian mercenaries whose services were obtained by England. To face them, Washington had about 23,000 men "on paper" who were mostly militia. He had some men on Manhattan while others were positioned on Long Island. In Upper Manhattan around 183rd St. was a large earthworks named Fort Washington. Across the Hudson from this point was another fort, at the time named Fort Constitution. With the British on Staten Island, Washington set up a 4-5,000 man "flying camp" of militia. Under the command of General Hugh Mercer, the men of the "flying camp" were positioned at Paulus Hook, Elizabethtown, Bergen Point, and Bergen Neck (Bayonne's 52nd St.) in order to protect New Jersey.

On August 22, 1776, Howe landed some 15,000 troops on the Long Island at Gravesend. To the north of Gravesend the Americans had a line of troops on the Heights of Guan. These hills ran roughly from the Gowanus Bay in Brooklyn to Jamaica, Queens. Behind these hills there was a second American position on the Brooklyn Heights. This line stretched from where the Brooklyn Navy Yard was down to the end of the Gowanus Canal. In order to attack Brooklyn Heights there were four passes through the Heights of Guan the British could use. The Americans protected the three to the west, but left the most eastward or Jamaica Pass undefended. On the night of the 16th, Howe snuck through the Jamaica Pass with 10,000 troops. The next morning other redcoats began to demonstrate in front of the Americans on the Heights of Guan. The Americans here realized Howe was behind them when his cannon began to fire. With the British and Hessians on both sides now the Americans here fled through the Gowanus Creek (today's canal) to the safety of Brooklyn Heights. To help them escape, General Williams Alexander aka Lord Stirling (a Basking Ridge resident) led 250 men against the larger enemy force. They made five different charges after which nearly all of the 250 men were either killed or captured. Lord Stirling was even taken prisoner during the fighting.

After this victory Howe now had some 22,000 men in front of the Brooklyn Heights. His officers wanted to storm them, but Howe still remembered Breed's Hill and refused. He could have brought ships up the East River behind the Americans, but did not because of a northeast wind. Washington soon crossed over from Manhattan with some reinforcements. Protected by a fog on the night of August 28th into the 29th, Washington evacuated Brooklyn Heights with boats. By the time the British investigated they saw Washington being rowed to Manhattan in the last boat.

On September 15th, Howe went up the East River and landed at Kip's Bay (34th St.) with 4,000 men. He could have cut off the Americans in Lower Manhattan, but decided to wait for reinforcements. In the meantime Howe and his officers ate cake and drank coffee at Mrs. Murray's house which wasted time. While the Americans in Lower Manhattan left behind 70 guns they were able to escape up towards Harlem Heights. By the end of the day Washington's 10,000 men were safely on the Harlem Heights (125th St.) with the British to the south. On September 20th there was a suspicious fire in Lower Manhattan which spread and destroyed about 500 buildings. With the British this close the "flying camp" evacuated from modern Bayonne and Paulus Hook.

On October 12th, with Washington still on the Harlem Heights, Howe landed on the Throg's Neck with 4,000 men. Howe was now to Washington's left and four miles behind him. On the 18th, Washington evacuated his men from the Harlem Heights after which they slowly headed north to White Plains. His men finally made it to White Plains on October 23rd followed by the British who encamped to the south. Behind him, Washington had left men at Fort Washington (183rd St.). General Lee returned from "his" victory at Charleston in late October. In his honor New Jersey's Fort Constitution was renamed Fort Lee. There was a small skirmish at White Plains which wasn't decisive for the British. On November 6th, Washington had a council of war during which he decided to split up his force of 14,000. Washington had General Heath take 4,000 men 18 miles above White Plains to Peekskill. General Lee went to New Castle with another 7,000 men. On November 10th, Washington crossed below Stony Point into New Jersey with 3,000 men. In addition there were still 3,000 men under General Nathaniel Greene at Forts Lee and Washington. After a nearly 70 mile march Washington camped at Hackensack near Fort Lee.

In order to help defend Fort Washington from an attack General Greene sent over another 1,500 men. The British and Hessians attacked Fort Washington on November 16th and forced its 3,000 defenders to surrender. On the night of the 19th General Cornwallis landed at Closter above Fort Lee with 4,000 men. He began a slow march south towards Fort Lee where General Greene would be pinned against the Hudson River. When the men at Fort Lee realized the British were coming they fled so fast that food was still cooking as the redcoats arrived. Along with the two forts, Washington lost 3,000 men killed or captured, 3,000 muskets, 150 cannon and 400,000 cartridges. He also lost valuable tents, blankets, and all the army's picks and shovels. With the British at Fort Lee the Americans set up across the Hackensack River at Hackensack. Washington decided not to make a stand here with his 3,500 men as their backs were to the Passaic River. On November 21st Washington's 3,500 men left Hackensack in the pouring rain. They burned the Acquackanonck Bridge over the Passaic and entered Newark. Washington by now has also sent a letter to General Lee to come to his aid with the 7,000 men from New Castle.

As Washington marched into Newark on November 22nd there was no warm reception. For the next five days though the British in Hackensack and Fort Lee left the Americans alone in Newark. Just as the British entered Newark from the north on November 28th, Washington exited to the south and continued into Elizabethtown. Here he was reinforced by General Stirling (recently exchanged) with 1,000 more men. Back in Newark there was a reception for the British who in turn plundered and looted houses of both patriots and loyalists. The next day Washington left Elizabethtown just as General Cornwallis marched in from Newark to the north. With the British in pursuit the Americans made it to New Brunswick where they crossed the Raritan River. While at New Brunswick, Washington sent some men down towards the Delaware River with instructions to gather all the boats within 30 miles of Trenton. In New Brunswick 1,000 men of the "flying camp" left for their homes as their enlistments expired. The Americans were damaging the bridge across the Raritan River when Cornwallis arrived on December 1st. There were a few cannon shots exchanged after which the Americans continued on down to Princeton via Route 27. General Cornwallis didn't advance past New Brunswick though as he had orders from Howe to wait for him. Washington's 3,000 men reached a nearly empty Princeton the following morning. He left General Stirling here with about 1,200 men while he went on to Trenton with the sick and wounded. After several requests from Washington to come and help, General Lee finally started to leave New Castle on December 2nd with his 3,000 men. It took General Howe four days to reach New Brunswick as the pursuit continued on December 7th. With the sick, wounded, and baggage across the Delaware River from Trenton, Washington returned back up to Princeton with a few hundred men. Cornwallis and Howe were headed down Route 27 though with 8,000 men so Washington and Stirling retreated back to Trenton. In

Princeton, the British loitered around for 17 hours before they headed down to Trenton. Just as the first British soldiers arrived the last Americans crossed the Delaware River on the last boat for 70 miles around. On the Pennsylvania side of the Delaware River Washington set up his 3,000 men between Yardley's Ferry (Yardley) and Coryell's Ferry (New Hope).

It had been 23 days since Washington's first request for help when his second in command, General Lee arrived in Chatham on December 8th. He still received additional letters from Washington to come on, but he stayed here for 3 more days. General Lee was in Morristown on December 12th which he left with his now 2,000 men to Vealtown (Bernardsville). In order to find better accommodations he left for Basking Ridge with a guard of about 15 men. They spent the night at Mrs. White's Tavern (no longer standing) at South Finley Avenue and Colonial Drive. General Howe, like Washington, had no idea where General Lee was. In order to find him, Howe had sent out a small group of horse mounted dragoons under Lt. Colonel Harcourt. They left Pennington where they spent the night of 12th near the Millstone River in Hillsborough. The following morning Harcourt sent a few of his dragoons up from Hillsborough under Banastre Tarleton to look for Lee. Along the way they caught an American dispatch rider who revealed Lee's location under the threat of harm. Up at Widow White's Tavern in Basking Ridge, Lee spent the morning eating breakfast and writing letters. His men were up and on a march from Vealtown (Bernardsville) to Pluckemin while Lee was still at White's Tavern at 10:00 a.m. Tarleton showed up with his six men and easily took care of Lee's few guards. Some shots were exchanged, but when Tarleton threatened to set the tavern on fire General Lee surrendered. He was placed on a horse and taken back to British held New Brunswick. Lee's second in command, General John Sullivan left Pluckemin with his 2,000 men and headed towards the Delaware River.

With Washington's depleted army across the Delaware River and Lee's capture, General Howe declared his 1776 campaign over. He had about an 80 mile long chain of posts set up from Fort Lee through Paulus Hook, Elizabethtown, Staten Island, Amboy, New Brunswick, Princeton, Trenton, and Bordentown. The Hessians were placed in Trenton and Bordentown under the commands of Colonel Rall and Colonel Von Donop respectively. In Trenton, Colonel Rall was big on parades, drills and inspections. During the day he would watch as the band played, his men marched, and his cannon were pulled back and forth. He made no trenches in Trenton and referred to the Americans across the Delaware as clowns, farmers, and clod-hoppers.

On the other side of the Delaware River in Bucks County, Washington was reinforced by General Sullivan's 2,000 soldiers (originally 7,000) and General Gate's 600 men from Fort Ticonderoga. Other men and militia also came up from Philadelphia. Washington now had about 7,000 men although many were sick with dysentery, ulcers, rashes, hepatitis, bronchitis. jaundice, and pneumonia. Many of the men in the December cold didn't even have shoes.

On December 17th about 800 British troops left Elizabethtown for Springfield where Major Oliver Spencer's Essex County militia was on their right flank. The local militia had been making pests of themselves in the form of little raids on British supplies. On December 11th for instance, the Morris County militia raided Woodbridge and returned back with 400 cattle and 200 sheep. As the British approached Springfield, the Essex County militia was reinforced by Colonel Jacob Ford's Morris County militia near Bryant's Tavern (Broad St. by Rt. 24 in Eastern Summit). There was a small skirmish which ended at dark as the disheartened Morris, Essex, and Sussex County militia fell back to Bryant's Tavern. They expected to fight the British regulars again the next day, but to their surprise the redcoats had retreated back to Elizabethtown. For the British this retreat from Springfield was the first time in N.J. that they ever had to fall back.

Back in Pennsylvania as Christmas Eve approached though Washington had come up with a plan. He would cross the Delaware River nine miles above Trenton with 2,500 men and attack Rall's Hessians. To cut off Rall's escape over the Assunpink Creek below Trenton, General James Ewing would cross here with 1,000 men. General John Cadwalader was to cross the Delaware at Dunk's Ferry and attack the other Hessians in Bordentown. Washington set his surprise attack to be on the day after Christmas.

Washington's 2,500 men, 200 horses, and 18 cannons began to cross the Delaware at 7 p.m. on Christmas Day at McConkey's Ferry (Washington Crossing State Park). This was actually the old Baker's Ferry which Samuel McConkey had purchased a couple years back. Those Durham boats came in handy as Washington's small force was poled across the ice choked the Delaware River. Nine miles to the south in Trenton at 7 p.m. Colonel Rall was drinking, toasting, eating, and playing cards. As midnight came around five hours later Rall was still carrying on and having a good time. Washington had planned to be completely across at midnight and on his way, but everything wasn't across and ready until 3 a.m. The weather was horrible with the cold and sleet mixed with snow. Due to the sleet the Americans would have to use bayonets as their powder would be wet and useless. Washington and his men began to march inland a bit to the Bear Tavern where they headed south. After a miserable four mile march through the sleet, rain, and snow, Washington's men reached the intersection of Bear Tavern Road and the Upper Ferry Road. Washington turned to the left so he could attack Trenton via the Pennington Road. General Sullivan turned right here so he could come in to Trenton from the west via the River Road. At around 8 a.m. both Washington's and Sullivan's soldiers attacked the Hessian picket posts in front of them. The column of soldiers who marched with George Washington was actually under the command of General Nathaniel Greene. Down in Trenton the Hessians who heard the first few shots began to turn out. If Colonel Rall heard the shots he probably thought it was just a few "farmers" as an aide went to his room three different times to inform him of the attack. In the meantime, General Greene set up his cannon above the town at the "Five Points" intersection where Pennington, Princeton, and Brunswick Avenues met King and Queen Streets (today's Warren and N. Broad Streets). While Rall was still getting dressed these guns began to fire shots down King and Queen Streets into the Hessians. Rall soon came outside and led his regiment up King Street which was repulsed. He then tried to march up Queen Street which also was turned back by cannon fire. Two of Rall's guns went into action against the American's cannons. Some men led by Captain William Washington and Lt. James Monroe charged down and captured the two Hessian cannon. Rall fell back to an orchard with his regiment to form them back up. At the same time, Somerset County's Frederick Frelinghuysen (his powder was dry) aimed, and hit Rall fatally wounding him. Rall's Hessians were soon surrounded and surrendered as did the others elsewhere. With Colonel Rall dying in Trenton, Washington began to recross the Delaware to Pennsylvania. About 30 Hessians were killed while 900+ were taken prisoner. Two Americans froze on the march and died while Captain Washington and Lt. Monroe (later the 5th U.S. President) were the only two wounded.

About 650 Hessians were able to escape to the south of Trenton as General Ewing did not cross due to the icy Delaware. General Cadwalader did not cross towards Bordentown either because of the ice. Cadwalader did cross on the 27th and found the Hessians had fled from the area. He sent word to Washington in Bucks County who recrossed with his men to Trenton where Cadwalader was. In the meantime, Lord Cornwallis completed a 50 mile march from New York to Princeton with his redcoats on New Year's Day 1777. There were now 8,000 British and Hessians in Princeton some 8 miles above Washington's 4,500 men in Trenton. Just below Maidenhead (now Lawrenceville) about 1,000 American riflemen were positioned by Route 206 and the Shabbakonk Creek. On January 2nd, Cornwallis left 1,200 men in Princeton as he moved south down Route 206. He left 1,500 more in Maidenhead with orders to move towards Trenton the next day. There had been a slight change in the temperature though from freezing to 50 degrees. This of course melted the snow which turned Route 206 into mud. Cornwallis began to move below Maidenhead with his 5,500 men as the riflemen opened fire. They began to fire and fall back which they did all afternoon. Impeded by the mud and Colonel Edward Hand's riflemen, Cornwallis's force didn't reach Trenton until late afternoon. Hand's riflemen continued to fall back down King and Queen Streets where they fought house to house towards the Assunpink Creek. Hand's men made it back across the bridge here where Washington's men were on the other side. The British and Hessians tried to cross the bridge, but were cut down by American cannons. It was dark now and Cornwallis had Washington pinned against the Delaware River with not enough time to recross to Pennsylvania. His officers wanted to attack in the dark to which Cornwallis replied "We've got the old fox safe now. We'll go over (the Assunpink Creek) and bag him in the morning."

Across the creek the British could see the American campfires as well as men digging with picks and shovels. Around midnight, Washington's men began to march eastward towards Hamilton and Mercerville. In the dark behind them were about 400 men in the dark who were digging, making noise, and tending the fires that the British were watching. In modern Mercerville, Washington turned left and marched towards Princeton via Route 533. Washington split his force by the Stony Brook with General Sullivan and General Greene going by different routes. General Mercer's 120 men led Greene's column followed next by General Cadwalader with his militiamen. As Mercer approached Princeton, British Lt. Colonel Charles Mawhood marched out towards Cornwallis with the 17th and 55th Regiments. Behind in Princeton he left the 40th Regiment. Mawhood spotted Mercer enroute to Princeton which led him to order the 55th to return back. Mawhood attacked Mercer with the 275 or so men of the 17th. Mercer's men spotted Mawhood though after which they took the high ground above the Stony Brook (Battlefield Park). They fired on Mawhood's redcoats from behind a fence in Thomas Clark's orchard. Mawhood's men charged Mercer's position with bayonets who then fell back. Mercer fell off his horse during the fray and was clubbed and bayoneted 13 times. By now Cadwalader's men had joined Mercer's in a retreat. Washington rode up in an attempt to rally the men with some reinforcements. With Washington in the middle of the two forces his men fired a volley followed by the British. As the smoke cleared Washington was still in between on his horse. He led an American bayonet charge which panicked the 17th into a complete retreat. The 40th and 55th British Regiments also retreated on their own towards New Brunswick. During the Battle of Princeton the Americans had 40 casualties which included General Hugh Mercer who would die 9 days later. He is still honored with Mercer County, Port Mercer, Lake Mercer,

Mercerville, as well as many streets in New Jersey. The British had 28 killed, about 60 wounded, and dozens who were taken prisoner.

Washington's men had won the battle, but they were tired from the 16 mile march, hungry, and cold. Lord Cornwallis in Trenton had turned back around and was headed to Princeton. As Washington left Princeton Cornwallis entered behind him. Past Kingston and in Rocky Hill Washington paused for a conference. They could continue on towards New Brunswick where General Lee was a prisoner, but Cornwallis was on his way up to Princeton. Rather than going towards New Brunswick, Washington turned left and spent the night at Somerset County Courthouse (Millstone). Cornwallis thought Washington was enroute to New Brunswick and he continued on towards it. The next day the Americans marched through Hillsborough stopping in Pluckemin as Cornwallis set up in New Brunswick. The Americans spent a second night in Pluckemin and marched into Vealtown (Bernardsville) on January 5th.

Washington's tired army finally reached a snow covered Morristown on January 6th. For the 45 year old Washington this was also his 18th year wedding anniversary. With a population of 250 people, Morristown was protected by the Great Swamp in modern Chatham, Harding, and Long Hill Townships. Morristown was also located behind three different Watchung Mountains. The First Watchung Mountain in this area runs from Paterson down through the Oranges (South Mountain Reservation) where there is a "gap" in the Millburn/Summit area. First Watchung Mountain continues on from Summit where it runs next to Route 22 through Mountainside, Watchung, Warren, Bridgewater, and Pluckemin. The Second Watchung Mountain parallels the first from Summit, but through New Providence (Mountain Ave.), Berkeley Heights, and Warren enroute to Pluckemin. The Third Watchung Mountain aka The Long Hill runs from Chatham on the border with Summit and New Providence (Fairmont Ave.) through Long Hill Township into Basking Ridge. In addition to these barriers, Morristown was ideal due to the closeness of the numerous farms, mills, forges, and furnaces nearby. Washington had access to Elizabethtown (modern Morris Avenue) and he could also keep an eye on the 10,000 British in New Brunswick and Perth Amboy.

Washington made his headquarters during this Loantaka Encampment at Arnold's Tavern (not standing) near the Morristown Green. There were only several thousand men in the camp who stayed in local buildings and homes. In order to protect Washington in Morristown, General Benjamin Lincoln was positioned in Bound Brook with about 500 men. On April 13, 1777 (Palm Sunday) the British and Hessians made a four pronged attack on Bound Brook to capture both Generals Benjamin Lincoln and Anthony Wayne. As the Battle of Bound Brook started, Benjamin Lincoln fled out of the Van Horne House without his pants on. There were several casualties in the battle which ended as General Greene came down from Basking Ridge and the British returned back to New Brunswick.

Inspired by the victories at Trenton and Princeton, more men arrived in Morristown to where Washington had about 10,000 (on paper) by May of 1777. At the end of May, the army left Morristown and camped at Middlebrook just above Bound Brook. Washington could keep an eye (from Washington Rock) on the 16,000 British and Hessians in New Brunswick. In order to lure Washington's 6,000 men into an open battle, General Howe moved much of his army from New Brunswick on June 12th. They reached Somerset Court House (Millstone) on the 14th, and camped below Manville on both sides of the Raritan River. Washington stayed at Middlebrook and the British returned to New Brunswick on

June 19th. Howe could not march across New Jersey to take Philadelphia with Washington on his right flank. On June 26th it looked as though the British and Hessians were going to depart from New Brunswick and Perth Amboy. With nearly 17,000 enemy troops in this area, Lord Stirling came down towards the Edison area with 1,980 men to harass them as they left. Instead of leaving though Howe's larger force turned back at Lord Stirling. Stirling's men retreated into Scotch Plain's Ash Brook Swamp (the reservation) with the redcoats in pursuit. Washington in turn came down from Middlebrook into the Piscataway area. During the Battle of the Short Hills, Stirling's small force held off the British so Washington could retire to the safety of Middlebrook without being trapped. Casualties were few, but Howe still could not take Philadelphia by a march across N.J. with Washington in Middlebrook to his right. Tired of this cat and mouse game, Howe's 15,000 or so men finally evacuated New Brunswick and Perth Amboy to Staten Island. His large force was soon onboard ships off of Sandy Hook.

Howe might be enroute to Charleston, Philadelphia, or up the Hudson River to help General Burgoyne. Burgoyne had started what he thought would be a three pronged invasion of New York State towards Albany. Burgoyne's 7,000 men began to move south from Lake Champlain to Albany. Lt. Colonel Barry St. Leger with 1,000 Iroquois Indians headed towards Albany from Lake Ontario. Burgoyne thought that Howe was going to sail up the Hudson River to Albany from the south. Burgoyne's plan would isolate New England and win the war. Howe though had been playing games since April with Washington in New Jersey. Washington left Middlebrook in late June and marched up to Pompton to counter Howe's Hudson River move. At the end of July Howe's 260+ ships were sighted off the Delaware Bay. To protect Philadelphia, Washington marched back down to Coryell's Ferry. He crossed over the Delaware River and marched to Philadelphia. Howe left the Delaware Bay and disappeared. Washington started to turn back to N.J. when Howe entered the Chesapeake Bay. Howe did not sail up the Delaware to Philadelphia because of three forts on the water's edge. In N.J., there was Fort Mercer at Red Bank and Fort Billings at the mouth of Mantua Creek. Across from Fort Mercer on Mud Island was another works named Fort Mifflin. In between Forts Mercer and Mifflin were underwater obstructions with spikes that faced upward to damage ships. Howe had to land 55 miles below Philadelphia and march up overland. Washington made a stand below Philadelphia with his 16,000 men.

Up in New York State, Burgoyne's 2nd "prong" that consisted of St. Leger with 1,000 Indians had been defeated. After the violent battle of Oriskany, St. Leger's Indians abandoned him so he turned back. With no sign of Howe or General Clinton's 7,000 men left in New York City, Burgoyne was on his own.

On September 10th, Howe's army of 15,000+ camped seven miles below Brandywine Creek where Washington's 11,000 men were set up below Philadelphia. The next day Howe had 5,000 men demonstrate in front of the center of the American lines. With this distraction, Cornwallis and Howe took 10,000 men around the American right flank to hit it from behind. The defeated Americans were able to retreat towards Philadelphia with 800 casualties to the British's 600. As Howe's army approached Philadelphia in early October of 1777, Washington came up with a plan that consisted of a four pronged attack on Howe at Germantown. Early on it looked like a rout as Howe's redcoats fled in disorder right past him. There was a lot of fog though along with the smoke which caused two American columns to fire on each other. Some American units got lost while much of the rest lost time trying to dislodge 120 redcoats from the Chew Mansion. Germantown ended in another

American defeat which let Howe march into Philadelphia. Washington positioned his men above Philadelphia to the north. Congress already had fled from the Philadelphia and reconvened up in York. Howe still couldn't supply Philadelphia from the Delaware River though with those forts on its banks. The Americans already abandoned the fort in Billingsport which left two others Howe still had to deal with.

With Howe down in Philadelphia, Burgoyne's 5,000 man army finally had to surrender up in New York at Saratoga. Howe sent about 2,000 Hessians against New Jersey's Fort Mercer at Red Bank held by 400 Americans. The Americans positioned themselves up in one section of the large fort. The Hessians came in and were hit hard at close range with muskets and cannon shots. They took 400 casualties while the rest retreated. Howe was finally able to take Fort Mifflin on November 15th which the Americans abandoned and set on fire. With the British in control of this fort, Fort Mercer across from it in New Jersey had to be abandoned. Howe could now finally bring supplies up the Delaware to Philadelphia. It was now November though and the British simply remained in Philadelphia. A tired General Howe wintered here and went to parties, but sent word to England that he wanted to be relieved of his command.

Washington's army made its way some 20 miles above Philadelphia to Valley Forge shortly before Christmas 1777. The men built huts and had to deal with shortages of food and supplies as well as sickness and disease. France had gotten word of the American victory up in Saratoga after which they recognized the United States as a nation. The French would soon send a naval fleet across the Atlantic to assist America. In February of 1778, a German volunteer named Frederick William Augustus Henry Ferdinand aka Baron von Steuben arrived at Valley Forge with a letter from Ben Franklin from France. As he had served as a general under the King of Prussia, von Steuben was given the title of Inspector General. He spoke not a word of English, but began to instruct (with interpreters) the Americans in European military drill. He taught a small unit of Americans on marching, turning, and even the bayonet. These men in turn later trained the others. He turned out to be a fraud, but performed a miracle and Washington didn't seem to mind. He also didn't seem to mind General Charles Lee who arrived in Valley Forge during May of 1778 after a prisoner exchange.

Down in Philadelphia, Howe got word from England that General Henry Clinton was on his way to replace him. Clinton soon arrived in the city which he would abandon as the French fleet was on its way. Clinton started his evacuation on June 16th, 17th, and 18th as his men crossed the Delaware River to New Jersey. The British didn't leave Philadelphia on ships because the loyalists, some Hessians, and plunder left on them. The Americans entered Philadelphia and found that Clinton had indeed left. Benedict Arnold would be Philadelphia's Military Governor. The British spent the 19th in the area of Mt. Laurel and Moorestown. Their march with a 12 mile long baggage train to the northeast was hampered as New Jersey's General William Maxwell's men cut down trees across the roads. On June 21st Washington crossed the Delaware River at Coryell's Ferry. His army, trained well by von Steuben now numbered at around 13,000. On June 23rd and 24th the Americans stayed in Hopewell while the British camped down in Allentown. With Washington to his left, Clinton couldn't go towards Sandy Hook by way of Princeton. He instead had to go to Sandy Hook via Monmouth Count Court House (Freehold). On June 24th a small force of 1,500 men was sent ahead under the young Lafayette. It was offered to Lee who deferred to a younger Lafayette. As Clinton headed towards Sandy Hook he placed his 1,500 wagons up in front with Cornwallis's elite troops in the rear. The advance British units reached Monmouth County Courthouse on June 26th while Washington stayed behind them in Cranbury. On the 17th, Lafayette's advance force that now numbered 5,000 reached Englishtown and some fighting soon followed. General Lee changed his mind and rode up to take charge of Lafayette's men. Washington had told him to attack the British the following morning. With the wagon train in front of Cornwallis, there could be no retreat up the one land road to Sandy Hook. The redcoats and Hessians in front of the wagons could not turn around to help Cornwallis.

On June 28th at 4 a.m., Clinton's advance units left for Sandy Hook with the wagon train behind them. Cornwallis's rear guard soon followed on the road as Lee's advance unit appeared. Cornwallis turned back and General Lee ordered a retreat before even a shot could be fired. Lee had missed Trenton, Princeton, and von Steuben's training. Lee retreated back along the Englishtown Road where he was met by an angry Washington. Lee was ordered to the rear as Washington reformed up the men for battle. The Battle of Monmouth raged in the 100 degree heat until late afternoon. Both sides were tired from the heat and the fight and there was no further action after dark. There were about 350 casualties on each side with many from the heat. At midnight, Clinton's men snuck off to Sandy Hook and left the 13,000 Americans behind them in the dark. The British then left New Jersey from Sandy Hook for New York City and Staten Island. General Lee requested a court martial where he was found guilty of insubordination and negligence. He was relieved of his command for one year.

Washington stayed here for another day after which his army marched from Freehold up to New Brunswick. They stayed here a few days and even celebrated the 4th of July. Washington continued on through Totowa enroute to Paramus. He continued on across the Hudson River where he met up with General Gate's army. The Americans now had a large force of some 20,000 men up in White Plains. The French fleet under the Admiral Comte D'Estaing appeared off Sandy Hook with 16 ships and 4,000 troops. D'Estaing would not advance onward to attack Clinton in New York because he was afraid his ships would run aground between Sandy Hook and Staten Island. D'Estaing's fleet stayed here for about ten days after which they sailed for Newport, Rhode Island where General John Sullivan had about 10,000 men and militia. D'Estaing arrived outside Newport to coordinate an attack with General Sullivan. Sullivan attacked one day earlier than planned which insulted Admiral D'Estaing. Sullivan's men had to retreat while the French fleet maneuvered to fight with several British ships. A storm blew in though which damaged both British and French ships. The British ships left for New York while the French fleet retired to Boston for repairs. As winter approached in November the French ships left for the West Indies.

Around the same time General Clinton sent Lt. Colonel Campbell with 3,500 men from New York to attack Savannah in Georgia.

Washington returned to Middlebrook on December 11, 1778 for the second time. He spent much of his time at the Wallace House in Somerville as did his wife Martha. Generals Greene and Wayne each spent time at Bridgewater's Van Veghten House. Lord Stirling also stayed in Bridgewater at the Van Vorne House at 900 Main Street. General von Steuben slept at the Staats House in South Bound Brook nearby. General Knox set up shop in Pluckemin. During the summertime, loyalists and Indians attacked the Wyoming Valley in Pennsylvania where they burned 1,000 homes and killed 200+ men, women, and children. Loyalists working with Indians also did similar raids in New York State as well. Congress and Washington both had enough of this and a plan was developed at the Wallace House. General John Sullivan would lead 5,000 men on an invasion of the Iroquois homeland.

Down to the south, Lt. Colonel Campbell captured Savannah on December 29th. General Prevost led another army up from Florida to Savannah after which the combined British force took Augusta, Georgia. The British now had control of Georgia.

In May of 1778, General Clinton took 6,000 men up the Hudson River. They captured two small forts at Stony Point and Verplanck's Ferry. To Washington it looked as though Clinton was getting ready to attack West Point to the north of these forts. In early June, Washington left Middlebrook to position himself between Clinton and West Point. Clinton soon headed back to New York City leaving a few redcoats behind. At around 1 a.m. on July 16th, General Anthony Wayne (who Wayne is named after) led about 1,300 men in a bayonet attack on British held Stony Point. Wayne's men killed 63 British and took 543 prisoners. As a reward for the Elizabethtown troops who stood by in reserve, Washington gave them a small cannon from Stony Point. This same gun is still outside in front of the Union County Courthouse in Elizabeth. It was also the gun that killed General Richard Montgomery during the failed 1775 attack on Quebec. The fort was abandoned by the Americans afterwards as per Washington.

Down in New Jersey the last British "base" was on Paulus Hook. On August 19th, Major Harry "Light Horse" Lee attacked Paulus Hook at 3 a.m. and took about 160 prisoners before withdrawing. Harry Lee was not related to Charles Lee, but his son who would come later was Robert E. Lee.

In September, the French Admiral D' Estaing appeared off of Georgia's coast with his 4,000 troops. He was there to help General Benjamin Lincoln with the siege of Savannah. The siege went slowly for several weeks when a hurried D' Estaing wanted to attack. During the American and French attack the allies lost 800 casualties. Among the dead was the Polish volunteer Count Casimir Pulaski after whom the Pulaski Skyway is named. With hurricane season on the way, the French fleet again sailed away which forced General Lincoln to abandon his siege. Lincoln then withdrew to Charleston in South Carolina.

Washington returned back to Morristown on December 1, 1779 with his 13,000 men. He stayed in the elegant Ford Mansion (still standing) with some of his staff officers who shared the house with the Ford family. General Arthur St. Clair stayed at Henry Wick's house in Jockey Hollow which is still open to the public. The 13,000 men began to construct a massive log hut city in Jockey Hollow to protect them from the weather. The winter of 1779-80 was the worst of the century. There were more than two dozen snowstorms which dumped at least six feet of snow on the Morristown area. With all the snow the roads in and out of Morristown were impassable which led to supply problems. Amongst the troops there were problems with smallpox, sickness, disease, and a lack of food and clothing.

With the French back in the West Indies, General Clinton had about 30,000 soldiers and sailors in New York City. Clinton left New York with Cornwallis and 16,500 men and sailed southward towards Charleston. Back in New York, the Hessian General Wilhelm von Knyphausen was left in charge. The winter wasn't any easier in New York as the Hudson and East Rivers and the New York Harbor froze solid in the zero degree weather.

After the British evacuated Philadelphia in 1778 Benedict Arnold became its military governor. He had some questionable business dealings in which he abused his position. He had a court martial in Morristown at Norris's Tavern. He was found guilty on four of eight counts and given a slight reprimand by George Washington.

In the zero degree temperatures the Arthur Kill also froze between Elizabethtown and Staten Island. Lord Stirling left Morristown on January 14th with 2,000 men, 300 sleighs, and 6 cannon for Elizabethtown. On January 15th they attacked Decker's Ferry (Port Richmond) across the frozen Arthur Kill. Spies informed the British of the attack and they simply fell behind their fortifications. Stirling's men retreated with food, clothing, and blankets although 500 of them got frostbite. In retaliation, Cornelius Hatfield Jr. came across to Elizabethtown on January 25th. His loyalists burned the Elizabethtown Courthouse (where the current one stands) and the First Presbyterian Church that was next door. His father, Cornelius Hatfield Sr. let the local residents use his storehouse as a temporary church.

On May 10th, Lafayette arrived in Morristown after a trip to France. He brought Washington word that the Count de Rochambeau was on his way with 6,000 French troops. Down in Charleston, General Clinton's siege ended with the capture of the city as well as Benjamin Lincoln's army of 6,000 Americans. Back in Morristown, the soldiers endured horrible conditions with little food and no pay. It resulted in a mutiny of two Connecticut regiments which was quickly subdued.

Back in New York City, General Knyphausen realized there were indeed problems in Morristown which could be exploited. On the night of June 6, 1780, the first of 5,000 enemy troops began to cross from Staten Island to Elizabethtown Point. After midnight, British General Thomas Stirling (no relation to Lord Stirling) began to lead 1,500 troops from the water's edge towards Elizabethtown. Spies had already warned Elizabethtown's Colonel Elias Dayton who positioned a dozen or so men at the end of New Point Road (where the minuteman statue is). As Stirling led his column out of the darkness the Americans here fired shots and fell back. General Stirling fell wounded after which it was decided to wait until morning before continuing on the gap in the Short Hills. From here it was about 15 miles to Morristown. As more redcoats landed from Staten Island there were only about 600 locals under Colonel Dayton and General Maxwell to stop them. They positioned themselves across Morris Avenue between Governor Livingston's mansion (Liberty Hall) and where Kean University is. A message from Colonel Dayton was sent off with a rider to inform Washington back in Morristown. To alert the local militia word was also sent to "the Heights Above Springfield" at the eastern edge of modern Summit. Here a signal cannon named "Old Sow" was fired and a beacon was set alite. This beacon was a tall pyramid shaped structure made of logs with tinder which was set on fire. In the darkness it would alert the nearby Essex, Morris, Middlesex, and Somerset County Militias which would respond.

The men set up by Liberty Hall opened fire as the British and Hessians appeared. They fell back down Morris Avenue and kept firing to slow the enemy march. The other militiamen had been gathering and were waiting in Connecticut Farms (Union Township). The Hessians and British arrived were they fought with the militia here for several hours with no progress. Much of Connecticut Farm's residents had fled, but Hannah Caldwell stayed behind. Her husband was the Reverend James Caldwell who preached at Elizabethtown's First Presbyterian Church. The parsonage though for safety was located in Connecticut Farms. During a house to house sweep a British soldier fired into the parsonage. Mrs. Caldwell was inside where she was shot and killed while holding her baby. Her body was stripped and dumped outside while the parsonage was ransacked and set on fire. Other buildings were also set on fire. Even 400 trees in an orchard were chopped down. The British and Hessians drove the militia back towards Springfield when Washington arrived with his 156 member Life Guard around 3 p.m. The angry militia, inspired by Washington drove Knyphausen's 5,000 men back towards Connecticut Farms as darkness fell. As the enemy pulled back, Washington and the militia set up in Springfield around the Rahway River. Knyphausen hadn't counted on the militia putting up such a strong resistance as he was told it would be very light. In the darkness his 5,000 men snuck back to Elizabethtown Point on the Arthur Kill.

Back in Charleston, General Clinton had left Lord Cornwallis with 6,000 men and set sail back to New York City. Clinton was aware that since his court martial, Benedict Arnold, now in charge of West Point was ready to switch sides. When Clinton returned on June 18th he found Knyphausen's harassed men on the shores of the Arthur Kill.

After he returned to New York with his 4,000 troops, General Clinton launched another plan. On June 23rd, he made it look as though his men were sailing up the Hudson to attack West Point. To counter this move, Washington took a couple thousand troops up towards Rockaway enroute to West Point. At the same time though General Knyphausen again marched towards Connecticut Farms with 6,000 men. The militia that was ready slowed his march down towards Springfield. Back in Springfield, Washington left General Nathaniel Greene with 2,500 Continentals. Again the nearby beacons were set on fire and "Old Sow" was shot off. Soon more of the nearby 5,000 local militiamen began to turn out. Knyphausen continued on down Morris Avenue with some of his men while the other half of his force marched down the Vaux Hall Road. The two columns could then converge on Springfield from different directions.

At the bridge over the Rahway River were Colonel Israel Angell's Rhode Island Continentals. Colonel Dayton's men fell back, joined them, and together they held up Knyphausen's column here for nearly an hour before they withdrew back into Springfield. Here they crossed another bridge over a stream (Mountain Avenue area) where Colonel Israel Shreve's N.J. Continentals were set up. Above them at the Vaux Hall Road Bridge, Colonel Matthias Ogden's Continentals and "Light Horse" Harry Lee's men were holding out still. As the battle raged down in Springfield, the Americans began to run out of paper wadding which was rammed down their muskets with the ball and powder. Parson Caldwell, still angry over his wife's death, ran to the Presbyterian Church in Springfield and came back with Watt's Hymnals. He handed out the paper pages yelling "Give em' Watts, boys." Eventually all of Greene's men in Springfield and up at the Vaux Hall Road Bridge fell back into the hills (on the border with Summit). Rather than attempt to attack Greene's men in the hillsides above Springfield, Knyphausen began to march back to Elizabethtown. Before he left though his men burned much of Springfield with the exception of a few loyalist houses. They even set fire to the Springfield Presbyterian Church which burned to the ground. In case he continued on to Morristown, Washington had turned back from Rockaway and set up here. A harassed Knyphausen fell back to the Arthur Kill where his men crossed over to Staten Island.

The British had left Newport prior to the arrival of Rochambeau's 6,000 French troops in July. The French would stay here in Rhode Island while Washington spent the summer of 1780 in the Pompton/Wayne/Totawa area. During August, Benedict Arnold assumed command at West Point.

After General Benjamin Lincoln surrendered Charleston, Congress sent General Horatio Gates to win back the south. Gates picked up militiamen along the way and soon he had about 5,000 men. Gate's army headed towards Camden in South Carolina where there were

1,000 of his men. For Gates, the Battle of Camden went badly as the militia ran away throwing down their unfired muskets. As his continentals also fled, Gates followed on his horse. He rode past his entire army and didn't stop until 180 miles later. Lord Cornwallis was now free to invade North Carolina.

Back in New York, Benedict Arnold wrote to General Clinton in code that he would sell West Point for £20,000. On September 20, 1780, a British Major John Andre went up the Hudson on a ship named the Vulture. He was rowed ashore about 18 miles below West Point where he met with Arnold on the New York side. Arnold had already weakened the walls in the form of construction. He then gave Major Andre the plans for West Point which he placed in his boot. The British would attack West Point in a few days during which Arnold would send his units all over the place. Washington himself would probably lead a rescue party and he would be captured. Major Andre stayed hidden in a nearby house during the daylight hours of the 21st. Some Americans though fired upon the Vulture which was forced to depart. Major Andre now had to travel back down to New York City by land. Prior to leaving from New York, General Clinton told Andre not to remove his British uniform and not to take any papers. On Arnold's instructions, Andre changed into some civilian clothes and left with a pass from Arnold. Three militiamen robbed Major Andre and the plot was soon discovered. The next day Arnold received word of Andre's capture as he ate with Washington and Lafayette. Arnold quickly left and fled to the Vulture as Washington went to inspect West Point. He was angry that Arnold wasn't there, but was soon informed of Major Andre's and Arnold's plans. On October 2nd, Major Andre was hanged as a spy. Had he been caught in his officer's uniform he probably wouldn't have been executed in Tappan where Washington's army now was. Benedict Arnold was now a British general.

Cornwallis down south was on his way towards North Carolina with his left flank protected by Major Patrick Ferguson's 1,000 loyalists. Cornwallis was in the Charlotte, North Carolina area as Ferguson set up on King's Mountain. He was attacked by 3,000 locals who killed 224 loyalists (including Ferguson) and either wounded or captured the rest. Cornwallis could no longer count on a loyalist uprising in North Carolina. He returned to South Carolina in October. As General Gates had been recalled by Congress, Major General Nathaniel Greene was sent down south as a replacement.

As 1781 began, Washington's army was positioned above West Point at New Windsor, New York. General Anthony Wayne's 10 Pennsylvania Regiments were down in Morristown's Jockey Hollow. His men had not been paid for a year and there was a lack of food, blankets, and clothing. Their enlistments were already up as several regiments mutinied and began to march off. Two officers were wounded while another was killed in an attempt to stop the mutineers. They marched to Princeton where General Wayne met with them at Nassau Hall. Congress also sent some delegates who gave the mutineers amnesty. The men with expired enlistments could leave although most simply just rejoined.

Down to the south, Lord Cornwallis was in Winnsboro, South Carolina. General Greene sent General Daniel Morgan towards him with about 800 men. Cornwallis in turn sent out Colonel Banastre Tarleton to attack Morgan. Morgan set up his men against the Broad River in three lines. Tarleton advanced on the first line of riflemen who fell back to the second line of militiamen. The militiamen fired two volleys and also fell back. It looked like a retreat and Tarleton's men were hit by the Continentals in the third line. The militia continued to retreat behind the continentals who also began to fall back. Tarleton ordered his men forward as the entire force of Continentals and militia opened fire at once. At the Cowpens the British lost 110 killed, 200 wounded, and 800 prisoners. Tarleton escaped, but Cornwallis lost 25% of his force. General Clinton sent him another 2,500 men under General Alexander Leslie. Clinton also sent General Benedict Arnold with another 1,200 redcoats to Virginia.

Up in New Jersey on January 20th, 160 men of the N.J. Brigade mutinied in Pompton. They marched to Chatham to get others to join them. Washington sent down General Robert Howe (no relation) with 500 New England soldiers who arrested the mutineers in Chatham. On January 27th, two of the mutiny's leaders were hanged in Bloomingdale as an example.

On February 1st, an angry Cornwallis began to chase Greene up through North Carolina. Greene and Morgan's small army stayed one day ahead of Cornwallis as they marched up to the Dan River on the North Carolina/Virginia border. Cornwallis followed them for two weeks and even burned most of his army's baggage for speed. Greene's men crossed the Dan River to Virginia and took up all the nearby boats. Cornwallis had to return back to Hillsboro where his supply lines were harassed. Greene soon recrossed the Dan River and started back down into North Carolina. General Greene waited for Cornwallis to attack him at Guilford Courthouse. Cornwallis attacked on March 15th, and began to lose the battle so he ordered his cannon to fire into the fray. He shot down men on both sides. Cornwallis won the battle, but lost 500 casualties compared to 79 Americans. Cornwallis then turned and headed for Virginia. Since December, Benedict Arnold had been in Virginia launching raids and burning houses. In response, Washington sent down Lafayette and General von Steuben to stop Arnold's 5,000 men. In May, Cornwallis joined Arnold's force and combined now numbered around 7,200. Lafayette and von Steuben had about 3,000 men who were reinforced by Anthony Wayne's men and the local militia.

Cornwallis set up his headquarters at Williamsburg, Virginia in June of 1781. Lafayette's force camped inland close to Cornwallis. Cornwallis then sent Benedict Arnold back to New York and moved his army to Yorktown. This was located on a peninsula between the James and York Rivers and the Chesapeake Bay.

In the meantime Washington met up with Rochambeau's French Army. Washington was told that the French Admiral De Grasse was coming up from the West Indies with his ships and 3,000 more troops. Washington's army crossed the Hudson River at King's Bridge followed by the French. Washington marched to the Summit and Short Hills Mall area on August 26th. Washington made sure that letters from him which detailed an invasion of New York City were found by the British. It looked like a siege was coming as the Americans built huge bake ovens in the Chatham area. On the night of August 28th, Washington snuck out of Chatham, went through Green Village, and stopped in Bound Brook. The residents in Chatham, woke up and found the Americans were gone. Washington continued on and crossed the Delaware into Pennsylvania. Back in New York City, General Clinton sent a letter to Cornwallis on the 29th which stated Washington "...still remains in the neighbourhood of Chatham." On August 31st, Admiral De Grasses's French ships blockaded Cornwallis in from the Chesapeake Bay. British Admiral Graves arrived with his ships and the two navies tried to set up for battle out at sea. Another French Admiral the Count de Barres arrived from Newport with the siege guns. He too went into the Chesapeake Bay. Graves had to return to New York for repairs as De Grasse also went into the bay. Graves was back in New York around the 23rd where Clinton was getting ready to rescue Cornwallis with 5,000 men.

By September 26th there were now 16,000 French and American troops at Williamsburg. On September 28th they began to march from Williamsburg in order to surround Cornwallis. On the 30th, Cornwallis abandoned his outer trenches which the allies took over. They moved heavy guns in closer. The allies began to fire thousands of shells and shots into the enemy in Yorktown. By mid-October the allies were only 400 yards away from Cornwallis. With no signs of Clinton, Cornwallis surrendered his army of 8,000 men on October 19th. The French ships soon left for the West Indies while the French troops stayed in Yorktown. The American troops with Washington returned back up to the Hudson Highlands at Newburgh. Washington left for several months to stay in Philadelphia. He returned back to Newburgh in March of 1782. In May, General Clinton was recalled and replaced by Sir Guy Carleton. The British evacuated Savannah during July of 1782. A provisional peace treaty was signed in Paris during November of 1782. In December the British evacuated Charleston although they still remained in New York City. Congress ratified the provisional treaty on April 15, 1783. The majority of the Continental Army was disbanded at Newburgh, New York on June 15, 1783. At around the same time the Congress moved from Philadelphia to Princeton which then became the temporary capitol of the U.S. Washington arrived in August, but there was no rooms available in Princeton. Washington stayed four miles away at Rockingham. The official peace treaty was signed over in Paris on September 3, 1783. At Rockingham, Washington delivered his farewell address to his troops in November of 1783. Washington left Rocky Hill and returned to West Point on November 13th. On November 22nd the British withdrew from Paulus Hook and New Jersey was finally free. The last remaining British troops in New York City left on November 25th. As they left Lower Manhattan, Washington entered New York City. The last British ships sailed away on December 4th. Washington gave his farewell address on December 4th at Manhattan's Fraunces Tavern (Pearl and Broad Streets) to his officers. He left Lower Manhattan via the Paulus Hook Ferry enroute to Philadelphia which he reached on the 8th. Congress was at its temporary capitol of Annapolis, Maryland as Washington settled his expenses for seven days. He traveled through Baltimore and reached Annapolis on December 21st. He resigned before Congress on December 22nd. Washington rode home to Mount Vernon which he reached in time for Christmas.

Paul Revere's Ride - April 19, 1775
Drawn by Charles G. Bush From Harper's Weekly June 29, 1867

CHAPTER THREE

Steamboats and Turnpikes

By 1784 things in New Jersey had started to return back to normal. With the Revolutionary War officially over and the British gone, traffic increased on water as well as land. A person could have gone to New York City on ferryboats that ran from Weehawken, Hoboken, Paulus Hook, and Elizabethtown. In N.J. there were more stagecoaches with cushioned seats, hard tops, and even an early strap form of suspension. Once again the roads and highways in New Jersey were filled with stagecoaches. With peace there was also an increase in the freight hauled between New York City and Philadelphia which of course came through New Jersey. The large Conestoga wagons pulled by four or six horses were again on the roads in great numbers.

I'd like to go back real quick to 1769 when John Fitch arrived in New Jersey from Connecticut. He settled in Trenton where he tried several things without success. When the war started, Fitch and Stacey Potts made buttons and fixed weapons. When the British and Hessians came he lost everything. Now on August 29, 1785, he applied to Congress for protection of an idea in the form of a model brass boat with side paddle wheels. In March of 1786, the New Jersey Legislature awarded Fitch the first grant in the U.S. for steam navigation. Fitch had exclusive rights to build, employ, and navigate steamboats in New Jersey's waters until 1800.

One of the problems in the country at the time was that the government since 1781 under the Articles of Confederation was weak. There was no executive branch, no separation of powers, and each state regulated its own trade. If a New Jersey farmer brought apples into New York City to sell them, New York could impose a duty as though the apples came from another country. Issues like this led to Virginia's James Madison who called for a convention of all the states. This convention, held in Annapolis during September of 1786 was attended by only a dozen men from just five states which included New Jersey. As nothing could be done it was decided to meet again in 1787.

Back in New Jersey during May of 1787 some property went up for auction. William Bayard was a wealthy New Yorker who lived in the 14th Street area of Manhattan. He owned several hundred acres in old Bergen County across the Hudson in New Jersey. During the war though he remained loyal to the British and would now have to pay the price. His various land holdings in New Jersey were confiscated and put up for auction. On May 15, 1787, Colonel John Stevens bought 564 of Bayard's acres in the Hoboken area.

Across from New Jersey in Philadelphia, the Constitutional Convention was set to begin during May of 1787. It was here where the founding fathers agreed upon a bicameral legislative branch. The lower chamber or House of Representatives is where seats for a state are determined by its population. The upper chamber or Senate was set up so that each state had two seats regardless of size. In addition there was an executive branch with a President. A judicial branch was also created which included the Supreme Court. To keep one particular branch from getting too strong, a system of checks and balances and separation of powers was placed in the Constitution. I mentioned the Constitutional Convention because John Fitch's steamboat was ready in August of 1787. Some of the delegates took a break as John Fitch gave them a ride in his new steamboat.

In order for the new Constitution to take effect though it had to now be ratified by at least nine states. Delaware was first followed by Pennsylvania. In New Jersey, at Trenton's Blazing Star Tavern, 39 delegates met for this purpose during December of 1787. As John Stevens presided, the delegates unanimously voted for ratification on December 18, 1787. New Hampshire was the ninth state to do so followed by Virginia and New York for emphasis. The outgoing Confederation Congress selected New York City as the temporary capitol of the United States.

During 1788 on the Delaware River, John Fitch had started to take some passengers on his steamboat from Philadelphia to Burlington, Bordentown, and Trenton. Fitch's steamboat ran at about seven miles per hour. John Stevens saw Fitch's steamboat in action which caused him to start to think of something.

In November of 1788, Governor William Livingston and the Council selected N.J.'s first two senators. Dr. Jonathan Elmer from Cumberland County and William Paterson of Princeton were chosen and soon crossed over to New York City. During January of 1789, Governor Livingston and the Council selected six electors to vote for a president. The next month these six electors cast their ballots which were forwarded via ferry to the U.S. Senate in Lower Manhattan. The Senate counted the ballots after which there were 69 votes for George Washington and 34 for John Adams. Washington had been unanimously chosen as the first President of the United States. With no telephones back then, a committee crossed to New Jersey on the Paulus Hook Ferry enroute to Virginia to inform Washington. After he received the news, he left Mount Vernon on April 16, 1789 for a week long trip to New York City. He was cheered by crowds of people who lined the roads. Washington crossed the Delaware River at Trenton and proceeded up Route 27 to Princeton. He continued to New Brunswick and Woodbridge where there was a reception at the Cross and Key Tavern. After he spent the night, Washington reached Elizabethtown the next day where there was a reception at the Red Lion. From here there was a lavish luncheon at Elias Boudinot's mansion (1703 E. Jersey Street) attended by Henry Knox, John Jay, Elias Boudinot, and others. Washington proceeded to the ferry dock on the Arthur Kill where a nicely decorated barge with thirteen oarsmen was waiting. The barge was rowed into the Newark Bay and through the Kill Van Kull on its way to Manhattan's Wall Street Pier. On April 30th, George Washington was sworn in as the first President of the United States. Chancellor Robert R. Livingston administered the oath.

By 1790 John Fitch had stopped his steamboat runs between Trenton and Philadelphia. During 1789-91 Colonel John Stevens had the rights to the Hoboken Ferry. Stevens obtained a patent in 1791 for a steam boiler he came up with. He was actually instrumental in getting the U.S. Congress to enact some of the first patent laws.

By 1792 John Fitch was broke in Philadelphia and loitering around. He needed funds, but after he was ignored by everyone he left for Kentucky.

Prior to 1793 a few people had experimented with hot air balloons in Europe, but not in the United States. On January 9, 1793, a Frenchman name Jean Pierre Blanchard was in Philadelphia about to take off in his green and yellow silk balloon. Blanchard spoke no English so President Washington gave him a letter that instructed people to provide assistance upon landing. Blanchard took off on what was the first balloon flight in the U.S. About 45 minutes later he landed in Gloucester County across the Delaware River. The N.J. residents here read Washington's letter after which Blanchard was given a meal at a tavern. He was then taken by coach to the Delaware where he took a ferryboat across to Philadelphia.

Up in Elizabethtown, Edward Thomas died during 1795. After the war he ran the ferry from Elizabethtown to New York City. General William Crane took over this ferry which was now called Crane's Ferry.

Stagecoach travel was even faster as a new wooden bridge opened across the Raritan River on November 2, 1795. The N.J. Legislature also gave charters for toll bridges across both the Hackensack and Passaic Rivers. With bridges like these the old ferries across these rivers were made obsolete.

In 1798 a broken John Fitch committed suicide. It was a sad ending for the man who invented the steamboat. In New Jersey, Colonel Stevens was hard at work on his own steamboat. In 1801 President Thomas Jefferson appointed Robert R. Livingston as his Minister to France. While in France, Livingston met with two Americans named Robert Fulton and Joel Barlow. Fulton was there to study painting, but had started to work on an experimental steamboat with Barlow. Before long all three Americans were all hard at work together.

When people even outside of New Jersey think "turnpike" the New Jersey Turnpike often gets mentioned. New Jersey's first "turnpike" though was another one. The Morris Turnpike was chartered by the N.J. Legislature in 1801, and would follow the Lenape's Minisink Trail route from Elizabethtown to Morristown via Springfield, Chatham, and Bottle Hill (Madison). By 1804 the Morris Turnpike was completed between Elizabethtown and Morristown. Every six miles there were "pikes" or long wooden poles across the road. When the small toll was paid the "pike" was "turned" so the person or vehicle could pass. To get around the tolls other roads or "shunpikes" were used in Springfield and Chatham. Farmers even drove cattle, sheep, and hogs along the Morris Turnpike to get them to market. Some exceptions to the tolls were if you were going to church, on farm business, or on the way to a militia muster. Thousands of people still drive this same route today along Morris Avenue (Route 82) from Elizabeth through Union, Springfield, and Millburn. Past Millburn it continues on as Route 124 and Main Street in Chatham and Madison into Morristown.

In 1804, Colonel Stevens became the first person to successfully test a steamboat with a four blade turn screw propeller. The propeller idea worked out, but Stevens thought paddle wheels were the way to go. He named his steamboat "Little Juliana" after his daughter. General Crane sold his Elizabethtown Ferry to Johnathan Dayton, Aaron Ogden, and Dr. John Stites. Stites soon sold his share to Dayton and Ogden. Dayton them sold his share to Thomas Gibbons who in turn leased this share to Ogden for ten years.

By 1806 the Morris Turnpike had been extended from Morristown out to Sussex County. This wasn't New Jersey's only turnpike though as there were others. The Bergen Turnpike ran between Bull's Ferry (Hackensack) and Hoboken. The Essex and Middlesex Turnpike connected New Brunswick with Phillipsburg. From Morristown, the Washington Turnpike ran out towards Schooley's Mountain. The Trenton and New Brunswick Turnpike ran via Princeton and Kingston.

With turnpikes like these the first major bridge opened across the Delaware River in 1806. The 1,000 foot covered bridge cost about $180,000 to build. It made stagecoach travel easier between New York City and Philadelphia.

On August 17, 1807, Robert Fulton made the first successful commercial steamboat trip between New York City and Albany. Fulton's "North River Steamboat of Clermont" left Cortland Street on the 17th and reached Albany on the 19th (with stops).

In 1808 Colonel Steven's steamboat "Phoenix" was ready to go. Stevens started an Elizabethtown to New York City steamboat run which was also the first regular steamboat service in the United States. New York State soon granted Robert Fulton and Robert R. Livingston monopolistic rights to steamboats on the Hudson River for 30 years. Stevens decided to take his 100 foot long "Phoenix" over to the Delaware River where it could run between Philadelphia and Trenton. When he made his trip to the Delaware via the Atlantic Ocean, Stevens became the first person in the U.S. to run a steamboat on the Atlantic Ocean.

There were still other sail ferries on the Hudson River though. In 1810 for instance, Cornelius Vanderbilt borrowed some money from his mother which he used to start a sail ferry from Staten Island to New York City.

By this point Colonel Stevens had the rights back to the Hoboken Ferry. He was still thinking though of using steam power on a "railroad." In 1811, he asked the N.J. Legislature for their permission to build a railroad from New Brunswick to Trenton. His request didn't sound like a good idea and was denied. Colonel Stevens became the first person in the U.S. to ask for a railroad charter.

Up on the Hudson River, Livingston and Fulton still had their steamboat monopoly as per New York State. The New Jersey Legislature passed a law where if a N.J. resident running a steamboat was stopped by New York "monopolists", they were entitled to damages. In 1811, Robert Fulton and several others assumed the lease of the Paulus Hook Ferry. Around the same time the New Jersey Legislature gave Colonel Stevens a charter to run ferryboats from Hoboken to Barclay St. in Lower Manhattan.

Aaron Ogden obtained a charter to run a steamboat from Elizabethtown to New York City. His "Sea Horse" from Elizabethtown led New York to pass a law where any steamboat that infringed on the Livingston/Fulton monopoly could be seized. By the Fall of 1811, Stevens began his ferry service from Hoboken to Manhattan. He put a steam engine on his "Juliana" which was connected to the side paddlewheels. Colonel Stevens was the first person to start steamboat service from Hoboken.

Down on the Delaware River at Coryell's Ferry there was a new wooden bridge between New Jersey and Pennsylvania. While the bridge was a benefit for stagecoaches it made the old ferry obsolete. As more stagecoaches carried mail into New Jersey's towns it led to post offices being established. Senator John Lambert helped Coryell's Ferry obtain its own post office. In response, the appreciative residents changed the town name to Lambert's Ville.

For Colonel Stevens, 1812 was a good year on the Hudson River with "Juliana." As the following spring came around he was served with an injunction against "Juliana" from New York. Rather than fight, "Juliana" simply went up to the Connecticut River. Protected by New York's monopoly granted to him, Robert Fulton soon had the steamboats "The Jersey" and "The York" in service from Paulus Hook. Stevens still had a ferryboat on the Hudson River powered by horses. This "steamboat" or "houseboat" had several horses onboard who walked on a small circular base. It turned several shafts that moved the paddlewheels.

Aaron Ogden became Governor of New Jersey, but still maintained his interest in steamboats. He even declined President Madison's nomination of him as a major general. New Jersey passed "Ogden's Law" which gave him a steamboat monopoly in its waters. John R. Livingston then bought control of the Robert Fulton/Robert R. Livingston steamboat monopoly. Ogden's steamboat "Seahorse" stayed in N.J.'s water between Elizabethtown and Jersey City where a horse boat then took his passenger to Manhattan. Livingston's steamboat in turn was kept between Staten Island and Manhattan after which his passengers took a horse boat to New Jersey.

During 1814, Colonel Steven's railroad survey between New Brunswick and Trenton was the first in the United States. The next year Stevens was given the country's first railroad charter. It went nowhere as investors didn't give any support.

With influential friends in New Jersey, John R. Livingston was able to get Ogden's Law repealed. Ogden tried the same thing in New York with the Livingston monopoly, but was unsuccessful. New York did give Ogden permission to run his steamboat between Elizabethtown and Manhattan for ten years, if he paid Livingston $800 a year. His steamboat "Seahorse" could now run without a problem, but issues arose with Thomas Gibbons. Gibbons wanted Ogden to either buy him out or let him purchase Ogden's share. When neither happened, Gibbons ran sailboats from Elizabethtown to Manhattan to annoy Ogden. Gibbons even tried to start a rate war with Ogden with his own steamboat "Mouse of the Mountain" between Elizabethtown and Manhattan. It didn't bother Livingston, but Ogden went to New York and obtained an injunction against Gibbon's steamboat. Ogden's new steamboat "Atalanta" ran between Elizabethtown and Manhattan while "Seahorse" covered Elizabethtown to Amboy. To carry their passengers, Ogden had a contract with the stagecoach company that had a route from Philadelphia to Amboy. In 1818 his creditors forced Ogden to sell off "Seahorse" after which he lost the stage contract. Gibbons then took over control of this steamboat route. Cornelius Vanderbilt sold off his interest in the Staten Island Ferry and worked as Gibbon's steamboat captain. With New York's injunction against him, Gibbon's steamboat carried passengers between Amboy and Paulus Hook.

To add to the fray, New York claimed all the waters between the two states as "theirs." John R. Livingston was able to get an injunction through New York that prohibited anyone except Aaron Ogden from operating a steamboat in these "New York" waters. New Jersey passed a law where steamboats with only New York licenses could be seized if they came to its shores. New Jersey passed a steamboat injunction against Livingston which forced him to bring passengers across on sailboats. New Jersey even slapped Aaron Ogden with an injunction against his steamboat "Atalanta" which prevented its use in the Hudson River area.

As the 1820's started, Jonathan Pitney from Morris County decided to settle down on Absegami Island. He thought the salt air was healthy and decided to start some kind of bathing resort on the island.

During 1820, a Morristown resident named George MacCulloch was on a fishing trip at Morris County's Great Pond. He came up with an idea to raise the water level of Great Pond after which a canal could be built through it from the Delaware River to Newark.

After an agreement was worked out with the Livingstons in 1821, Colonel Stevens was able to run steamboats on the Hudson River. In November of 1821 Stevens incorporated the Hoboken Steam Ferryboat Company. His steam ferry-boat aptly named "Hoboken" soon began taking passengers between Hoboken and Barclay Street.

Back in Morristown during 1822, George MacCulloch proposed his idea for a canal across Northern New Jersey during a local meeting. Prior to this time goods moved across New Jersey on wagons which weren't exactly fast. With a canal across Morris County, products could be moved somewhat quicker. Ephraim Beach was hired as an engineer and he began to survey a possible route.

During 1824, Aaron Ogden and Thomas Gibbon's dispute made it all the way to the U.S. Supreme Court. In the case of Gibbons vs. Ogden, Chief Justice John Marshall ruled that only Congress could regulate inter-state commerce which included passengers as well as freight. As a result, there would be no more watercraft monopolies anywhere in the United States.

On December 31, 1824, an act was passed which incorporated the Morris Canal and Banking Company. In July of 1825, work on the Morris and Essex Canal began as Great Pond was damned at its southern end. When the water level rose and joined the smaller pond next to it, Lake Hopatcong was created in Morris County.

Michael E. Ferlise

CHAPTER FOUR

New Jersey's
Early Railroads

I decided to start this chapter in 1825 with Colonel John Stevens. In Hoboken, he became the first person to run a steam engine on a track. Colonel Stevens had a 630 foot long circle of track on which his steam engine chugged along at six miles per hour. He demonstrated his idea for the public and potential investors in order to attract capital. Unfortunately the investors thought that the Morris Canal sounded like a better idea. For now there would be no steam engines running across New Jersey on tracks.

At the same time in New York State the Erie Canal opened up. It ran from Buffalo on Lake Erie to Albany at the Hudson River. At an approximate cost of $7.6 million, the Erie Canal was the biggest engineering project in the United States at the time. One of the benefits was that the Erie Canal provided access from the Hudson River to the Great Lakes.

Staying in New York State, the future New York Central Railroad got its start on April 17, 1826. This was when the New York State Legislature chartered the Mohawk and Hudson Railroad. With its various locks, the Erie Canal took about forty miles to cover the distance between Albany and Schenectady. The Mohawk and Hudson Railroad could cut this distance to only sixteen miles. The canal interests got their say in as the railroad's charter allowed for passenger traffic only.

To the south of New Jersey on February 28, 1827, the charter for the Baltimore and Ohio Railroad was approved. This charter allowed for a railroad to be built between the Baltimore and the Ohio Rivers. On July 4, 1828 the first stone of the Baltimore and Ohio was laid. The honor went to Charles Carrol. He was the last living signer of the Declaration of Independence.

During 1829 Peter Cooper of New York built the B & O's first steam engine named "Tom Thumb." The one ton engine had a top speed of 18 miles per hour. The "Tom Thumb" was the first American built steam engine to run on an American railroad. As the year ended the B & O had almost 15 miles of track laid from Baltimore. Both the "Tom Thumb" as well as horses pulled cars for the B & O. The little railroad started excursions which made it the first railroad in the U.S. to carry revenue paying passengers.

On February 4, 1830, the first railroad in New Jersey was chartered with the Camden and Amboy Railroad and Transportation Company. This was also the first commercial railroad charter in the United States. After the Baltimore and Ohio, the Camden and Amboy was the second major railroad in the United States. There would now be a rail link between the Delaware River to the southwest and the Raritan Bay. On the same day in 1830, the New Jersey Legislature chartered our second canal. The Delaware and Raritan Canal would link the Delaware River with the Raritan Bay to the northeast. It seems at the time there were two camps as to how to how to get from the Delaware River to the Raritan Bay. On one side, Robert F. Stockton and James Neilson lobbied for the Delaware and Raritan Canal. On the other side, Colonel John Steven's two sons Robert Livingston Stevens and Edwin Stevens argued for the Camden and Amboy Railroad.

In the Spring of 1830, the Camden and Amboy Railroad was organized with Robert Livingston Stevens as President and Edwin Stevens as Treasurer. The Camden and Amboy Railroad's $1,000,000 in stock was bought up in about ten minutes. The Delaware and Raritan Canal was only able to sell about 10% of its stock and the rest went slowly. During 1830 the route for the Camden and Amboy Railroad was surveyed between Bordentown and Camden and from Bordentown to South Amboy. In order to buy a steam engine and some rails Robert Livingston Stevens departed for England. While on his way across the Atlantic

The History of Transportation In New Jersey

Ocean Robert designed the "T" rail that is still used to this day. He also designed the iron railroad spike, the fish bar, and the bolts and nuts used to hold the "T" rails together.

Meanwhile in Elizabethtown, several men were chosen to approach the New Jersey Legislature in order to ask for a railroad. William Chetwood, Edward Price, William Starkweather, and Isaac H. Williamson were selected to ask for an Elizabethtown to Somerville railroad route. Isaac H. Williamson was New Jersey's Governor between 1817 and 1829.

On January 21, 1831, New Jersey's second railroad charter went to the Paterson and Hudson River Railroad. This railroad was planned to run from Paterson to Jersey City. The Paterson and Ramapo Railroad was also chartered in New Jersey.

On February 9, 1831, the New Jersey Legislature chartered the Elizabethtown and Somerville Railroad. The first President of the Elizabethtown and Somerville Railroad was Isaac H. Williamson. The ex-New Jersey Governor became the Mayor of Elizabethtown in 1831. The charter allowed for $200,000 to be raised through stock. As per the charter, the Elizabethtown and Somerville Railroad could charge no more than .06¢ per mile. So long as a person paid the "toll" they could use this "public highway."

On February 15, 1831, a "Marriage Act" was passed to prevent a fatal competition between the Camden and Amboy Railroad and the Delaware and Raritan Canal. The Joint Companies kept their old organizational set ups and officers, but the total revenue from the two was shared. The Joint Companies gave New Jersey 1,000 shares of stock. In return, New Jersey granted that for the thirty years of the charter, no other railroad could compete with the Camden and Amboy on the Philadelphia to Amboy route. The Camden and Amboy had a monopoly for the time being on this route.

In New Jersey the Somerville and Easton Railroad got its start on February 26, 1831.

Starting in May 1831, the Camden and Amboy Railroad's first of more than twenty shipments of "T" rail arrived from England. While he was in England, Robert Stevens also met with George Stephenson who built steam locomotives. In August of 1831, an unassembled ten ton steam locomotive arrived in Bordentown from England. A twenty-three year old handyman named Isaac Dripps put the parts together by trial and error.

Up in New York State on August 9, 1831 the Mohawk and Hudson Railroad officially opened. Its first steam locomotive the "DeWitt Clinton" was named in honor of a man who promoted the Erie Canal. Nearly twelve feet long and weighing 6,800 pounds, the "DeWitt Clinton" was the first steam locomotive in New York State. On opening day, it chugged along at fifteen miles per hour with three "stagecoach" passenger cars in tow.

Down in Bordentown, the Camden and Amboy Railroad had nearly one mile of its new "T" rail laid down. Without the aid of any blueprints, Isaac Dripps had the Camden and Amboy's steam locomotive assembled by November of 1831. Imported from England it was aptly name the "John Bull". After an initial test run, the "John Bull" was ready for its first public demonstration on November 12, 1831. The "John Bull" had a tender which consisted of a flat car with a whiskey barrel as a water tank, and two "stagecoach" passenger cars. Each of the two coaches sat thirty people. The "John Bull" pulled them about thirty miles per hour back and forth on the mile long test track.

In November of 1831, the Morris and Essex Canal opened between Phillipsburg and Newark. Due to geography, New Jersey's oldest and longest artificial waterway had twenty-three inclined planes. There were twelve inclined planes to the east of Lake Hopatcong with eleven to the west. These allowed canal boats to travel the 914 feet up or down from Lake

Hopatcong which is still New Jersey's largest lake. At a cost of about $2.1 million, the nearly 99 mile canal allowed for a five day trip from the Delaware River to Jersey City. Canal boats loaded with anthracite coal from the Lehigh Valley gave a nice boost to the iron industry in Morris and modern Passaic Counties. With coal, the numerous iron furnaces could use it to smelt iron ore instead of charcoal for which hundreds of nearby trees were cut down and fired. Besides coal though iron ore, lumber, lime, and various farmed goods crossed New Jersey on the Morris and Essex Canal.

The future Lackawanna Railroad got its early beginnings during 1832 when the Ligett's Gap Railroad was incorporated. This coal and iron carrying road was conceived by brothers George and Seldon Scranton. The Ligett's Gap Railroad ran from Scranton to Great Bend in Pennsylvania.

Back in New Jersey, the New Jersey Railroad and Transportation Company was chartered on March 7, 1832. This company wanted to run its tracks from Jersey City to New Brunswick, but first had to discuss this plan with the Camden and Amboy Railroad. Before any work could start, the Hackensack and Passaic Bridge Company had to be bought out. Several thousand cedar logs as well as a lot of fill had to be placed in the Hackensack marshes for the future roadbed.

Up in New York State, the New York and Erie Railroad was chartered on April 24, 1832. It was planned to run between Piermont on the New York side of the Hudson River and Lake Erie. As per the charter, the railroad had to be contained to New York only with no connections to Pennsylvania and New Jersey.

By the end of September, the Camden and Amboy Railroad had tracks laid from Bordentown to Hightstown. As December that year came to a close, the Camden and Amboy's tracks reached all the way up to South Amboy on the Raritan Bay. The Camden and Amboy gave the State of New Jersey 1,000 shares of its stock again. There was promised dividend of $30,000+ per year which equaled the State of New Jersey's operating costs. In one way this was good for residents as there was no need for New Jersey to enact any new taxes. In return for the stocks it was given, the State of New Jersey confirmed the Camden and Amboy's railroad monopoly between the Delaware River and the Raritan Bay.

During 1832 the Paterson and Hudson Railroad had tracks laid from Paterson to Acquackanock (modern Passaic). Coaches here were pulled by horses as opposed to steam powered locomotives.

In 1833 the Baltimore and Ohio Railroad's Mount Clare engine repair shops were the first ever in the United States.

By September of 1833, the Camden and Amboy Railroad had runs between Bordentown on the Delaware River and South Amboy on the Raritan Bay. On its first trip the "John Bull" ran into a pig which caused the engine to run into a ditch. By January of 1834 there was a new track that ran south from Bordentown to Camden. With this, the Camden and Amboy Railroad now had a single track between Camden and South Amboy that was approximately sixty-one miles long. Passenger coaches could be pulled by either horses or the locomotive "John Bull", which was somewhat faster. The Camden and Amboy Railroad enjoyed its monopoly along this area through New Jersey which included control of the steamboats at either end.

By May of 1834, the Delaware and Raritan Canal opened up between Trenton and New Brunswick. Built by Irish laborers with picks and shovels, the D & R Canal was about forty-three miles long, seventy-five feet wide, and eight to nine feet deep. Prior to this second canal in New Jersey, goods shipped on the water between Philadelphia and New York had to go around Cape May. With the D & R Canal, coal and other products crossed through New Jersey in barges pulled by mules along the tow path in two days. There were fourteen locks and no inclined planes.

On September 1, 1834, the New Jersey Railroad's first horse drawn car "The Washington" was pulled from Newark to Bergen Hill in Jersey City. There was no tunnel yet so this had to do for now. As 1834 came to a close the New Jersey Railroad's tracks reached Elizabethtown. At the same time, the Paterson and Hudson River Railroad was finally into Jersey City.

Four years after its charter, work was ready to begin on the Elizabethtown and Somerville Railroad. A civil engineer named James Moore came to Elizabethtown where he began work at the end of Broadway on the Arthur Kill.

While the Morris Canal was nice, it completely bypassed Morristown as well as the portion of Essex County where modern Union County is. To help with the problem, the N.J. Legislature chartered the Morris and Essex Railroad on January 29, 1835. The M & E was planned to run from Morristown into Essex County. Of course the M & E could always meet up with the NJRR's tracks which were already here. In March of 1835, one of the M & E's new directors was Jonathan Crane Bonnel (1798-1865) of Summit. He had a sawmill in Chatham, and had recently purchased a 200 acre farm in New Providence Township where Summit is. He offered the M & E a free right of way if the route was changed to run over "the summit" and by his sawmill. The M & E was the first railroad in New Jersey that would cut across a mountain.

By August of 1835 the Baltimore and Ohio had its tracks out to Washington D.C. In New York State, the New York and Erie Railroad had started to dig at Piermont on the west bank of the Hudson River. Up at Lake Erie work started in the Dunkirk area. New York State did allow an adjustment to the charter so the New York and Erie could cross a little bit into Pennsylvania.

On November 19, 1835, horse drawn cars on the Morris and Essex started to run from Newark to Orange. During early December, the NJRR's engine "The Newark" made it over Bergen Hill with the aid of some horses. By the end of 1835 the NJRR had its tracks from here to Rahway. On December 31, 1835, the NJRR made its first run out to Rahway. The engine made its way along with four passenger cars filled with dignitaries. On the return trip its baggage car overturned although nobody was seriously injured. By July of 1836 the NJRR had tracks out to New Brunswick. They now had a link with the Camden and Amboy Railroad and access to the Delaware River.

During August of 1836, the Elizabethtown and Somerville RR started service. Horses pulled passengers between the Elizabethport Ferry and Broad Street.

By October of 1836, the Morris and Essex's passengers started using the NJRR's tracks to ride into the newly incorporated Jersey City. The Paulus Hook Ferry still departed from here, but was now referred to as The Jersey City Ferry. On November 19, 1836, the M & E RR's line between Newark and Orange opened with horse drawn cars for passenger service. This wasn't the answer and Newark's Seth Boyden was asked by the M & E to build them a steam locomotive. Nearby, the Morris and Essex Canal built an eight mile extension from the Newark Bay through Jersey City. This made it easier for coal from Pennsylvania carried on the Morris and Essex Canal to reach the New York City market. The canal now crossed 60 miles of New Jersey via nearly 107 miles of land.

Down in Southwestern New Jersey, the Camden and Philadelphia Steamboat Ferries started service on the Delaware. This gave Camden and Amboy/NJRR passengers quick access to Philadelphia. A little to the north along the Delaware River, the Belvidere and Delaware Railroad was incorporated during 1836. The Bel-Del shared its right of way with the Delaware and Raritan Canal located just several feet away.

Seth Boyden's steam locomotive for the M & E was ready by July of 1837. At six tons, "The Orange" which cost nearly $7,000 to build, was ready for use on the M & E. During the Fall of 1837, "The Orange" began running through what was then North Orange, South Orange, Millville (Millburn), and "The Summit" in the Watchung Mountains. Early on though "The Orange" needed help from oxen in order to get to where modern Summit is today. The coming of the M & E RR through this area gave a boost to the paper mills in Millville (Millburn). It also helped the numerous hat factories in The Oranges where even the Stetson Family made their hats.

As January of 1838 came around, the M & E had tracks from "The Summit" through Chatham and into Madison. The M & E turned this little farm village into the modern Borough of Madison we know today. The wholesale growing of roses started which were then brought to New York City via the M & E's tracks. This resulted in Madison earning the nickname of "Rose City."

There was another interesting side note that occurred nearby in Morristown that improved communication quite a bit. Since 1837, an NYU art professor named Samuel F. B. Morse was working on a telegraph with Alfred Vail. Their little project was financially backed by Vail's father who was a wealthy judge. Judge Vail wanted a demonstration to see where his money was going. In early January of 1838, Vail and Morse strung three miles of wire around the Speedwell Ironworks. Judge Vail gave Alfred a note with "A patient waiter is no loser" written on it. Vail sent it through the wires which didn't touch each other, after which Morse read "A patient waiter is not loser" aloud. They came up with the first electromagnetic telegraph anywhere. Vail went on to work out the telegraph transmitter as well as a new alphabet called "Morse Code" with dots and dashes.

The Elizabethtown and Somerville Railroad had tracks out to Plainfield. Back then there were three engines named "General Wall", "Eagle," and "Philadelphia." The E & S's rolling stock early on consisted of one passenger car along with several boxcars and flatcars. The first train from Elizabethtown to Plainfield ran on January 1, 1839. Engineer Henry Frazer was at the controls of the engine "Eagle" with Ogden Smith as his conductor. There would soon be ferry service from Elizabethport where the E & S tracks ended to New York City with "Water Witch" and "Cinderella." The Elizabethtown and Somerville tracks out to Plainfield somewhat paralleled The Old York Road (Route 28). and began to make stagecoaches obsolete in this area.

By January of 1840, the Elizabethtown and Somerville Railroad had tracks out to Bound Brook in Somerset County. Prior to 1840, the Camden and Amboy Railroad ran from Camden to South Amboy via the way of Bordentown, Hightstown, Jamesburg, Helmetta, and Old Bridge. The original route was later shifted so it ran north from Trenton to New Brunswick via Princeton and Monmouth Junction. Once in New Brunswick, Camden and Amboy customers could continue on with the New Jersey Railroad's line through Elizabethtown, Newark, and Jersey City. Today's Northeast Corridor in New Jersey still follows the Camden and Amboy's newer route along with the New Jersey Railroad's above it. The original sixty-two mile Camden and Amboy right of way is somewhat shorter today in the form of Conrail's Amboy Secondary between Monroe Township and South Amboy.

In 1841, the New Jersey Railroad leased the Paulus Hook Ferry with its four ferryboats from the Associates of Jersey City. By 1842, the Elizabethtown and Somerville Railroad was out as far as Somerville with an eye towards the Delaware River. During the early 1840's Samuel Morse was stringing telegraph wires on poles along the Baltimore and Ohio's tracks between Baltimore and Washington D.C. By the spring of 1844, Morse's telegraph line was ready for a test. On May 24, 1844, the message of "What hath God wrought?" was sent over this line from the Supreme Court building in Washington D.C. to the B & O's Pratt Street Station in Baltimore. In September of 1845, the Morris and Essex Railroad decided to extend its tracks through Denville to Dover, but via Rockaway. The following year Samuel Morse's telegraph line stretched from Washington D.C. to Jersey City.

Around 1846 the State of New York lifted the "New York only" restriction placed upon the N.Y. & Erie Railroad. It was now able to cross in and out of Pennsylvania in the Port Jervis area of New York State. Due to an increase in British rail trackage, an English manufacturer was unable to deliver 12,000 tons of "T" rail the N.Y. & Erie needed. The railroad then turned to the two Scranton Brothers in Pennsylvania. Prior to this time they made nails, but had also experimented with the use of anthracite coat to smelt iron ore into "T" rails. The Scrantons were able to provide the Erie with the "T" rail it needed so work could continue.

By 1847 the Elizabethtown and Somerville Railroad was in financial straits as its income did not match expenses. At a public auction, the little road was sold to John Stearns and Coffin Colket. On February 20, 1847, it was rechartered and renamed The Central Railroad of New Jersey. That day the N.J. Legislature also chartered The Somerville and Eastern Railroad. This road was planned to run from Somerville to Phillipsburg on the Delaware River. By the end of the year the N.Y. & Erie had its tracks out to Port Jervis.

During the summer of 1848 the Morris and Essex R.R. had service from Newark out to Denville via Rockaway. Shortly afterwards the Paterson and Ramapo and the Paterson and Hudson River Railroads would open up for service.

On February 22, 1849, the two charters of the Central Railroad of NJ and the Somerville and Easton Railroads were adjusted whereby each bought and assumed control of the other. In April the two lines merged together in the form of the Central Railroad of N.J. This merger would eventually allow for access to the coal fields of Pennsylvania. The CRRNJ had service sixty-three miles across New Jersey by 1851. From Elizabeth its tracks ran through Westfield, Plainfield, Somerville, Clinton, and Bloomsbury to Phillipsburg. The CRRNJ could now haul coal eastward from Easton just across the Delaware River.

In Pennsylvania, George Scranton's Ligett's Gap Railroad opened between Scranton and Great Bend some fifty miles away. There was a name change though from the Ligett's Gap RR to the Lackawanna and Western RR.

During 1851, the New York and Erie RR was completed from Dunkirk on Lake Erie to Piermont some twenty-four miles above New York City on the western shore of the Hudson River. At the time the New York and Erie was the longest railroad in the World. On May 14th and 15th U.S. President Millard Fillmore with some of his cabinet took a ride on the

N.Y. & Erie's first run. A steamboat took these special guests on the 1 ½ hour ride from Lower Manhattan to Piermont where the train was then taken.

George Scranton's Lackawanna and Western RR was in action several months later to Great Bend where its six foot gauge tracks met the NY & Erie's six foot gauge tracks. George Scranton could now bring his coal towards New York via the NY & Erie. The Lackawanna and Western's early steam locomotives with names like "Lackawanna", "Capouse", "Tunkannock", and "Wyoming" were made in Paterson.

Passengers on the NY & Erie RR soon grew tired of the 1 ½ hour ferry ride from Piermont to Lower Manhattan or vice versa. In place of the ferry ride they started to use the Paterson and Ramapo RR and the Paterson and Hudson River RR. The NY & Erie RR still had its charter restriction which kept it in New York State. The New York & Erie leased the Paterson & Ramapo and the Paterson & Hudson River Railroads. It also chartered the one mile long Union Railroad between Suffern (where its passengers had been getting off) and the Paterson & Ramapo RR. Because the NY & Erie was six foot or broad gauge and the other two were four foot eight and one-half inch or standard gauge, a third rail had to be laid down to Jersey City.

The future Montclair Branch of New Jersey Transit got its start in 1852 as the Newark and Bloomfield RR was chartered.

Down in South Jersey, the promoters of the Camden and Atlantic Railroad met to discuss ending their future line at Absegami Island. They opened a map drawn up by their engineer, saw "Atlantic City" written across it, and the name stuck.

In March of 1853, the Pennsylvania Legislature allowed the Lackawanna and Western RR to merge with the Delaware and Cobb's Gap RR. The new name was now the Delaware Lackawanna and Western RR.

One month later in New York, all of the small railroads between Albany and Buffalo came together with a merger and the new name of New York Central.

By October of 1853 the NY & Erie had a third rail from Suffern down to Jersey City. On November 21, 1853, its first train ran direct from Suffern to Jersey City.

Down in Jersey City the NJRR had a line from here to Newark and New Brunswick already. At a cost of $485,000, the NJRR purchased the rights to the Jersey City Ferry along with some of the local waterfront from the Jersey City Associates. The NJRR now assumed control of what used to be the old Paulus Hook Ferry for access to Manhattan.

By 1854 the M & E's tracks were as far out as Hackettstown. Due to competition with the M & E, the Morris Turnpike Corporation decided it could no longer keep up with the Morris Turnpike's repairs. As a result, local towns like Union, Springfield, Chatham, and Madison took over the old Morris Turnpike which is still around in the form of Morris Avenue and Main Street. Some local residents will even notice the old "shunpikes" still carry the name of Shunpike.

At this point in time the Camden and Amboy RR had one single track between Amboy and Bordentown. The Raritan and Delaware Bay RR was chartered by the NJ Legislature on March 3, 1854. It was planned to cut across New Jersey between these two bays.

On July 1, 1854, the first train of the Camden and Atlantic RR took 600 passengers from Camden to Atlantic City. There were no bridges at either end of the C & A yet so ferries were used by the passengers. While the Camden and Amboy wasn't happy about the Raritan and Delaware Bay RR, it didn't seem to view the Camden and Atlantic as competition. On

July 4th, regular service started for passengers between Camden and Atlantic City which had just incorporated on March 3rd.

To the north of Atlantic City in what was Essex County, Elizabeth was now a city. Nearby Hoboken incorporated the following year in 1855. At the same time, the NY & Erie RR purchased 212 acres of land and waterfront in Jersey City/Hoboken. The NY & Erie's Long Dock Company was chartered by the NJ Legislature to improve the land in this area.

NJ Transit's Montclair Branch got its start during 1856 in the form of the Newark and Bloomfield RR. It ran from West Bloomfield (Montclair) down to Newark where it connected with the M & E at Roseville Avenue. The Pascack Valley Line's early beginnings also go back to 1856 when the NJ Legislature chartered the Hackensack & NY RR.

With an increase in ferryboats around New Jersey, there were bound to be accidents. On March 15, 1856, the ferryboat "New Jersey" had a fire start onboard halfway between Philadelphia and Camden. Sixty passengers died after the fire started.

Two months later construction started at Port Monmouth for the Raritan and Delaware Bay RR.

At the same time, the DL & W in Pennsylvania was completed to the Delaware River at the Water Gap where New Jersey was reached by a new bridge. John Blair built an 18 mile railroad from here through Warren County. This met the CRRNJ's line across New Jersey at Hampton. The DL & W worked out a contract with the CRRNJ which allowed it to use their line. The CRRNJ in turn added a third rail to its tracks to accommodate the DL & W's broad gauge trains.

As June of 1856 started, the NY & Erie's Long Dock Company began work on a mile long tunnel under Bergen Hill. This would allow access between the Paterson and Hudson River RR's tracks and the Long Dock Company on the other side. Nearby in Jersey City, the NJRR's new Exchange Place Terminal opened up.

Back in 1853 Pope Pius IX established New Jersey's first Catholic diocese in Newark. New Jersey's first Bishop here was James Roosevelt Bayley. He went out to Madison and founded the first diocesan college in the U.S. along the M & E's tracks. Bishop Bayley started Seton Hall here which he named after his aunt, St. Elizabeth Ann Seton.

Today's Black River & Western RR can trace its roots back to 1857 when the Bel-Del RR built a 12 mile branch out to Ringoes.

Due to financial problems the NY & Erie RR went into receivership in 1859.

Seton Hall by now had relocated up the Morris and Essex to South Orange where the modern university is today.

As the 1860's started, the CRRNJ was burning more coal in its locomotives instead of wood. In the New Jersey/New York area more people and industries were also using more coal. With the increased demand for coal from Pennsylvania, the CRRNJ was on its way to becoming a large coal carrier.

The Raritan and Delaware Bay was already complete from Port Monmouth to Eatontown when a branch from here to Long Branch was built in June of 1860.

Elsewhere in the United States though things were getting heated. South Carolina seceded from the U.S. in December of 1860. President Elect Abraham Lincoln departed from Springfield, Illinois on a cross country trip to Washington D.C. Lincoln's train from Jersey City arrived in Newark at the M & E's Broad St. Station in February 1861. He made a speech after which he departed on another train for Trenton. Seven days later, Jefferson Davis in the South was elected President of the Confederate States of America. Lincoln finally arrived in Washington D.C. on February 23rd on a Baltimore and Ohio train. The Civil War began on April 12th when South Carolina bombarded Fort Sumter.

In early 1861, the NY & Erie was reorganized and renamed the Erie Railway Company. After 57 deaths and 5 years of construction the Erie's tunnel through Bergen Hill was finally completed. On the side of the tunnel entrance just below NJ Transit's Bergen Tunnels is still carved "Long Dock Company Incorporated 1856." Along the Hudson River in Pavonia the Erie RR's terminal also opened. The Erie no longer had to use the NJRR's Exchange Place Terminal in Jersey City anymore. The Erie RR also started up the Pavonia Ferry Company that was chartered by King George II back in 1733. For its Pavonia Ferry the Erie RR leased two of the NJRR's ferryboats. The Pavonia Ferry's first run was on May 1, 1861. Service was provided to Manhattan's Chambers Street.

With the U.S. Civil War underway some of the Hudson River ferryboats in N.J. were seized by the Federal Government. The CRRNJ's "Kill Van Kull" was one while the Hoboken Steam Ferry Company's "Hoboken" was another. The NJRR sold its ferryboat "John P. Jackson to the U.S. Government as well. Within a year though "Hoboken" would be lost. With the increases in coal and freight the CRRNJ double-tracked its Main Line across New Jersey between Phillipsburg and Raritan.

During 1862 the Camden and Amboy RR's tracks were realigned so they now ran between New Brunswick and Trenton. At Princeton Junction, a three mile branch line was built for service to the college. This new alignment is the modern Northeast Corridor Line used by Amtrak, Conrail, and NJ Transit.

By August of 1862 the Raritan and Delaware Bay RR had worked its way down to where Wharton State Forest is.

By this time the CRRNJ had grown tired of sending its cars from Elizabethport to Jersey City on the NJRR. The CRRNJ came up the idea of bridge across the Newark Bay between Elizabeth and Bergen Neck (Bayonne). Once on the other side of Newark Bay the tracks could run up the peninsula to Jersey City. Of course the Erie's Pavonia Terminal and the NJRR's Exchange Place Terminal were already here. The CRRNJ would have to construct theirs where Communipaw Bay or the South Cove was. It had to be filled in first with New York City garbage.

Millionaire Cornelius Vanderbilt was able to gain control over the New York & Harlem and the Hudson River Railroads. The New York Central's freight was normally shipped down the Hudson River from Albany to Manhattan. When the Hudson River froze, the NY Central used these two smaller railroads to access Manhattan by rail. The Hudson River froze as usual, but Vanderbilt decided to refuse the NY Central access to his two railroads. When the NY Central's freight piled up, its stock plunged after which Vanderbilt bought it up. After a deal was worked out with the NYC, the stock went up which made Vanderbilt even richer.

In 1863 the M & E RR stopped using the NJRR's Exchange Place Terminal. The M & E started to use the Erie's Bergen Hill Tunnel to get to its own tracks in Hoboken. Here it built a terminal at Newark St. near where the Hoboken Ferry Company was.

As the Civil War continued on, the U.S. Government allowed the upstart Raritan and Delaware Bay RR to carry Union troops and supplies. The Camden & Amboy didn't like losing its old monopoly. It even introduced a bill in the Congress to force the R & DB to turn over all its profits.

The mining industry in the Lake Hopatcong area had the Morris Canal, but lacked any railroad connection. This was taken care of though when the Ogden Mine RR was chartered.

In the summer of 1864, the CRRNJ's "South Branch" from Somerville to Flemington was ready for use. On its Main Line the town of Craneville changed its name to today's Cranford. The CRRNJ's new terminal at Communipaw Cove was still being constructed in Jersey City as the two mile long drawbridge over the Newark Bay was finished between Elizabethport (by the Jersey Gardens Mall) and modern Bayonne.

JOHN STEVENS
Father of the American Railroad System

The Original "John Bull" Train—Built in 1831

John Bull 1831

Baltimore and Ohio RR

*Here is Jersey Central's first train, consisting of a loco-
motive, a wood car and one coach. The locomotive is the
"Eagle," built by Baldwin at Philadelphia in 1838. It pulled
the first train to Plainfield January 1, 1839.*

CHAPTER FIVE

Railroads and other things

in New Jersey

Now that the Civil War was over the United States started the rebuilding process. The U.S. Government returned the New Jersey Railroad's two ferryboats "Philadelphia" and "John P. Jackson." During 1865 the Camden and Amboy Railroad opened a three mile long branch line to Princeton. The modern "Princeton Line" is half a mile shorter, but it still follows this same route. New Jersey Transit has one car nicknamed the "Dinky" that shuttles passengers between Princeton Junction on the Northeast Corridor with Princeton Station. Down the shore a second railroad reached Long Branch. People left New York City on ferryboats that steamed down to Sandy Hook. From Sandy Hook, trains of the new Long Branch and Seashore Railroad followed the coastline to Long Branch. The engines and cars were provided by the Camden and Amboy Railroad. This line now competed with a branch line of the Raritan and Delaware Bay Railroad. This railroad already had a line from Eatontown to Long Branch prior to the Long Branch and Seashore Railroad.

On August 2, 1865, the Central Railroad of New Jersey's passenger and ferry buildings in Jersey City formally opened. On the opposite side of the Hudson River in Lower Manhattan the CRRNJ's Liberty Street Terminal opened. Ferry service in between was initially performed by the ferryboats "Communipaw" and "Central." The CRRNJ built stations in Bayonne, Greenville, and Flemington as well as a freight house in Jersey City. After six years of work the CRRNJ's new "High Bridge" over the Raritan River was completed. The older bridge over the Raritan River was covered with dirt and filled in.

During 1865 the Morris and Essex Railroad completed its link between Phillipsburg and Hackettstown. By this time, Morris and Essex trains ran to Hoboken via the Erie's Bergen Hill Tunnel completed in 1862. On November 23, 1865, the first coal train ran from Phillipsburg to Hoboken. Wood burning locomotives though had trouble hauling heavy coal loads over the hill between Chatham and "The Summit" in New Providence Township. The long coal trains had to be broken up and brought over the hill in sections. The now coal carrying Morris and Essex Railroad directly competed with the Morris Canal.

In Morris County, the Ogden Mine Railroad was completed for the moment. It ran from the mines above Lake Hopatcong and down to Nolan's Point on the lake. From this point the iron ore traveled by barge over the Morris Canal.

In 1867 the Morris and Essex Railroad built a branch from Denville to Boonton. During that time Boonton was a bustling iron production center. Prior to the Morris Canal, charcoal was used to heat up iron ore in order to extract the iron. Charcoal was made by chopping down acres of trees and firing them. After a while though there were fewer and fewer trees. Like the Morris Canal, the Morris and Essex Railroad could now bring coal to the Boonton area for this purpose.

According to the story, the CRRNJ's President John Taylor Johnston decided to name a station after his daughter Fanny Wood. In Westfield Township a Central Railroad station soon carried the name of Fanwood. The modern Borough of Fanwood started to develop around this station named after Fanny Wood.

It was around now when the New Jersey Railroad and Transportation Company became part of the United Companies of New Jersey. This company already included the Camden and Amboy Railroad as well as the Delaware and Raritan Canal. Across the Hudson River in New York a group of people controlled almost half of the New York Central's stock. This group asked Cornelius Vanderbilt to become President to which he agreed.

In 1868 at Hoboken the railroad and ferry terminals were replaced with a larger one. Standard gauge Morris and Essex Railroad trains brought passengers eastward into

Hoboken. From here railroad passengers used the Hoboken Ferry Company's boats to cross the Hudson River to New York City. Back then Montclair was known as West Bloomfield. The Newark and Bloomfield Railroad had been planned to run from Bloomfield to Jersey City. When West Bloomfield didn't figure into the plans it left in the form of Montclair. In 1868 the Morris and Essex took control of the Newark and Bloomfield Railroad. In Morris County the Chester Branch was built down from the Dover area to the iron mines in Chester.

In 1868 a third railroad to Long Branch was chartered with the New York and Long Branch. This CRRNJ concern was chartered to run from Amboy to Long Branch. Prior to this railroad, the second route to Long Branch was the Long Branch and Seashore Railroad that ran from Sandy Hook downward. In wintertime there was a chance steamboat service between New York City and Sandy Hook might be halted. The New York and Long Branch's rail connection above Amboy could provide year round service to Jersey City. In order to access the Hudson River from Pennsylvania, the Lackawanna had been using the CRRNJ's Mainline since the 1850's. The CRRNJ laid a third rail along side its track for broad gauge D L & W trains. To improve its access to the east, the Lackawanna leased the Morris and Essex RR along with its terminal on the Hudson in Hoboken.

By 1869 the CRRNJ had passenger service on its little Newark and New York Railroad. These tracks ran from the Communipaw Terminal through Jersey City, Kearny, and Newark where they ran to Broad Street. With this "railroad" the CRRNJ was able to provide service to its terminal from Newark.

Across the Hudson River in New York, Cornelius Vanderbilt merged the New York Central with the Hudson River Railroad. With this merger the railroad had a new name of the New York Central and Hudson River Railroad. In New York City, steam locomotives were not allowed below 42nd Street. New York residents pretty much lived on the lower portion of Manhattan Island, but some people had started to move up to this area. At 42nd Street and 4th Avenue Vanderbilt had construction started on the new Grand Central Depot.

For several years prior to 1869 the Hackensack and New York Railroad had service between Hackensack and Jersey City. In 1869 this railroad expanded north to the Erie Railroad's tracks in Hillsdale. That same year the Erie Railroad gained control of the Hackensack and New York Railroad.

On February 15, 1870, the Passaic Valley and Peapack Railroad was chartered and construction started from Summit to Bernardsville. The railroad's surveyor George Howell got the tracks to pass through the Cornish Family's farm a little past New Providence Township. Howell then named the area "Gillette" in honor of his wife Rachel Gilette Cornish.

By 1870 in Atlantic City, Conductor Alex Boardman from the Camden and Atlantic Railroad had finally grown tired of sweeping sand from his cars that passengers tracked in. Boardman spoke with a local hotel employee named Jacob Keim who also hated cleaning up sand. After some discussion they came up with the idea of using a pathway of small boards laid on the beach. "Boardman's Walk" as it was called opened in Atlantic City during June of 1870. This was actually the first "boardwalk" in the United States.

For the CRRNJ, it opened a new passenger station in Newark at Ferry Street. This was built on the branch from Broad Street to the terminal in Jersey City. New tracks later ran from this line down to the south where they connected with the Mainline that ran through Elizabethport. From Elizabethport other new tracks continued south to Perth Amboy. The CRRNJ had an eye towards Long Branch which by now had a reputation as a health resort with its cool ocean breeze. Even U.S. President Ulysses S. Grant came to Long Branch in order to escape the sweltering air back at Washington D.C. His house at 991 Ocean Avenue was known locally as the "Summer Capitol." With the new Monmouth Park Race Track more people came down to Long Branch. President Grant even had his own box in which to watch the action.

During the late 1860's a young Thomas Edison worked in New York City for the stock ticker company of Gold Indicator. He worked in New York City, but lived in Elizabeth on Morris Avenue with fellow employee Franklin Pope. The two men started their own company in Jersey City which Western Union then acquired. Edison made some improvements on Western Union's stock ticker for which he was given $40,000. Edison took his money, purchased some supplies, and rented two buildings in Newark where he made stock tickers.

After its foreclosure in New Jersey, the old Raritan and Delaware Bay Railroad had a name change to the New Jersey Southern Railroad Company.

After the Lackawanna took over the Morris and Essex Railroad it started to work on some improvements. In order to divert heavier freight trains off of the Morristown Line, new tracks were laid from Denville through Boonton to Paterson. From here trains could run towards Secaucus and Hoboken (or vice versa) via Passaic. At the same time new tracks were laid between Denville and Dover. This allowed Rockaway to be bypassed. To use the Morris and Essex's tracks which were standard gauge, the Lackawanna had to add a third rail for its broad gauge equipment. Soon the Lackawanna had its trains using the terminal in Hoboken.

During the spring of 1871 the CRRNJ leased the Lehigh and Susquehanna Railroad that ran between Easton and Wilkes-Barre in Pennsylvania. With its tracks already in Phillipsburg, the CRRNJ could now bring coal east to New York City.

Across the Hudson River in the 42nd Street area the $3 million Grand Central Depot opened up for passenger service in 1871.

On June 30, 1871, the Pennsylvania Railroad leased the United Companies for 999 years. The PRR now had control over the old Camden and Amboy Railroad, the New Jersey Railroad, and the Delaware and Raritan Canal. This gave the PRR access to Jersey City and New York City from Pennsylvania via Trenton, New Brunswick, Elizabeth, and Newark.

The Lehigh Valley Railroad in turn leased the Morris Canal for 999 years. This eliminated it as coal carrying competition. From this point on, the once great Morris Canal would never again show a profit. During the 1870's the Lehigh Valley Railroad started work on its own tracks from the Delaware River. They ran across New Jersey via Somerset County.

On December 23, 1871, the first train ran from Basking Ridge to Summit. By the end of January in 1872, regular passenger service started on these tracks out to Bernardsville. One of the people that the future Gladstone Branch bought out to this area the President of the Metropolitan Bank of New York, George I. Seney. Other wealthy New Yorkers followed the tracks out into the Somerset Hills where they too built huge mansions and estates.

There were no automobiles yet, but as a sign of things to come John D. Rockefeller purchased land on Bayonne's Constable Hook in 1872. To the north of Constable Hook during June of 1873, the second terminal in Hoboken was destroyed in a fire. As a replacement, a temporary structure was built for the Lackawanna's passengers who crossed the Hudson River at Hoboken.

For the CRRNJ at this time its smaller lines were consolidated into the larger company. The CRRNJ "acquired" the Newark and New York Railroad which ran from Jersey City to Newark with a little branch between Newark and Elizabethport. The CRRNJ also absorbed its small line from Elizabethport that ran south to Perth Amboy.

Inspired by the technology used to construct a tunnel underneath the Thames River in England, Colonel DeWitt Clinton Haskin had an idea to do the same thing under the Hudson River. In Jersey City at 15th Street, Colonel Haskin sank a shaft. He planned to use compressed air to keep the water back during construction. Haskin stopped work because the Lackawanna obtained an injunction against the project.

By 1874 the CRRNJ's Main Line from Cranford was elevated for safety out to Plainfield. As the Lackawanna was now using the M & E RR, the CRRNJ was able to remove the third rail it had across New Jersey.

Up in Jersey City the Lackawanna had access to Hoboken via the Erie's tunnel through Bergen Hill. This wasn't the best arrangement however. This led to the Lackawanna building its own trestle over the Erie's tracks along with a new Bergen Hill tunnel.

With its Morris and Essex Lines, the Lackawanna was able to provide service to the iron industry in Morris County. The CRRNJ's Main Line past Somerville ran roughly along today's Route 78 corridor south of Morris County. In order to compete with the DL & W in Morris County, the CRRNJ's High Bridge RR opened from High Bridge towards Dover. 1875 was a good year for the CRRNJ as its New York and Long Branch RR was ready from Amboy down to Long Branch. For Long Branch this was the third railroad that provided service out to it. The first train to Long Branch on this new line ran on June 26, 1875 with President Ulysses S. Grant as a passenger.

Down in Southern N.J. the PRR leased the West Jersey RR in order to gain access to Atlantic City.

At around the same time a new railroad was being proposed to run between the Delaware River and Bound Brook where the CRRNJ's tracks were. The Delaware and Bound Brook RR would run via West Trenton, Belle Mead, and Hillsborough.

The first oil refinery on the East Coast was established in Bayonne during 1875. The Prentice Oil Company began to bring petroleum from Pennsylvania to Bayonne in railroad cars.

As 1876 came around the United States was now 100 years old. It was the year of Custer's Last Stand, Alexander Graham Bell's telephone, and Hopewell's Great Frog War. The Delaware and Bound Brook RR was working on its line between Philadelphia and Bound Brook via Hopewell. The PRR already had its own tracks through here and didn't like this new railroad. The D & B RR would have to build a "frog" or intersection across the PRR's tracks. To block construction of this frog, the PRR began to park an engine across the spot where it would go. If a PRR train had to go through, this engine was pulled into a siding after which it returned to its blocking duties. On January 5, 1876, this engine pulled into its siding when 200 men appeared and chained it down. They piled logs across the PRR tracks so the intersection could be built. A PRR engine left Millstone at 60 mph, rammed the log barricade and a D & BB locomotive. As armed men for both roads appeared, the Sheriff asked Governor Bedle for the militia. On January 8th there was a court ruling. It stated the PRR could not interfere with the D & BB's frog. That day one of its engines crossed the PRR's tracks at the completed frog.

Thomas Edison sold his Newark factory in 1876. He relocated to Menlo Park alongside the PRR's tracks (Northeast Corridor). Edison's Menlo Park factory was the first organized research facility in the world.

Colonel Maltby was the owner of several hotels in Sea Girt and Spring Lake. He let CRRNJ officials know that if the New York and Long Branch RR came down by his hotels that 150 brokers would ride to Wall Street from his hotels. In response, the CRRNJ extended its tracks from Long Branch to Sea Girt. Long Branch was still a popular resort as the new U.S. President Rutherford B. Hayes visited the town.

Up to this point in time the D L & W's tracks and equipment were broad or 6' gauge. This led to problems with the interchange of cars with standard gauge railroads. For 48 hours in March of 1876, the Lackawanna shut down while its equipment was readjusted. At the same time its tracks were changed to 4'8 1/2" or standard gauge. In May of 1877 the D L & W's first Bergen Hill Tunnel was ready for its Morris and Essex trains. This tunnel is still used by New Jersey Transit as we speak.

A second railroad started service between Camden and Atlantic City. The new Philadelphia and Atlantic City RR now competed with the Camden and Atlantic RR.

During 1878 in Bayonne, John D. Rockefeller purchased the Prentice Oil Company to make way for his Standard Oil Refinery. At the same time, Pennsylvania's Tidewater Oil Company also came up to Bayonne. Coal was still king for the moment, but it was fast losing its status. Railroads like the CRRNJ, PRR, Lackawanna, and Lehigh Valley still brought trains of coal cars eastward from Pennsylvania though.

During 1878 the PRR took over the Belvidere and Delaware RR which now became a branch of its new parent railroad.

Thomas Edison did not discover electricity. He did not invent either electric power or the electric lamp. While at Menlo Park though he did try to make it both cheaper and affordable. There were already electric arc lamps which were expensive, let out a foul odor, and were extremely bright. Edison tried dozens of filaments, but nothing seemed to work or last. He then took some common thread which he carbonized and shaped into a filament. He placed it in a bulb from which the air was taken out. It began to glow on October 19, 1879. It only burned out on the 21st when Edison increased the power. He then began to produce wire, switches, fuses, and generators. On December 31, 1879, Edison lit up his Menlo Park lab as well as the nearby homes. Edison had now made electricity practible and affordable.

Our current Gladstone Branch between Summit and Gladstone was originally named the NJ West Line. Towards the end of the 1870's it had money problems. This led to bankruptcy. It was sold to Roswell Rolston and renamed the Passaic and Delaware RR.

By 1880 the CRRNJ's New York and Long Branch RR now had service down to Manasquan.

In order to get more petroleum eastward, the Standard Oil Company's pipeline opened in 1880 between Pennsylvania and Bayonne.

During July of 1880 a third railroad reached Atlantic City in the form of a branch line of the West New Jersey Railroad. This West Jersey and Atlantic Railroad ran some 33 miles between Newfield and Atlantic City.

The Erie Railroad's most western terminal was now out to Chicago. In this part of the country, its line between Suffern and Jersey City was extremely busy. In order to bypass a congested Paterson, the Erie built the Bergen County RR between Ridgewood and Rutherford.

On March 4, 1881, James Garfield was inaugurated as the new U.S. President. On July 2, 1881, President Garfield was at the PRR's station in Washington D.C. when he was shot by Charles Guiteau. He lingered for a bit without his health improving as his weight fell from 200 to 130 pounds. His doctors felt it might be a good idea if the ailing Garfield left Washington D.C. for the cool ocean breezes of Long Branch. On September 5th, a message was sent to the CRRNJ in Jersey City by telegraph that Garfield would be coming the next day. President Garfield was coming to stay at a cottage in Long Branch. The cottage though was located one mile from the NY and Long Branch's tracks. In order to avoid a rough carriage ride for Garfield, a railroad spur had to built overnight. Some tracks were removed from the Westfield area and brought to Long Branch via Elizabeth. During the afternoon several hundred men began to build the railroad spur. As the night wore on they were joined by 2,000 volunteers. On September 6th, Garfield left Washington in the morning and reached Elberon around 1 p.m. His 3 car train was pushed by an engine down the completed spur towards the cottage. At one point it stalled and was pushed by 200 men. President Garfield died at the cottage at 10:35 p.m. on September 19th. He was removed 2 days later. Elsewhere, the CRRNJ leased the Ogden Mine RR which ran from Jefferson to Nolan's Point halfway up Lake Hopatcong. Nolan's Point became known as a resort area which brought more CRRNJ passengers to visit here. By 1882 the CRRNJ's NY and Long Branch's tracks reached down to Bay Head. As the PRR was going to build a parallel line down from Perth Amboy towards Bay Head, an agreement was worked out with the CRRNJ to avoid a suicidal competition. The 38 miles from Perth Amboy would now be double-tracked and shared by both the PRR and CRRNJ complete with interchangeable tickets.

By 1882 the Lackawanna leased the Passaic and Delaware RR better known as some of today's Gladstone Branch. At that point the tracks only ran out to Bernardsville. The Morris and Essex lines were already in Summit at the other end, so this now became the D L & W's Passaic and Delaware Branch.

Any New Jersey residents who took the ferryboats to lower Manhattan were in for a treat as Thomas Edison was ready for another demonstration. For several years he had been wiring up a small section of Lower Manhattan complete with underground wires. At Pearl Street he built the first power grid in the world. It powered several hundred of his electric bulbs in about 3 dozen buildings. Edison still had his detractors though who were mostly in the gas industry. These people felt that their gaslights were still the way to go. During the 1870's the CRRNJ's Mulford Station was moved a bit. It was renamed Roselle after John Pierre Roselle, a friend of the CRRNJ's President. Edison still needed to convince a skeptical public that his electric lights were more practical than gaslights or candles. Edison decided to use Roselle for another demonstration. He built a power station (NE corner of 1st Ave. and Locust St.), installed street lamps, and wired up 35 houses and businesses. In early 1883 Roselle became the first municipality anywhere with electric incandescent street lighting. The First Presbyterian Church (5th Ave. and Chestnut St.) became the first church with this kind of lighting. Charles Stone's Grocery Store near the CRRNJ's tracks became the first store in the world to be lit with incandescent lights. By 1883, the CRRNJ's Ogden Mine RR was extended from Nolan's Point up to an area above Lake Hopatcong. The CRRNJ brought thousands of people here during the summer.

During 1883 in South Jersey, the PRR bought out the Camden and Atlantic Railroad. The Philadelphia and Atlantic Railroad was sold at a foreclosure sale to the Reading.

The Baltimore and Ohio RR acquired the Staten Island Railroad along with its ferry operation.

In 1885 the Lackawanna's third temporary structure was replaced with a fourth terminal. Up in Weehawken the New York Central purchased the New York, West Shore, and Buffalo RR. This railroad had a line down the western shore of the Hudson River with a terminal at Weehawken. The new West Shore Line was now part of the New York Central. In 1886 the Hoboken Ferry's street trestle "Observer Highway" into the Lackawanna Terminal was completed. At the time it was the largest wrought iron structure in the world.

Many a ferryboat passenger traveling to Lower Manhattan from New Jersey gazed towards Bedloes Island as a $300,000 pedestal was being built. Frederic Auguste Bartholdi's statue soon arrived from France in 214 large crates. On October 28, 1886, the Statue of Liberty was officially dedicated in New York Harbor. It was a gift from France to commemorate the French and American alliance during the Revolutionary War.

During 1888 the Rockaway Valley RR was incorporated to run from the CRRNJ Main Line at White House into Morris County near Morristown. Due to the high volume of traffic on its Main Line there were now 4 tracks between Westfield and Cranford. Around 1889 the CRRNJ started a Jersey City to Atlantic City service. Its passengers left the CRRNJ's NY and Long Branch at Red Bank. From here they continued down through Lakewood to Winslow Junction. From here the CRRNJ reached Atlantic City via the Reading's tracks. Back in Jersey City the CRRNJ was also rebuilding its terminal on the Hudson River.

Underneath the Hudson River, an English company took over the unfinished tunnel. With his Greathead shield design, James Greathead increased the length of original tunnel under the Hudson to 2,000 feet. His shield was pushed forward with hydraulic rams after which the sand and silt came through openings in the shield. After it came through, the silt was hauled away by carts. Iron rings were placed around the tunnel's circumference. On the Hudson River itself, ferryboats with paddlewheels would soon be obsolete. The Hoboken Ferry Company's "Bergen" was the first double-ended ferryboat in the world with a single shaft screw propeller.

By 1890 the Reading RR was out of bankruptcy and looking to make a move into New Jersey. The CRRNJ agreed to lease itself to the Reading for 999 years after its stockholders were promised a yearly dividend of 7%. During 1890 the CRRNJ continued to expand. The High Bridge Branch off its Main Line was completed from High Bridge up to Hibernia. There were also new stations built at Raritan and Lebanon.

In 1890 the Baltimore and Ohio's "Royal Blue Line" was complete up to Philadelphia. Once across the Delaware River, the B & O used the Reading RR's tracks up to Bound Brook, followed by the CRRNJ's Main Line in order to access the Hudson River.

The PRR replaced its 1856 terminal with a new 12 track terminal at Exchange Place. To the north of Exchange Place, the Erie RR constructed its terminal near Pavonia Avenue at a cost of $200,000.

In the meantime the Lackawanna organized the Passaic and Delaware Corporation. It was put together so the tracks from Bernardsville could be extended out to Gladstone. The extension was completed in October of 1890 out to Gladstone. With this seven miles of new track more bankers, stock brokers, and millionaires came out to the Somerset Hills to build huge estates.

During 1891 the CRRNJ built its West 8th station in Bayonne. Over in Elizabeth it constructed a passenger station on the Main Line at West Grand and Broad Streets. Still standing today, this station is being refurbished as part of a Midtown Elizabeth redevelopment project. The following year another new station was placed out in Westfield along the four track Main Line. It was on these tracks that CRRNJ engine #385 (4-4-0) ran from Jersey City to Philadelphia and back in 4 hours and 25 minutes. At some points the little engine clicked off 2 miles every 75 seconds at speeds of 105 miles per hour, then a world record. In 1894 the CRRNJ's Netherwood Station, still standing today, was built in Plainfield. During the 1890's the Mesabi Iron Range was discovered out in Minnesota. As a result, iron mining activity began to decline in the Chester area of Morris County. This in turn led to a decline in freight traffic on the CRRNJ's Hackle Barney Branch off of its High Bridge RR. To the north, the Lackawanna also saw a freight reduction on its Chester Branch off of the Morris and Essex.

One of the problems of the Lackawanna's Morris and Essex lines was that it (as did the Morris Canal) bypassed the Hanover/Whippany area. In order to provide the numerous mills here with rail service, a four mile long railroad was built between Morristown and Whippany. The Whippany River RR had money problems after which the McEwen Brothers took it over.

Down in South Jersey during 1896, the PRR got a jump on the Reading RR when its Delair Bridge across the Delaware River opened. The PRR no longer needed a ferry for its passengers bound for Atlantic City.

At this point the B & O Railroad used the CRRNJ's Communipaw Terminal, but still wanted direct access to Manhattan. It placed two new ferries "Mauch Chunk" and "Easton" on its Whitehall Line later known as the Royal Blue Ferry. B & O passengers now used these boats to continue on to Manhattan. It wasn't until January 1, 1898 when New York City officially consisted of the five boroughs as we know it today. In 1898 the B & O began to run its "Royal Limited" with all Pullman cars. The "Royal Limited" brought people from Washington D.C. to Jersey City in about 5 hours.

The Lackawanna's extension out to Gladstone on its Passaic and Delaware Branch continued to bring the wealthy out to this area. In 1898 a wealthy investment banker named Clinton Ledyard Blair came out to Peapack. He purchased 423 acres and began to build his huge estate known later as "Blairsden." He created Ravine Lake after a dam was built across the North Branch of the Raritan River. He brought in full grown trees for his property as work started on "Blairsden." He had a full sized pool built in his basement along with more than two dozen fireplaces. He had about 75 servants who saw to his every need. If Blair got bored, he could simply ride in his own private railroad coach to Hoboken. Among his neighbors he could count Julius Stursberg who already had a mansion named "Stonehyrst." In nearby Bernardsville U.S. Senator John Dryden (he helped found Prudential Insurance) built his stone estate named "The Stronghold." His son-in-law also lived in Bernardsville in a massive house named "Faircourt." Colonel Anthony R. Kuser also owned land up in Sussex County. He gave New Jersey some 11,000 acres in 1923 for High Point State Park. With so many wealthy Lackawanna passengers out here, they rode on a special train dubbed the "Millionaires Express."

The Lackawanna brought other millionaires out to Morristown on its M & E Lines. There were about 100 millionaires in the Morristown area alone. Hamilton and Florence Twombly (worth only $70 million) bought 900 acres out here for their 100 room summer house named "Florham (For Florence and Hamilton) Farms." The little town of Afton changed its name to Florham Park. The Park portion of the name came from their neighbor

Dr. Leslie Ward's estate "Brooklake Park." Geraldine Rockefeller Dodge and her husband Marcellus Hartley Dodge came out to Madison where they built "Giralda Farms." The Sisters of Charity of St. Elizabeth obtained the old Madison property along the M & E where Seton Hall was. Very close to the Convent Station stop, the College of St. Elizabeth was the first college for women in the United States. When the Lackawanna's more religious President Sam Sloane resigned, William H. Truesdale took his spot. With Truesdale in charge, the Lackawanna now had Sunday service. He spent several million dollars on upgrades such as new bridges and reballasting. A new passenger station was also constructed on New Providence.

This station though is not to be confused with the other one located in the Murray Hill section of New Providence. Several years before, Carl Schultz donated land as well as the money for a station along the Lackawanna's tracks in New Providence. His only condition was that the station bear the name of Murray Hill after his favorite area in New York City.

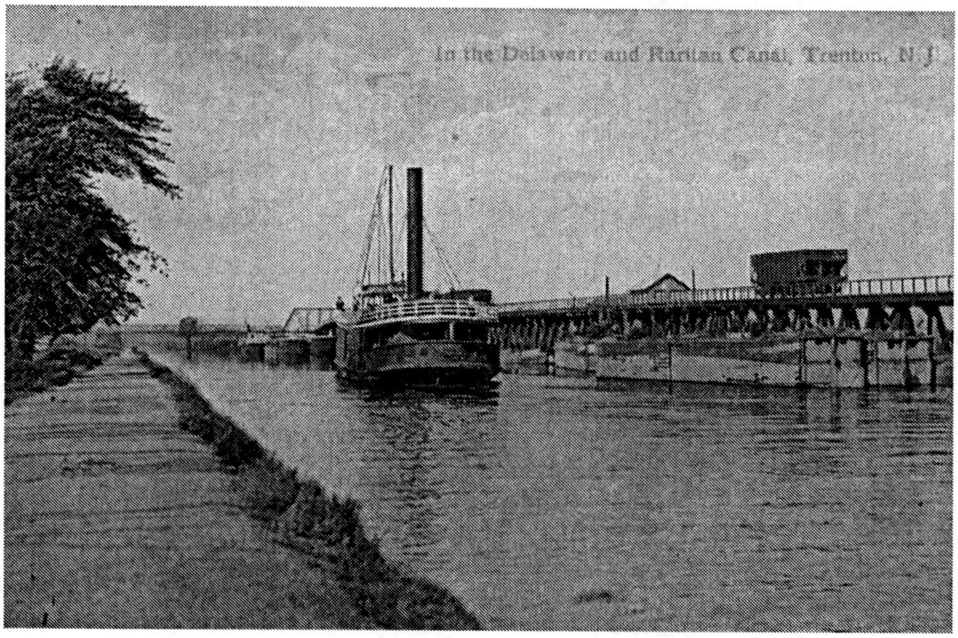
In the Delaware and Raritan Canal, Trenton, N.J.

Michael E. Ferlise

G—Form 28.

Pennsylvania Railroad Company.

....*Division.*

....*18*

TIME REPORT OF FREIGHT TRAINS.

From..................... *To*...................
Left.................. *Arrived*...............
Train,.........................
Engine,.........................
Engineman,.........................
Fireman,.........................
Correct,.........................*Yard Master.*

G—Form 28.

Pennsylvania Railroad Company.

....*Division.*

....*18*

TIME REPORT OF FREIGHT TRAINS.

From..................... *To*...................
Left.................. *Arrived*...............
Train,.........................
Engine,.........................
Engineman,.........................
Conductor,.........................
Flagman,.........................
Brakemen:

Conductors must deliver this Report to the Yard Master at the end of each trip, who will check and forward to the Superintendent.

66

M. W. 39.

PENNSYLVANIA RAILROAD COMPANY.

Distributing Train Conductors Daily Report, _____ Division, _____

DATE.	No. CAR.	No. TIES.	FROM WHERE TAKEN.	WHERE DELIVERED.	No. of CAR.	No. Ca. Yds. Ballast.	FROM WHERE TAKEN.	WHERE DELIVERED.	REMARKS

C. R.—Form 32.

32 12-28-86.

PENNSYLVANIA RAILROAD COMPANY.

N. C. R. W., P. W. & B. R. R., B. & P. R. R., A. & F. R. W., W. J. R. R., C. & A. R. R.
DIVISION.

Conductor's Daily Report of C. T. Cars Moved on Supervisor's Division No._____
Station,_____ 18___

_____ward. | _____ward.

INITIALS.	ENGINE NO.	WHERE FROM.	WHERE TO.	INITIALS.	ENGINE NO.	WHERE FROM.	WHERE TO.

	INITIALS.	Kind of Car. Wheels	NO. OF CAR.	Loaded Empty	Where From.	Where To.		INITIALS.	Kind of Car. Wheels	NO. OF CAR.	Loaded Empty	Where From.	Where To.
1							26						
2							27						
3							28						
4							29						
5							30						
6							31						
7							32						
8							33						
9							34						
10							35						
11							36						
12							37						
13							38						
14							39						
15							40						
16							41						
17							42						
18							43						
19							44						
20							45						
21							46						
22							47						
23							48						
24							49						
25							50						

OVER.

OVER.

Conductor.

NOTE.—This report must be made out in accordance with instructions given in Book C. R.—Form 76.

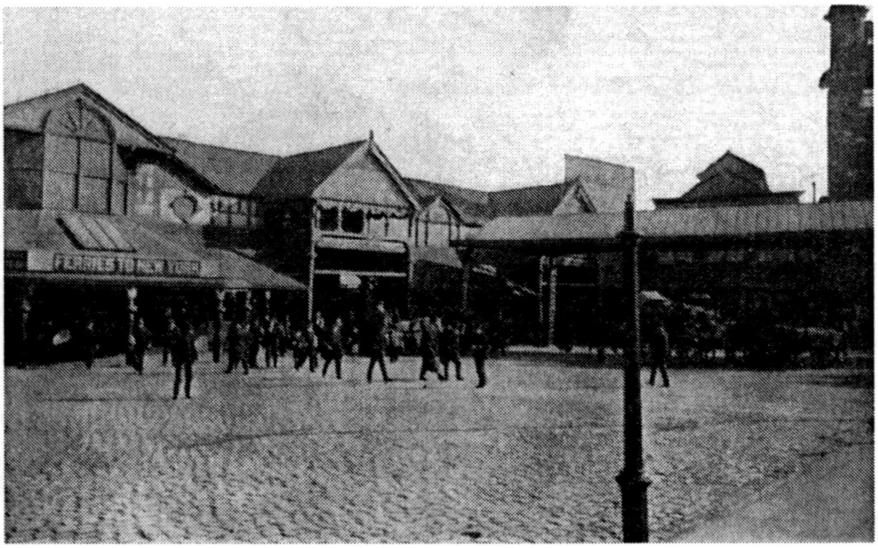
FERRIES TO NEW YORK

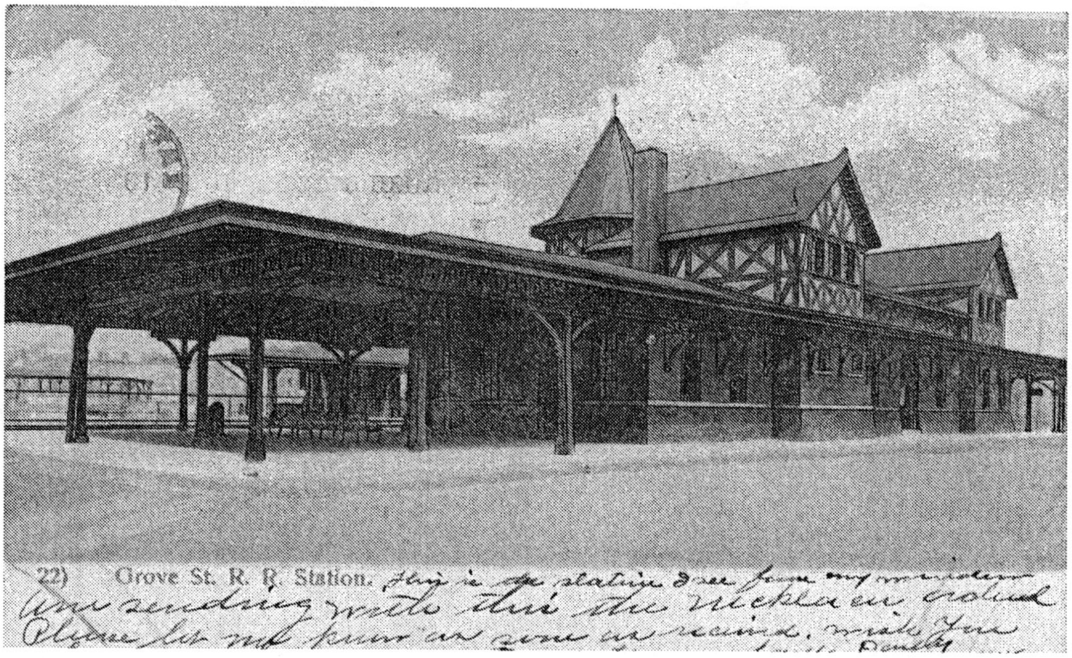
22) Grove St. R. R. Station.

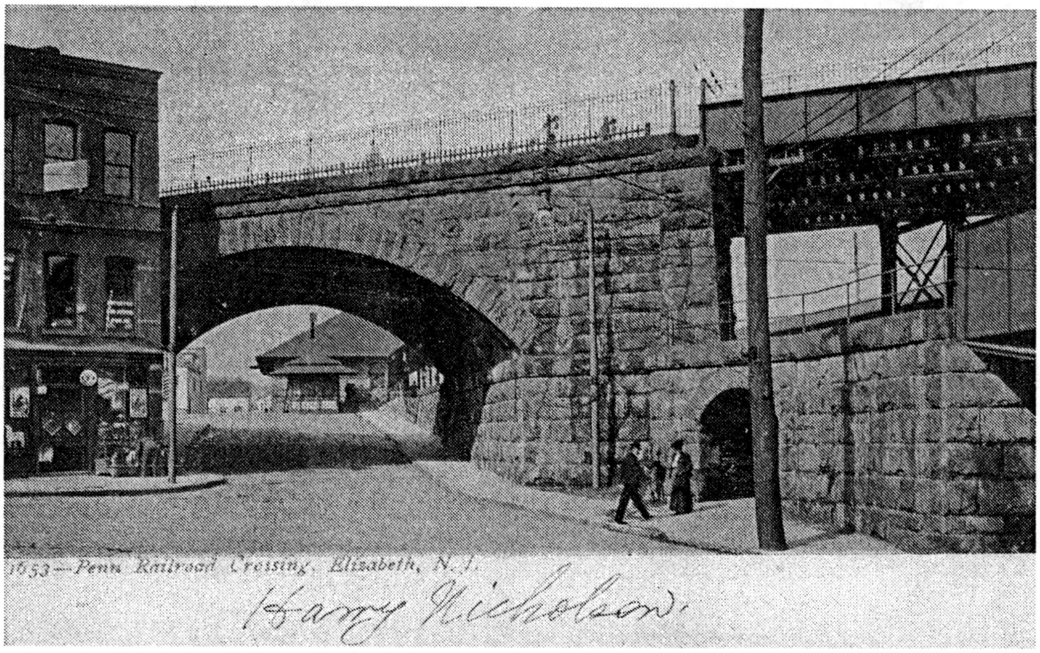
1653—Penn Railroad Crossing, Elizabeth, N. J.
Harry Nicholson

The Pennslyvania Limited—First Limited Train in America

The Broadway Limited—Leading Train of Today

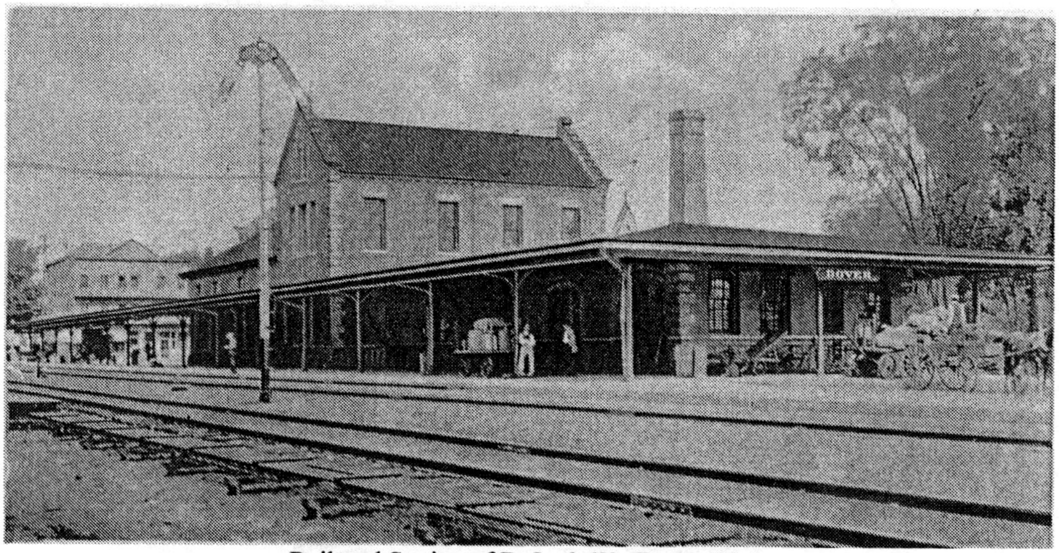
DOVER
Railroad Station of D. L. & W., Dover, N. J.

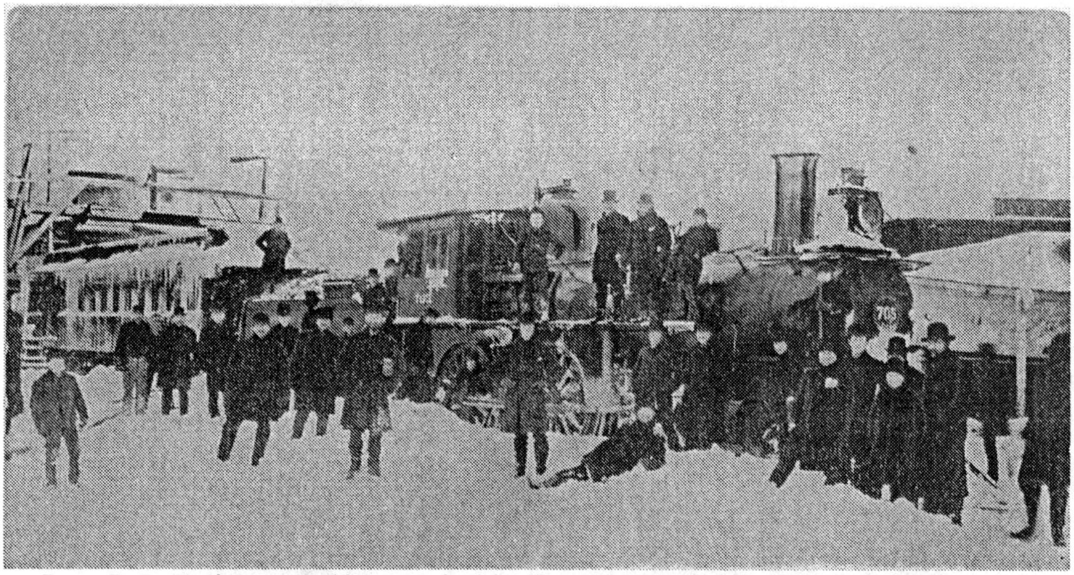
Penn. R. R. Engine stopped by snow in the Blizzard of March 12th, 1888, at Elizabeth, N. J.

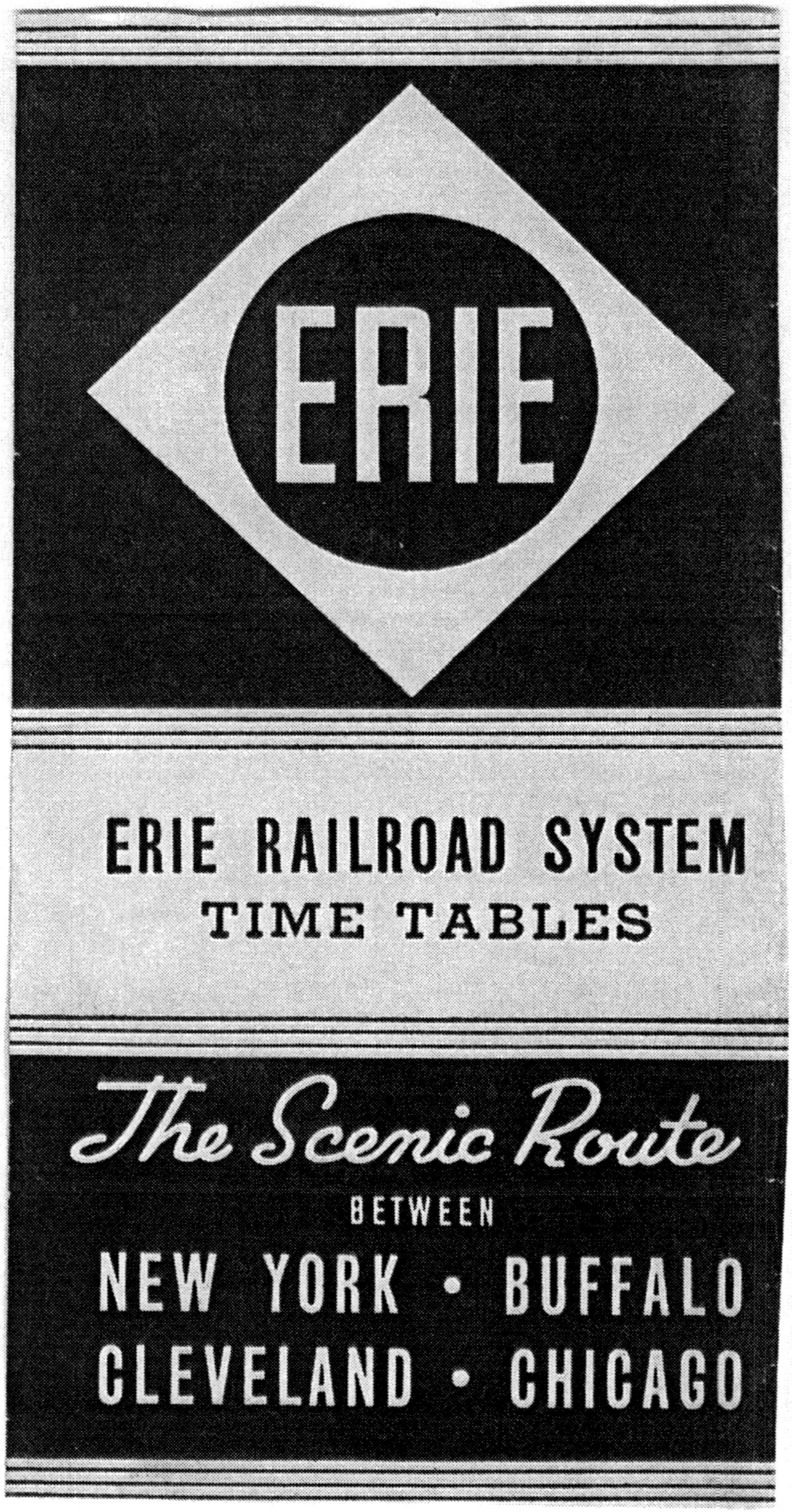
ERIE
ERIE RAILROAD SYSTEM
TIME TABLES
The Scenic Route
BETWEEN
NEW YORK • BUFFALO
CLEVELAND • CHICAGO

Will it Clear?

● Tremendous oversize loads will clear on the Erie, America's Heavy Duty Railroad. For clearances on the Erie, established in the days of broad gauge track, are *high* and *wide*.

Today, as industry hustles to outproduce the Axis, Erie's unusual heavy duty capacity is of greater importance than ever.

ERIE RAILROAD

THE HEAVY DUTY RAILROAD

ERIE

From Girders to Guns

● Uncle Sam needs guns and shells and tanks and planes. We hustle not only ore but also scrap, whether it be old bridge girders or junked automobiles, to the hungry mills. We speed steel to the fabricating plants. Then we rush the finished products on their way to meet the enemy.

Erie is prepared to "*keep 'em rolling.*" In war as in peace —you can expect fast, safe, dependable service whenever and whatever you ship via Erie.

For any transportation information see the local Erie man.

ERIE RAILROAD

THE HEAVY DUTY RAILROAD

ERIE
Keep 'em Rolling to Keep 'em Flying
● Many months ago all 22,000 of us on the Erie tightened up our belts and declared all-out for national defense. We ordered thousands of new cars, stepped up the modernization program which had long been under way.
Today, we are moving huge quantities of parts, machinery, and supplies to "keep 'em flying" as the new army slogan says. We are ever at the service of the military, of the government—and you, too, whether you ship airplane parts, fountain pens, or peanuts. Erie delivers the goods.
You can help to keep 'em rolling for defense by giving advance notice of car requirements, by loading and unloading promptly, by loading to the load limit, and many other ways that may speed shipments.
Let's all keep 'em rolling to keep 'em flying.
Carl Howe, *Vice President*
ERIE RAILROAD • CLEVELAND, OHIO
LET'S GO! U.S.A.
KEEP 'EM FLYING!
ERIE RAILROAD
THE SCENIC ROUTE OF THE EAST

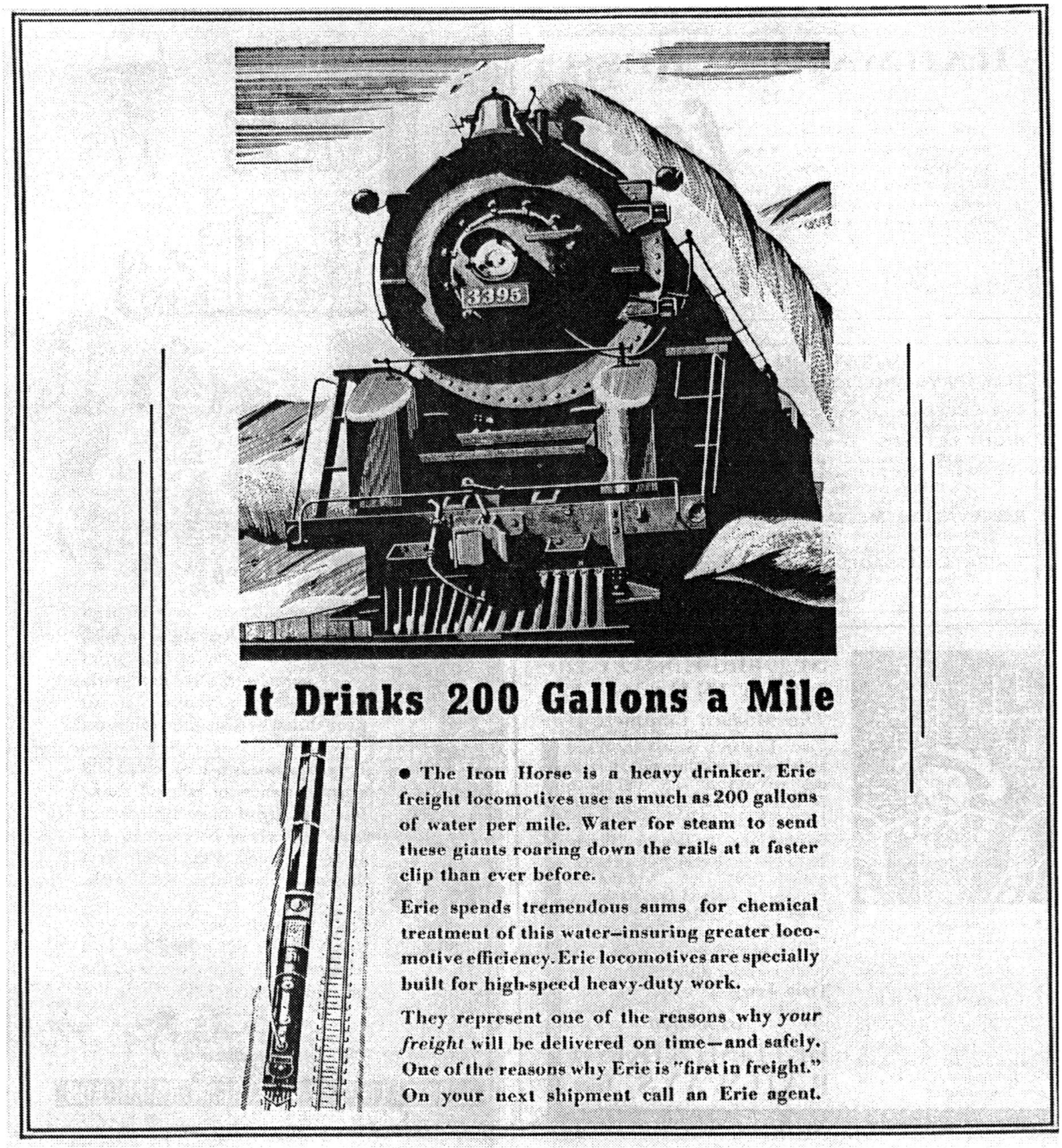
3395
It Drinks 200 Gallons a Mile
● The Iron Horse is a heavy drinker. Erie freight locomotives use as much as 200 gallons of water per mile. Water for steam to send these giants roaring down the rails at a faster clip than ever before.
Erie spends tremendous sums for chemical treatment of this water–insuring greater locomotive efficiency. Erie locomotives are specially built for high-speed heavy-duty work.
They represent one of the reasons why *your freight* will be delivered on time—and safely. One of the reasons why Erie is "first in freight." On your next shipment call an Erie agent.

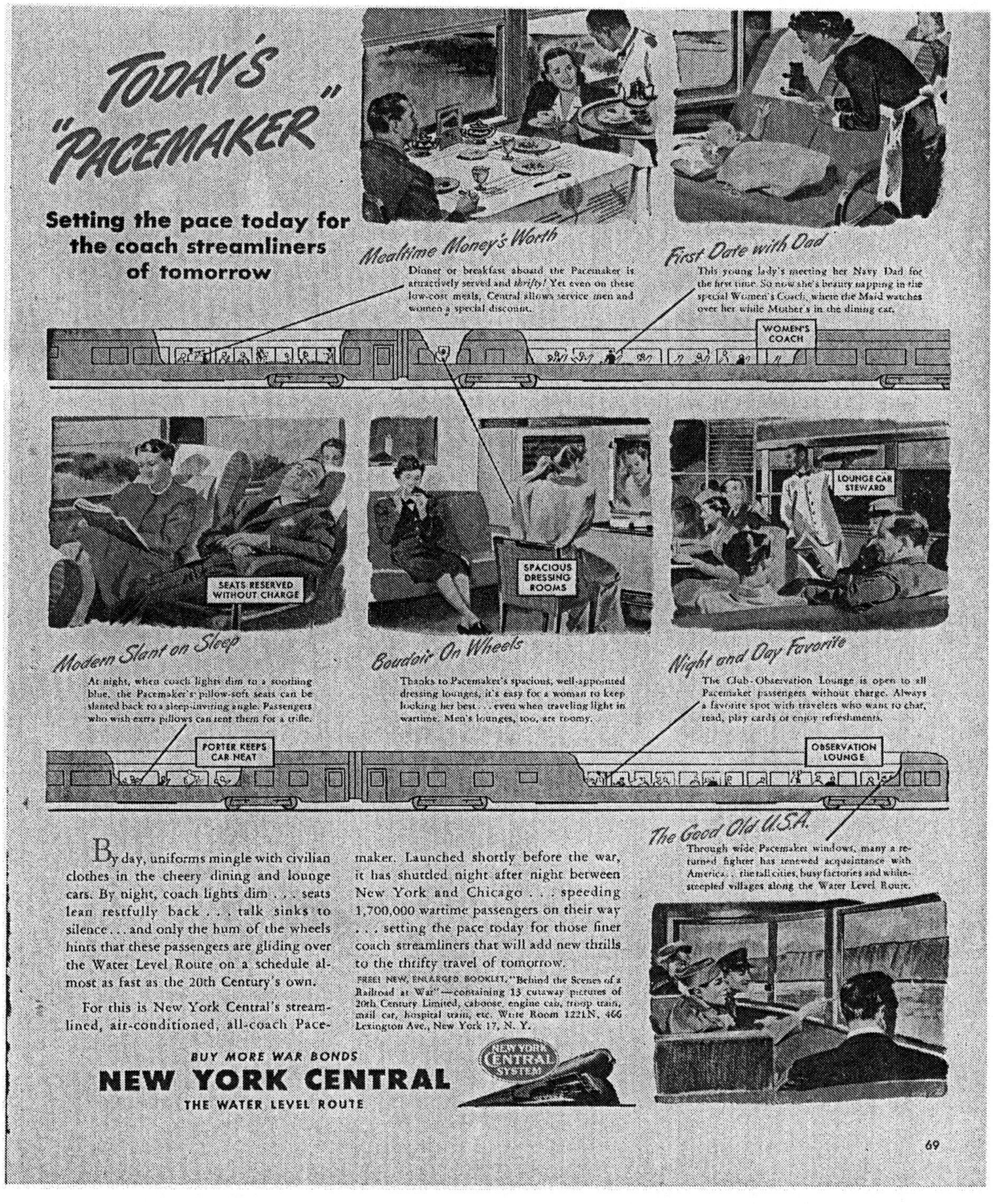
TODAY'S "PACEMAKER"
Setting the pace today for the coach streamliners of tomorrow
Mealtime Money's Worth
Dinner or breakfast aboard the Pacemaker is attractively served and *thrifty!* Yet even on these low-cost meals, Central allows service men and women a special discount.
First Date with Dad
This young lady's meeting her Navy Dad for the first time. So now she's beauty napping in the special Women's Coach, where the Maid watches over her while Mother's in the dining car.
WOMEN'S COACH
SEATS RESERVED WITHOUT CHARGE
SPACIOUS DRESSING ROOMS
LOUNGE CAR STEWARD
Modern Slant on Sleep
At night, when coach lights dim to a soothing blue, the Pacemaker's pillow-soft seats can be slanted back to a sleep-inviting angle. Passengers who wish extra pillows can rent them for a trifle.
Boudoir On Wheels
Thanks to Pacemaker's spacious, well-appointed dressing lounges, it's easy for a woman to keep looking her best . . . even when traveling light in wartime. Men's lounges, too, are roomy.
Night and Day Favorite
The Club-Observation Lounge is open to all Pacemaker passengers without charge. Always a favorite spot with travelers who want to chat, read, play cards or enjoy refreshments.
PORTER KEEPS CAR NEAT
OBSERVATION LOUNGE
The Good Old U.S.A.
Through wide Pacemaker windows, many a returned fighter has renewed acquaintance with America . . the tall cities, busy factories and white-steepled villages along the Water Level Route.
By day, uniforms mingle with civilian clothes in the cheery dining and lounge cars. By night, coach lights dim . . . seats lean restfully back . . . talk sinks to silence . . . and only the hum of the wheels hints that these passengers are gliding over the Water Level Route on a schedule almost as fast as the 20th Century's own.
For this is New York Central's streamlined, air-conditioned, all-coach Pacemaker. Launched shortly before the war, it has shuttled night after night between New York and Chicago . . . speeding 1,700,000 wartime passengers on their way . . . setting the pace today for those finer coach streamliners that will add new thrills to the thrifty travel of tomorrow.
FREE! NEW, ENLARGED BOOKLET, "Behind the Scenes of a Railroad at War" —containing 13 cutaway pictures of 20th Century Limited, caboose, engine cab, troop train, mail car, hospital train, etc. Write Room 1221N, 466 Lexington Ave., New York 17, N. Y.
BUY MORE WAR BONDS
NEW YORK CENTRAL
THE WATER LEVEL ROUTE
NEW YORK CENTRAL SYSTEM
69

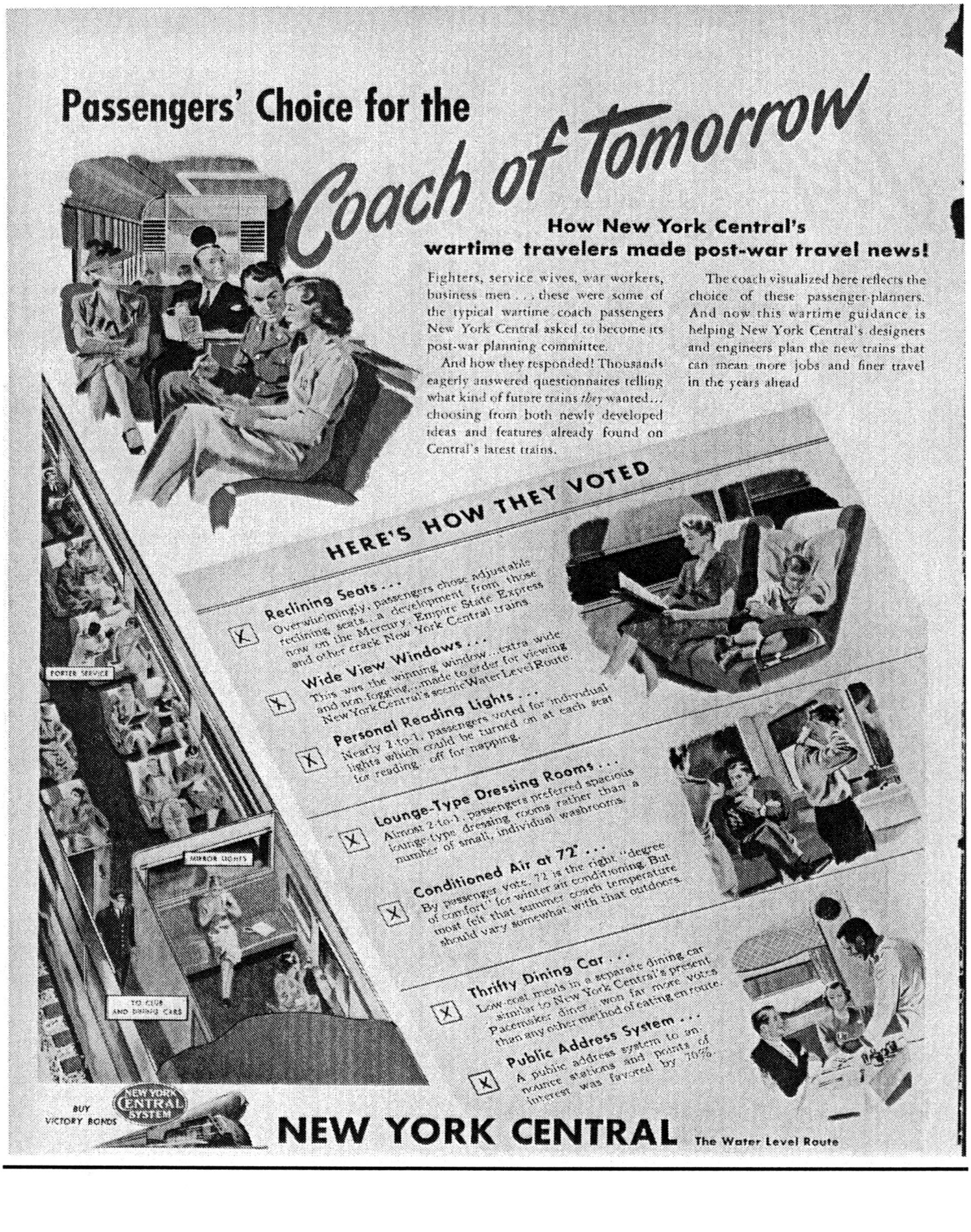
Passengers' Choice for the
Coach of Tomorrow
How New York Central's
wartime travelers made post-war travel news!
Fighters, service wives, war workers, business men . . . these were some of the typical wartime coach passengers New York Central asked to become its post-war planning committee.
And how they responded! Thousands eagerly answered questionnaires telling what kind of future trains *they* wanted . . . choosing from both newly developed ideas and features already found on Central's latest trains.
The coach visualized here reflects the choice of these passenger-planners. And now this wartime guidance is helping New York Central's designers and engineers plan the new trains that can mean more jobs and finer travel in the years ahead
HERE'S HOW THEY VOTED
X Reclining Seats . . .
Overwhelmingly, passengers chose adjustable reclining seats...a development from those now on the Mercury, Empire State Express and other crack New York Central trains
X Wide View Windows . . .
This was the winning window...extra wide and non-fogging...made to order for viewing New York Central's scenic Water Level Route.
X Personal Reading Lights . . .
Nearly 2-to-1, passengers voted for individual lights which could be turned on at each seat for reading, off for napping.
X Lounge-Type Dressing Rooms . . .
Almost 2-to-1, passengers preferred spacious lounge-type dressing rooms rather than a number of small, individual washrooms.
X Conditioned Air at 72° . . .
By passenger vote, 72 is the right "degree of comfort" for winter air conditioning. But most felt that summer coach temperature should vary somewhat with that outdoors.
X Thrifty Dining Car . . .
Low-cost meals in a separate dining car similar to New York Central's present Pacemaker diner...won far more votes than any other method of eating en route.
X Public Address System . . .
A public address system to an-
nounce stations and points of
interest was favored by 70%
PORTER SERVICE
MIRROR LIGHTS
TO CLUB AND DINING CARS
BUY VICTORY BONDS
NEW YORK CENTRAL SYSTEM
NEW YORK CENTRAL
The Water Level Route

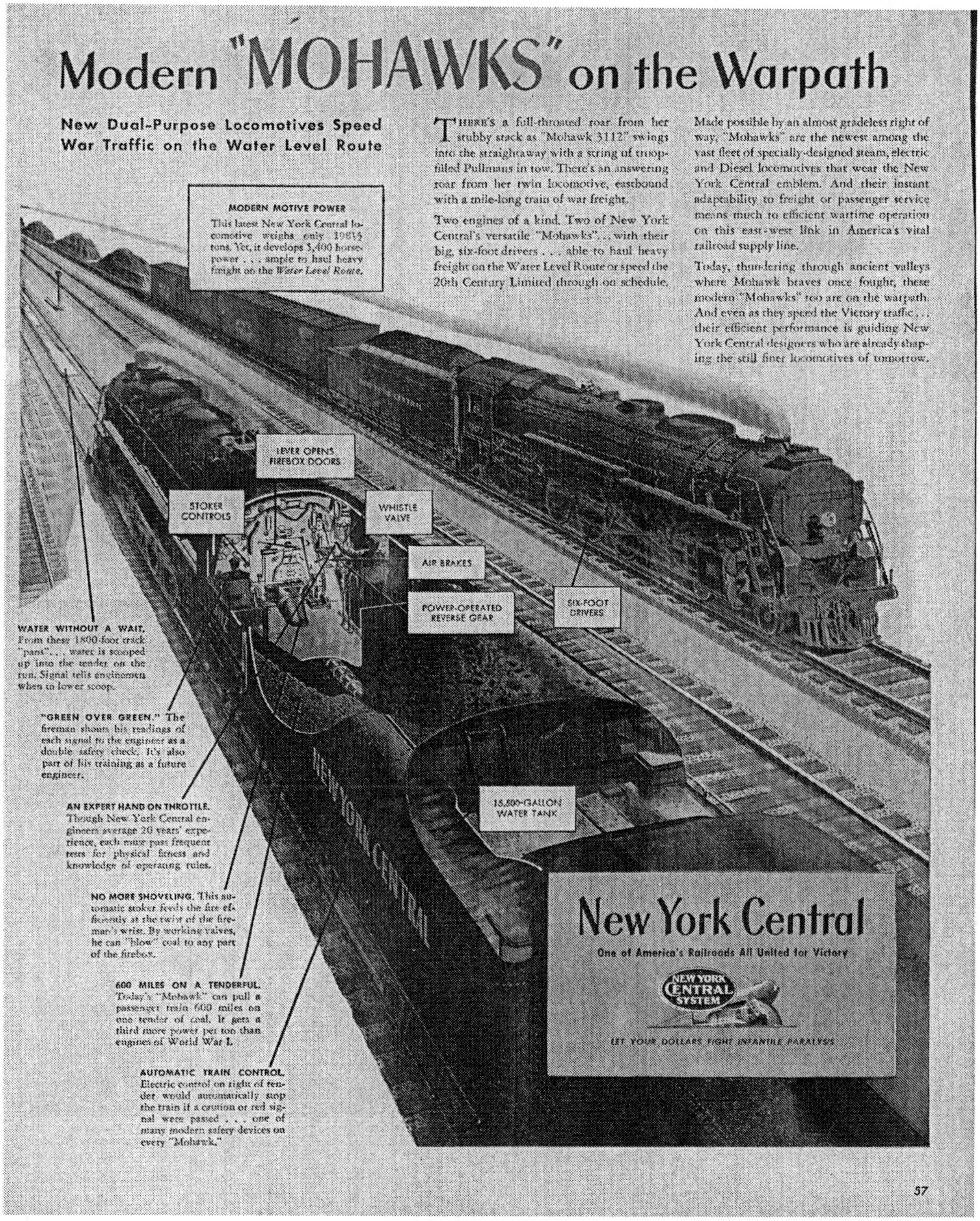
Modern "MOHAWKS" on the Warpath
New Dual-Purpose Locomotives Speed War Traffic on the Water Level Route
THERE'S a full-throated roar from her stubby stack as "Mohawk 3112" swings into the straightaway with a string of troop-filled Pullmans in tow. There's an answering roar from her twin locomotive, eastbound with a mile-long train of war freight.
Two engines of a kind. Two of New York Central's versatile "Mohawks"... with their big, six-foot drivers . . . able to haul heavy freight on the Water Level Route or speed the 20th Century Limited through on schedule.
Made possible by an almost gradeless right of way, "Mohawks" are the newest among the vast fleet of specially-designed steam, electric and Diesel locomotives that wear the New York Central emblem. And their instant adaptability to freight or passenger service means much to efficient wartime operation on this east-west link in America's vital railroad supply line.
Today, thundering through ancient valleys where Mohawk braves once fought, these modern "Mohawks" too are on the warpath. And even as they speed the Victory traffic... their efficient performance is guiding New York Central designers who are already shaping the still finer locomotives of tomorrow.
MODERN MOTIVE POWER
This latest New York Central locomotive weighs only 198½ tons. Yet, it develops 5,400 horsepower . . . ample to haul heavy freight on the Water Level Route.
LEVER OPENS FIREBOX DOORS
STOKER CONTROLS
WHISTLE VALVE
AIR BRAKES
POWER-OPERATED REVERSE GEAR
SIX-FOOT DRIVERS
15,800-GALLON WATER TANK
WATER WITHOUT A WAIT. From these 1800-foot track "pans"... water is scooped up into the tender on the run. Signal tells enginemen when to lower scoop.
"GREEN OVER GREEN." The fireman shouts his readings of each signal to the engineer as a double safety check. It's also part of his training as a future engineer.
AN EXPERT HAND ON THROTTLE. Though New York Central engineers average 20 years' experience, each must pass frequent tests for physical fitness and knowledge of operating rules.
NO MORE SHOVELING. This automatic stoker feeds the fire efficiently at the twist of the fireman's wrist. By working valves, he can "blow" coal to any part of the firebox.
600 MILES ON A TENDERFUL. Today's "Mohawk" can pull a passenger train 600 miles on one tender of coal. It gets a third more power per ton than engines of World War I.
AUTOMATIC TRAIN CONTROL. Electric control on right of tender would automatically stop the train if a caution or red signal were passed . . . one of many modern safety devices on every "Mohawk."
NEW YORK CENTRAL
New York Central
One of America's Railroads All United for Victory
NEW YORK CENTRAL SYSTEM
LET YOUR DOLLARS FIGHT INFANTILE PARALYSIS
57

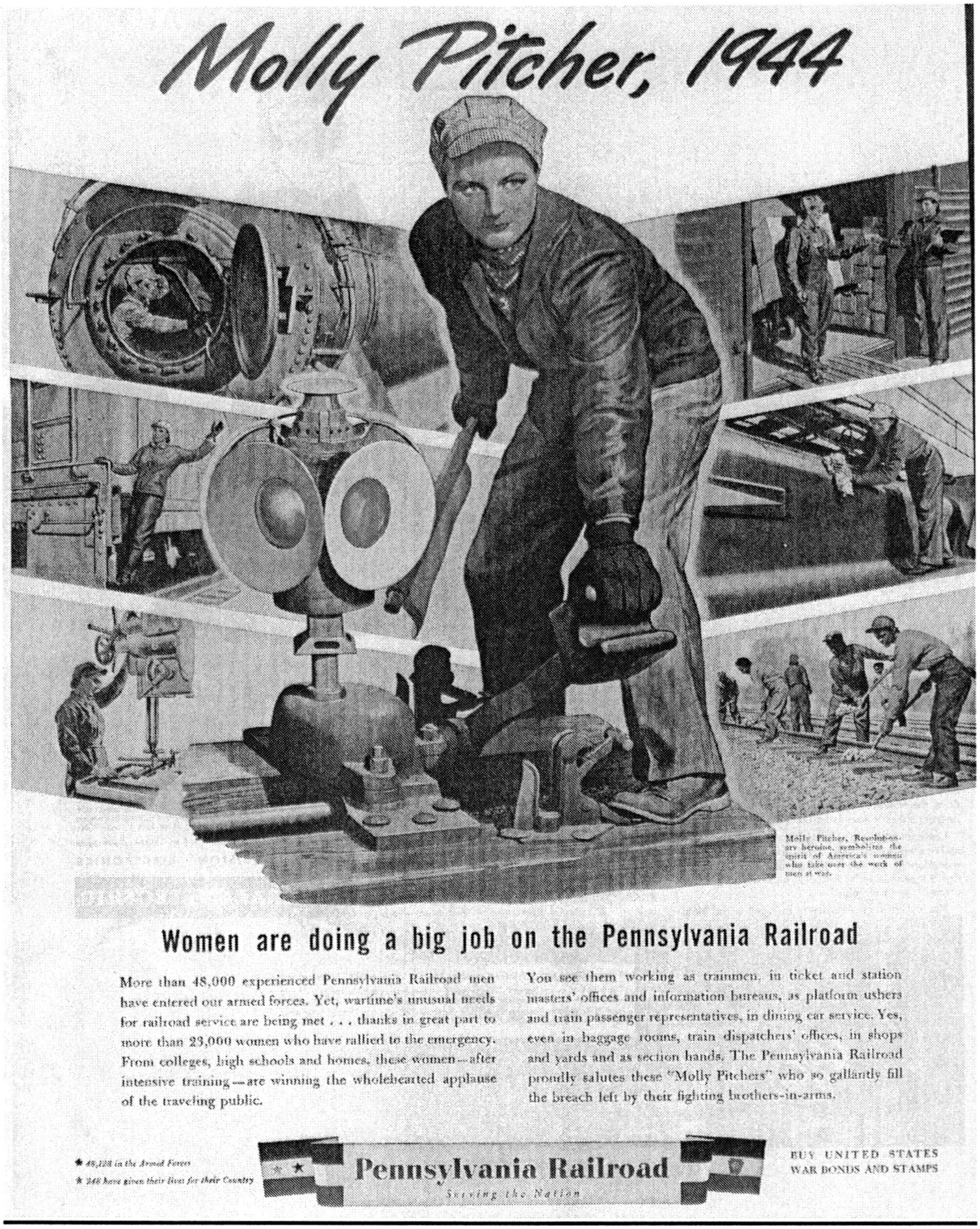
Molly Pitcher, 1944
Molly Pitcher, Revolutionary heroine, symbolizes the spirit of America's women who take over the work of men at war.
Women are doing a big job on the Pennsylvania Railroad
More than 48,000 experienced Pennsylvania Railroad men have entered our armed forces. Yet, wartime's unusual needs for railroad service are being met . . . thanks in great part to more than 23,000 women who have rallied to the emergency. From colleges, high schools and homes, these women—after intensive training—are winning the wholehearted applause of the traveling public.
You see them working as trainmen, in ticket and station masters' offices and information bureaus, as platform ushers and train passenger representatives, in dining car service. Yes, even in baggage rooms, train dispatchers' offices, in shops and yards and as section hands. The Pennsylvania Railroad proudly salutes these "Molly Pitchers" who so gallantly fill the breach left by their fighting brothers-in-arms.
★ 48,128 in the Armed Forces
★ 248 have given their lives for their Country
Pennsylvania Railroad
Serving the Nation
BUY UNITED STATES WAR BONDS AND STAMPS

What it takes to move a division

IF, like the eagle, you could look down on the amount of railroad equipment it takes to move a single armored division, here is what you would see . . . *75 trains!*

For a division takes all its equipment with it — tanks, jeeps, armored cars, supply trucks, tractors, anti-aircraft guns, many things. And its men, numbering about 12,000, need berths in which to sleep!

Those 75 trains *taken out* of civilian service and *put into military service*, are *about equal to* the number of passenger trains running daily over the Pennsylvania Railroad between *two of the busiest places on the face of the globe* — New York and Washington.

Multiply this one division by the many moving in this country and you can understand why . . . you may have difficulty getting a berth . . . or be obliged to stand in a coach . . . or arrive at your destination late. In fact, demand for equipment is now so great that on arriving at terminals cars must be put right back into service, so you may find them not quite so spic and span as we would like. Housekeeping facilities are adequate but there's not always time.

But Americans are taking all this like good soldiers. For they know this is a war of movement, and that movement begins right here — *in America, on the rails.*

 **PENNSYLVANIA RAILROAD** *Serving the Nation*

BUY UNITED STATES
WAR BONDS AND STAMPS

★ *27,917 in the Armed Forces* ★ *21 have given their lives for their country*

Bringing in the HARVEST

...SO VITAL TO VICTORY!

NEVER before in history has food figured so much in American calculations.

Today we are a rationed nation, sharing our food with our boys abroad and their comrades-in-arms.

In order that there may be food for all, the railroads not only are moving great quantities from canneries, packing plants, fruit and vegetable areas but are sending thousands of cars into the harvest fields to haul millions of bushels of grain—your daily bread.

You may wonder how the railroads can take on so big a job as the harvest these days and still keep the war effort rolling. Here is the answer in one word—*cooperation.*

The railroads work together. While crops are still ripening in the fields, their plans are already laid. When harvesting starts, Pennsylvania Railroad contributes a share of its freight cars, along with other railroads, to the great American car "pool"... and there's a reserve army of cars all mobilized to move the crops to elevators and ship sidings.

Result: Plenty of cars for agriculture, the load evenly distributed among many railroads.

It is this sort of teamwork, going on every day, that is enabling the railroads to do for their country what United States Senator Clyde M. Reed of Kansas described as "the most phenomenal job in their history."

 **PENNSYLVANIA RAILROAD**
Serving the Nation

BUY UNITED STATES
WAR BONDS AND STAMPS
★ *29,842 in the Armed Forces* ★ *26 have given their lives for their country*

Rushing the Rations
BUY WAR BONDS
PENNSYLVANIA
PENNSYLVANIA RAILROAD

IT is early morning. Stars still hang in the sky. Folks are deep in slumber. But at the many great freight terminals of the Pennsylvania Railroad all is bustle and activity . . . *the rations are rolling in!*

Fresh meats from great packing centers . . . crisp vegetables and juicy fruits from lands where the warm sun shines . . . butter from creameries . . . cases of canned goods from canneries . . . the foods so essential to wartime energy and health.

Over the lines of the Pennsylvania Railroad more food is moving than in any year within memory . . . particularly to great industrial centers and Atlantic ports, for shipment overseas.

But that is only half the story. In the face of rising costs, *the railroads today are hauling food at virtually the same low freight rates prevailing in 1939.* That helps materially to keep living costs down.

Of course, to keep this tremendous tide of food flowing in from every part of the country often means delays for passenger trains and less vital freight shipments. But these are days when "first things must come first." And food certainly is a *first.* So if your train should be a little late, please remember that vitamins for the overseas or home front may have had the right-of-way.

PENNSYLVANIA RAILROAD

Serving the Nation

BUY UNITED STATES WAR BONDS AND STAMPS

★ *34.742 in the Armed Forces* ☆ *47 have given their lives for their country*

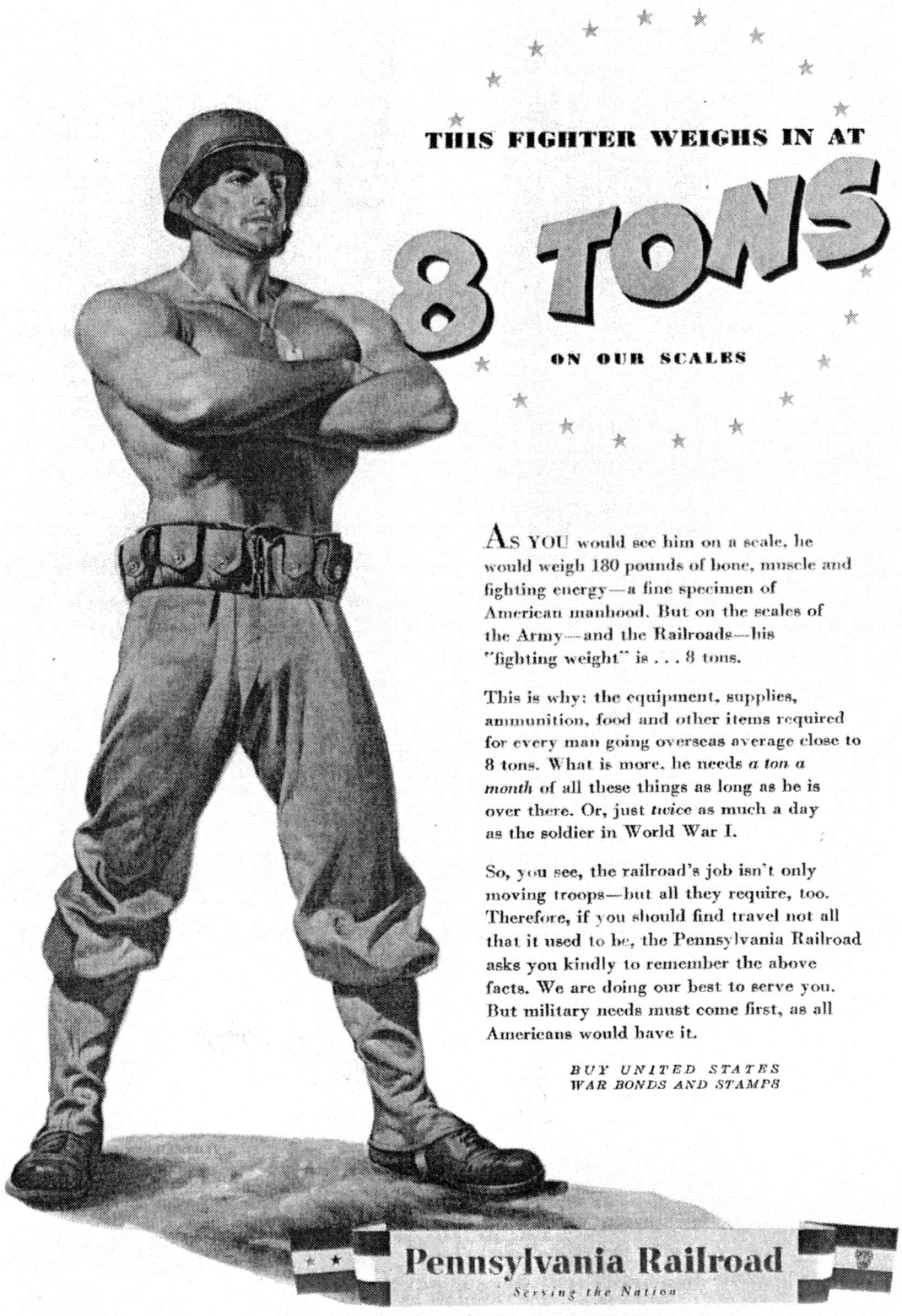

THIS FIGHTER WEIGHS IN AT

8 TONS

ON OUR SCALES

As YOU would see him on a scale, he would weigh 180 pounds of bone, muscle and fighting energy—a fine specimen of American manhood. But on the scales of the Army—and the Railroads—his "fighting weight" is . . . 8 tons.

This is why: the equipment, supplies, ammunition, food and other items required for every man going overseas average close to 8 tons. What is more, he needs *a ton a month* of all these things as long as he is over there. Or, just *twice* as much a day as the soldier in World War I.

So, you see, the railroad's job isn't only moving troops—but all they require, too. Therefore, if you should find travel not all that it used to be, the Pennsylvania Railroad asks you kindly to remember the above facts. We are doing our best to serve you. But military needs must come first, as all Americans would have it.

BUY UNITED STATES
WAR BONDS AND STAMPS

Pennsylvania Railroad
Serving the Nation

★ 43,867 in the Armed Forces   ★ 113 have given their lives for their country

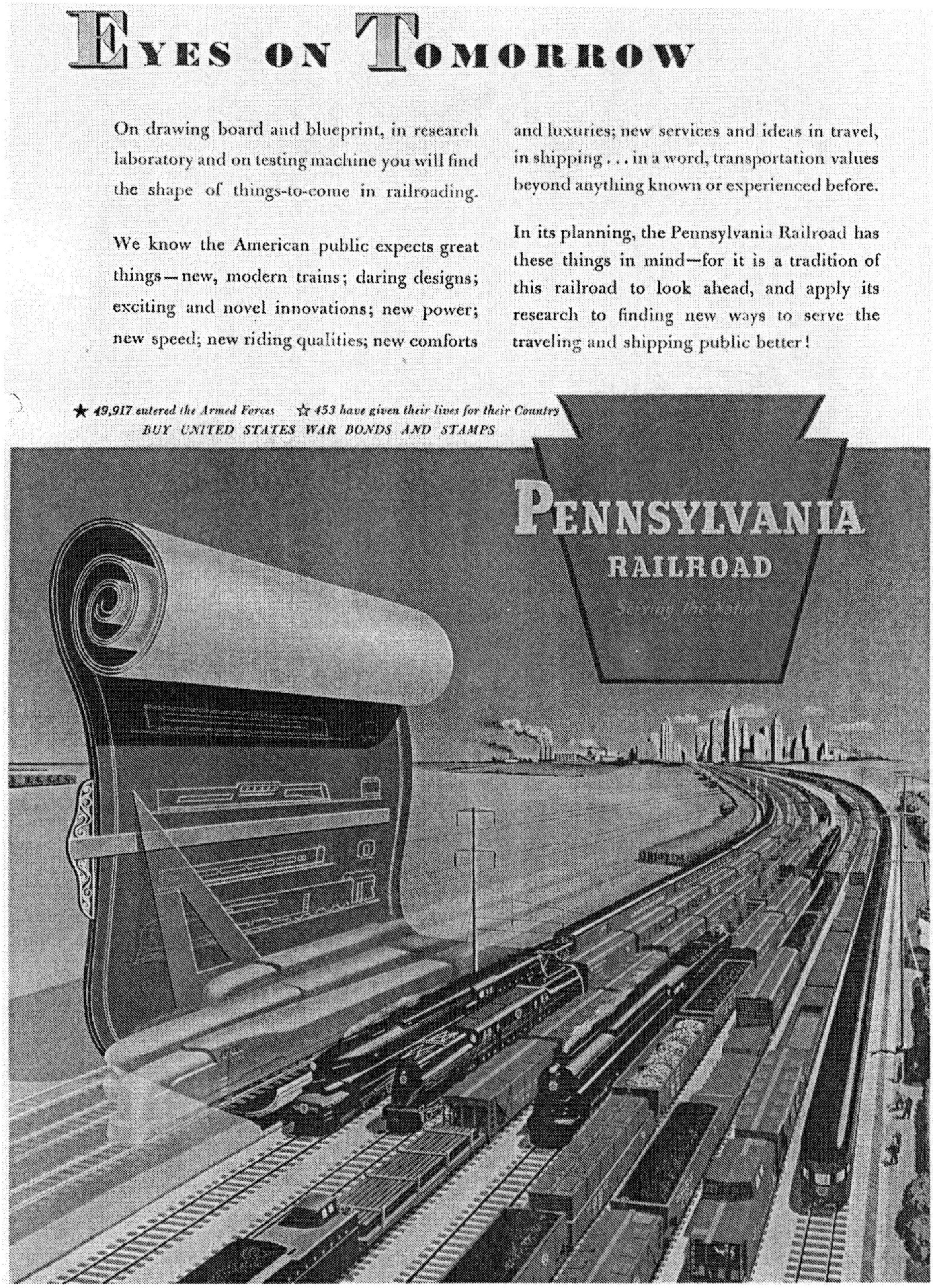
EYES ON TOMORROW
On drawing board and blueprint, in research laboratory and on testing machine you will find the shape of things-to-come in railroading.
We know the American public expects great things — new, modern trains; daring designs; exciting and novel innovations; new power; new speed; new riding qualities; new comforts and luxuries; new services and ideas in travel, in shipping . . . in a word, transportation values beyond anything known or experienced before.
In its planning, the Pennsylvania Railroad has these things in mind—for it is a tradition of this railroad to look ahead, and apply its research to finding new ways to serve the traveling and shipping public better!
★ 49,917 entered the Armed Forces ☆ 453 have given their lives for their Country
BUY UNITED STATES WAR BONDS AND STAMPS
PENNSYLVANIA
RAILROAD

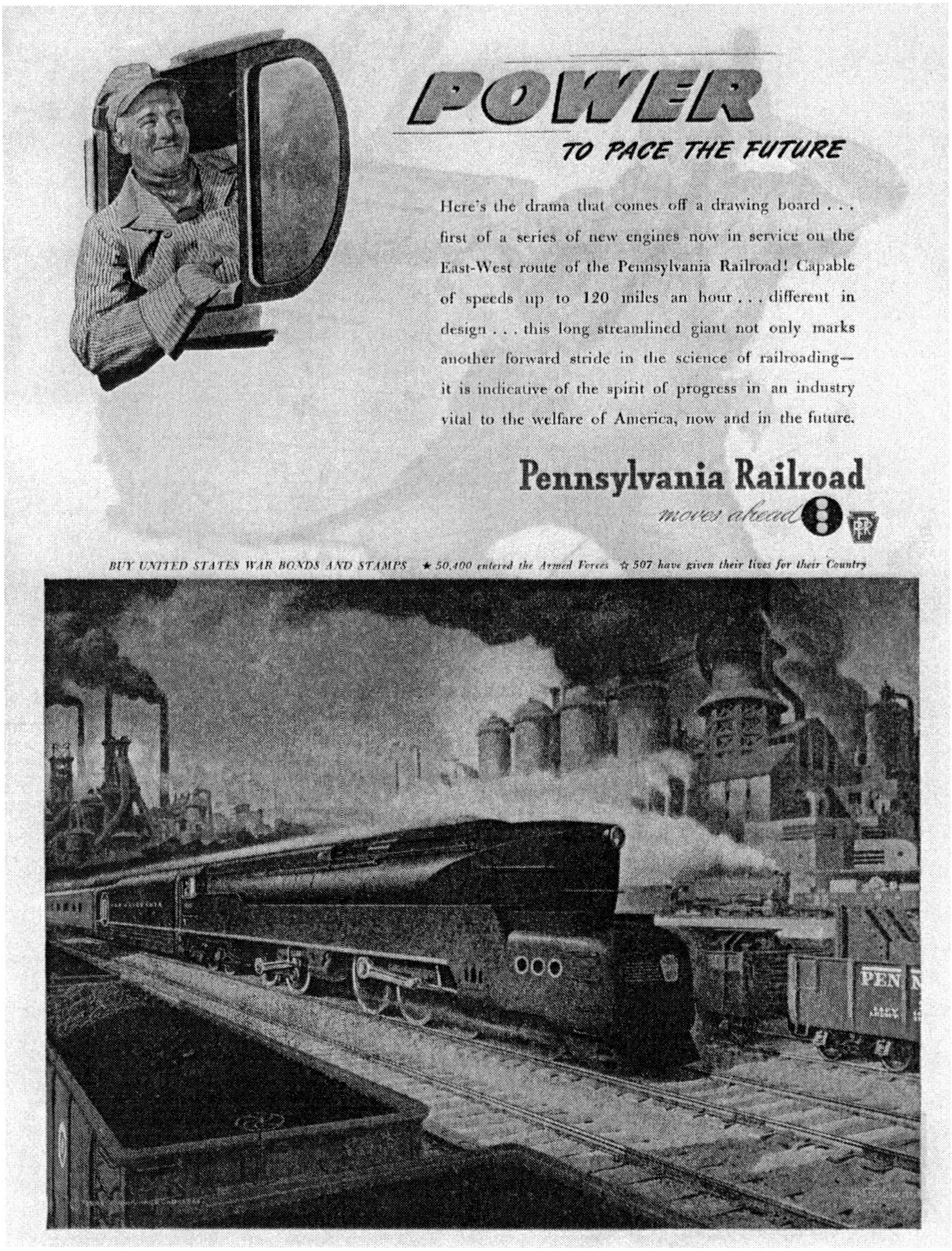
POWER
TO PACE THE FUTURE
Here's the drama that comes off a drawing board . . . first of a series of new engines now in service on the East-West route of the Pennsylvania Railroad! Capable of speeds up to 120 miles an hour . . . different in design . . . this long streamlined giant not only marks another forward stride in the science of railroading—it is indicative of the spirit of progress in an industry vital to the welfare of America, now and in the future.
Pennsylvania Railroad
moves ahead
BUY UNITED STATES WAR BONDS AND STAMPS ★ 50,400 entered the Armed Forces ☆ 507 have given their lives for their Country
PEN

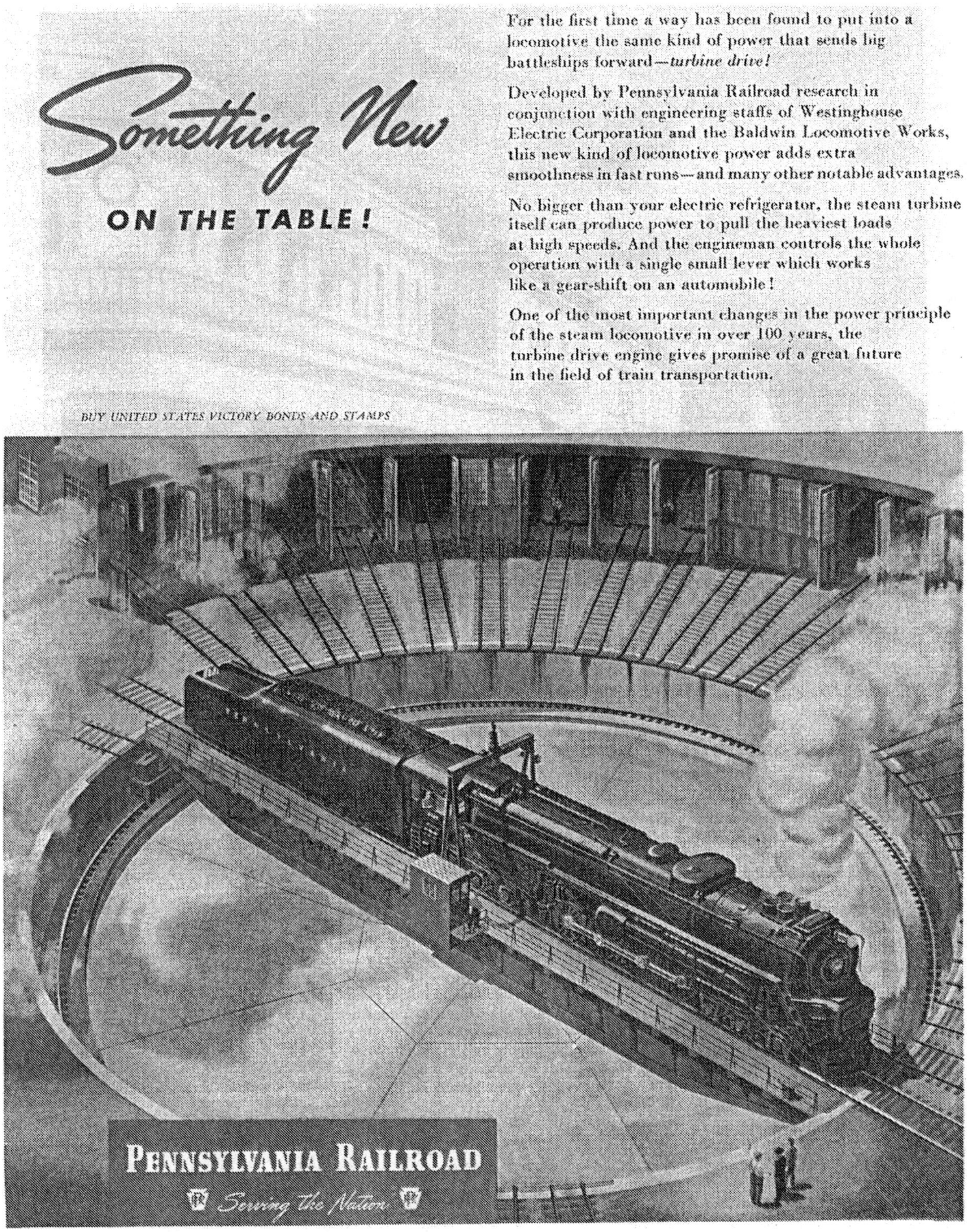
Something New
ON THE TABLE!
For the first time a way has been found to put into a locomotive the same kind of power that sends big battleships forward—*turbine drive!*
Developed by Pennsylvania Railroad research in conjunction with engineering staffs of Westinghouse Electric Corporation and the Baldwin Locomotive Works, this new kind of locomotive power adds extra smoothness in fast runs—and many other notable advantages.
No bigger than your electric refrigerator, the steam turbine itself can produce power to pull the heaviest loads at high speeds. And the engineman controls the whole operation with a single small lever which works like a gear-shift on an automobile!
One of the most important changes in the power principle of the steam locomotive in over 100 years, the turbine drive engine gives promise of a great future in the field of train transportation.
BUY UNITED STATES VICTORY BONDS AND STAMPS
PENNSYLVANIA RAILROAD
Serving the Nation

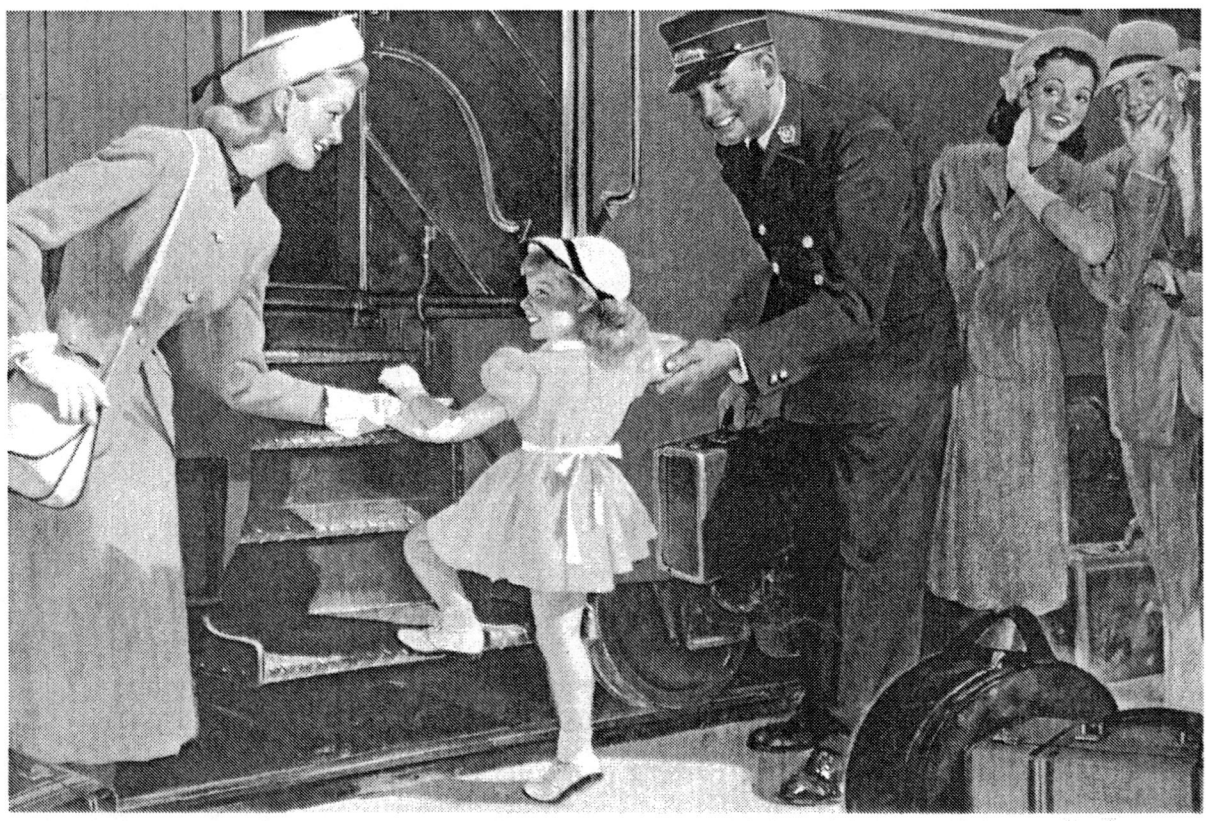

For a Carefree Vacation... GO BY TRAIN!

Yes, and like this little lady — go by Pennsylvania Railroad!

Our great passenger fleets offer a choice of 1,100 daily trains between East and West — North and South — scheduled for your convenience, equipped for your comfort... by day, by night. Whether you travel by sleeping car or coach, there is a train ready to take you when you are ready to go.

No better year — and no better way... whether you plan to visit New York, Washington or other eastern cities; a quiet resort, or the folks back home.

Enjoy the extra convenience and comforts the Pennsylvania Railroad now offers through its great network of through service. Coast-to-coast... to New England ...Eastern Canada...the South...the Southwest — *all without change of cars!*

To the grandeur of the Canadian Rockies... to America's inspiring National Parks, well-timed connections.

Our city ticket offices, travel bureaus and ticket agents are available to help you plan a carefree and relaxed vacation — *from the first to the final mile!*

PENNSYLVANIA RAILROAD
Serving the Nation

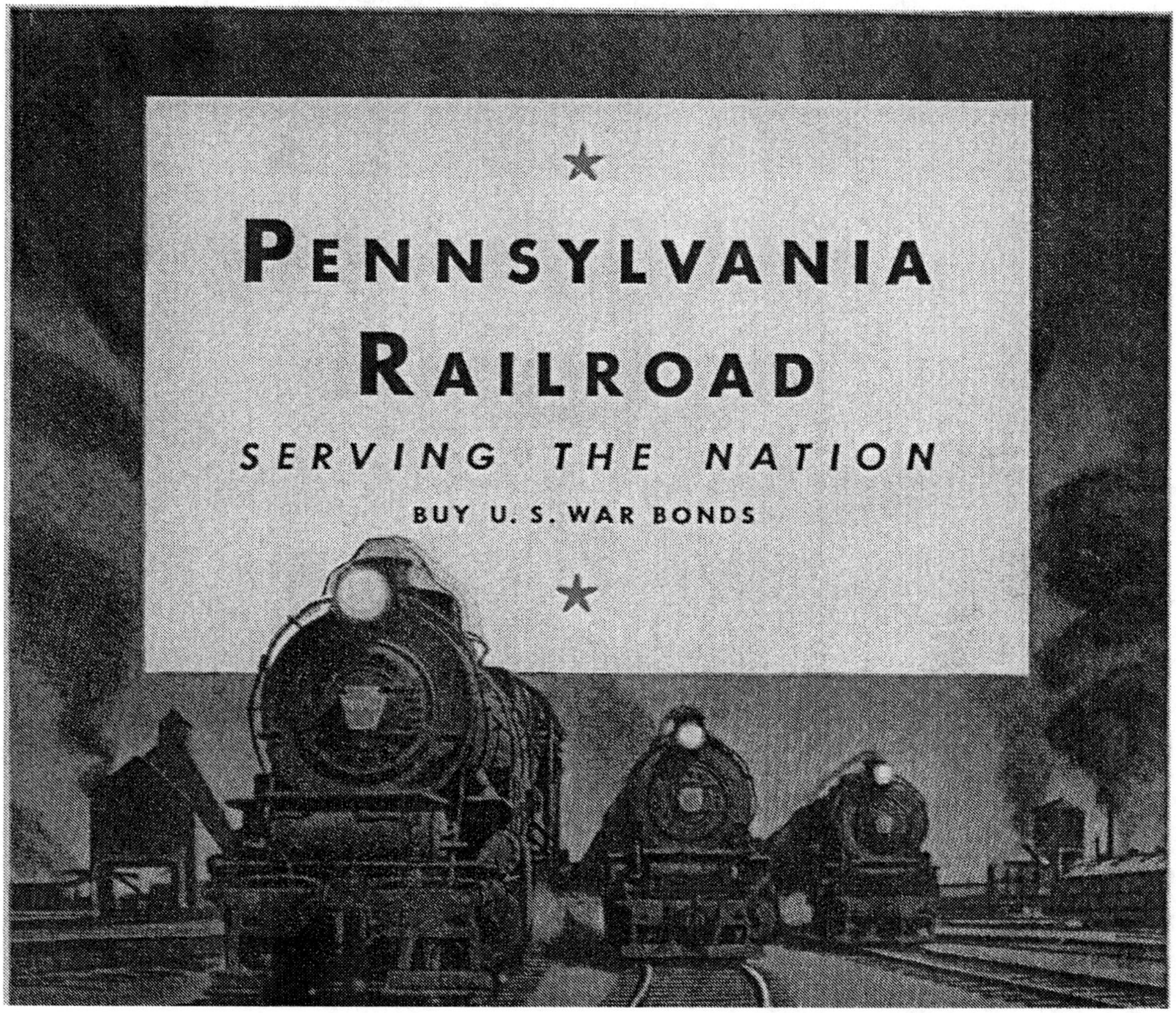
PENNSYLVANIA
RAILROAD
SERVING THE NATION
BUY U. S. WAR BONDS

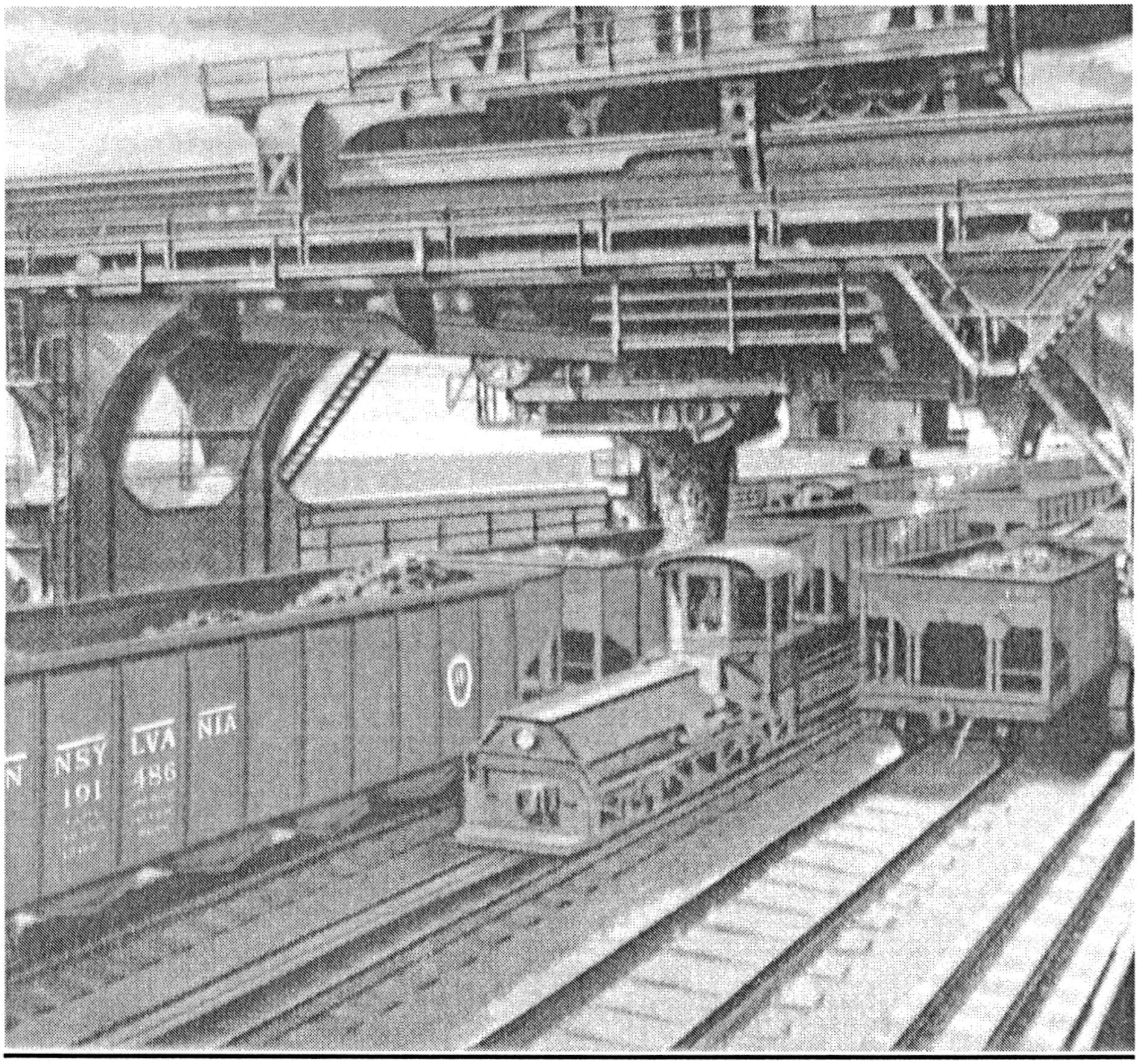
N NSY LVA NIA
101 486

Michael E. Ferlise

CHAPTER SIX

**New Jersey's Railroads
at Their Peak**

For the Central Railroad of New Jersey the 1900's started off on a bad note. The ferryboat "Plainfield" became a complete loss after there was a fire onboard off Jersey City. The iron mining industry in the Chester area declined as a result of the Mesabi Range in Minnesota. The CRRNJ then removed its tracks of the Hacklebarney Branch. After the year 1900 the Delaware and Raritan Canal never showed a profit.

During 1901 the DL & W built stations at Newark's Broad Street, Millington, and Bernardsville. At this point in time the Baltimore and Ohio Railroad had control over the CRRNJ. The B & O ran trains into the CRRNJ's Communipaw Terminal where its Royal Blue Ferry took passengers to Manhattan. The two Royal Blue ferryboats for this service were "Mauch Chunk" and "Easton." The Baltimore and Ohio Railroad also controlled the rail and ferry service of the Staten Island Rapid Transit Ferry Company. On June 14, 1901, the CRRNJ/B & O "Mauch Chunk" headed for Whitehall Street in Manhattan crashed into the Staten Island Ferry's "Northfield" that was leaving for New York City. There were almost 1,000 people on the "Northfield" and unfortunately four people died. This gave the State of New York a reason to start negotiations for a city takeover of the Staten Island Rapid Transit Ferry Company.

Even though in New York City the Park Avenue railroad tracks were sunken there were still accidents. On January 8, 1902, a New York Central locomotive ran past a red signal obscured by smoke and haze. It then rammed into an idle New Haven train which resulted in fifteen deaths. Something had to be done with the problem of smoke, haze, grime, and cinders. In 1902, the New York Central introduced its luxury train service between New York City and Chicago with the "20th Century Limited." To stay competitive the Pennsylvania Railroad introduced its new "Broadway Limited."

In late January of 1902, John Fairfield Dryden assumed the vacant U.S. Senate seat from New Jersey left when William Sewell died in December of 1901. Senator Dryden was both the founder and President of the Prudential Insurance Company in Newark.

In 1902 U.S. President Theodore Roosevelt signed the Sherman Anti-Trust Act. It had an impact on the Pennsylvania Railroad which was forced to give up majority control of the Baltimore and Ohio. The B & O was now free to go off on its own.

William McAdoo was getting the financial backing needed to restart the work on the tunnel under the Hudson River. The New York and Jersey Tunnel Company was organized in 1902 after which work under the Hudson River commenced.

Across the Hudson River at Liberty Street, the CRRNJ's new two ferry slip terminal opened. On this side of New Jersey their repair shops in Elizabethport opened as well as a new Plainfield station.

During 1902 the Whippany River Railroad expanded from Morristown towards Whippany. The Whippany and Passaic River Railroad was then incorporated to build another line from the Whippany River Railroad to the east where the Erie Railroad had a line in Essex Fells.

Since the 1890's CRRNJ President John Maxwell had been obtaining land in the Cranford/Westfield area. In order to develop the area the Garwood Land and Improvement Company was created. Samuel Garwood served as its first President. Along the CRRNJ Main Line on February 23, 1903, the Borough of Garwood was created from Westfield and Cranford.

In 1903, the Whippany River Railroad (Morristown to Whippany) was combined with the Whippany and Passaic River Railroad (Whippany to Essex Fells). It was renamed the

Morristown and Erie Railroad. Shortly afterwards, the Erie Railroad offered passenger and freight service from Morristown to Jersey City via its tracks at Essex Fells.

By this time in New Jersey there were so many little trolley companies with most in bad financial shape. The NJ State Attorney General Thomas McCarter left his position to organize the Public Service Corporation of New Jersey. The project was backed by the Prudential Insurance Company and the Fidelity Union Bank. The President of Prudential was U.S. Senator John Fairfield Dryden. With about $10 million in funding, Public Service was able to take over around 100 different trolley companies. Public Service also took in and consolidated several hundred little gas and electric companies. Public Service transported people around New Jersey on trolley lines from which gas and electricity were also provided to customers along the way. Thomas McCarter served as the first President of Public Service. In his place, the New Jersey Legislature appointed his brother Robert McCarter as the Attorney General of New Jersey.

By 1903 the D L & W took control of the Hoboken Ferry Company from the Eldridge family. At this point in the Newark area both the PRR and CRRNJ had their tracks elevated to prevent accidents. The D L & W did not and instead had street level grade crossings. This led to numerous accidents between D L & W trains and trolleys, buggies, and even pedestrians. One morning a trolley filled with Barringer High School students slid down Clifton Avenue on some ice where it stopped on the D L & W tracks. At the same time the Bernardsville Special was headed on these track going east. There was a crash which resulted in nine deaths and about thirty injuries. The D L & W then removed its grade crossings in Newark where the tracks would be elevated.

Back in 1904, Kenilworth in Union County was known as New Orange. At the time the New Orange Four Junction Railroad connected New Orange with the nearby tracks of the CRRNJ and Lehigh Valley Railroad. Louis Keller, the publisher for the "Social Register" in New York City gained control of the little railroad in 1904. Back in the late 1800's Baltusrol Golf Course was built on his farm in Springfield. The Rahway Valley Railroad was then extended from New Orange to his property in Springfield.

Underneath the Hudson River, William McAdoo's workmen from both sides finally met in March of 1904. With the north tunnel completed, it was the first time that people could cross between New Jersey and New York under the Hudson River. The Hudson and Manhattan Railroad Company was organized separate from the New York and New Jersey Tunnel Company. The first President was William McAdoo. With the first tunnel completed from Hoboken towards Midtown Manhattan, a second one was started next to it. The first tunnel was built with a shield that pushed forward one foot every hour. There were holes in this shield in which the mud and silt was pushed out from in front. The muck then had to be carried out of the tunnel by carts. As the shield moved forward each foot, iron rings were bolted around the circumference of the tunnel. The second tunnel was built with the shield's small doors for the silt closed. McAdoo now used powerful hydraulic jacks that simply pushed the shield forward and forced all the silt to the sides. Without having to carry the mud out of the tunnel work went faster the second time.

By now in New York City the IND or Interborough Rapid Transit "subway" was completed from Lower Manhattan to the Bronx. The D L & W now started to use "Phoebe Snow" with her white dress, hat, and gloves. This nicely dressed Lackawanna passenger advertised the railroad's clean burning anthracite coal locomotives. This was opposed to bituminous coal that was portrayed as dirty with soot and cinders. By the end of the year the

D L & W formally leased the Hoboken Ferry Company. At the same time, Lewis Keller's Rahway Valley Railroad from New Orange approached the Lackawanna's tracks in Summit.

In the early morning hours of August 7, 1905, there was a fire on the Lackawanna ferryboat "Hopatcong." As the boat burned, the wooden ferry terminal and railroad terminal in Hoboken caught fire and also burned. With no D L & W railroad terminal, other nearby terminals were used by Lackawanna trains. The Lackawanna ferries still used the ferry slips where passengers then took Public Service trolleys to the other terminals or Newark for D L & W trains. For a while now the Morris and Essex/Lackawanna Railroads brought wealthy people towards the Morristown area. With easy rail access to New York City dozens of very rich people now lived out in Morris County. By 1905 there were approximately 90 millionaires in Morristown alone.

Other wealthy people followed the Lackawanna's Passaic and Delaware Branch (Gladstone Branch) out into the Somerset Hills. By now C. Ledyard Blair already had his 423 acre estate "Blairsden" when he got new neighbors in 1906. Walter Graeme Ladd along with his wife Kate Macy Ladd built a forty room mansion on nearly 500 acres next to "Blairsden." The Ladd's estate was named "Natirar" which is Raritan spelled backwards. Wealthy people out this way could once again take the "Millionaire's Express" to Hoboken in 1907. On February 25, 1907, the Lackawanna's new terminal opened in Hoboken. Built with a minimal amount of wood, the new terminal had seventeen track platforms and six ferry slips. Designed in the beaux-arts style by architect Kenneth Murchison, it had a steel framework covered with copper. Above the terminal rose a 225 foot high clock tower with four clocks up top. The "Bush" style train shed had slits in the top so smoke from steam engines could escape. At Hoboken, the Lackawanna had three ferry routes across the Hudson River to Barclay Street, Christopher Street, and 23rd Street.

Underneath the Hudson River two more tunnels were built for the Hudson and Manhattan Railroad. These tunnels connected Exchange Place in Jersey City with Lower Manhattan. The H & M's massive "Powerhouse" was built in Jersey City. Inside, steam generators powered by coal energized turbines could put out 11,000 volts of alternating current.

Down in Washington D.C., Union Station opened in October of 1907. Prior to this time both the Pennsylvania and Baltimore and Ohio Railroads had their own stations here. It took an act of Congress back in 1903, but the new Union Station was jointly owned by both the PRR and the B & O. With twenty-two tracks, Union Station was built at a cost of $20 million. Service first started as B & O train number ten departed from Washington D.C. enroute towards New Jersey.

On February 25, 1908, U.S. President Theodore Roosevelt in Washington D.C. sent a signal to "the Powerhouse" in Jersey City. With this signal, the Hudson and Manhattan Railroad opened up service between New Jersey and Manhattan under the Hudson River. At that point in time the H & M upper route ran from Hoboken to Christopher Street where it ended at 19th Street.

In order to shorten the distance between Hoboken and Buffalo, the Lackawanna started work on its "New Jersey Cut-Off" between Port Morris N.J. and Slateford Junction in Pennsylvania. The twenty-nine mile "Cut-Off" removed nearly eleven miles off of the Lackawanna Main Line to Scranton in Pennsylvania. The New Jersey Cut-Off, built at a cost of $11 million had nearly seventy-five new bridges along its twenty-nine miles. The Lackawanna's Paulins Kill Viaduct built near Blairstown was 1,100 feet long with seven arches. At nearly 120 feet above the valley below, this was the longest viaduct in the entire world. It only held the record for a short time because the Lackawanna soon built a 110 foot high viaduct above Pennsylvania's Pequest Valley that was three miles long.

In 1908, the Lackawanna also started work on a second tunnel through Bergen Hill in Jersey City. This second Tunnel would allow for four D L & W tracks through Bergen Hill above the Erie's just below. Some of New Jersey Transit's trains that run to or from Hoboken still use these tunnels today. As per an earlier law in New York State, steam locomotives were banned below the Harlem River as of July 1, 1908. With electric engines in this area instead of steam locomotives there wouldn't be accidents caused by excessive smoke and haze.

By the following year the Hudson and Manhattan Railroad had new stations under the Erie's Pavonia Terminal, the Pennsylvania's Exchange Place Terminal, and Church Street in Lower Manhattan. During 1910 the H & M's tracks in Midtown Manhattan reached 33rd Street.

While the Hudson and Manhattan tubes were being built, the Pennsylvania Railroad was also digging under the Hudson River. By 1910 the PRR's tunnels between North Bergen and Midtown Manhattan were completed. The Pennsylvania Railroad could now provide direct rail access to New York City from New Jersey. With these tunnels, the PRR got ahead of the CRRNJ, Lackawanna, Reading, and the Baltimore and Ohio. In Midtown Manhattan between 31st and 33rd Streets the "first" Pennsylvania Station opened. The Romanesque style station designed by McKim, Mead, and White had exterior marble columns that rose sixty feet above the street. In addition to the two Hudson River tunnels, the PRR built three more under the East River between Manhattan and Queens. Across the East River in Queens the PRR constructed a large train yard. As per New York State law though steam locomotives were not permitted below the Harlem River anymore. PRR steam locomotives stopped at the "Manhattan Transfer" to the east of Newark. From here DD-1 electric engines brought the trains to Pennsylvania Station in Midtown. The Pennsylvania still kept its Exchange Place Terminal in Jersey City where commuters still crossed the Hudson River by ferryboat or via the H & M tubes. Several PRR passenger trains from Philadelphia continued to run to the Exchange Place Terminal.

During 1910 on its Main Line the CRRNJ built a passenger station at High Bridge. By 1911 the Hudson and Manhattan Railroad had tracks out to the Pennsylvania's "Manhattan Transfer." PRR passengers could take the Hudson and Manhattan's tubes to Manhattan in addition to PRR electrics to Pennsylvania Station in Midtown.

At this point in time the Lackawanna's tracks through Chatham Boro ran at street level. In November of 1911, Isadore Katz in a horse drawn carriage went across the Willow Street grade crossing in Chatham. Unfortunately Mr. Katz didn't notice the Easton Mail Express coming fast from Summit. There was an accident and Mr. Katz died from his injuries. Down the Lackawanna's line on December 24, 1911, the first train ran on the now completed D L & W "Cut-Off." Back to Chatham, the Lackawanna had a station where some passengers had to walk across the tracks in order to catch trains. In January of 1912 Harold Martin was killed by a westbound train that ran past an idle one. Chatham residents were concerned about these kinds of accidents. This led to a discussion of how to solve the problem. The Lackawanna's tracks through Chatham could either be elevated like in the Oranges or lowered like those in Summit. On the future Gladstone Branch in Somerset County the Lackawanna built a new station in Basking Ridge.

During the late 1800's, two men named H. W. Johns and C. B. Manville started a business where they made asbestos products. In 1912 they moved to a 328 acre farm in Hillsborough near the CRRNJ's Mainline. At the same time in Jersey City, the Hudson and Manhattan Railroad built its Summit Avenue Station where Journal Square is today.

In 1913 the PRR decided not to renew its permission for the Lehigh Valley Railroad to use the Exchange Place Terminal. The Lehigh Valley simply started to use the CRRNJ's Communipaw Terminal nearby. With the Reading, Baltimore and Ohio, and now the Lehigh Valley Railroads using its terminal, the CRRNJ was hard at work on improvements. In Aldene on the CRRNJ's Mainline (Roselle Park) the Marconi Wireless Telegraph Station started up. This spot is where the current Romerovski Brothers building is today. Further down the line the CRRNJ continued improvements with a new station at Bound Brook.

At this point in time the Lackawanna Railroad proposed new elevated tracks in Chatham. Chatham residents though wanted the Lackawanna to lower its tracks for safety. The case went as far as the New Jersey Supreme Court which dismissed it on behalf of the Lackawanna. In 1913, Lackawanna passengers who used the Barclay Street Ferry could walk to the new Woolworth Building in Lower Manhattan. The $13.5 million building was commissioned and paid for by Frank W. Woolworth. He was best known for his chain of 5 cent and 10 cent stores. When compared to modern skyscrapers it may not seem tall, but back in 1913 the Woolworth Building was the tallest building in the entire world.

Uptown in Manhattan during 1913, Grand Central Terminal was completed. Today everyone seems to refer to the building as Grand Central Station which is actually incorrect. Grand Central is not a station, but a terminal where trains end or terminate without continuing on through. At the same time the old New York Central and Hudson Railroad was reorganized with its smaller subsidiaries into the New York Central Railroad.

World War I may have started in Europe during 1914, but back in Jersey City the CRRNJ's improved Communipaw Terminal opened. In order to handle double decked ferryboats, the new copper covered ferry building now had two floors. With the additional B & O, Reading, and Lehigh Valley Railroad trains there were now twenty tracks instead of twelve. The new "Bush" style train shed that covered the terminal's tracks was made from concrete, iron, and steel.

Back then people referred to 5 cent coins as "jitneys." In the Newark area there were dozens of people who owned little buses on which they gave people rides. With the usual fare of 5 cents these small buses soon also started to be called "jitneys." Many people to this day almost 100 years later still call these little buses "jitneys."

The United States got closer to being involved in World War I as a German U-boat sank the British steamship "Lusitania" on May 7, 1915. About 1,200 people which included 128 Americans died when the "Lusitania" went down. The ship had been enroute to England from New York.

The Lackawanna continued with improvements as a new passenger station was built at Far Hills during 1914. While its tracks through Chatham were being elevated and realigned, another new station opened here for passengers on June 19, 1914. In 1915 two more new passenger stations opened nearby in Morristown and Morris Plains. During 1916 the Lackawanna's station in Madison just past Chatham opened. When people think of Broad Street in Newark the New Jersey Transit (old Lackawanna) station comes to mind. Back in 1916 the CRRNJ built its own station in a little from Broad Street and Lafayette Streets.

During October of 1917 the New Jersey Southern Railroad was absorbed by the CRRNJ. After this merger the old New Jersey Southern became the CRRNJ's Southern Division. It joined the CRRNJ's New York and Long Branch Railroad at Red Bank where it ran to the southwest. From Red Bank it ran down to Lakewood and Lakehurst where the Barnegat Branch headed to Barnegat. From Lakehurst it continued through the Pine Barrens to Winslow Junction where the Reading Railroad's Atlantic City Railroad headed to Atlantic City. After Winslow Junction it headed towards the Delaware Bay via Vineland and Bridgeton.

As the United States became involved in World War I, U.S. President Woodrow Wilson issued a proclamation. On December 28th every transportation system in the country would be under U.S. Government control. The new nationalized system of all the U.S. railroads was placed under the control of President Wilson's son in law William G. McAdoo. In New Jersey, the new owner of the Rockaway Valley Railroad, Frank Allen dismantled everything and sold the rails for wartime scrap. With anti-German sentiment in the area the Lackawanna renamed its boats Hamburg and Bremen to Chatham and Maplewood respectively. On the CRRNJ's Mainline the town of German Valley changed its name to Long Valley.

The U.S. Railroad Administration decided it would be better if Baltimore and Ohio as well as Lehigh Valley Railroad trains now terminated at the PRR's New York Pennsylvania Station. The switch from the CRRNJ's terminal in Jersey City for these two railroads was permanent for the moment. During 1918 in Orange the Lackawanna's new station at Highland Avenue opened.

With airplanes becoming prevalent the very first municipal airport in the world opened at Atlantic City's Bader Field. For the Rahway Valley Railroad in Union County 1919 was its last year of passenger service.

With World War I over, all the U.S. railroads were returned to their own control as of February 19, 1920. For the Rahway Valley Railroad, the man responsible for bringing it from Aldene to Summit where the Lackawanna was died. With the death of Louis Keller, Roger Clark and his son George took over. The little Union County railroad was in bad shape, but Clark and his son gave it a little boost. On April 30, 1921, an interstate agency between New York and New Jersey was created in the form of the Port of New York Authority. It wasn't until 1972 when the name was changed to the Port Authority of New York and New Jersey. To avoid confusion I am going to simply use the current name from this point on. This agency formed between New York and New Jersey was the first of its kind in the United States.

With all the ships in the Newark Bay during World War I, the CRRNJ's drawbridge across it was an inconvenience. During the early 1920's the CRRNJ started to improve its Newark Bay Drawbridge between Elizabeth and Bayonne.

During 1922 the State of New Jersey took over control of the now outdated Morris Canal. The following year the Lackawanna built its East Orange and Brick Church (also in East Orange) passenger stations. At the same time in 1923, the State of New York passed a law that banned all steam locomotives from the New York City area. In May of 1923, the Baltimore and Ohio Railroad started its Capitol Limited service between Washington D.C. and Chicago. This was an attempt by the B & O to compete with the PRR's Broadway Limited and the New York Centrals "20th Century." By 1924 the old Morris Canal was officially put to rest and drained in various parts.

In the meantime, the CRRNJ saw an oil-electric engine that was demonstrated by both General Electric and Ingersoll Rand. This could help as a solution to the steam locomotive ban in New York City that was about to take effect. On October 22, 1925, the CRRNJ's new diesel switcher # 1000 started work in their Bronx Freight Terminal. It was the first use ever in the United States of a diesel locomotive. At 60 tons and 300 horsepower, the diesel switcher was built by General Electric, Ingersoll Rand, and the American Locomotive Company or ALCO.

With more motor vehicles on New Jersey's roads the first traffic circle in the United States was built in Pennsauken. On July 1, 1926, U.S. President Calvin Coolidge officially opened the Delaware River Bridge between Camden and Philadelphia. At the time this was the longest suspension bridge in the entire world. With the bridge open there was an increase in automobile, bus, and truck traffic between New Jersey and Philadelphia. This in turn led to a decrease in revenue for the Pennsylvania and Reading Railroads on their Philadelphia to Atlantic City routes. Buses in particular took a lot of railroad passengers away from the PRR and the Reading between Philadelphia and Atlantic City.

In August of 1926, the Pennsylvania Railroad decided to refuse the Baltimore and Ohio access to its Pennsylvania Station in New York City. By the end of August, Baltimore and Ohio passenger trains were again ending at the CRRNJ's Communipaw Terminal in Jersey City. The B & O used the Reading's tracks from Philadelphia to Bound Brook. From here they ran to Jersey City via the CRRNJ's tracks through Elizabeth. Once in Jersey City at Communipaw, B & O passengers got on B & O buses that crossed the Hudson River on the CRRNJ's ferryboats. For B & O passengers these buses that traveled across the Hudson River were free of charge.

On November 27, 1926, New Jersey Governor A. Harry Moore dedicated the CRRNJ's new Newark Bay Lift Bridge which cost $14 million to build. It provided the CRRNJ four tracks across the Newark Bay between Elizabeth and Bayonne near 5th Street. At that time it was the longest four track railroad bridge in the entire world.

In the City of Newark the old Morris Canal had pretty much been abandoned and drained. Newark decided to spend $425,000 to purchase the Morris Canal's bed through the city. Newark would build a subway if Public Service would maintain and operate it. By this point the Public Service Coordinated Transit Company had been set aside from the Public Service Electric and Gas Company to handle buses and Trolleys.

In May of 1927, Charles A. Lindbergh made the first solo airplane ride across the Atlantic Ocean. Airline travel started to come of age soon after Lindbergh's flight in his "Spirit of St. Louis" to Paris. Afterwards, Lindbergh returned back to Washington D.C. where he was welcomed back as a hero. Newsreels were taken of Lindbergh's return which were then rushed off to New York City via the Pennsylvania Railroad. The film of his return to Washington D.C. was developed along the way in a baggage car that was temporarily turned into a darkroom. The 215 mile trip via New Jersey was completed in 175 minutes courtesy of engine # 460.

At 12:01 a.m. on November 13, 1927, the Holland Tunnel opened up for motor vehicles underneath the Hudson River between Jersey City and Lower Manhattan. The Holland Tunnel was the first motor vehicle tunnel underneath water in the United States. A truck enroute to Bloomingdales in Manhattan became the first to cross under the Hudson River. Built over a seven year period at a cost of $45 million, it was named in honor of Clifford Holland. Holland's design idea consisted of two tubes which each had two lanes for motor vehicles. The Holland Tunnel made it easier for cars, trucks, and buses to travel between New Jersey and New York City. It was bad news for the Lackawanna Railroad which saw a quick 40% drop in its ferry traffic across the Hudson River. The Erie Railroad also experienced a similar drop in its ferry service as well. With people using the Holland Tunnel, the Hudson and Manhattan Railroad had a sharp decrease in its ridership underneath the Hudson River. If this wasn't bed enough work had just started on the George Washington Bridge between Fort Lee and Upper Manhattan.

With more people traveling to Lake Hopatcong by car the CRRNJ decided to discontinue its passenger service to this area in 1927.

Back in Newark, work was underway on the old Morris Canal bed which was being widened for the future subway. The fill that was taken up was hauled to the marshes on the Newark/Elizabeth border for an airport. Around the same time the Newark Bay was also being widened to accommodate more ships. The muck that was dredged up was piped to the same marshland for the future Newark Airport.

In order to reduce smoke, cinders, dirt, and congestion the Lackawanna Railroad decided to electrify some of its tracks in 1928. For safety, the Lackawanna wanted an overhead caternary instead of a third rail at track level. Work was planned to begin during the summer of 1929 on its three lines out towards Morristown, Gladstone, and Montclair. In the meantime, the Lackawanna built a drawbridge over the Hackensack River between Jersey City and Kearny. This three track vertical-lift bridge is still used by NJ Transit today.

On June 29, 1928, the Port Authority opened two bridges across the Arthur Kill between New Jersey and Staten Island. The Goethals Bridge was built between Elizabeth and Howland Hook in Staten Island. At 135 feet above the Arthur Kill, it honored Major General George W. Goethels. He built the Panama Canal. The second bridge between Perth Amboy and Tottenville in Staten Island was the Outerbridge Crossing. While this is the Port Authority's outermost bridge it was actually named after the agency's first chairman Eugenius H. Outerbridge. With more motor vehicles in this part of New Jersey the first traffic "cloverleaf" in the United States was constructed in Woodbridge at Routes 1 and 35. The downside to more automobiles was that the Morristown and Erie Railroad had to discontinue passenger service. This left it as simply a freight railroad.

By the summer of 1928 Newark Airport started out as a 1,600 foot cinder runway. There weren't a lot of runways in the country and this was the first commercial landing strip in the United States.

The CRRNJ started its famous "Blue Comet" luxury train service from Jersey City to Atlantic City on February 21, 1929. The comfortable blue coaches were complete with blue upholstery and carpeting. These passenger cars carried the name of comets such as Haley, Tuttle, Biela, Faye, and Spitaler. From the Liberty Street Ferry, "Blue Comet" passengers left Jersey City courtesy of a steam locomotive and traveled through Elizabethport, Amboy, and Red Bank. From here the "Blue Comet" continued south via the old New Jersey Southern Railroad through Lakewood and the Pine Barrens to Winslow Junction. From here the Reading Railroad's Line to Atlantic City was used to complete the trip to Atlantic City.

Unfortunately for most of the people in the United States, the Great Depression started in October of 1929 as stocks crashed. This didn't stop the CRRNJ from introducing its new passenger train named "The Bullet" on November 7, 1929. "The Bullet" had a running time of four hours between Jersey City and Wilkes-Barre in Pennsylvania.

In Cranford the CRRNJ had elevated its track and built an elevated passenger station here. In fact "1929" is still etched in the concrete railroad overpasses that run through Cranford. Further down the line in Hillsborough there were about 5,000 people living near the Johns-Manville asbestos plant. Much of the mail that these people received was addressed to "Johns-Manville" instead of Hillsborough. In 1929 Manville officially separated from Hillsborough.

During 1929 the Lackawanna started its electrification project from Bloomfield Junction to Montclair. On September 3, 1930, the first electric train left Hoboken for Montclair with Thomas Edison at the controls. On September 22, 1930, the first electric train ran down the Lackawanna's tracks to South Orange. By the end of December the Lackawanna could run electric trains out to Morristown. By January 6, 1931, the Passaic and Delaware Branch from Summit to Gladstone was fully electrified. Towards the end of January, the electrification project reached Dover M.U. service began to Montclair, Dover, and Gladstone. In Montclair the Lackawanna built a six platform passenger station and a small one at Lyons. By now the Rahway Valley Railroad had linked up with Lackawanna in Summit. Its tracks still ran through Springfield and Kenilworth to Roselle where they linked up with the CRRNJ.

From the New Jersey side of the Hudson River the skyline of Manhattan was changing. In 1930, the Chrysler Building at 42nd Street and Lexington Avenue replaced the Woolworth Building as the tallest building in the world. In 1931 the Empire State Building replaced the Chrysler Building. It was built at 5th Avenue and 33rd Street.

After four years of construction, the George Washington Bridge opened up across the Hudson River on October 25, 1931. At a cost of about $59 million, the 3,500 foot "GWB" was the longest suspension bridge anywhere at that time. On November 15, 1931, the Bayonne Bridge opened between Bayonne and Staten Island. The $13 million bridge over the Kill Van Kull was the longest bridge of this type in the world.

In Newark a new street opened over what used to be a section of the old Morris Canal. Raymond Boulevard was named in honor of ex-mayor Thomas L. Raymond. Just above a portion of Raymond Boulevard the new Pulaski Skyway opened for motor vehicles on November 24, 1932. At a cost of about $21 million, the Pulaski Skyway across the marshes between Newark and Jersey City was the most expensive "highway" to be constructed at that time.

As the "Great Depression" continued throughout the country the Reading Railroad was losing money down in South Jersey. This resulted in the Pennsylvania, Reading, West Jersey and Seashore, and the Atlantic City Railroads coming together down here to form the new Pennsylvania Reading Seashore Lines. The PRSL was 2/3rds owned by the Pennsylvania. The other 1/3rd belonged to the Reading. With this merger in South Jersey, the Reading and the Pennsylvania could eliminate duplicate trackage in order to cut financial losses.

In New Jersey 1between New York's Pennsylvania Station and Philadelphia's Broad Street Station, the PRR had been electrifying the tracks. The PRR's first electric train from New York's Pennsylvania Station to Broad Street in Philadelphia made a run on January 16, 1933. Early on, PRR's electrics covered the ninety mile trip via New Jersey in just under two hours. The PRSL started service officially on June 25, 1933.

In 1934 the State of New Jersey took over control of the old Delaware and Raritan Canal. Some of the D & R Canal in Trenton had been filled in during a WPA project. Much of the canal between Mercer and Middlesex Counties was left alone after New Jersey's takeover.

Due to a decline in passengers the CRRNJ only had one "Blue Comet" train from Jersey City to Atlantic City by 1934. For the Rahway Valley Railroad in Union County, 1934 was the first year where the little road had a profit.

By April of 1935 the Pennsylvania Railroad had electric service between New York City and Washington D.C. As part of its electrification project the PRR built Newark's Pennsylvania Station which was ready in 1935. The Pennsylvania also electrified the tracks between Rahway and South Amboy. From Newark's Pennsylvania Station the Newark Subway opened for its first four miles through the old Morris Canal bed. In order to compete with the PRR's electric service, the Baltimore and Ohio introduced its "Royal Blue" service between Jersey City and Washington D.C. on June 24, 1935.

Due to a decline in mining activity around Lake Hopatcong, the CRRNJ abandoned the northern section of the Ogden Mine Railroad form Nolan's Point to the Edison area.

With GG1 electric locomotives the PRR had the trip from New York City to Philadelphia down to ninety-five minutes. As the summer of 1937 started, the Hudson and Manhattan Railroad had tracks to Newark's Pennsylvania Station. There was no longer a need for the H & M station at Park Place which was then torn down. In order to compete with the PRR's fully electrified line between New York City and Washington D.C., the Reading Railroad started its "Crusader" on December 13, 1937. The steam locomotives (there were two) and tenders were covered with stainless steel for a streamlined look. The passenger cars were also made with a stainless steel exterior for the same look. The "Crusader" made two round trips everyday (except Sunday) between Jersey City and Philadelphia. Due to continued operating losses, the CRRNJ's last "Blue Comet" ran from Jersey City to Atlantic City in September of 1941. The CRRNJ also discontinued its ferry service to Manhattan's 23rd Street.

In anticipation of being dragged into World War II the United State's industrial machine was already in action. In New Jersey, local factories, plants, and industries that produced commercial items instead turned out military products. New Jersey's vast transportation system of railroads along with its large ports contributed to the U.S. war effort. Things became more urgent after December 7, 1941 when Japan launched a surprise attack on Pearl Harbor. The U.S. declared war on Japan and entered World War II. The U.S. was also soon at war with Germany.

The U.S. Government took over control of Newark Airport and built Morristown Airport in Hanover. In Kearny the Federal Shipbuilding & Dry-dock Co. started to turn out ships 24 hours a day and seven days a week. In nearby Bayonne, while the U.S. Navy took control of the Port Terminal, patrol torpedo boats or PT Boats were made on Avenue E. Just off the PRR's tracks in Linden, Wildcat fighter aircraft were produced at the General Motors Plant. These fighters were tested just across Routes 1 & 9 from what later became Linden Airport. Industries like these that ran around the clock needed oil, coal, iron, steel, and all sorts of materials. Items like these were brought to New Jersey's plants by railroads like the Erie, CRRNJ, Lackawanna, Lehigh Valley, Reading, and Pennsylvania. In order to get the finished war products to ports in Camden, Newark, or Elizabeth these same railroads were used. The war production picture in New Jersey becomes even larger when Philadelphia and New York City at both ends are figured in. Coal and petroleum from Pennsylvania was brought by rail to New York. From here all manner of war related products left the Port of

New York destined for Europe of the Pacific. Hundreds of thousands of soldiers and sailors made their way to New York City via New Jersey's railroads and ferryboats.

Over in the Philippines the Japanese defeated the British and Americans. General Macarthur was able to escape in one of those PT boats made back in Bayonne. In revenge for Pearl Harbor, LT. Colonel Doolittle took off from the U.S.S. Hornet in a B-25 700 miles away from Japan. Doolittle was followed by 15 other B-25's. On April 18, 1942. They dropped some bombs on Tokyo and a few other Japanese cities. While the damage was light it did give a boost to American morale. Doolittle's B-25's were each powered by two Curtiss-Wright engines made back in New Jersey.

With World War II there was soon a need to expand Hoboken's 14th Street shipyard. The DL & W had some ferry service from here to Manhattan which had to be discontinued on April 27, 1942.

In June of 1942, four German-American saboteurs departed from a U-Boat off New York where they landed on the beach in a rubber raft. They buried some explosives and had plans to blow up Pennsylvania Station in Newark, the Hell's Gate Railroad Bridge in New York, and several other targets. Four other Germans landed off Florida after which they were to head up to New Jersey. Here in Irvington a Nazi sympathizer (who was a minister) was going to help them. All the potential saboteurs including the Irvington minister were arrested after which six were executed.

In July of 1942, the Erie's Pavonia Ferry Company stopped its service to Manhattan's 23rd Street. Two Erie ferryboats "Goshen" and "Rutherford" were also sold to the U.S. Government for use in Florida.

One month later, Hillsdale's Captain Frank Hill became the first American pilot to shoot down a German fighter aircraft. In October of 1942, the 102nd Cavalry Regiment from Essex County was the first American cavalry unit to land in Europe.

On December 7, 1942, the U.S. Navy launched the largest of its Iowa Class battleships aptly named the USS New Jersey. The other massive battleships in this class were named the Iowa, Missouri, Wisconsin, Illinois, and Kentucky. These huge battleships each had eight boilers that were manufactured here in Bayonne. The USS New Jersey would go on to earn 11 battle stars in World War II, 4 in Korea, and 2 during Vietnam. After its 57 years of service the USS New Jersey was the most decorated ship in the history of the U.S. Navy.

As the war raged on, back in New Jersey the CRRNJ continued to bring trains of petroleum filled tank cars to Bayonne, Carteret, and Linden. To help service Standard Oil's Bayway Refinery in Linden, the Tremley RR Yard opened in August of 1943. The CRRNJ brought millions of barrels of oil here to Tremley. It was also the largest tank car yard in the world.

In Europe the tide of war turned against Germany which led to Hitler's suicide on April 30, 1945. While the war was over in Europe it still continued to rage in the Pacific with the Japanese. The Americans "island hopped" towards Japan and had taken Okinawa by early July of 1945. Japan refused to give in which led to plans for a possible Allied invasion of Japan itself. With fanatical Japanese resistance the Allies faced the possibility of taking one million casualties. To end the war quicker the Americans had an alternative. On August 6, 1945, a B-29 Superfortress "Enola Gay" flew over the Japanese city Hiroshima and dropped the first atomic bomb. Even though about 150,000 people were killed or wounded Japan still refused to surrender. This led to a second B-29 "Bocks car" which dropped a second atomic bomb on Nagasaki. These two B-29's were powered by four Curtiss-Wright engines made back in New Jersey. Japan surrendered and World War II ended.

Plainfield Railroad Station, C.R.R. of N.J., Plainfield, N.J.

Along the Erie R.R.

Lackawanna Station, Newark, N.J.

Pennsylvania Station, New York City.

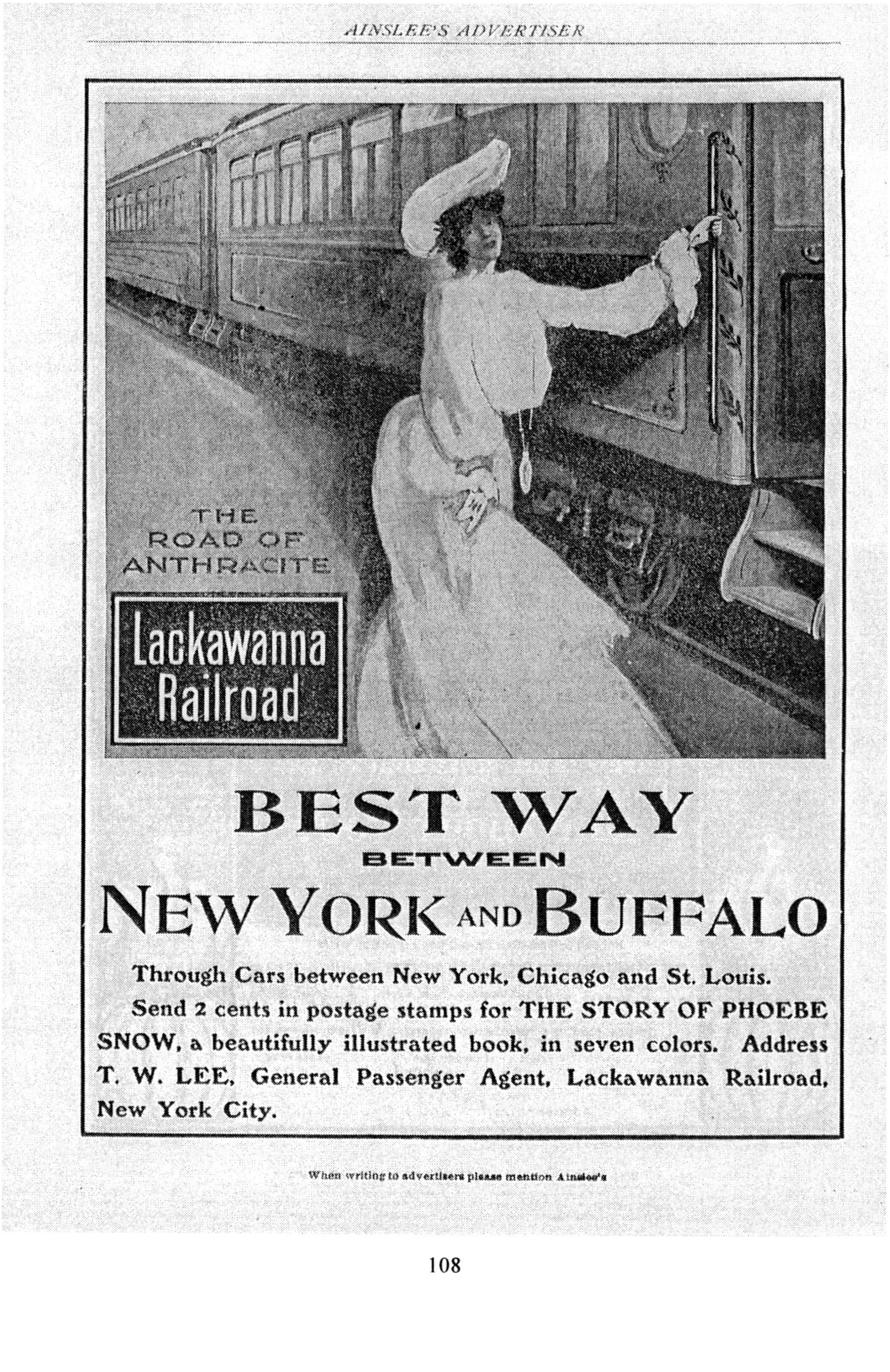
AINSLEE'S ADVERTISER
THE ROAD OF ANTHRACITE
Lackawanna Railroad
BEST WAY
BETWEEN
NEW YORK AND BUFFALO
Through Cars between New York, Chicago and St. Louis.
Send 2 cents in postage stamps for THE STORY OF PHOEBE SNOW, a beautifully illustrated book, in seven colors. Address T. W. LEE, General Passenger Agent, Lackawanna Railroad, New York City.
When writing to advertisers please mention Ainslee's

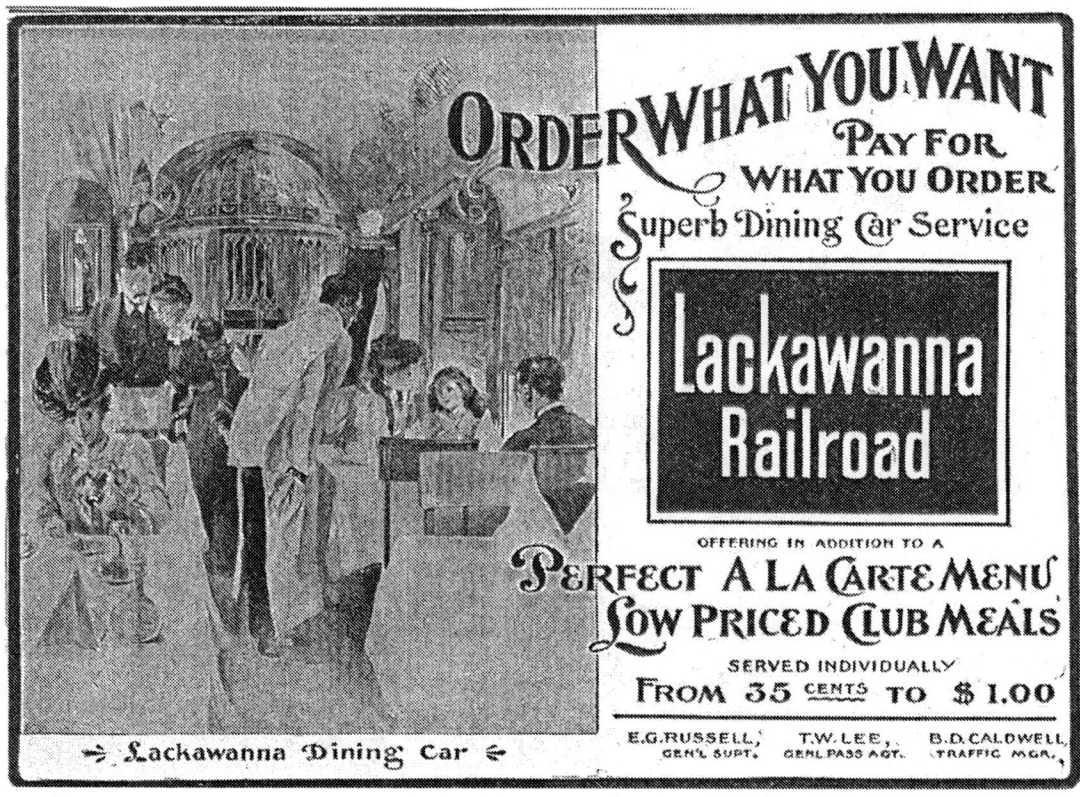

ORDER WHAT YOU WANT PAY FOR WHAT YOU ORDER
Superb Dining Car Service

Lackawanna Railroad

OFFERING IN ADDITION TO A

PERFECT A LA CARTE MENU LOW PRICED CLUB MEALS

SERVED INDIVIDUALLY FROM 35 CENTS TO $1.00

E.G. RUSSELL, GEN'L SUPT.   T.W. LEE, GEN'L PASS AGT.   B.D. CALDWELL, TRAFFIC MGR.

↦ Lackawanna Dining Car ↤

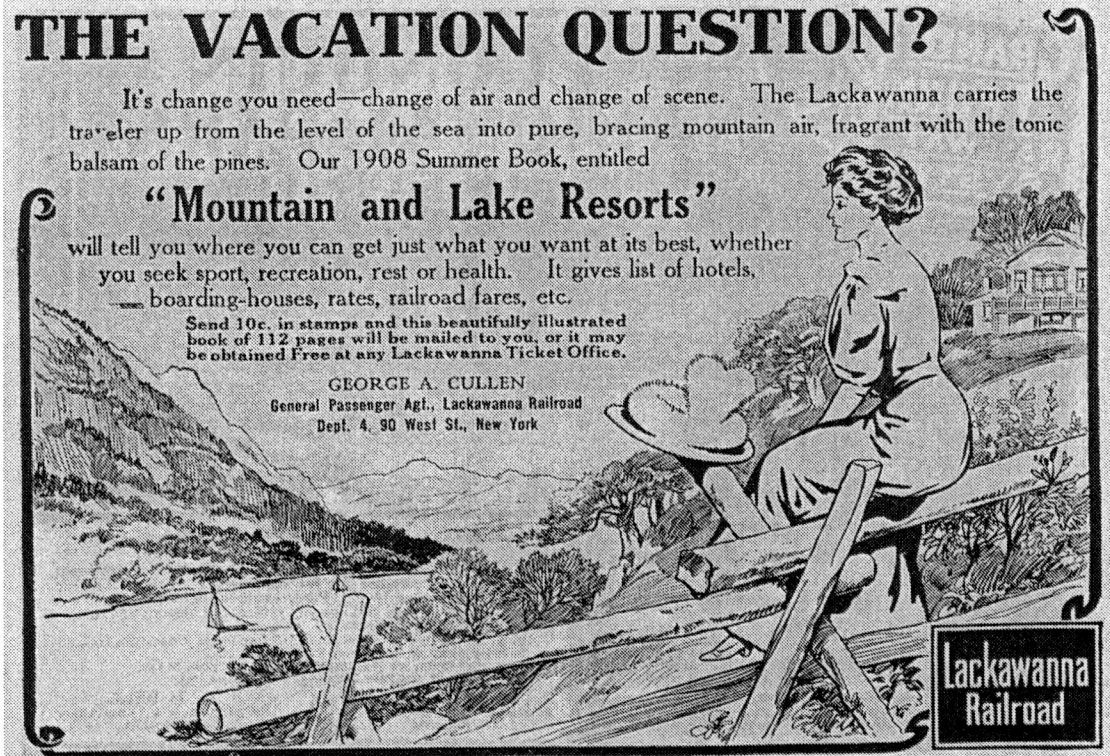

THE VACATION QUESTION?

It's change you need—change of air and change of scene. The Lackawanna carries the traveler up from the level of the sea into pure, bracing mountain air, fragrant with the tonic balsam of the pines. Our 1908 Summer Book, entitled

"Mountain and Lake Resorts"

will tell you where you can get just what you want at its best, whether you seek sport, recreation, rest or health. It gives list of hotels, boarding-houses, rates, railroad fares, etc.

Send 10c. in stamps and this beautifully illustrated book of 112 pages will be mailed to you, or it may be obtained Free at any Lackawanna Ticket Office.

GEORGE A. CULLEN
General Passenger Agt., Lackawanna Railroad
Dept. 4, 90 West St., New York

Lackawanna Railroad

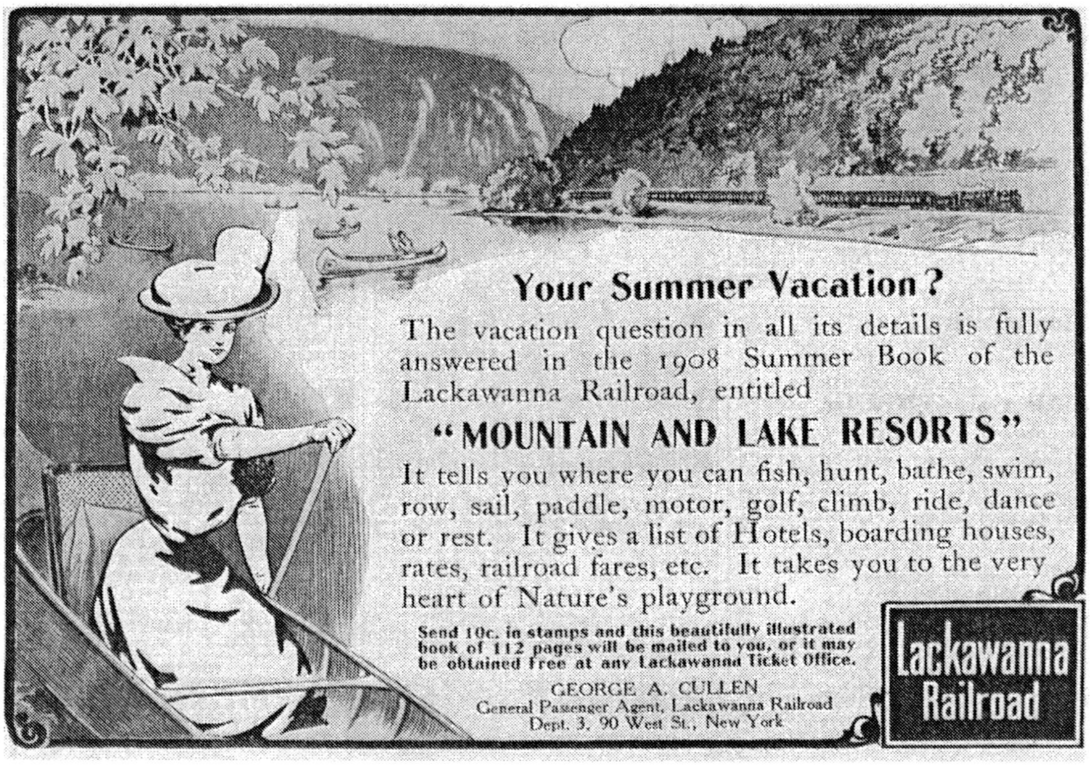
Your Summer Vacation?
The vacation question in all its details is fully answered in the 1908 Summer Book of the Lackawanna Railroad, entitled
"MOUNTAIN AND LAKE RESORTS"
It tells you where you can fish, hunt, bathe, swim, row, sail, paddle, motor, golf, climb, ride, dance or rest. It gives a list of Hotels, boarding houses, rates, railroad fares, etc. It takes you to the very heart of Nature's playground.
Send 10c. in stamps and this beautifully illustrated book of 112 pages will be mailed to you, or it may be obtained free at any Lackawanna Ticket Office.
GEORGE A. CULLEN
General Passenger Agent, Lackawanna Railroad
Dept. 3, 90 West St., New York
Lackawanna Railroad

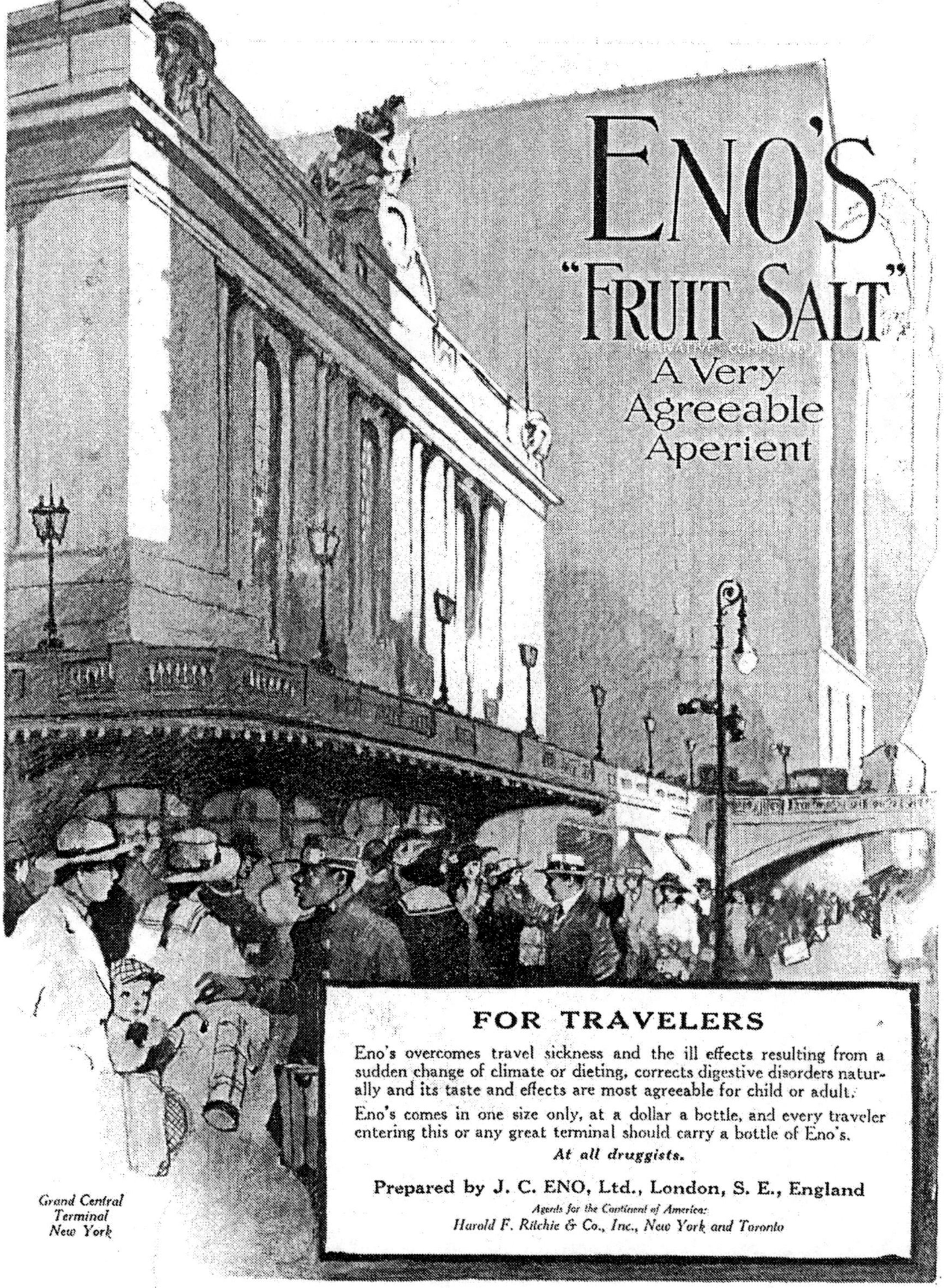
ENO'S
"FRUIT SALT"
A Very
Agreeable
Aperient
FOR TRAVELERS
Eno's overcomes travel sickness and the ill effects resulting from a sudden change of climate or dieting, corrects digestive disorders naturally and its taste and effects are most agreeable for child or adult.
Eno's comes in one size only, at a dollar a bottle, and every traveler entering this or any great terminal should carry a bottle of Eno's.
At all druggists.
Prepared by J. C. ENO, Ltd., London, S. E., England
Agents for the Continent of America:
Harold F. Ritchie & Co., Inc., New York and Toronto
Grand Central Terminal New York

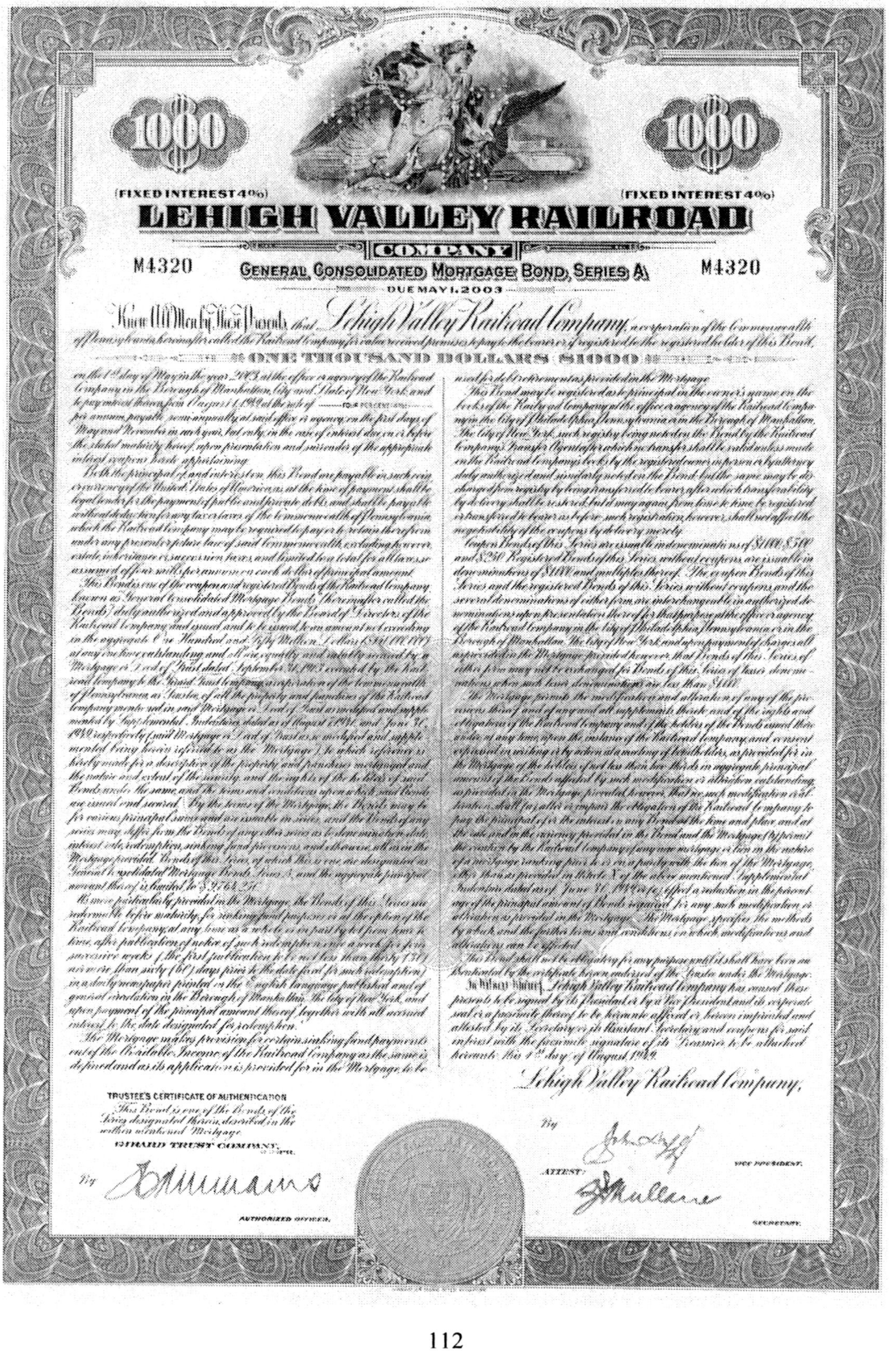

(FIXED INTEREST 4%) (FIXED INTEREST 4%)

1000 1000

LEHIGH VALLEY RAILROAD COMPANY

M4320 GENERAL CONSOLIDATED MORTGAGE BOND, SERIES A M4320

DUE MAY 1, 2003

Know All Men by These Presents that Lehigh Valley Railroad Company, a corporation of the Commonwealth of Pennsylvania, hereinafter called the Railroad Company, for value received, promises to pay to the bearer or, if registered, to the registered holder of this Bond,

ONE THOUSAND DOLLARS $1000

TRUSTEE'S CERTIFICATE OF AUTHENTICATION

This Bond is one of the Bonds of the Series designated therein, described in the within mentioned Mortgage.

GIRARD TRUST COMPANY, TRUSTEE.

By

AUTHORIZED OFFICER.

Lehigh Valley Railroad Company,

By

VICE PRESIDENT.

ATTEST:

SECRETARY.

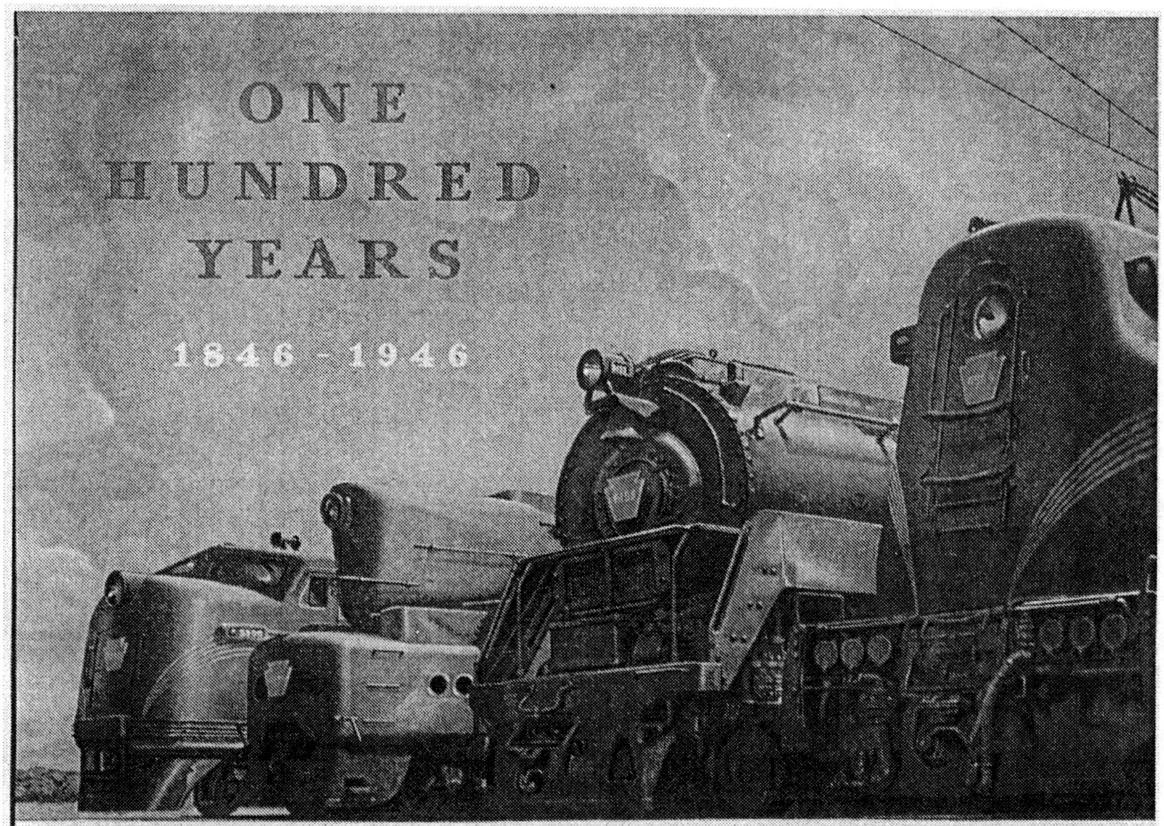
ONE
HUNDRED
YEARS
1846 - 1946

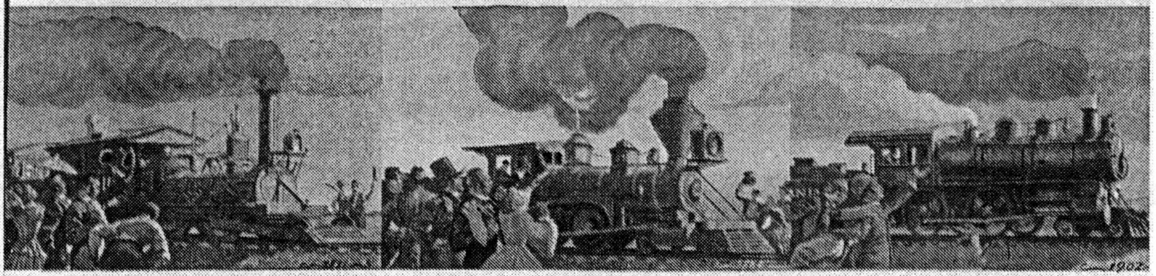

The "John Bull," built in 1831—America's oldest original locomotive

A Pennsylvania Railroad locomotive of 1865

Power in 1902 for the Pennsylvania Special, forerunner of the Broadway Limited

THIS YEAR—1946—marks a century of progress by the Pennsylvania Railroad in service to the American people. Reflecting the tremendous industrial growth of the Country itself, this service has steadily advanced from a few trains a day to 1,340 passenger trains and 3,170 freight trains daily, operating over 10,114 miles of line extending from the Atlantic to the Mississippi. Now, as we prepare to move into a second century, our combined research, engineering and shop facilities are producing new trains, new locomotives, new cars, new comforts and new technical achievements . . . to add another chapter of transportation progress that has continued for one hundred years.

PENNSYLVANIA RAILROAD

Serving the Nation

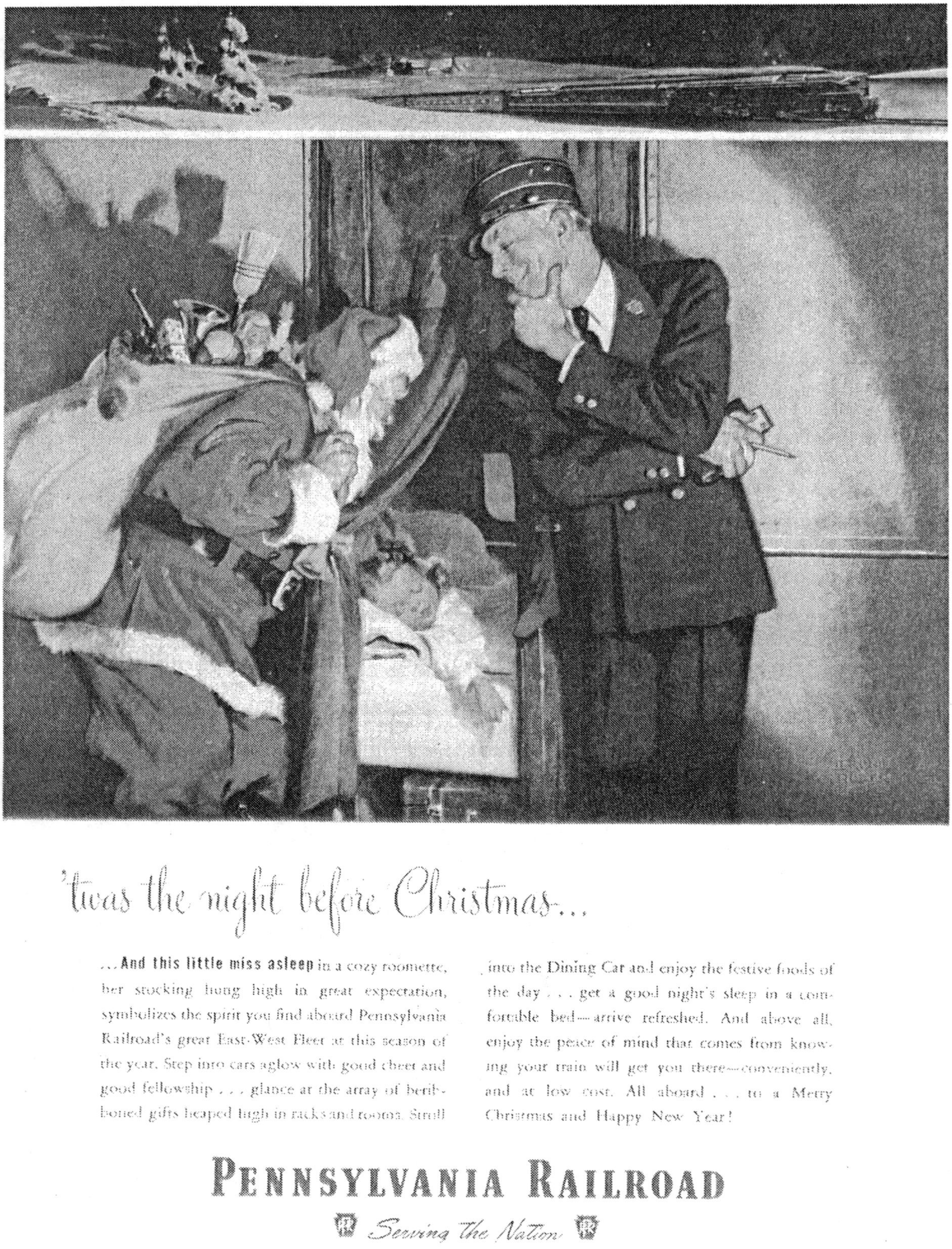
'twas the night before Christmas...
...And this little miss asleep in a cozy roomette, her stocking hung high in great expectation, symbolizes the spirit you find aboard Pennsylvania Railroad's great East-West Fleet at this season of the year. Step into cars aglow with good cheer and good fellowship . . . glance at the array of berib-boned gifts heaped high in racks and rooms. Stroll into the Dining Car and enjoy the festive foods of the day . . . get a good night's sleep in a com-fortable bed—arrive refreshed. And above all, enjoy the peace of mind that comes from know-ing your train will get you there—conveniently, and at low cost. All aboard . . . to a Merry Christmas and Happy New Year!
PENNSYLVANIA RAILROAD
Serving the Nation

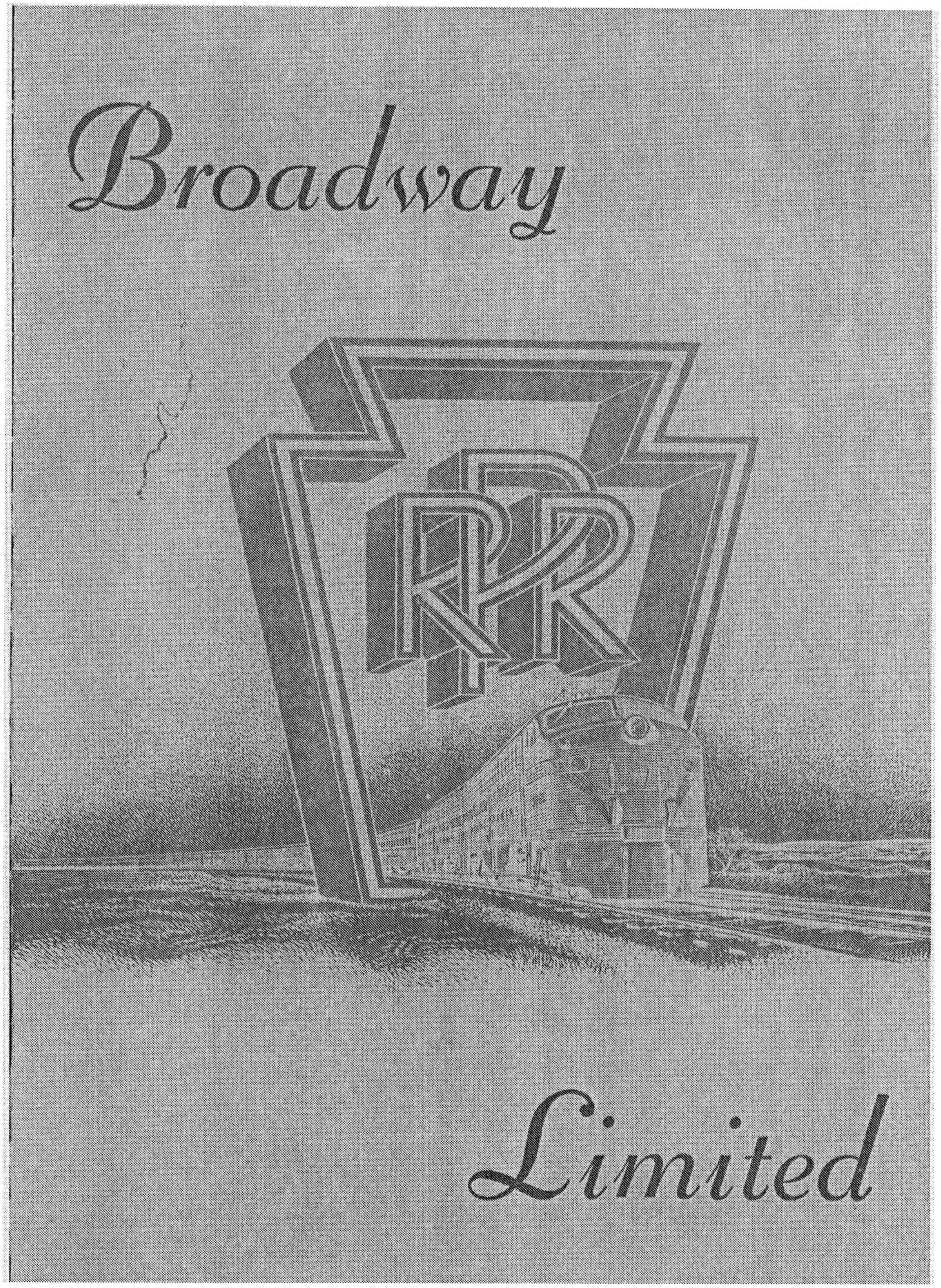
Broadway
Limited

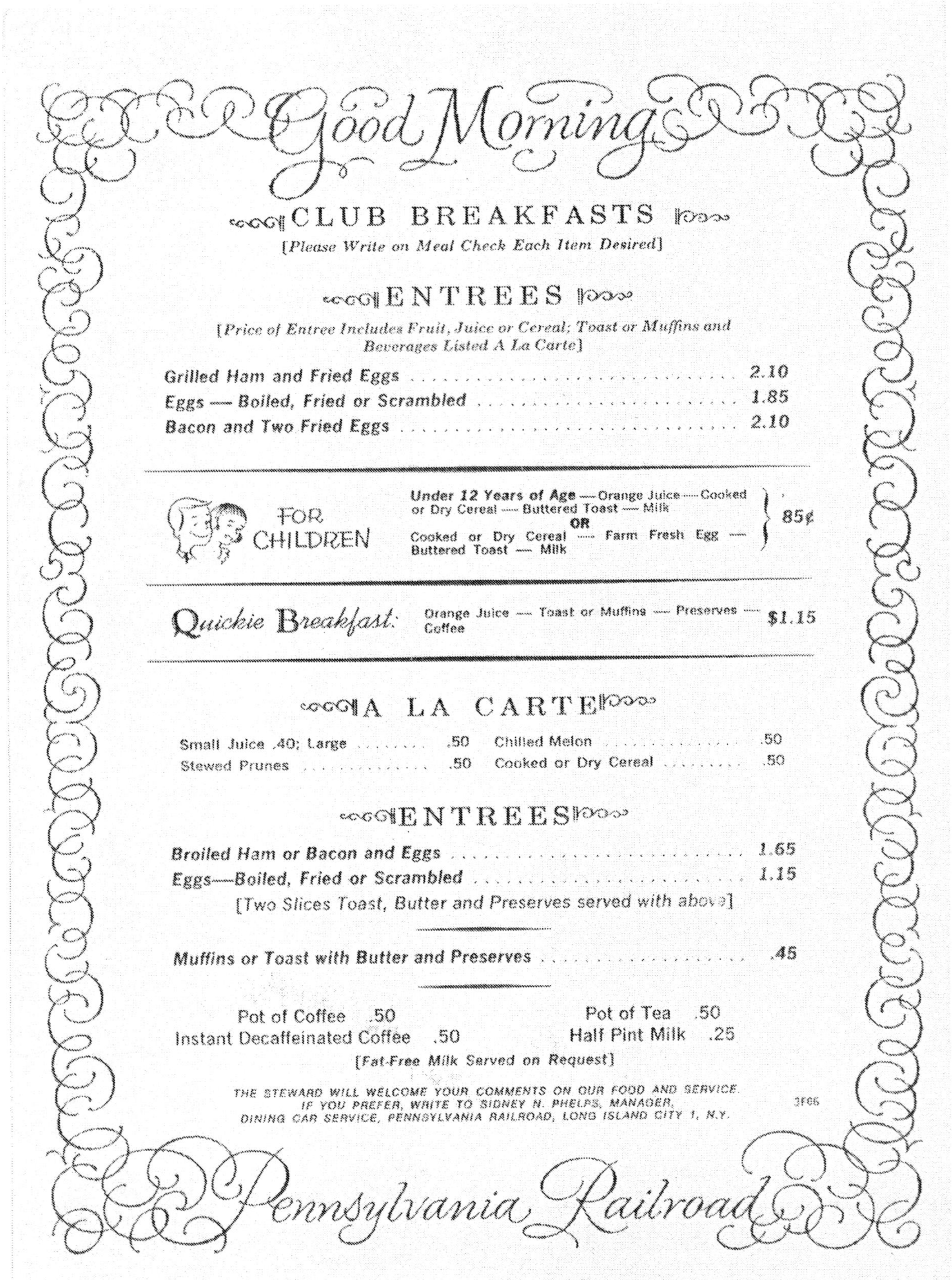

Good Morning

CLUB BREAKFASTS

[Please Write on Meal Check Each Item Desired]

ENTREES

[Price of Entree Includes Fruit, Juice or Cereal; Toast or Muffins and Beverages Listed A La Carte]

Grilled Ham and Fried Eggs	***2.10***
Eggs — Boiled, Fried or Scrambled	***1.85***
Bacon and Two Fried Eggs	***2.10***

FOR CHILDREN

Under 12 Years of Age — Orange Juice — Cooked or Dry Cereal — Buttered Toast — Milk
OR
Cooked or Dry Cereal — Farm Fresh Egg — Buttered Toast — Milk
85¢

Quickie Breakfast: Orange Juice — Toast or Muffins — Preserves — Coffee **$1.15**

A LA CARTE

Small Juice .40; Large	.50	Chilled Melon	.50
Stewed Prunes	.50	Cooked or Dry Cereal	.50

ENTREES

Broiled Ham or Bacon and Eggs	***1.65***
Eggs—Boiled, Fried or Scrambled	***1.15***

[Two Slices Toast, Butter and Preserves served with above]

Muffins or Toast with Butter and Preserves ... ***.45***

Pot of Coffee .50
Instant Decaffeinated Coffee .50
Pot of Tea .50
Half Pint Milk .25

[Fat-Free Milk Served on Request]

THE STEWARD WILL WELCOME YOUR COMMENTS ON OUR FOOD AND SERVICE. IF YOU PREFER, WRITE TO SIDNEY N. PHELPS, MANAGER, DINING CAR SERVICE, PENNSYLVANIA RAILROAD, LONG ISLAND CITY 1, N.Y.

3F66

Pennsylvania Railroad

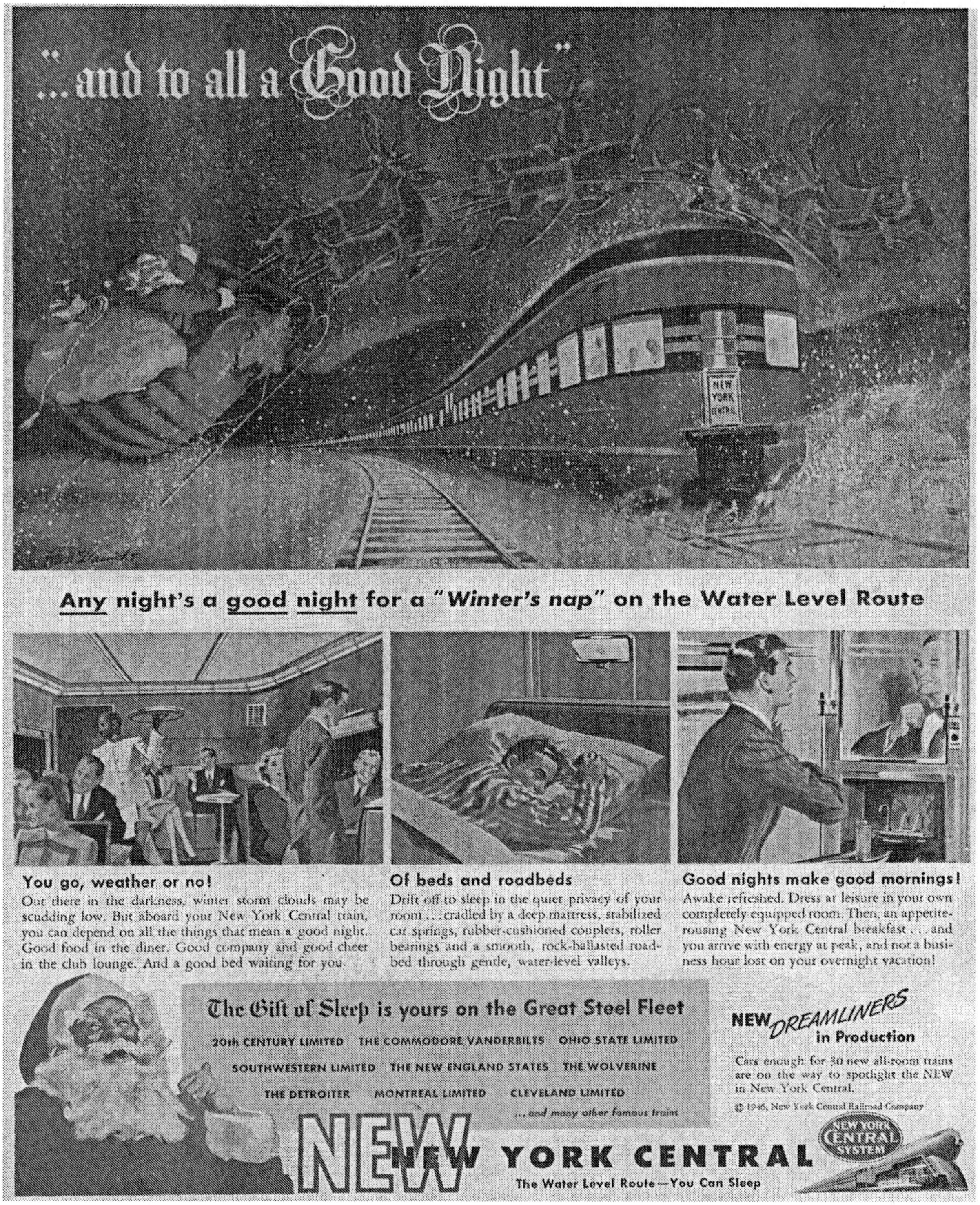
"...and to all a Good Night"
Any night's a good night for a "Winter's nap" on the Water Level Route
You go, weather or no!
Out there in the darkness, winter storm clouds may be scudding low. But aboard your New York Central train, you can depend on all the things that mean a good night. Good food in the diner. Good company and good cheer in the club lounge. And a good bed waiting for you.
Of beds and roadbeds
Drift off to sleep in the quiet privacy of your room . . . cradled by a deep mattress, stabilized car springs, rubber-cushioned couplers, roller bearings and a smooth, rock-ballasted roadbed through gentle, water-level valleys.
Good nights make good mornings!
Awake refreshed. Dress at leisure in your own completely equipped room. Then, an appetite-rousing New York Central breakfast . . . and you arrive with energy at peak, and not a business hour lost on your overnight vacation!
The Gift of Sleep is yours on the Great Steel Fleet
20th CENTURY LIMITED THE COMMODORE VANDERBILTS OHIO STATE LIMITED
SOUTHWESTERN LIMITED THE NEW ENGLAND STATES THE WOLVERINE
THE DETROITER MONTREAL LIMITED CLEVELAND LIMITED
...and many other famous trains
NEW DREAMLINERS in Production
Cars enough for 30 new all-room trains are on the way to spotlight the NEW in New York Central.
© 1946, New York Central Railroad Company
NEW
NEW YORK CENTRAL
The Water Level Route—You Can Sleep
NEW YORK CENTRAL SYSTEM

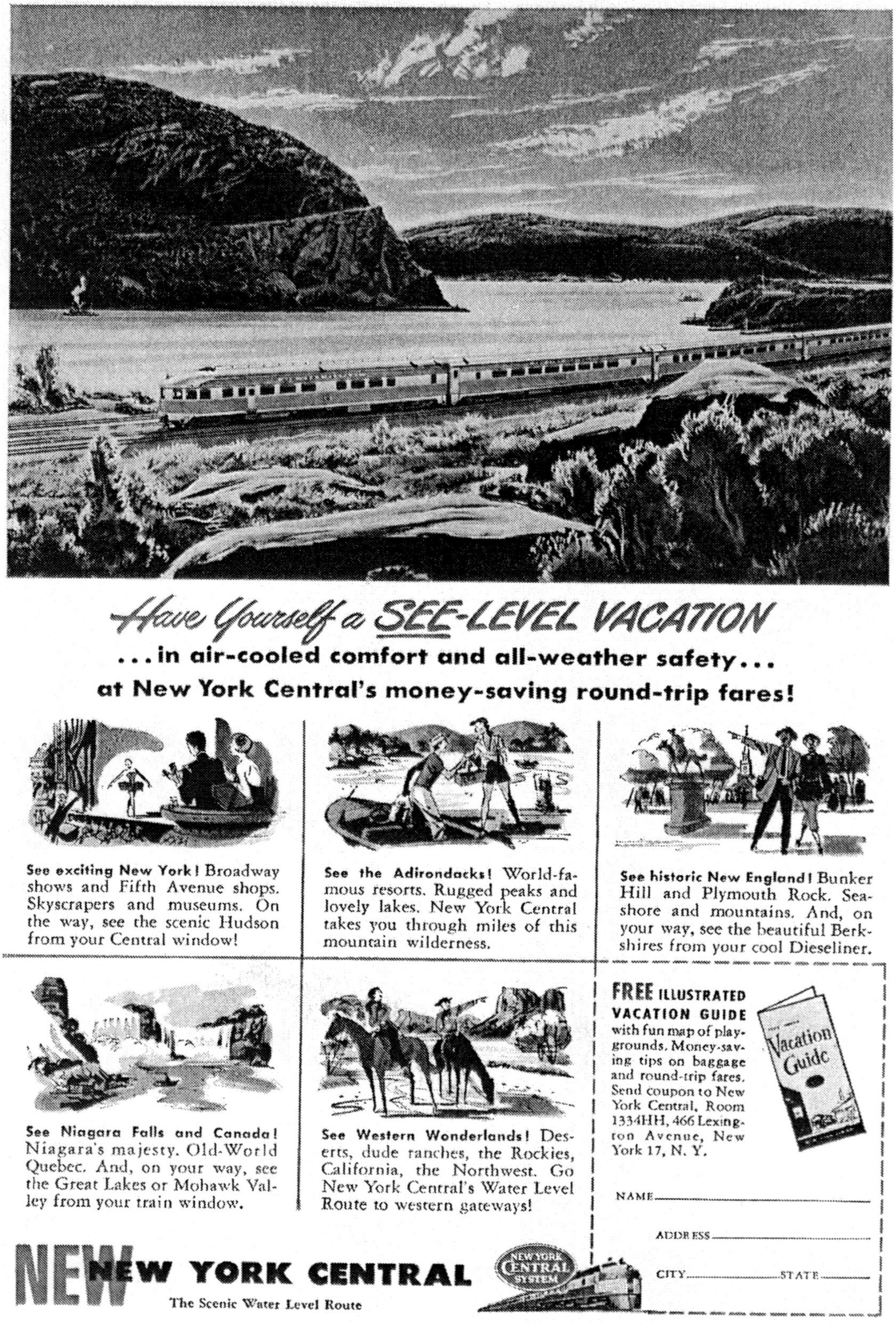
Have Yourself a SEE-LEVEL VACATION
...in air-cooled comfort and all-weather safety...
at New York Central's money-saving round-trip fares!
See exciting New York! Broadway shows and Fifth Avenue shops. Skyscrapers and museums. On the way, see the scenic Hudson from your Central window!
See the Adirondacks! World-famous resorts. Rugged peaks and lovely lakes. New York Central takes you through miles of this mountain wilderness.
See historic New England! Bunker Hill and Plymouth Rock. Seashore and mountains. And, on your way, see the beautiful Berkshires from your cool Dieseliner.
See Niagara Falls and Canada! Niagara's majesty. Old-World Quebec. And, on your way, see the Great Lakes or Mohawk Valley from your train window.
See Western Wonderlands! Deserts, dude ranches, the Rockies, California, the Northwest. Go New York Central's Water Level Route to western gateways!
FREE ILLUSTRATED VACATION GUIDE
with fun map of playgrounds. Money-saving tips on baggage and round-trip fares. Send coupon to New York Central, Room 1334HH, 466 Lexington Avenue, New York 17, N. Y.
Vacation Guide
NAME
ADDRESS
CITY
STATE
NEW YORK CENTRAL
The Scenic Water Level Route
NEW YORK CENTRAL SYSTEM

Big Deal For Dad's Little Wheels

They go one way free on the Central

Next time, take the family on your business trip. The pleasure begins with the planning. Once on board, the youngsters settle right into the adventure—watching the world through picture windows built to fit wide eyes. Mom and Dad have room to roam and all the comforts only train travel offers.

And the savings! When one parent pays the regular round-trip fare, the other parent and children (12-21) pay only one-way fare for round trip. Youngsters under 12 go for half the one-way fare. *Small fry under 5 go scot-free!*

Step off the train into a rental car. Convenient for business calls and sightseeing excursions. You make arrangements when you buy your tickets.

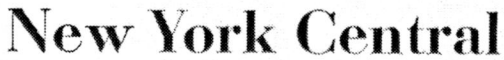

Easy Does It…when the family goes New York Central

Easy on Dad! No traffic to tire him. No white line to watch. When New York Central does the driving, he's free to read, nap, or enjoy the wonderful *Water Level Route* scenery that parades past his big picture window.

Easy on Mother, because her mind's at ease about the youngsters. No back-seat fidgets. No frequent roadside stops. Everything the children need is right at hand. And they couldn't be safer at home!

Easy on the Kids! They don't have to stay put in their seats. There's plenty of room to move about. And there's the extra thrill of those famous New York Central meals in the diner, with their own, thrifty Children's Menu to choose from.

Easy on the Budget! Round-trip coach fares are low. And special Family Tickets cut them as much as 50% or even more. Ask your New York Central ticket agent all about them.

New York Central

The Scenic Water Level Route

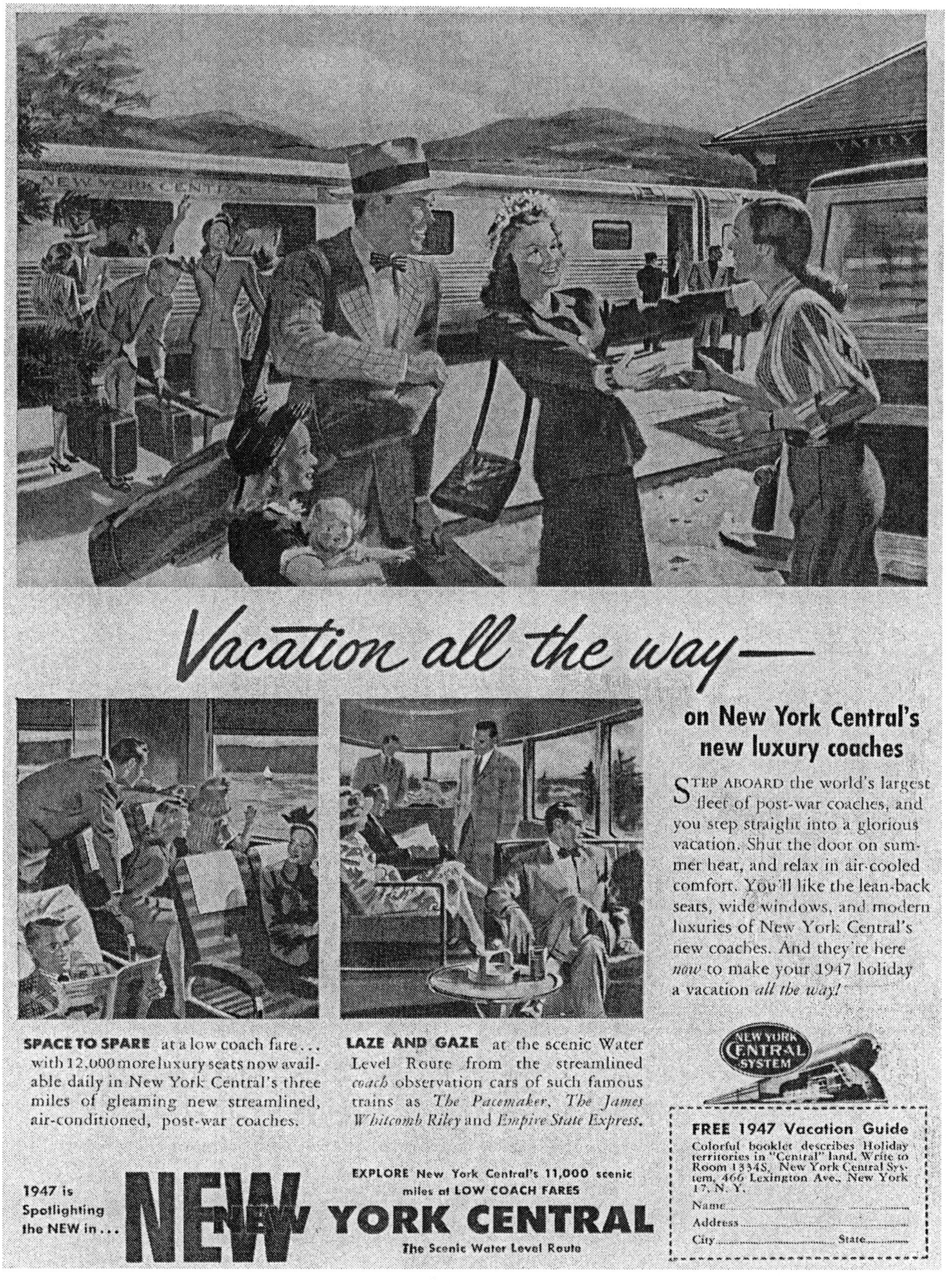
NEW YORK CENTRAL
Vacation all the way—
on New York Central's new luxury coaches
STEP ABOARD the world's largest fleet of post-war coaches, and you step straight into a glorious vacation. Shut the door on summer heat, and relax in air-cooled comfort. You'll like the lean-back seats, wide windows, and modern luxuries of New York Central's new coaches. And they're here now to make your 1947 holiday a vacation all the way!
SPACE TO SPARE at a low coach fare... with 12,000 more luxury seats now available daily in New York Central's three miles of gleaming new streamlined, air-conditioned, post-war coaches.
LAZE AND GAZE at the scenic Water Level Route from the streamlined coach observation cars of such famous trains as The Pacemaker, The James Whitcomb Riley and Empire State Express.
NEW YORK CENTRAL SYSTEM
FREE 1947 Vacation Guide
Colorful booklet describes Holiday territories in "Central" land. Write to Room 1334S, New York Central System, 466 Lexington Ave., New York 17, N. Y.
Name
Address
City
State
1947 is Spotlighting the NEW in...
NEW
EXPLORE New York Central's 11,000 scenic miles at LOW COACH FARES
NEW YORK CENTRAL
The Scenic Water Level Route

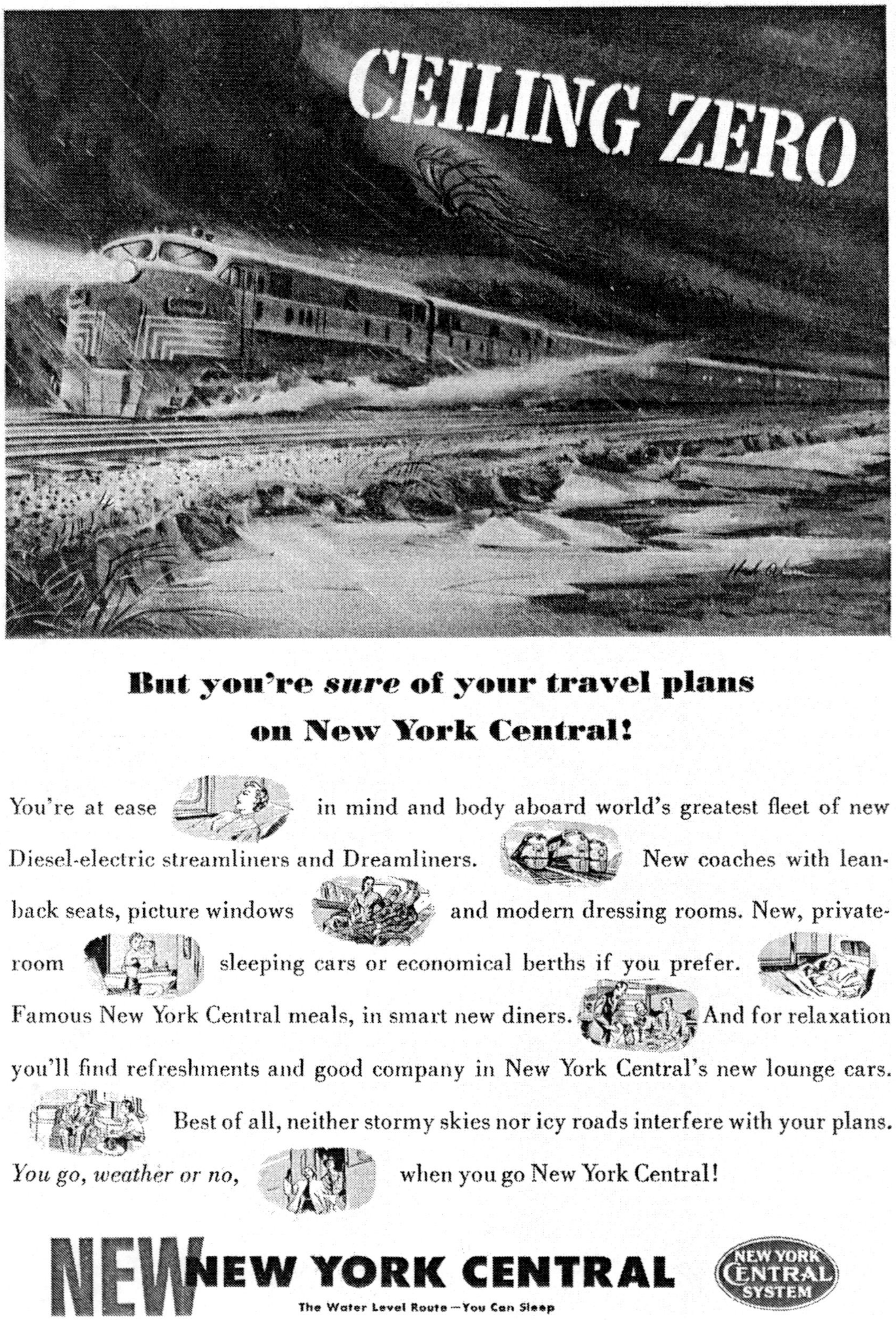
CEILING ZERO
But you're *sure* of your travel plans on New York Central!
You're at ease in mind and body aboard world's greatest fleet of new Diesel-electric streamliners and Dreamliners. New coaches with lean-back seats, picture windows and modern dressing rooms. New, private-room sleeping cars or economical berths if you prefer. Famous New York Central meals, in smart new diners. And for relaxation you'll find refreshments and good company in New York Central's new lounge cars. Best of all, neither stormy skies nor icy roads interfere with your plans. *You go, weather or no,* when you go New York Central!
NEW NEW YORK CENTRAL
The Water Level Route—You Can Sleep
NEW YORK CENTRAL SYSTEM

From Head Start...

to Happy Ending

You get more vacation relaxation on NEW YORK CENTRAL

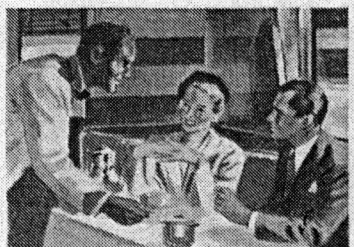  

Weatherproof Start! Why let stormy skies delay your start? Leave on time, in all-weather safety and comfort ... aboard a New York Central Dieseliner.

Cool Off Right Off! Relax in Central's air-cooled weather. See the Hudson and Mohawk Valleys, the Berkshires and Great Lakes thru wide picture windows.

Many Happy Returns! Why travel a way that gets you home tired and tense? For a happier return, go New York Central...and get back with vacation vim intact!

FREE VACATION GUIDE
to New York, New England, Canada, the Great Lakes and Western Wonderlands. Send coupon for your copy now!

New York Central, Room 1334B
466 Lexington Ave., New York 17, N. Y.
Please send free Guide and money-saving facts about round-trip fares.

NAME ....
ADDRESS ....
CITY .... STATE ....

NEW YORK CENTRAL
NEW **YORK CENTRAL**
The Scenic Water Level Route

NEW YORK CENTRAL SYSTEM

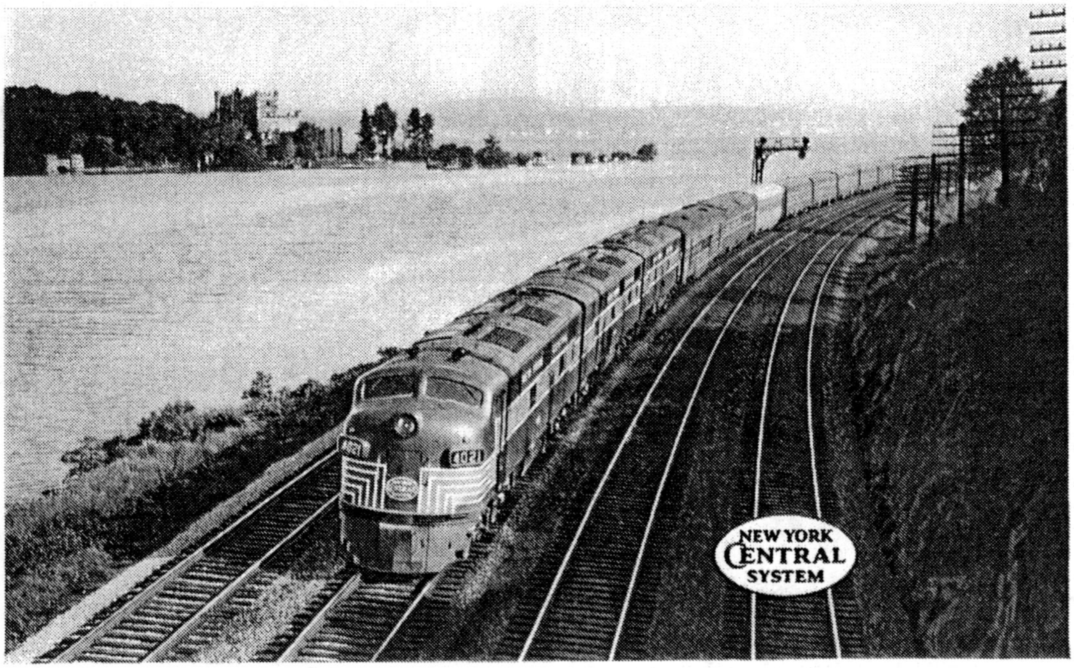
NEW YORK
CENTRAL
SYSTEM

Bruning Copying Machines Streamline Paperwork for Fast-Moving Railroad!

The progressive New York Central System, famous for fast, efficient trains like the 20th Century Limited, has streamlined paperwork, too, with modern Bruning Copyflex copying machines.

In New York Central's accounting operations, many reports and statements are reproduced by Copyflex directly from original work sheets. Cumulative reports are prepared by posting new entries on work sheets and making new Copyflex copies. This has completely eliminated clerical rewriting, retyping, proofreading. Reports go out hours to days earlier.

You, too, can save time and money with Copyflex on almost any paperwork in your business. Copyflex machines are clean, odorless, economical — letter-size copies cost less than a penny each for materials. Mail coupon below for special literature offer.

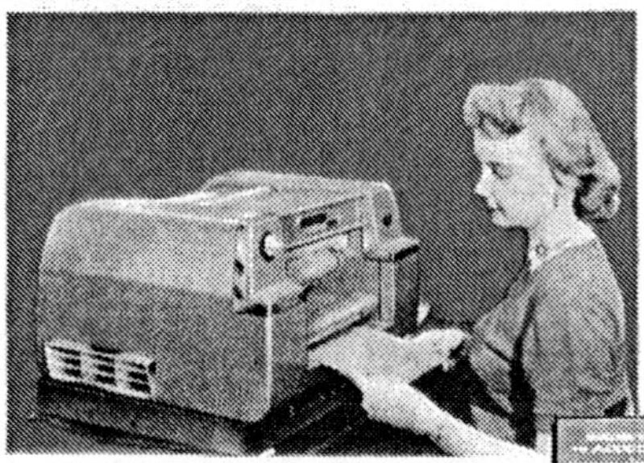

Desk Top Model, $555. Larger Models Available.

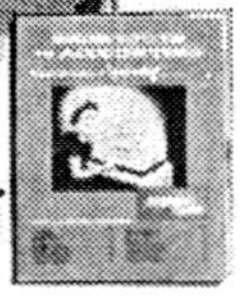

BRUNING
Copyflex

Offices in Principal U. S. Cities

Send for your free copy!

Charles Bruning Company, Inc., Dept. 21-NG
1800 Central Rd., Mount Prospect, Ill.
In Canada: 105 Church Street, Toronto 1, Ont.

Please send me my free copy of "Shortcuts to Accounting" and further information on Copyflex.

Name ____________ Title ____________

Company ____________

Address ____________

City ____________ County ____________ State ____________

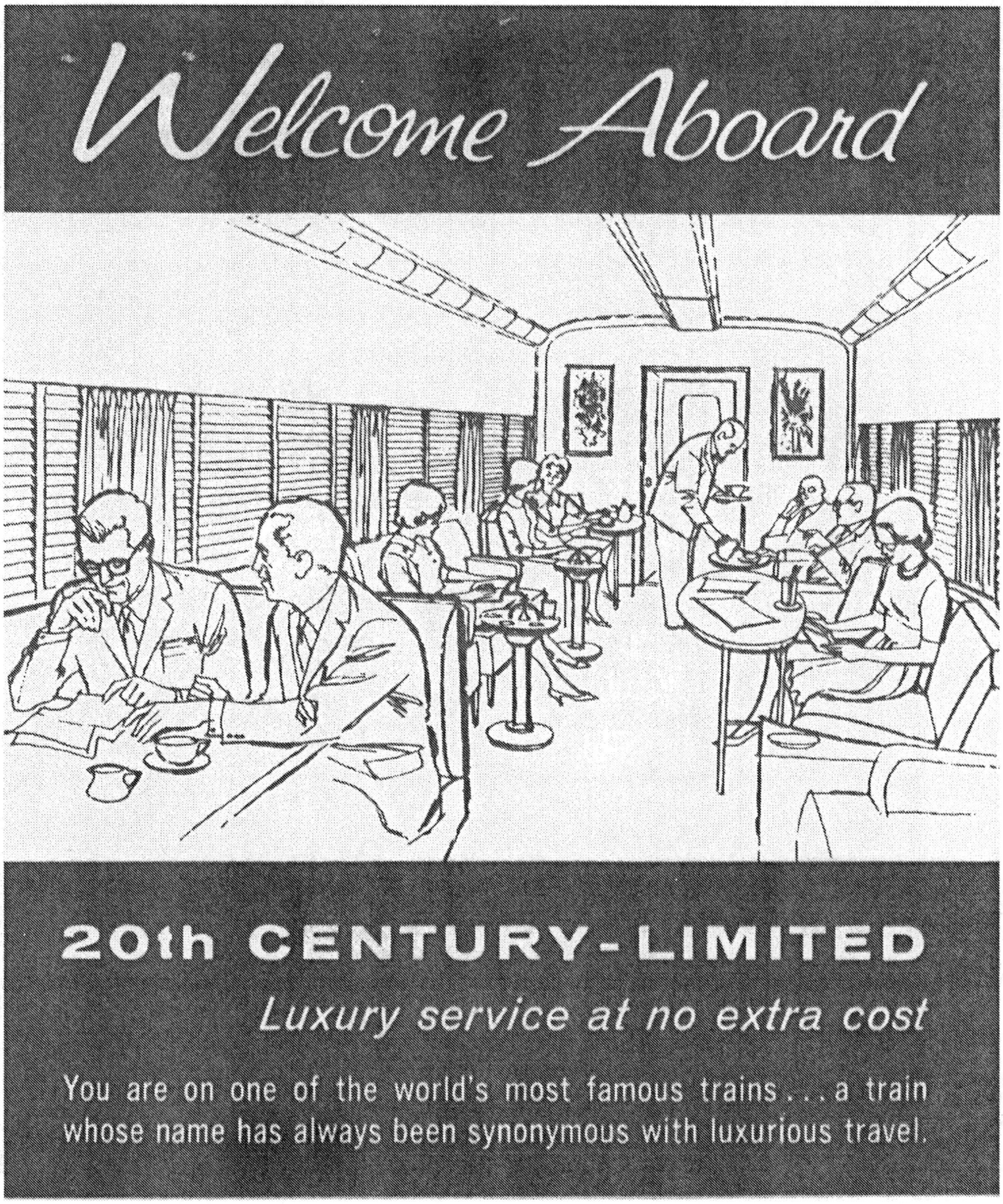
Welcome Aboard
20th CENTURY-LIMITED
Luxury service at no extra cost
You are on one of the world's most famous trains . . . a train whose name has always been synonymous with luxurious travel.

20th Century Limited . . . services

The 20th Century-Limited is known for three things — the dependability of its schedule, the tasteful elegance of its appointments, and the variety of special services it offers to make your trip comfortable, convenient and completely enjoyable.

These services include —

Dining Car Service for dinner and breakfast both eastbound and westbound. Enjoy our recorded music with your dinner. Corsages are provided ladies at dinner, and boutonnieres to gentlemen at breakfast in dining car—"compliments of the 20th Century."

Two Lounge Cars . . . the comfortable mid-train lounge and the observation Lookout Lounge (recorded music) . . . both well stocked with newspapers, current magazines and refreshments. Hotel Red Book, Official Railway Guide and stationery also available. You will enjoy the complimentary hors d'oeuvres served in the lounge cars before dinner.

Typewriter. Check the availability of the Underwood with your porter.

Valet Service at modest prices. Your porter will arrange it.

Room Service . . . Refreshments and meal service will be provided to you in your room if you so desire. There is a small extra charge for this service.

Shoe Shine. Place your shoes in the shoe box on retiring and find them gleaming in the morning . . . courtesy of your porter.

Electric Shaver. Remington Roll-A-Matic. Ask your porter for it.

Your Own Newspaper will be in your shoe box in the morning.

Baggage Transfer. Your porter can supply a tag to mark your luggage for automatic transfer to the station taxicab stand in Chicago or New York. Also, if you leave Chicago the same day, you can check your luggage direct to your reserved space on selected outgoing trains.

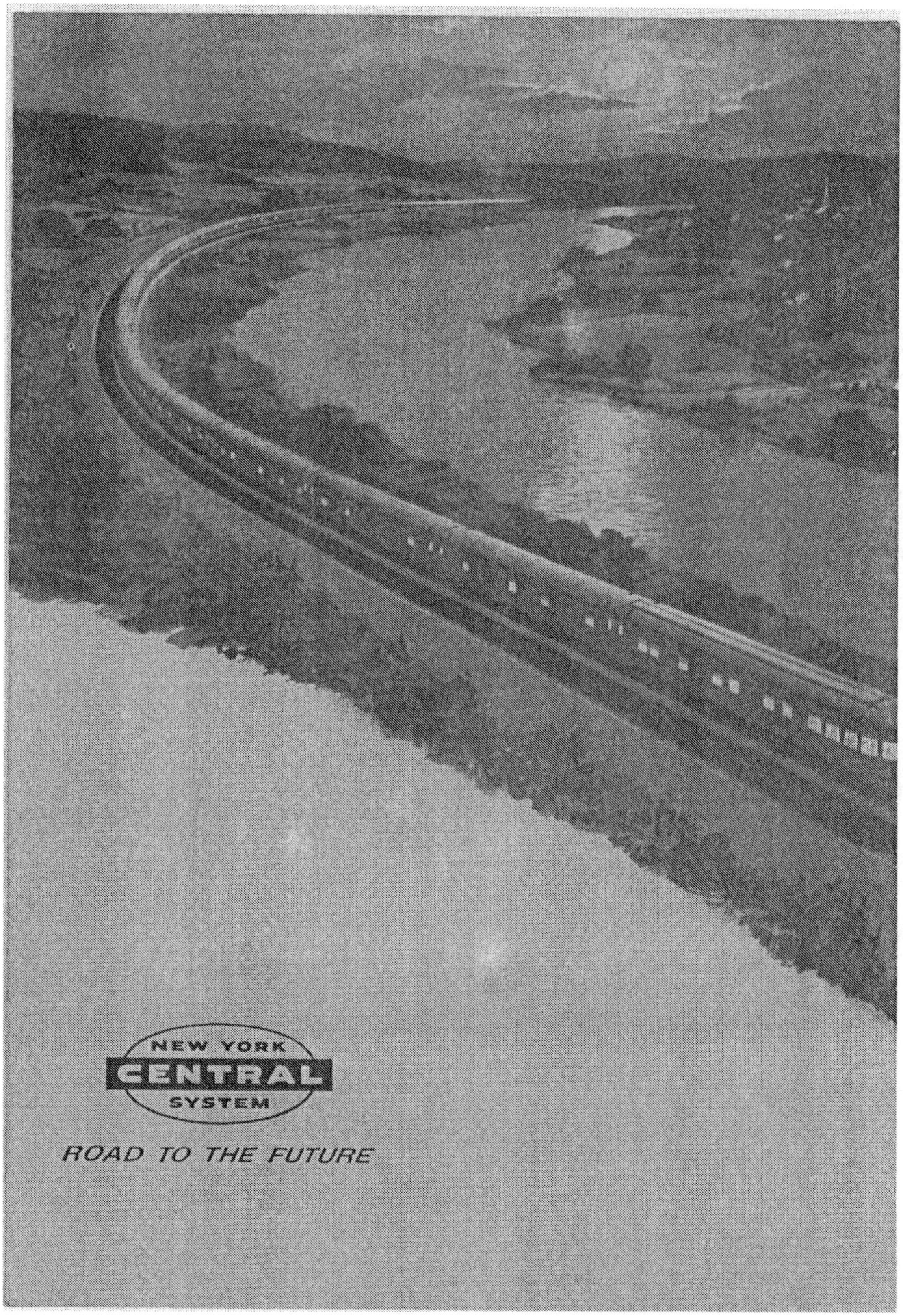
NEW YORK
CENTRAL
SYSTEM
ROAD TO THE FUTURE

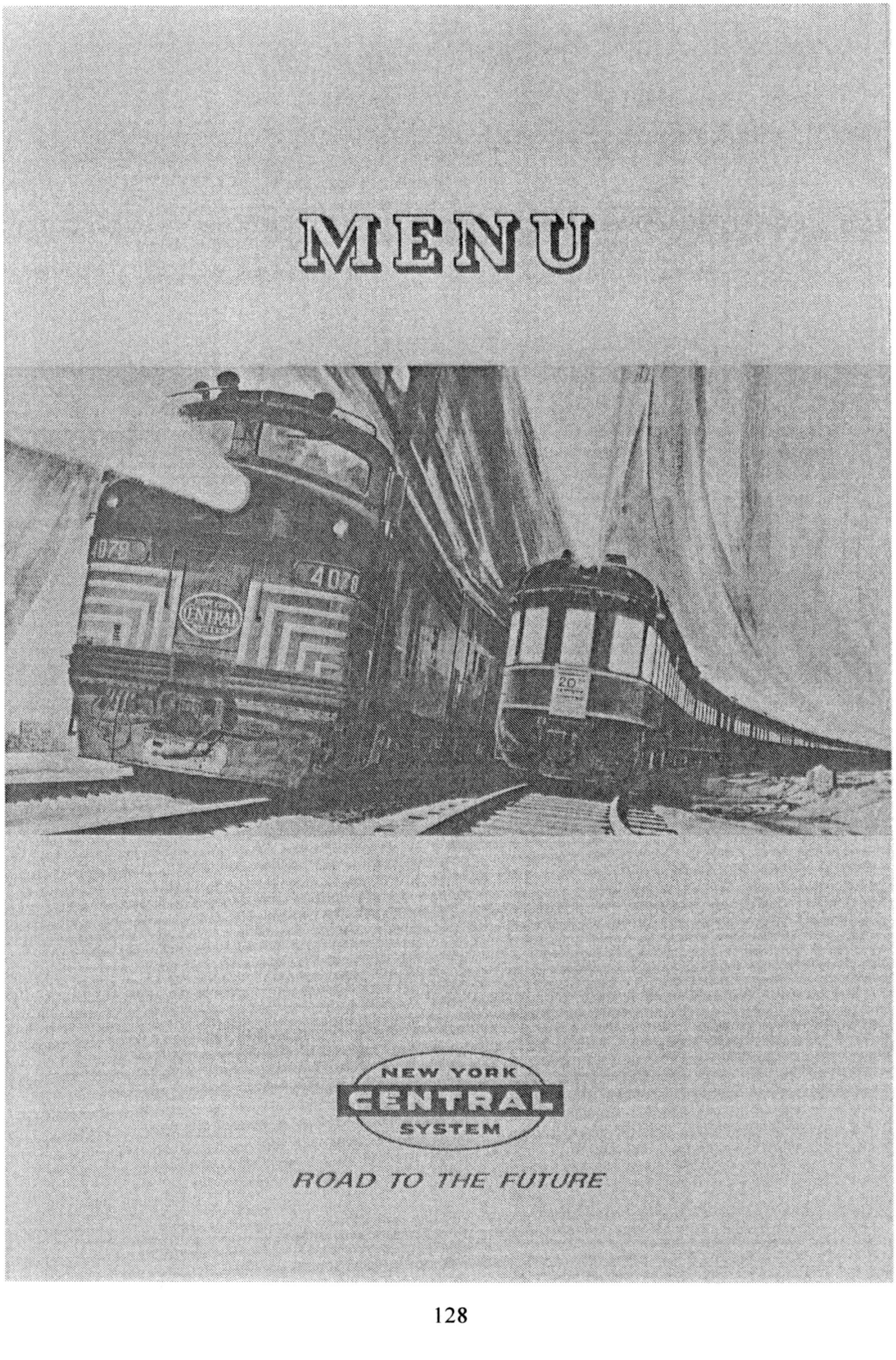
MENU
NEW YORK
CENTRAL
SYSTEM
ROAD TO THE FUTURE

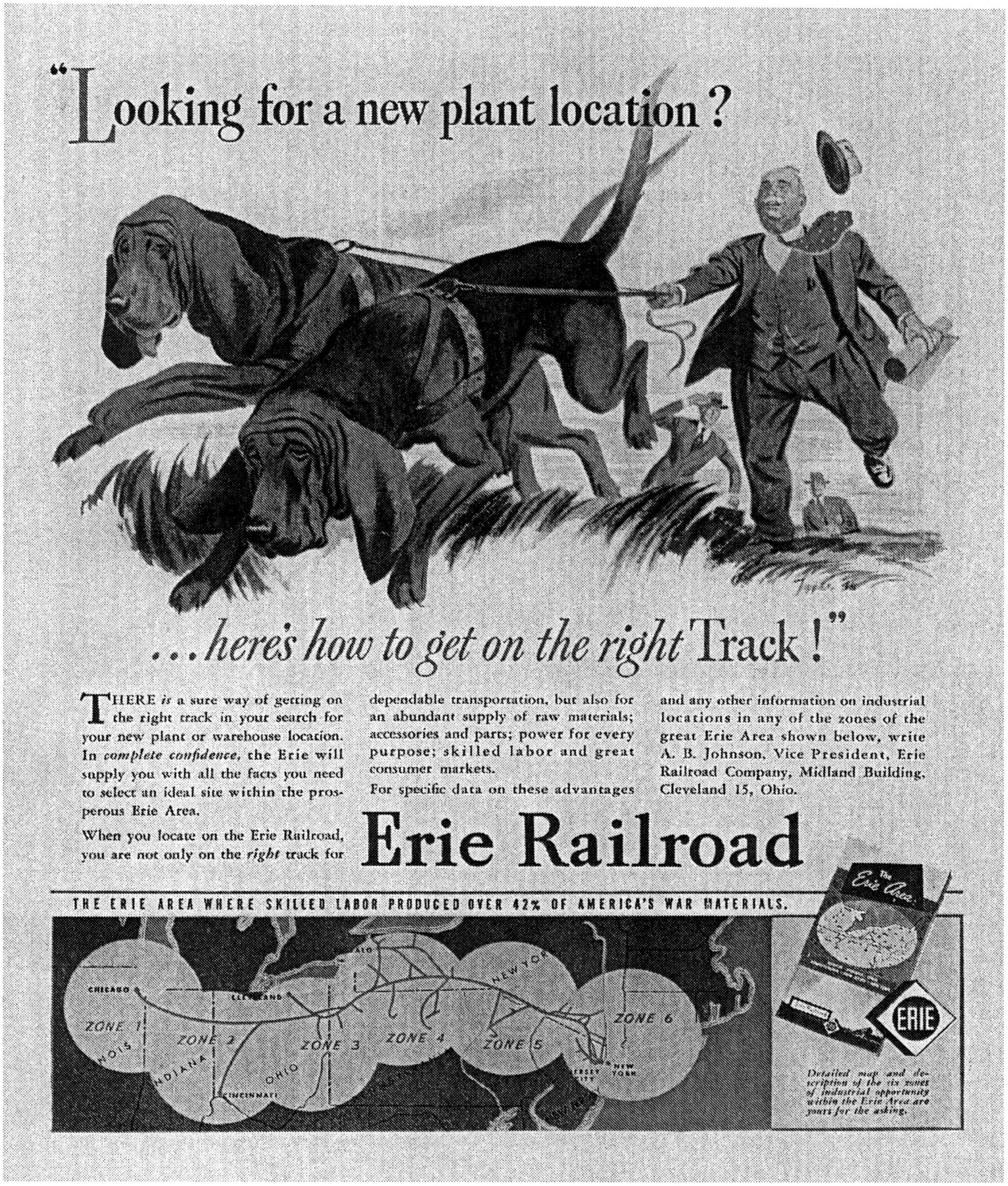
"Looking for a new plant location?
. . . here's how to get on the right Track!"
THERE *is* a sure way of getting on the right track in your search for your new plant or warehouse location. In *complete confidence*, the Erie will supply you with all the facts you need to select an ideal site within the prosperous Erie Area.
When you locate on the Erie Railroad, you are not only on the *right* track for dependable transportation, but also for an abundant supply of raw materials; accessories and parts; power for every purpose; skilled labor and great consumer markets.
For specific data on these advantages and any other information on industrial locations in any of the zones of the great Erie Area shown below, write A. B. Johnson, Vice President, Erie Railroad Company, Midland Building, Cleveland 15, Ohio.
Erie Railroad
THE ERIE AREA WHERE SKILLED LABOR PRODUCED OVER 42% OF AMERICA'S WAR MATERIALS.
CHICAGO
ZONE 1
ZONE 2
INDIANA
OHIO
CINCINNATI
ZONE 3
ZONE 4
NEW YORK
ZONE 5
ZONE 6
NEW YORK
ERIE
Detailed map and description of the six zones of industrial opportunity within the Erie Area are yours for the asking.

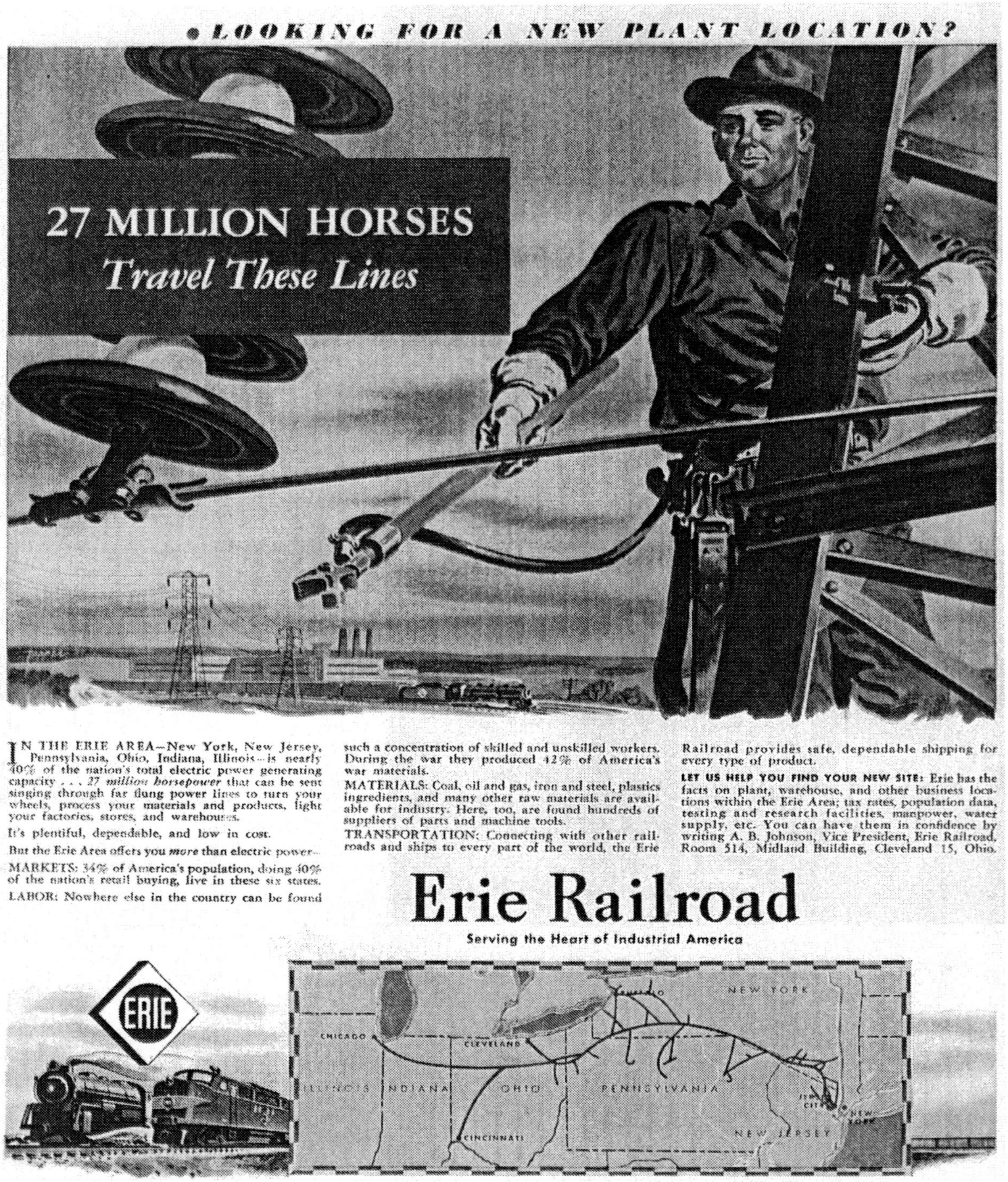

• LOOKING FOR A NEW PLANT LOCATION?
27 MILLION HORSES
Travel These Lines
IN THE ERIE AREA—New York, New Jersey, Pennsylvania, Ohio, Indiana, Illinois—is nearly 40% of the nation's total electric power generating capacity . . . 27 million horsepower that can be sent singing through far flung power lines to turn your wheels, process your materials and products, light your factories, stores, and warehouses.
It's plentiful, dependable, and low in cost.
But the Erie Area offers you more than electric power—
MARKETS: 34% of America's population, doing 40% of the nation's retail buying, live in these six states.
LABOR: Nowhere else in the country can be found such a concentration of skilled and unskilled workers. During the war they produced 42% of America's war materials.
MATERIALS: Coal, oil and gas, iron and steel, plastics ingredients, and many other raw materials are available for industry. Here, too, are found hundreds of suppliers of parts and machine tools.
TRANSPORTATION: Connecting with other railroads and ships to every part of the world, the Erie Railroad provides safe, dependable shipping for every type of product.
LET US HELP YOU FIND YOUR NEW SITE: Erie has the facts on plant, warehouse, and other business locations within the Erie Area; tax rates, population data, testing and research facilities, manpower, water supply, etc. You can have them in confidence by writing A. B. Johnson, Vice President, Erie Railroad, Room 514, Midland Building, Cleveland 15, Ohio.
Erie Railroad
Serving the Heart of Industrial America
ERIE
CHICAGO
CLEVELAND
NEW YORK
ILLINOIS
INDIANA
OHIO
PENNSYLVANIA
NEW JERSEY
CINCINNATI

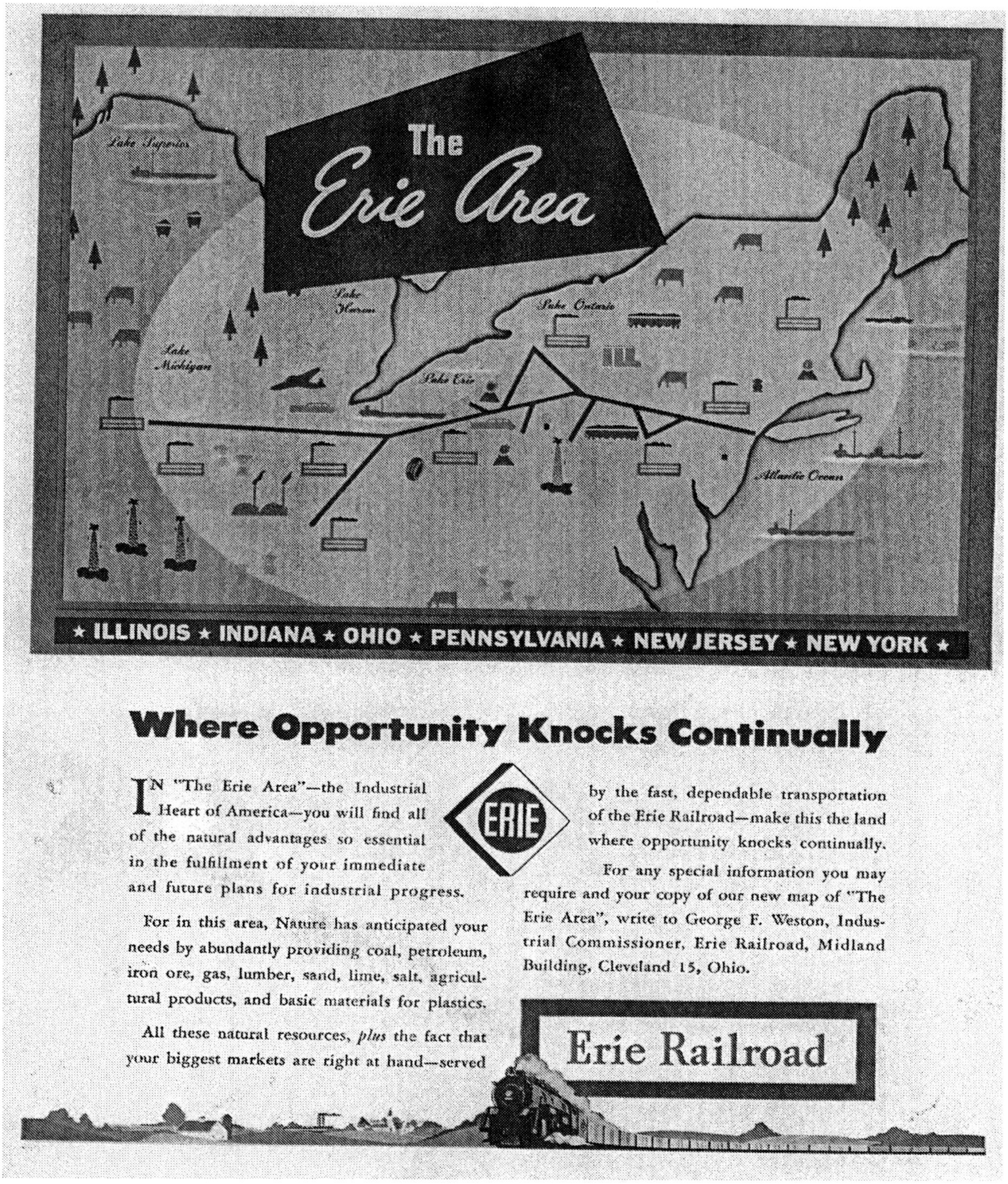
The Erie Area
★ ILLINOIS ★ INDIANA ★ OHIO ★ PENNSYLVANIA ★ NEW JERSEY ★ NEW YORK ★
Where Opportunity Knocks Continually
ERIE
IN "The Erie Area"—the Industrial Heart of America—you will find all of the natural advantages so essential in the fulfillment of your immediate and future plans for industrial progress.
For in this area, Nature has anticipated your needs by abundantly providing coal, petroleum, iron ore, gas, lumber, sand, lime, salt, agricultural products, and basic materials for plastics.
All these natural resources, *plus* the fact that your biggest markets are right at hand—served by the fast, dependable transportation of the Erie Railroad—make this the land where opportunity knocks continually.
For any special information you may require and your copy of our new map of "The Erie Area", write to George F. Weston, Industrial Commissioner, Erie Railroad, Midland Building, Cleveland 15, Ohio.
Erie Railroad

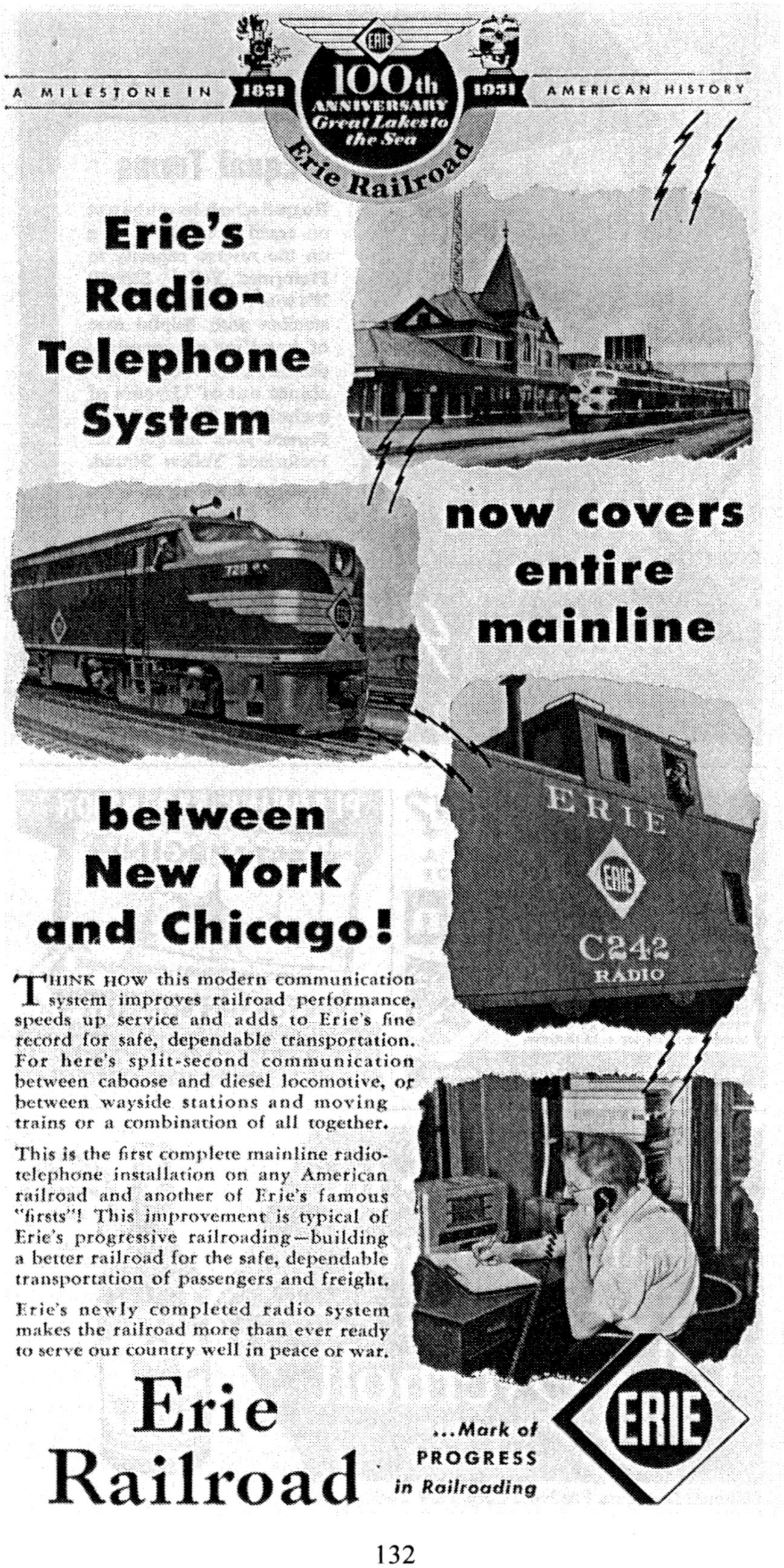
A MILESTONE IN
1831
100th ANNIVERSARY
Great Lakes to the Sea
1951
AMERICAN HISTORY
Erie Railroad
Erie's Radio-Telephone System
now covers entire mainline
between New York and Chicago!
ERIE
C242
RADIO
THINK HOW this modern communication system improves railroad performance, speeds up service and adds to Erie's fine record for safe, dependable transportation. For here's split-second communication between caboose and diesel locomotive, or between wayside stations and moving trains or a combination of all together.
This is the first complete mainline radio-telephone installation on any American railroad and another of Erie's famous "firsts"! This improvement is typical of Erie's progressive railroading—building a better railroad for the safe, dependable transportation of passengers and freight.
Erie's newly completed radio system makes the railroad more than ever ready to serve our country well in peace or war.
Erie Railroad
...Mark of PROGRESS in Railroading
ERIE

ERIE . . . Mark of PROGRESS in Railroading

The flame with the 14-mile reach

As you rode a train on a cold winter's night, you may have caught sight of a bundled-up trackman standing near a switch with a lighted torch. His job is to make sure that ice and snow don't lock the switch in one position.

The Erie Railroad has improved on this practice by installing remote-control gas heaters on switches. These are operated by a dispatcher from a control point as far away as 14 miles—or even farther!

As he traces the progress of the train over his control board, the dispatcher starts the heaters by turning a control switch. Electric current ignites the gas and the flame shoots along the under part of the railhead. Away go the ice and snow, leaving the switch clear for safe operation!

These gas heaters are already installed at key points on the railroad, with more to come. Here is another example of Erie's progressive railroading—the continuous search to improve the safe, dependable transportation of passengers and freight.

Erie Railroad

Serving the Heart of Industrial America

WISC.
MICHIGAN
BUFFALO
ROCHESTER
NEW YORK
VT.
MASS.
CONN.
CHICAGO
CLEVELAND
YOUNGSTOWN
SCRANTON
ILLINOIS
INDIANA
OHIO
PENNSYLVANIA
NEW JERSEY
NEW YORK
JERSEY CITY
INDIANAPOLIS
CINCINNATI

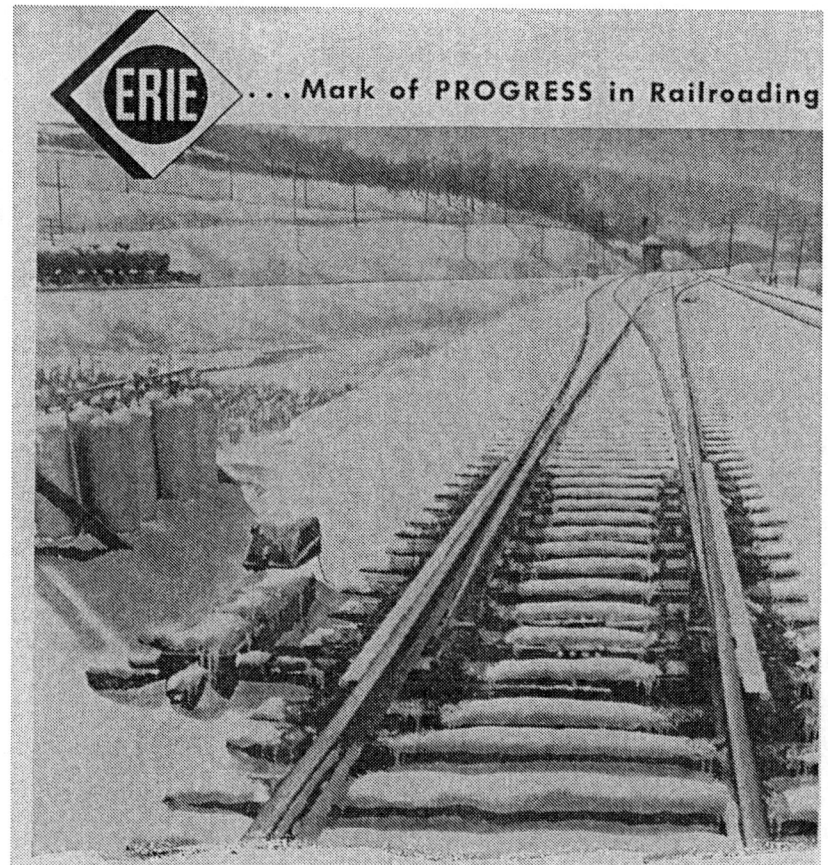

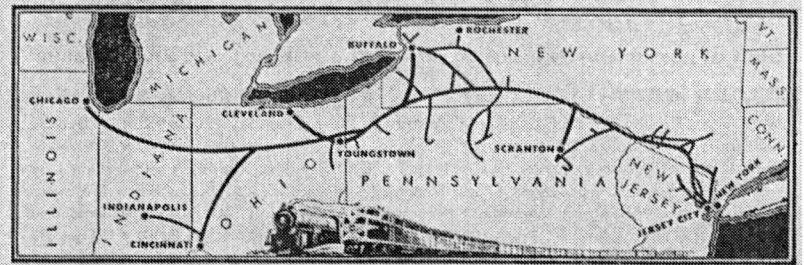

Phoebe Snow
rubbed
her eyes !
814
Lackawanna Railroad
814
BUFFALO
SYRACUSE
UTICA
ITHACA
NEW YORK
CORNING
ELMIRA
BINGHAMTON
SCRANTON
PENNSYLVANIA
NORTHUMBERLAND
NEW JERSEY

BACK around 1900, when the Lackawanna Railroad was winding up its first half-century, a lovely character called "Phoebe Snow" made her bow upon the scene of American folklore. In her immaculate white gown and adorned by a dainty corsage of violets, she symbolized the cleanliness of passenger travel on the Lackawanna—"the Road of Anthracite."

Two years ago, the Lackawanna proudly put into service between New York and Buffalo, its new de luxe Diesel-powered streamliner—the PHOEBE SNOW. Aboard, on its inaugural trip, was the living lady of the part...*Phoebe Snow*, herself! Her eyes popped with delight as she went from one end of the train to the other. Here, indeed, was the last word in modern travel luxury.

It's a far cry from the days of Lackawanna's first little steam engine, the Spitfire, with its old wooden bench coaches, to the comforts and conveniences of the modern PHOEBE SNOW. And it's a far cry, too, from the old-fashioned methods of handling freight to the fast, efficient and dependable service which the Lackawanna Railroad provides for today's shippers.

We, the men and women of the Lackawanna, look back with pride to the accomplishments of the past. Now, as our railroad enters its second century, we pledge ourselves to provide even better transportation service in the years to come.

1851 1951

Lackawanna Centennial

Lackawanna Railroad

THE ROUTE OF PHOEBE SNOW

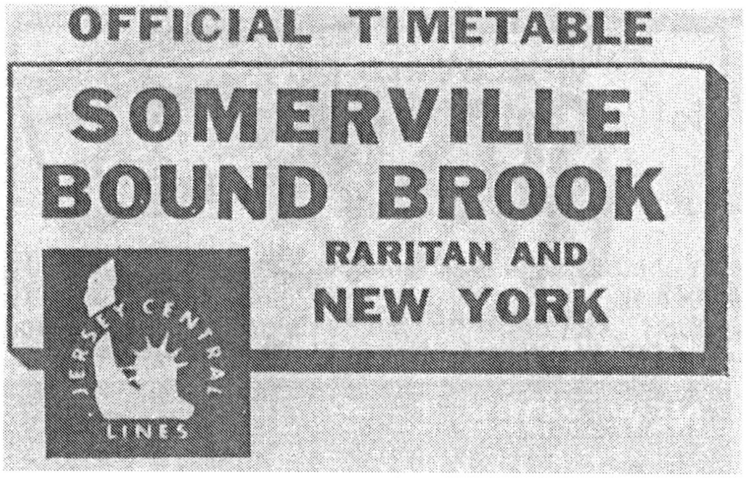
OFFICIAL TIMETABLE
SOMERVILLE
BOUND BROOK
RARITAN AND
NEW YORK
JERSEY CENTRAL
LINES

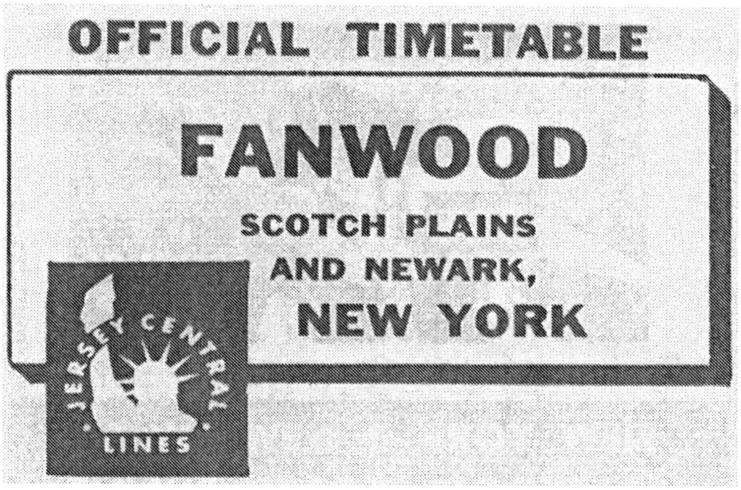
OFFICIAL TIMETABLE
FANWOOD
SCOTCH PLAINS
AND NEWARK,
NEW YORK
JERSEY CENTRAL
LINES

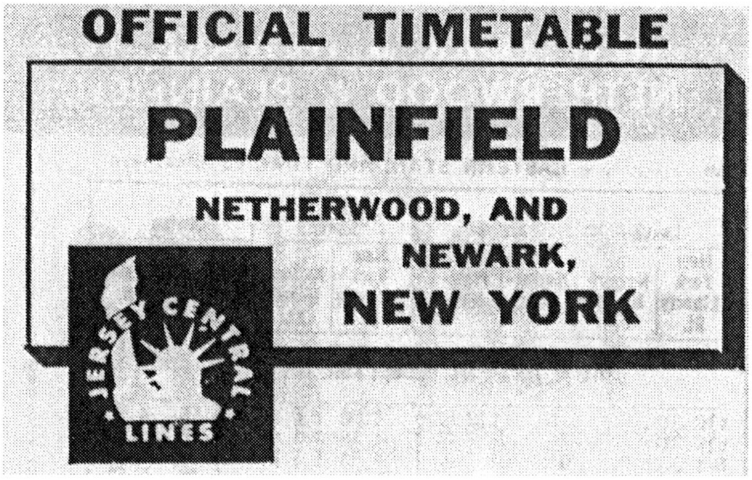
OFFICIAL TIMETABLE
PLAINFIELD
NETHERWOOD, AND
NEWARK,
NEW YORK
JERSEY CENTRAL
LINES

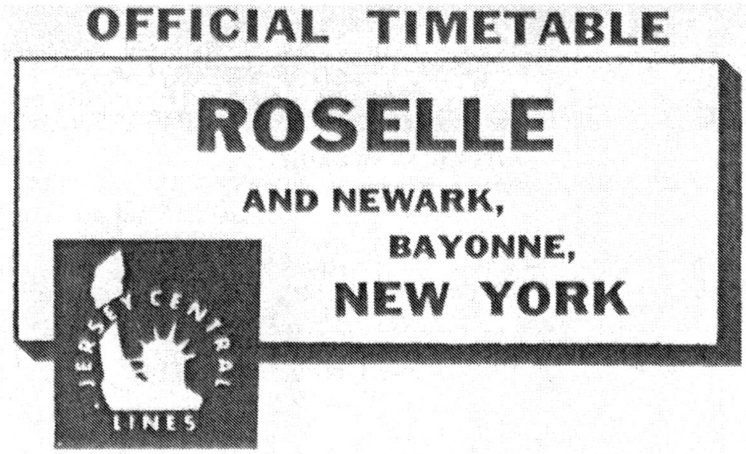
OFFICIAL TIMETABLE
ROSELLE
AND NEWARK,
BAYONNE,
NEW YORK
JERSEY CENTRAL
LINES

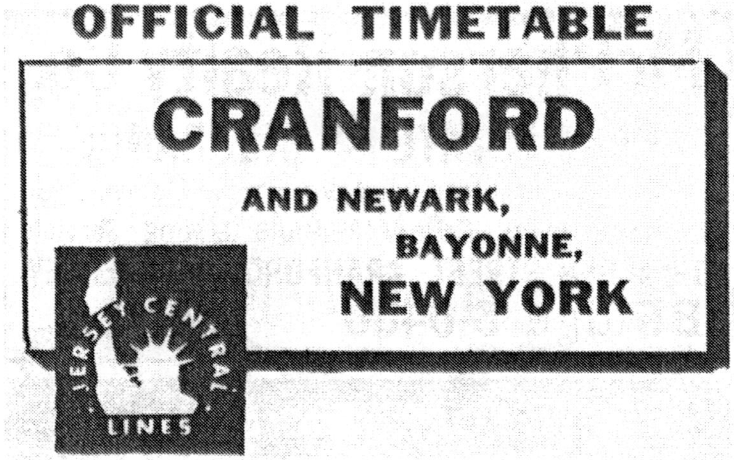
OFFICIAL TIMETABLE
CRANFORD
AND NEWARK,
BAYONNE,
NEW YORK
JERSEY CENTRAL
LINES

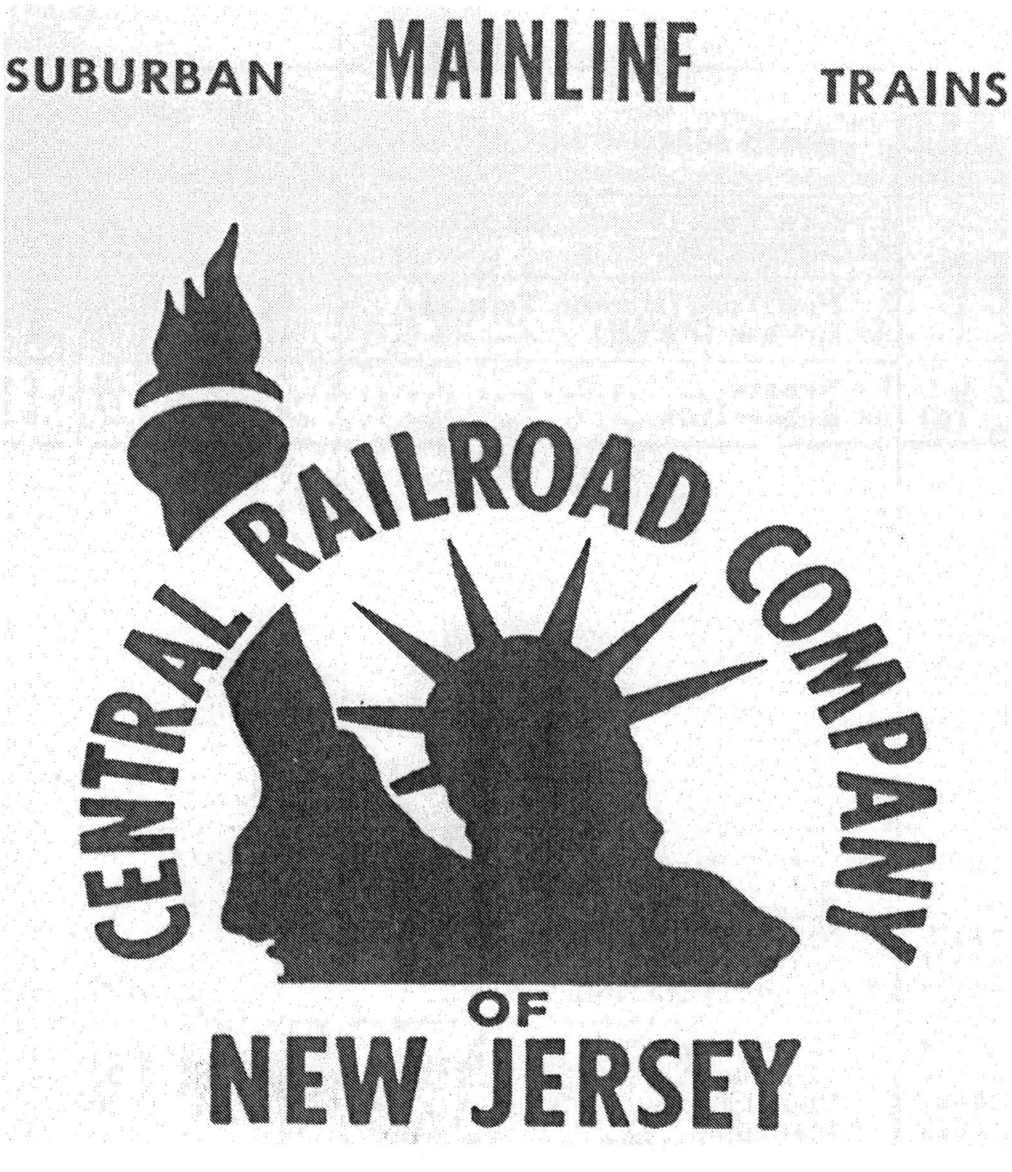
SUBURBAN MAINLINE TRAINS
CENTRAL RAILROAD COMPANY
OF
NEW JERSEY

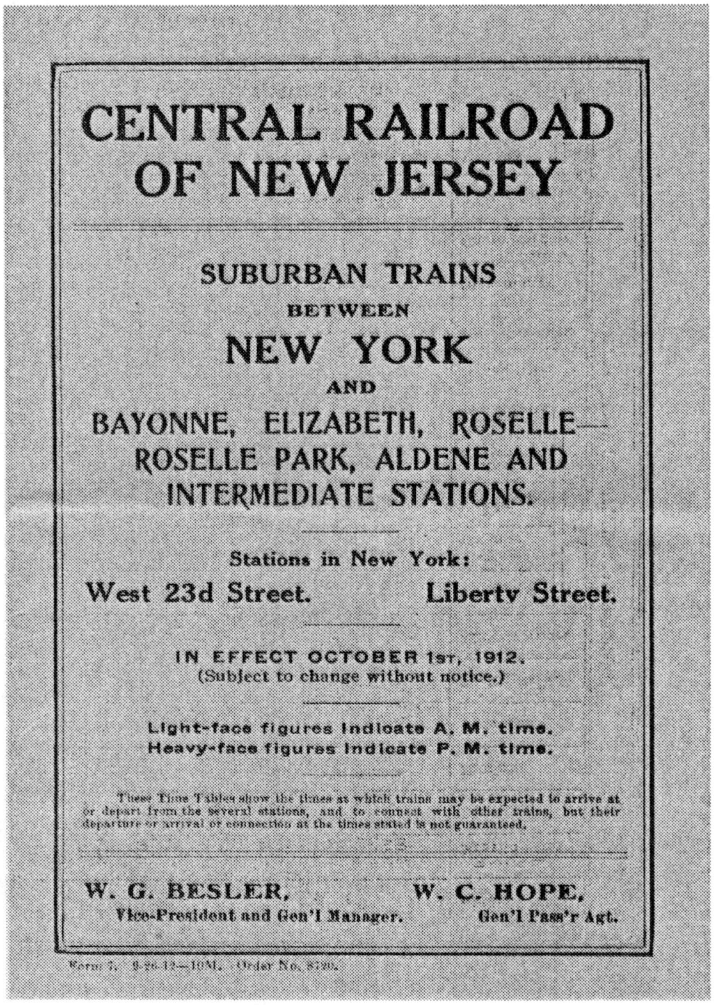

CENTRAL RAILROAD OF NEW JERSEY

SUBURBAN TRAINS
BETWEEN
NEW YORK
AND
BAYONNE, ELIZABETH, ROSELLE—ROSELLE PARK, ALDENE AND INTERMEDIATE STATIONS.

Stations in New York:
West 23d Street. Libertv Street.

IN EFFECT OCTOBER 1st, 1912.
(Subject to change without notice.)

Light-face figures indicate A. M. time.
Heavy-face figures indicate P. M. time.

These Time Tables show the times at which trains may be expected to arrive at or depart from the several stations, and to connect with other trains, but their departure or arrival or connection at the times stated is not guaranteed.

W. G. BESLER, Vice-President and Gen'l Manager.
W. C. HOPE, Gen'l Pass'r Agt.

Form 7. 9-26-12—10M. Order No. 8720.

DEPARTMENT OF PROGRESSIVE ADVERTISERS
DELAWARE WATER GAP
Lackawanna Railroad
In the Blue Ridge Mountains of Pennsylvania, surrounded by delightful resorts at Stroudsburg and throughout the Delaware Valley; an ideal region for spring and summer. A beautifully illustrated book describing these resorts and containing a fascinating love story entitled "For Reasons of State," will be sent on receipt of 4 cents in stamps. Address T. W. LEE, General Passenger Agent, Lackawanna Railroad, New York City.

NUMBER
THE
NEW YORK CENTRAL
AND
HUDSON RIVER
RAILROAD COMPANY
$1000
MORTGAGE
THREE AND ONE-HALF PER CENT.
COUPON GOLD BOND.
PRINCIPAL DUE
1997.
INTEREST PAYABLE
JANUARY 1ST & JULY 1ST
PRINCIPAL AND INTEREST PAYABLE
City of New York.
TRUSTEE'S CERTIFICATE.
This bond is one of a series of bonds described in the within mentioned mortgage or deed of trust, executed by The New York Central and Hudson River Railroad Company to the undersigned, as Trustee.
Central Trust Company of New York,
TRUSTEE.
By
VICE PRESIDENT.
1000

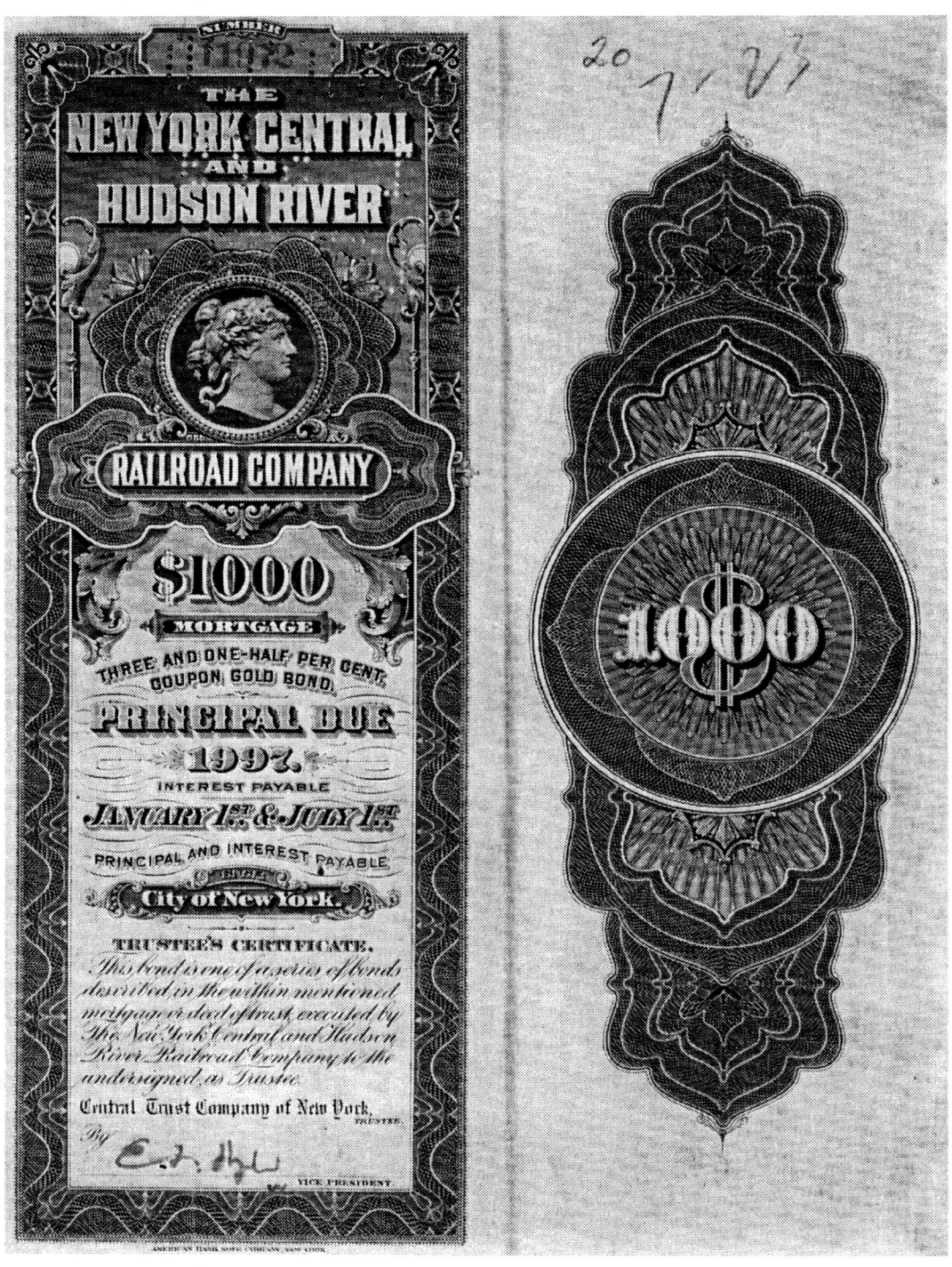

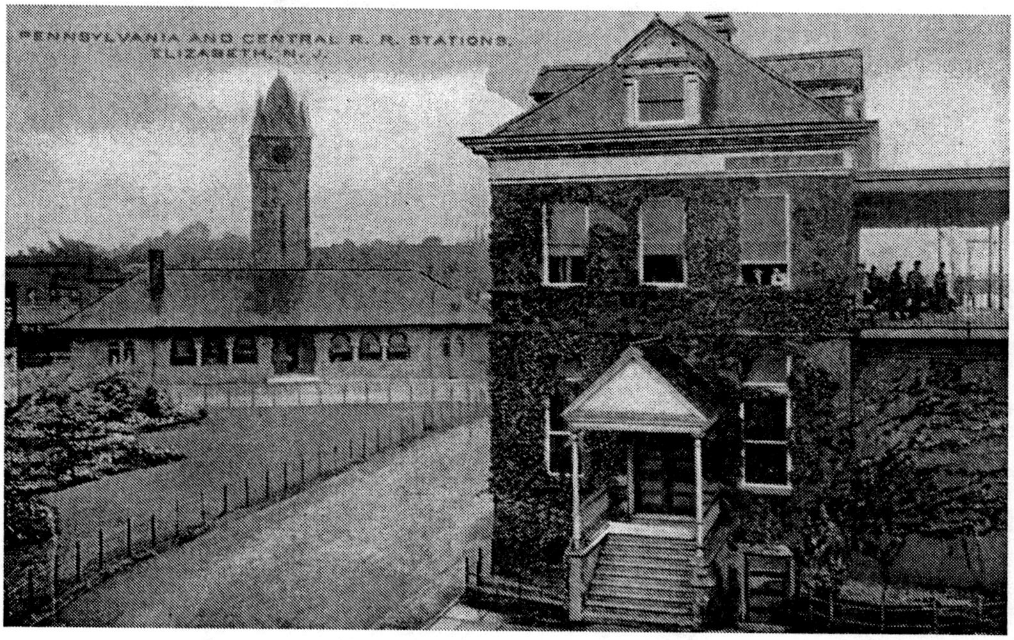
PENNSYLVANIA AND CENTRAL R. R. STATIONS,
ELIZABETH, N. J.

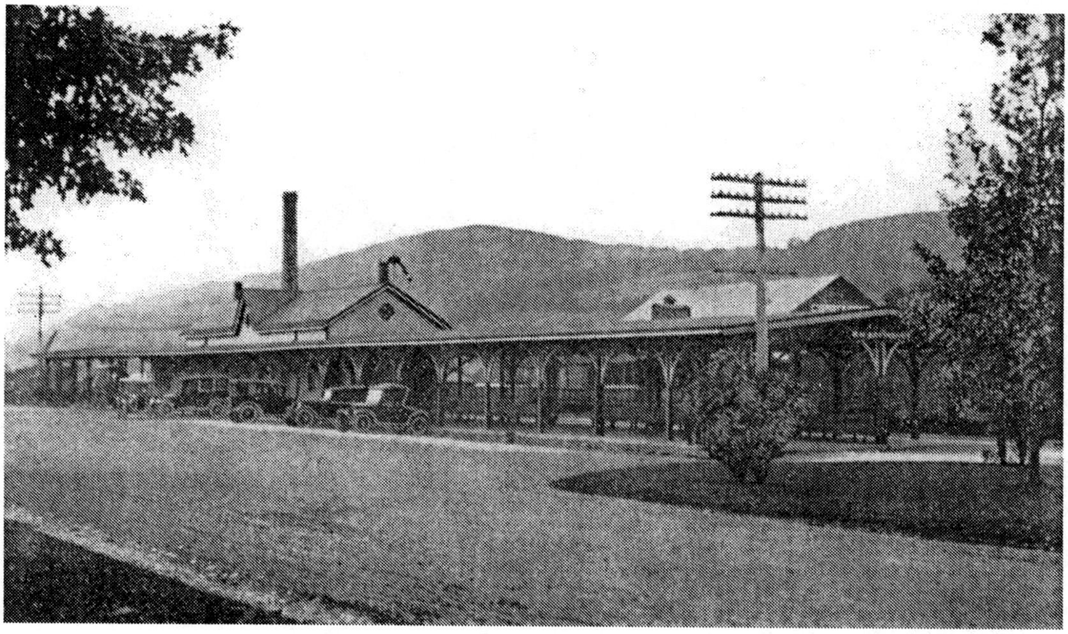

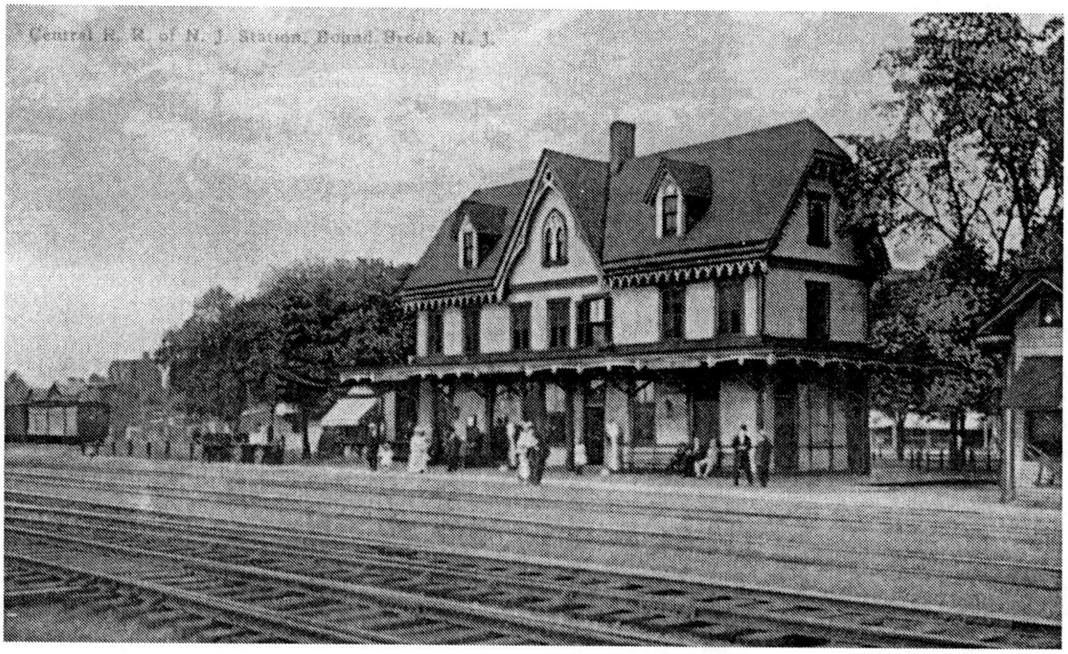
Central R. R. of N. J. Station, Bound Brook, N. J.

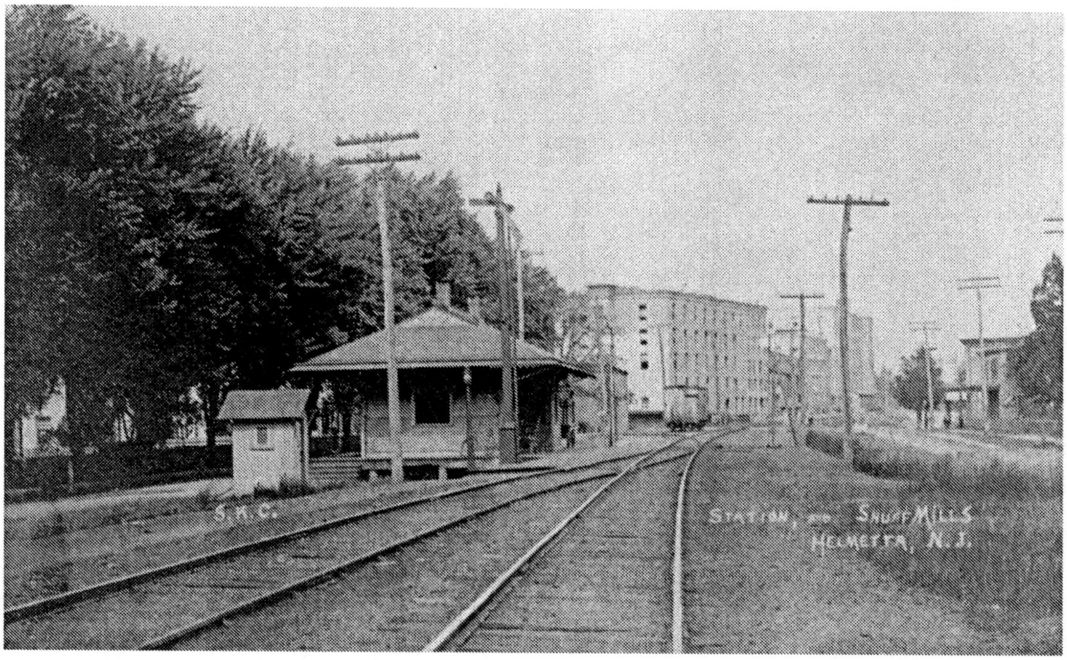
S.H.C.
STATION, AND SNUFF MILLS
HELMETTA, N.J.

Netcong-Stanhope R. R. Station.

ARRIVAL OF 5 P. M. TRAIN, BERNARDSVILLE, N. J.

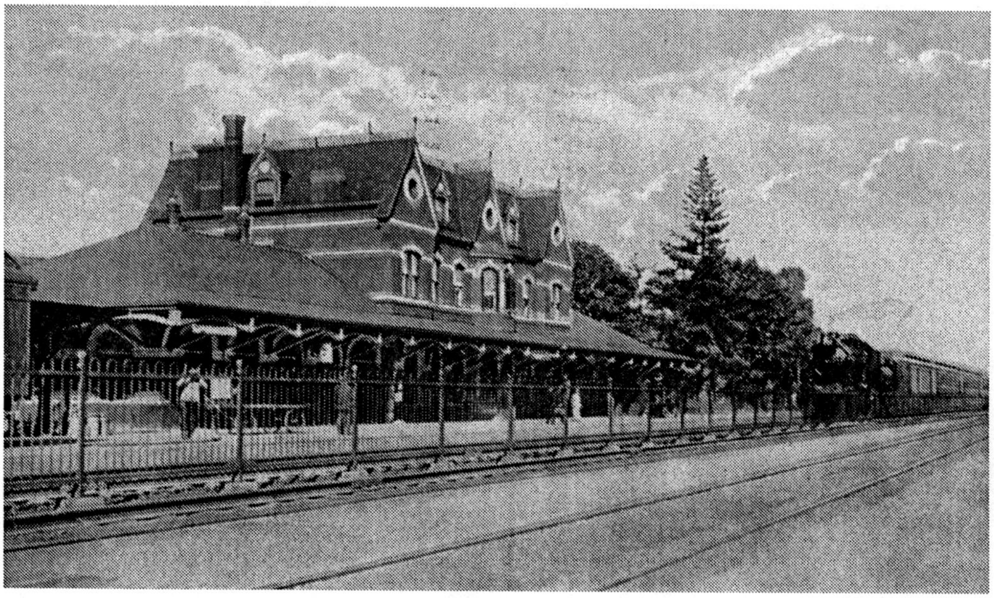

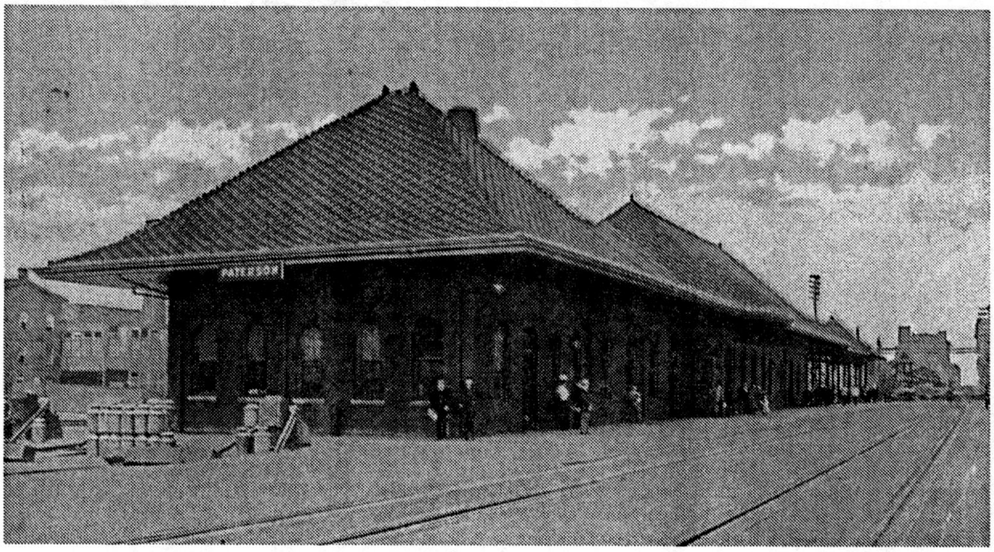
PATERSON

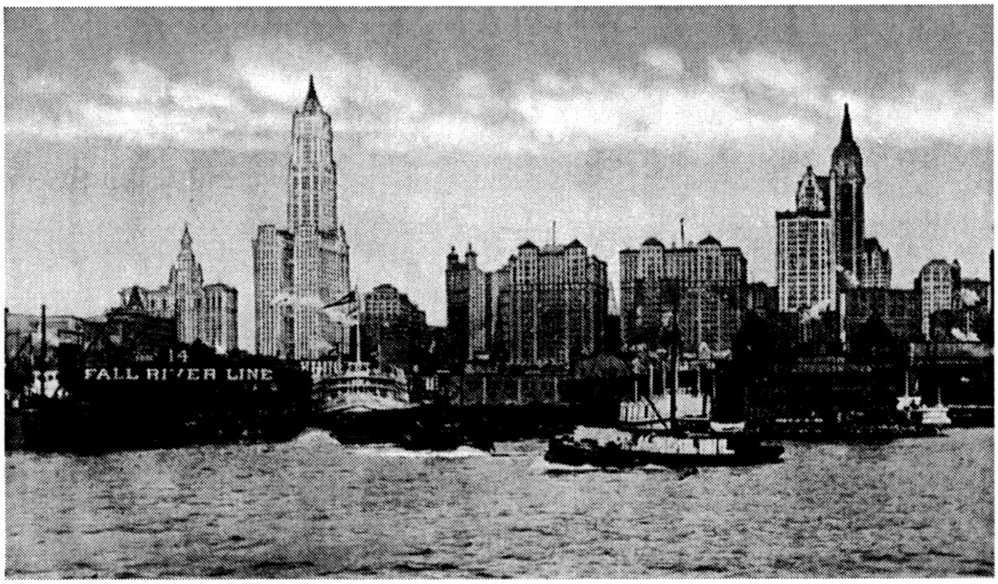
14
FALL RIVER LINE

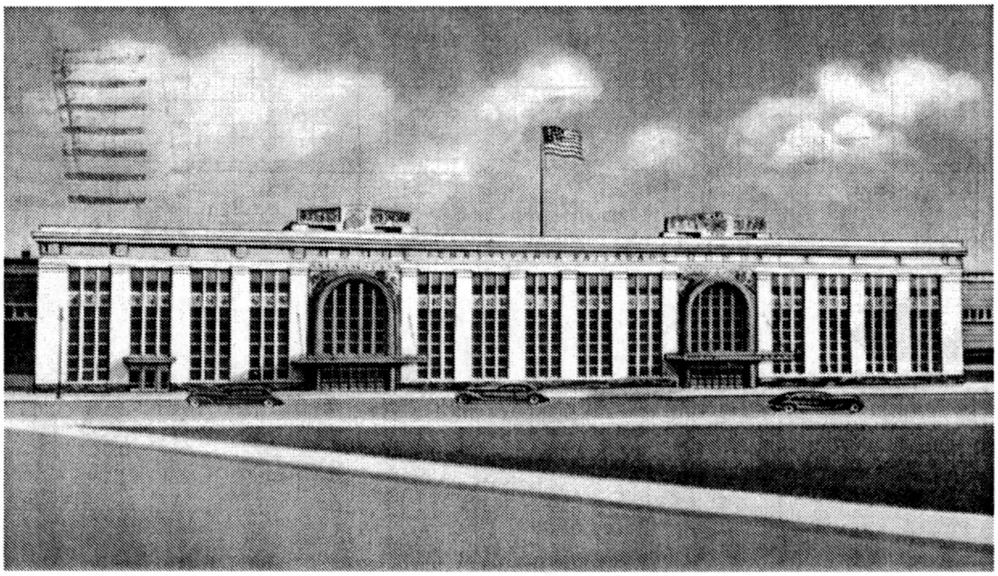

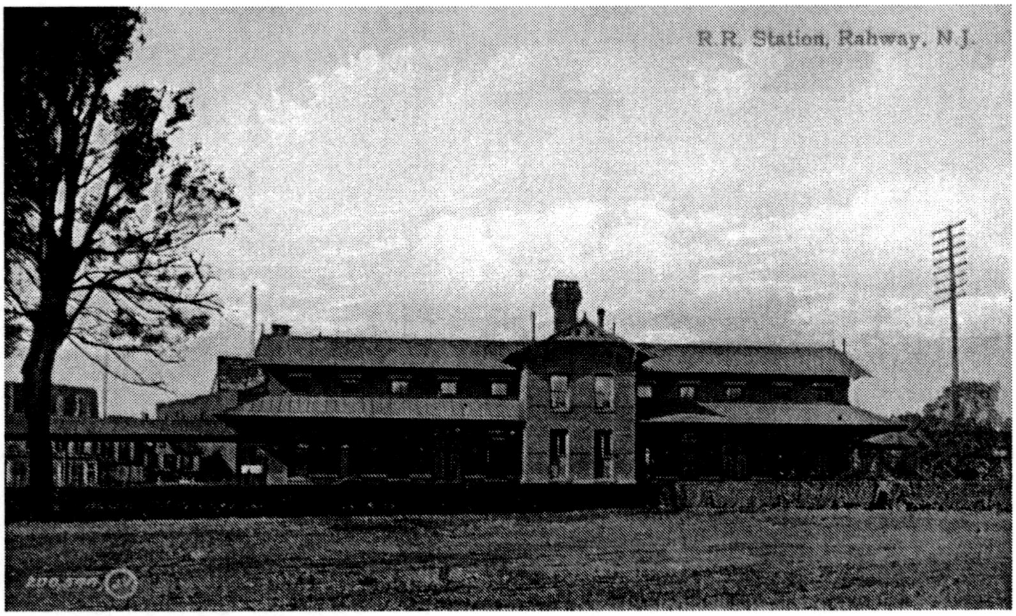
R.R. Station, Rahway, N.J.

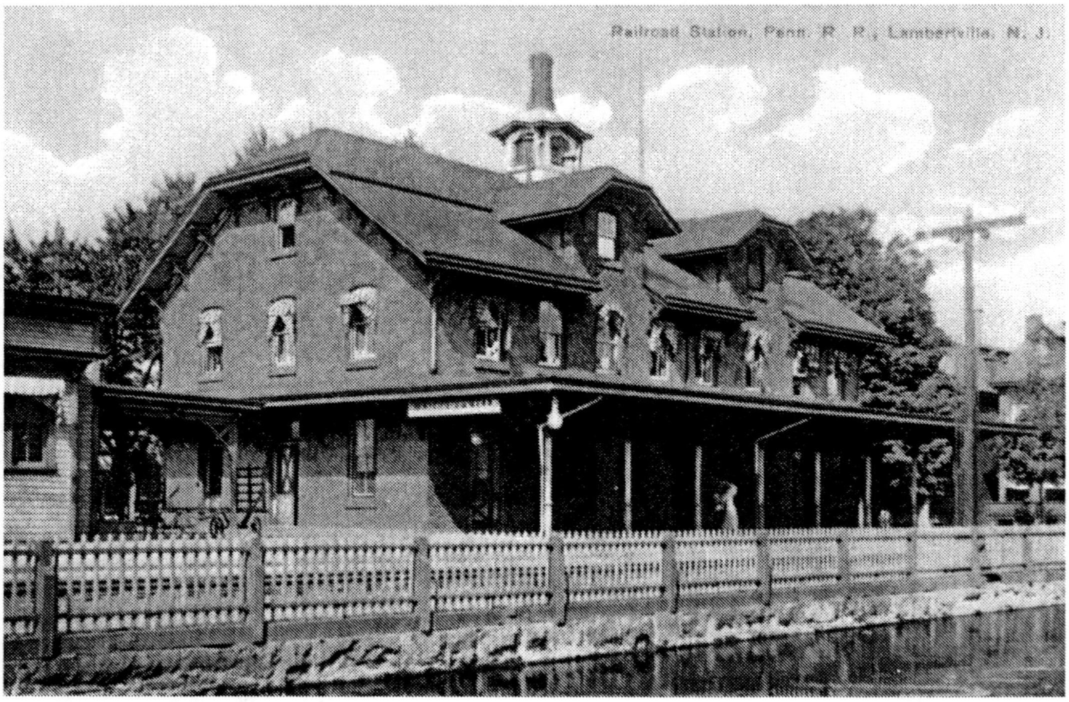
Railroad Station, Penn. R. R., Lambertville, N. J.

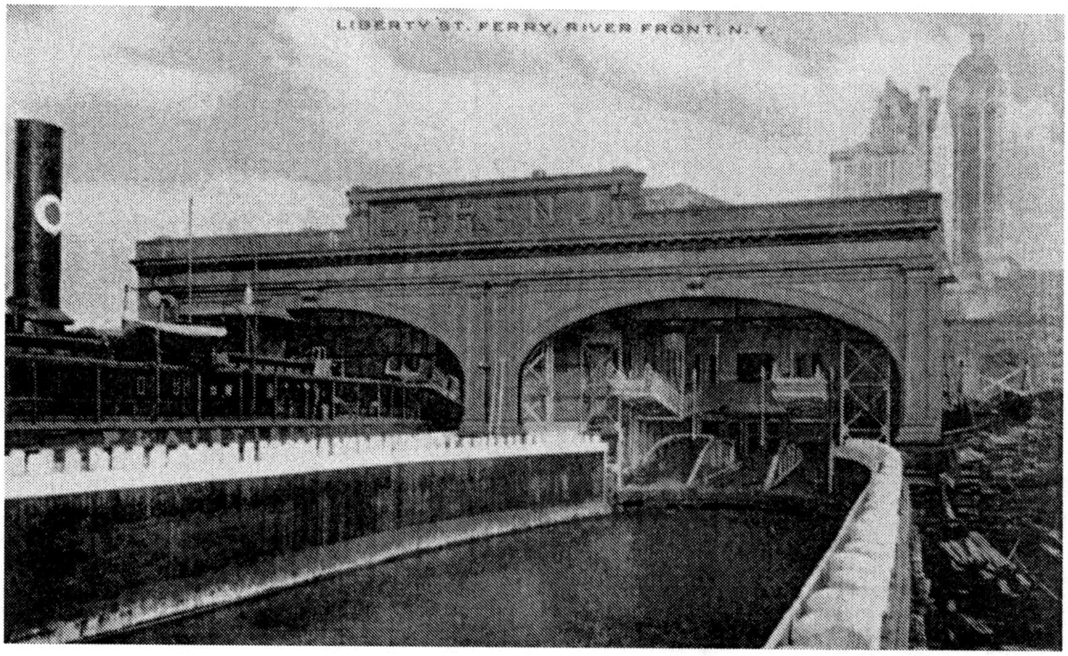
LIBERTY ST. FERRY, RIVER FRONT, N. Y.

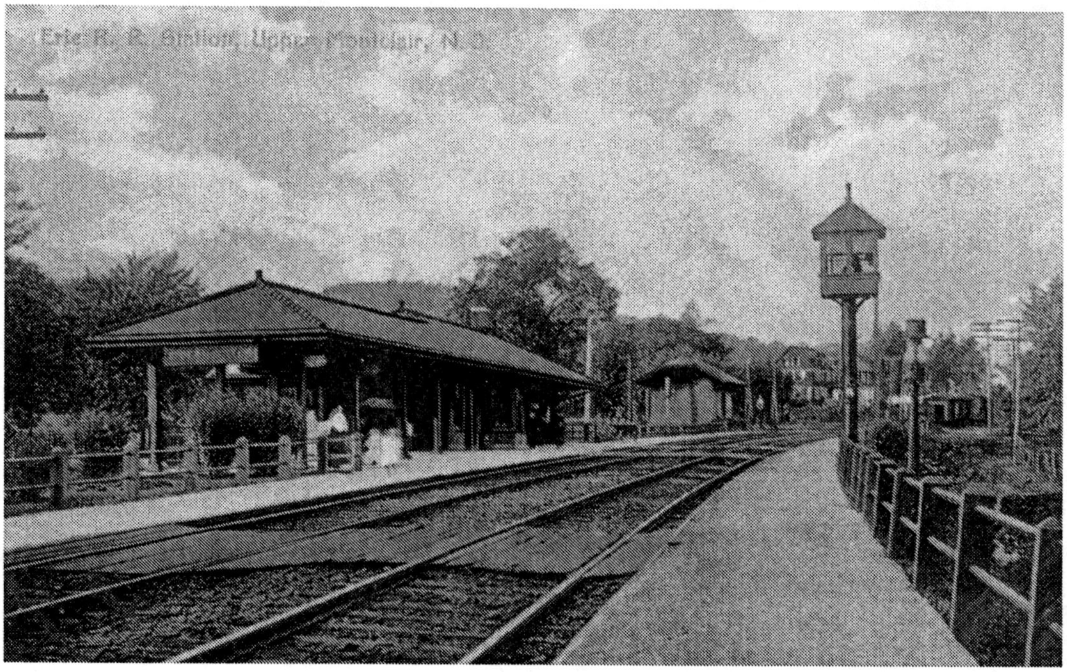
Erie R. R. Station, Upper Montclair, N. J.

Central Railroad Station, High Bridge, N. J.

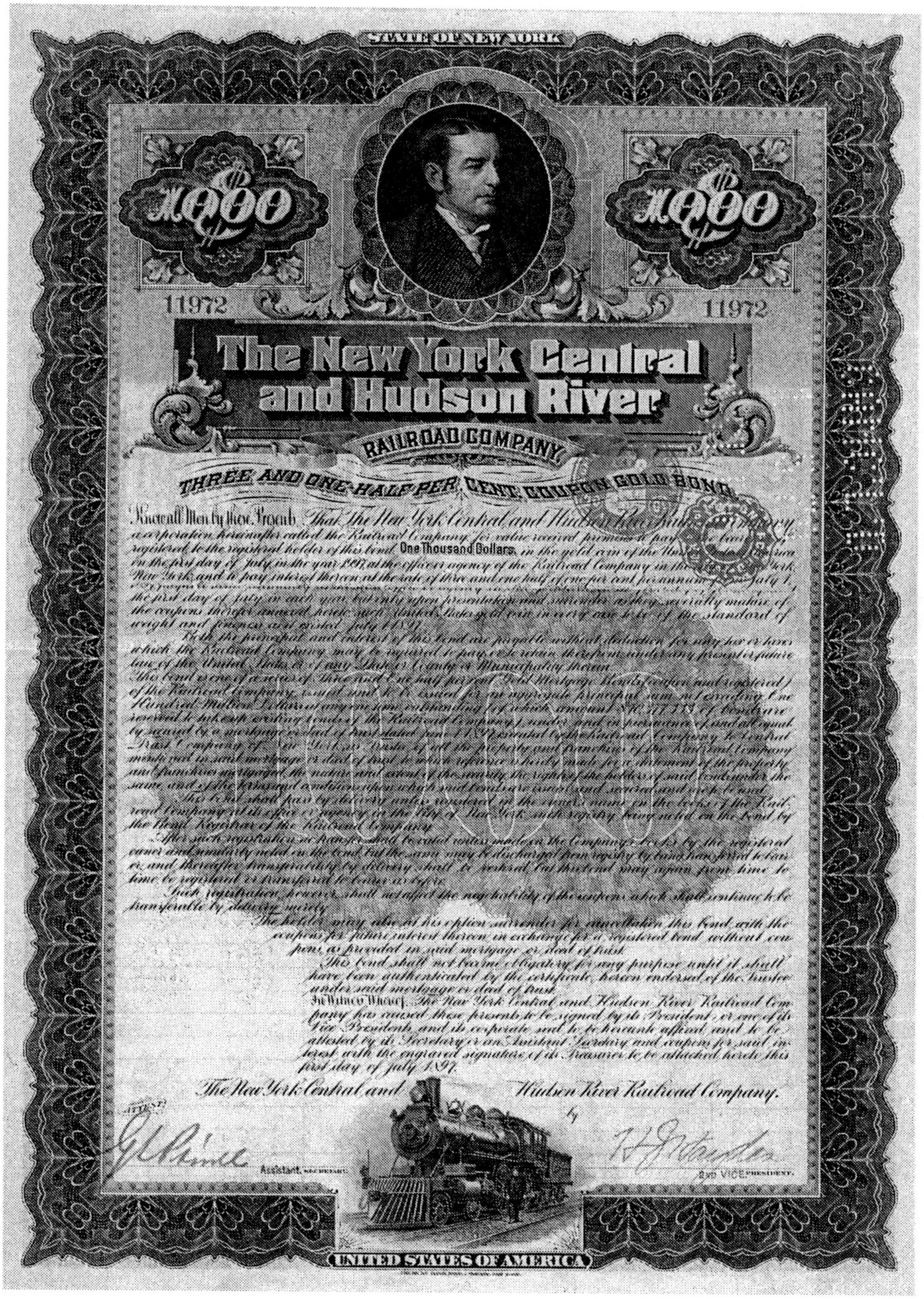
STATE OF NEW YORK
$1000
$1000
11972
11972
The New York Central and Hudson River
RAILROAD COMPANY
THREE AND ONE-HALF PER CENT COUPON GOLD BOND
One Thousand Dollars
The New York Central and Hudson River Railroad Company.
UNITED STATES OF AMERICA

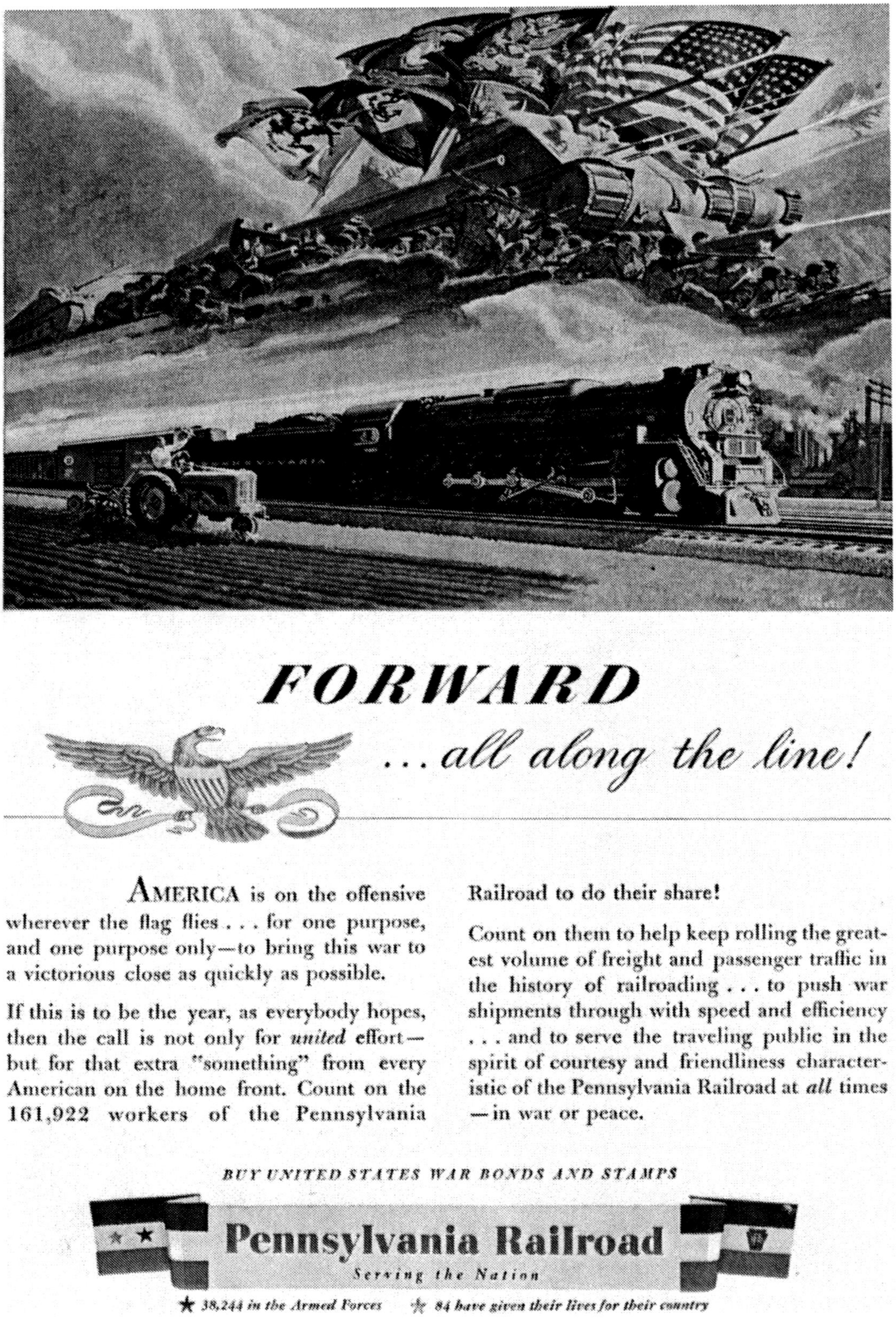
FORWARD
...all along the line!
AMERICA is on the offensive wherever the flag flies . . . for one purpose, and one purpose only—to bring this war to a victorious close as quickly as possible.
If this is to be the year, as everybody hopes, then the call is not only for *united* effort—but for that extra "something" from every American on the home front. Count on the 161,922 workers of the Pennsylvania Railroad to do their share!
Count on them to help keep rolling the greatest volume of freight and passenger traffic in the history of railroading . . . to push war shipments through with speed and efficiency . . . and to serve the traveling public in the spirit of courtesy and friendliness characteristic of the Pennsylvania Railroad at *all* times—in war or peace.
BUY UNITED STATES WAR BONDS AND STAMPS
Pennsylvania Railroad
Serving the Nation
★ 38,244 in the Armed Forces ★ 84 have given their lives for their country

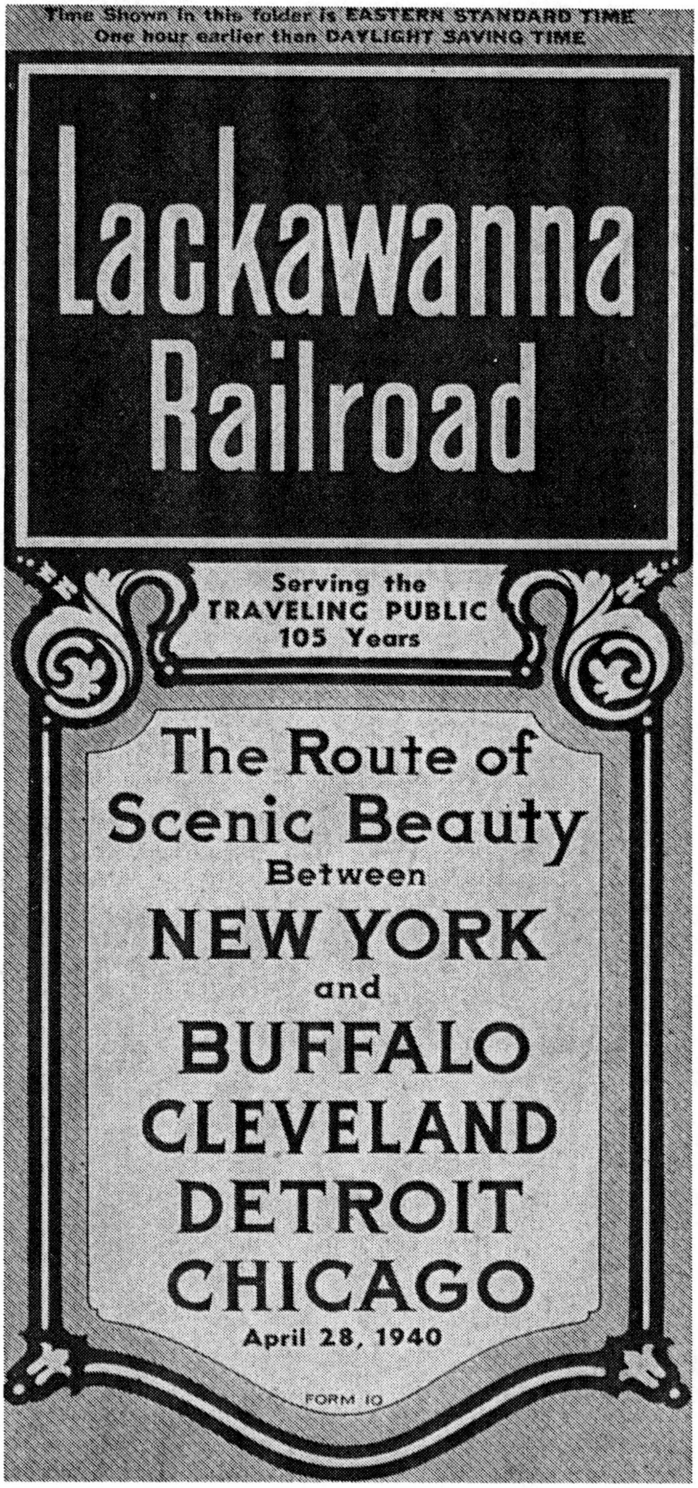
Time Shown in this folder is EASTERN STANDARD TIME
One hour earlier than DAYLIGHT SAVING TIME
Lackawanna
Railroad
Serving the
TRAVELING PUBLIC
105 Years
The Route of
Scenic Beauty
Between
NEW YORK
and
BUFFALO
CLEVELAND
DETROIT
CHICAGO
April 28, 1940
FORM 10

A Brief Review of...

Room Accommodations
IN PENNSYLVANIA RAILROAD'S 142 LIGHT-WEIGHT SLEEPING CARS PLACED IN SERVICE DURING THE YEARS 1938-1940

MASTER ROOM
FOR ONE OR TWO PERSONS

DAY

NIGHT

Most complete of all private accommodations, the stately Master Room provides unexcelled comforts and conveniences for the traveler. Four arm chairs provide an air of restful informality. These are collapsible and may be folded away at night. Connecting bathroom has a shower and complete toilet and lavatory facilities. Full-length mirrors; individual air-conditioning, heat and light control. Individual radio is also provided.

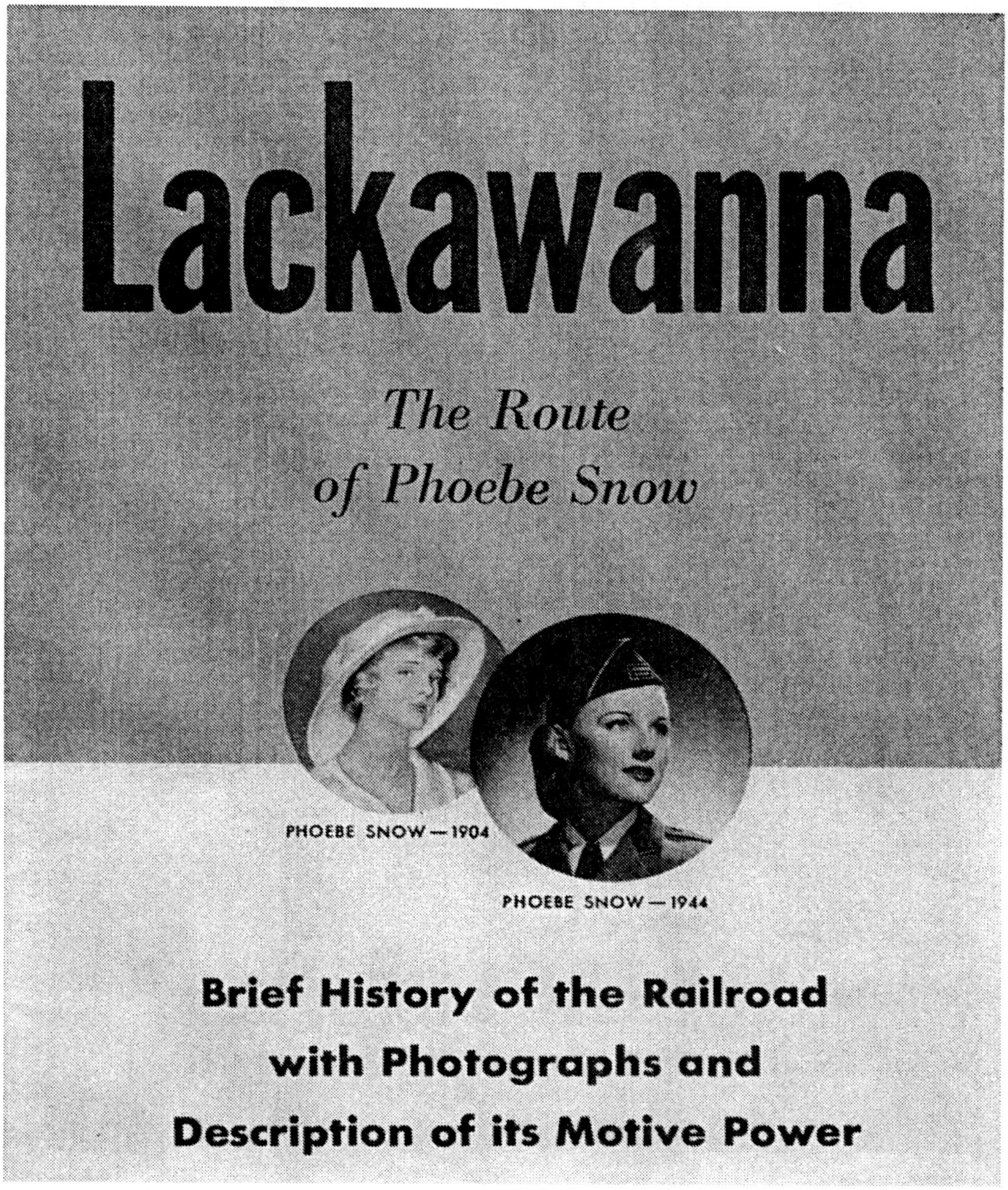
Lackawanna
The Route
of Phoebe Snow
PHOEBE SNOW—1904
PHOEBE SNOW—1944
Brief History of the Railroad
with Photographs and
Description of its Motive Power

previously stated, was reached by using the tracks of the New York and Erie between Great Bend and Owego.

Stock control of the Syracuse, Binghamton and New York Railroad, extending from Binghamton to Syracuse, was acquired in January, 1869; and, in September, 1912, that railroad was leased by the Lackawanna. The Oswego and Syracuse Railroad was leased in February, 1869. The Valley Railroad between Great Bend and Binghamton, a link in the main line, was also started in 1869.

In April, 1870, the Greene Railroad and the Utica, Chenango and Susquehanna Valley Railroad were leased.

In 1873, the Lackawanna and Bloomsburg Railroad, between Scranton and Northumberland, which line served the upper anthracite fields south of Scranton, was acquired by the Lackawanna.

In 1882, the largest single link in the Company, the New York, Lackawanna and Western Railroad Company, extending from Binghamton to Buffalo—two hundreds miles—was thrown open to traffic. These latter two links thus established the Company as a trunk line road, providing direct rail service between the Atlantic seaboard and the Niagara frontier, at Buffalo.

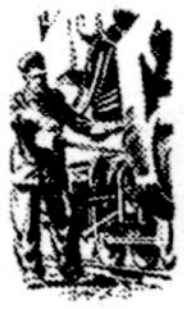

The Modern Railroad

• In addition to the main line extending from Hoboken to Buffalo, the Company operates 561 miles of branch lines. Chief of these are the branches running from Scranton to Bloomsburg and Northumberland, from Binghamton to Syracuse, Oswego and Utica, and from Owego to Ithaca.

The entire main line of the road is of multiple track construction and it is laid with heavy-section rail. From Hoboken to Dover, the area of densest traffic, there are three tracks via much of the Newark-Dover line and on the Boonton line.

Among the Company's notable engineering achievements are Tunkhannock Viaduct, largest concrete viaduct in the world, nineteen miles west of Scranton, and Pequest Fill, greatest railroad embankment in the world, near Slateford Junction, New Jersey.

The rolling stock includes 403 locomotives, 749 passenger cars, 519 company cars, and 17,196 freight cars of all classifications.

The Marine Department operates 216 tugs, lighters, barges, coal and grain boats and auxiliary equipment. This department, operating thirteen ferry boats, transports daily thousands of passengers across the Hudson River. More than 650 marine employes are required to operate the fleet.

Total capital expenditures by the Company to 1933 amounted to more than $332,000,000. This sum represented an investment of approximately $332,000 for each mile of the Company's 998 miles of roadway then operated, indicating a high degree of development.

The Lackawanna has on its payrolls 15,000 employes earning about $2,750,000 monthly.

The Lackawanna has important freight terminals at Hoboken, also piers on both sides of the Hudson River, on the Harlem River, the East River and in Brooklyn, serving shippers and receivers in the Metropolitan area. At Buffalo, on Lake Erie, and at Oswego, on Lake Ontario, the Company also operates port and terminal facilities.

Two ticket offices in New York City in addition to passenger terminals at West 23rd Street, Christopher Street and Barclay Street, provide convenient service for the traveler. The Company's centrally located passenger station in Buffalo is used by the Nickel Plate and the Baltimore and Ohio railroads.

The largest freight and passenger terminals on the railroad are in Hoboken. They cover 225 acres. The passenger terminal is served by seventeen tracks and six ferry slips. The freight terminal, bordering on the Hudson River, has a capacity of 3,100 cars.

Lackawanna Terminal Warehouse, bordering on the freight yards in Jersey City, is a fire-proof structure containing more than 1,250,000 square feet of floor space.

The commuter traffic of the Lackawanna is among the densest anywhere. Each business day more than 72,000 passengers are transported to and from Greater New York.

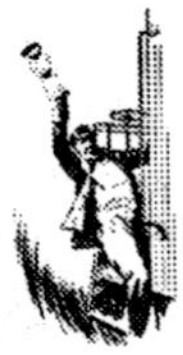

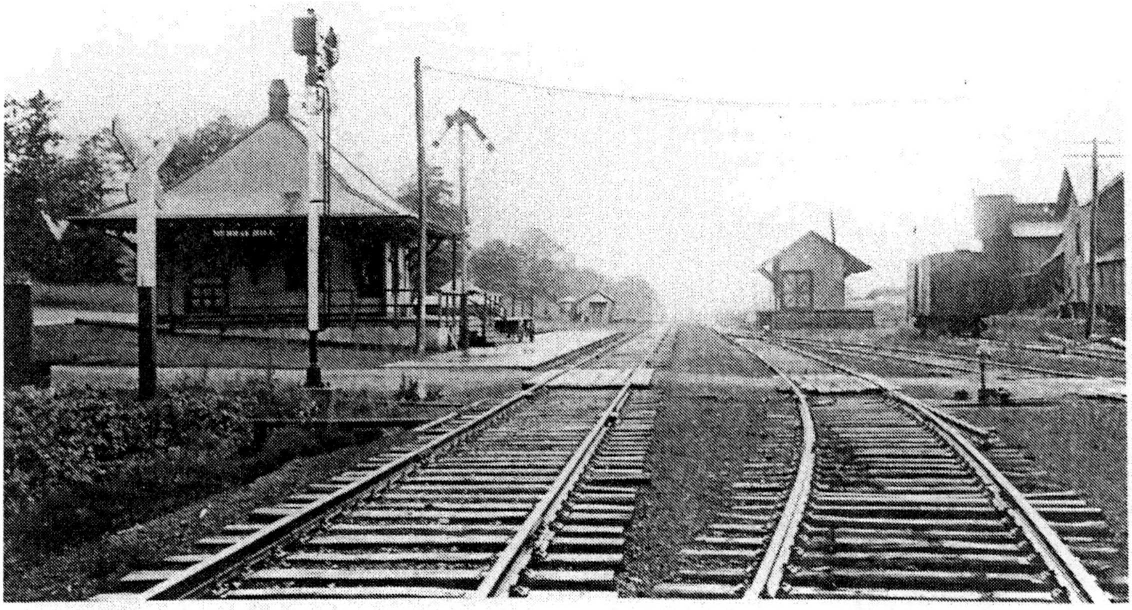

The Murray Hill passenger station and freight house at about 1915. This station is actually located in New Providence. Note the chewed ties in the foreground where a car ran off the track when the derail was open.

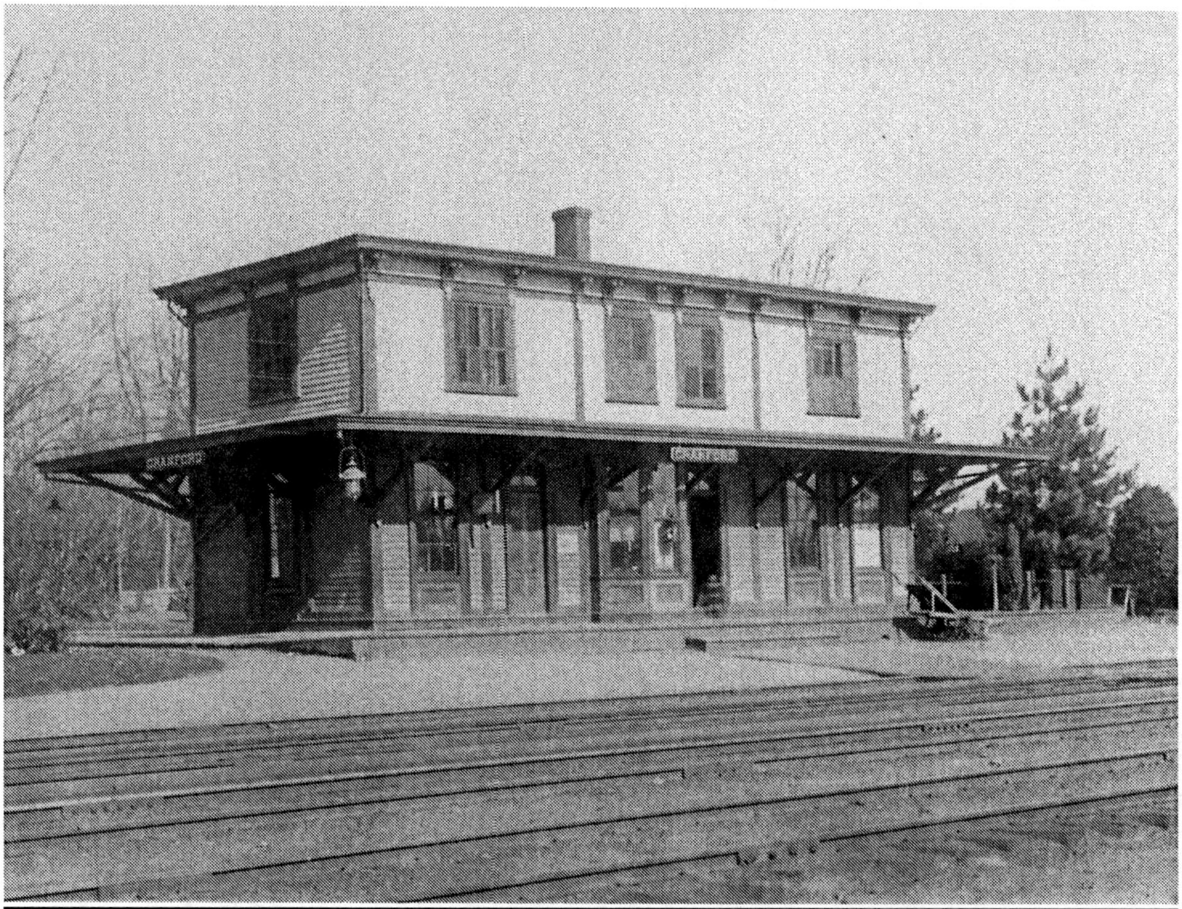

Michael E. Ferlise

CHAPTER SEVEN

Bankruptcy All Around

As World War II drew to a close in 1944-5, the Central Railroad of New Jersey adopted the Statue of Liberty as its official emblem. It was now out of bankruptcy. Along with these changes came the new name of The Jersey Central Lines. When World War II was finally over the Lackawanna discontinued its ferry service to 23rd Street in New York City. The Pennsylvania Railroad at this point only had ferry service between Exchange Place in Jersey City and Cortland Street in Lower Manhattan.

By 1946 the Erie Railroad and Jersey City were fighting over the wooden firetrap that was Pavonia Terminal. The Erie wanted to discontinue its ferry service on the Hudson River which Jersey City rebuffed. Jersey City wanted the old station demolished and replaced with a new one. Rather than build a new terminal, the Erie Railroad wanted to simply relocate to where the Hudson and Manhattan Railroad had its tubes nearby.

The Jersey Central had to discontinue service between Jersey City and Newark when a boat in the Hackensack River damaged two spans over it between Kearny and Jersey City. The damage might have been repaired, but when the United States government wanted the bridge rebuilt higher the Jersey Central didn't bother. The CNJ did provide a shuttle between the Communipaw terminal and the Hackensack River. Due to Western Electric being located here there was a similar shuttle between Newark and the southern tip of Kearny.

By August, the Jersey Central also had a problem with New Jersey where the railroad taxes were the highest in the nation. In an attempt to shelter its Pennsylvania earnings from the State of New Jersey, the CNJ transferred all of the leased Lehigh and Susquehanna Lines to the Central Railroad Company of Pennsylvania or CRP. This started a court battle between the CNJ and the State of New Jersey over whether or not these earnings could be taxed by the Garden State. With no 23rd Street ferry service, the CNJ get rid of the ferryboats "Bayonne" and "Elizabeth."

In 1948 the CNJ installed its first automatic crossing gates complete with lights and bells. They were placed at Flemington Road near White House in response to an accident there in which a woman was killed. Another improvement took place in Fanwood where the pedestrian overpass was covered as it still is today. Due to a lack of passengers on the shuttle between the Hackensack River and the Communipaw Terminal this service was discontinued by the CNJ. Across the Hudson River, U.S. President Dwight D. Eisenhower inaugurated the New York Central's "Twentieth Century Limited" streamliner.

On November 9, 1949, the Lackawanna introduced its new "Phoebe Snow" train. The name for this Hoboken to Buffalo service came from the old advertisement of Phoebe Snow. If for example the "Phoebe Snow" left Hoboken at 10:30 a.m, it arrived in Buffalo before 7 p.m. The "Phoebe Snow" made the return trip back to Hoboken the following day.

By now New Jersey's once extensive system of trolley lines was already being dismantled. With more automobiles and especially buses, N.J. residents were no longer taking the trolley for local travel. Today, NJ Transit's Newark City Subway is all that remains of the state's old system of trolley lines.

The CNJ probably regretted getting rid of those two ferryboats in 1947 as the "Lakewood" burned in a fire. The downside to the location of the CNJ's Communipaw Terminal was that it had no direct access to the Hudson and Manhattan Railroad tubes. The nearest H & M stations were across the Morris Canal Big Basin at Grove Street and Exchange Place. With no direct "tube" access to Manhattan the damaged "Lakewood" had to be rebuilt. After it was repaired this boat became the third to carry the name "Elizabeth II."

On December 31, 1949, the Pennsylvania Railroad discontinued what was left of its Hudson River ferry service from Exchange Place. When the PRR stopped the Exchange Place to Cortland Street ferry there was no Paulus Hook ferry for the first time since 1760.

You might recall how I earlier mentioned the millionaire investment banker C. Ledyard Blair. He built a huge mansion "Blairsden" in Peapack and Gladstone on the DL & W's Passaic and Delaware Branch. He died in 1949 after which his heirs sold "Blairsden" to the Sisters of St. John the Baptist.

As the 1950's got underway railroads in New Jersey, like the rest of the United States were no longer using coal. More and more railroads were using diesels instead of coal burning locomotives. New Jersey residents, like the rest of the country were using natural gas or oil in their homes. With no more widespread coal use the Lehigh Valley Railroad shut down its coal terminal in Perth Amboy. To make matters worse for New Jersey's railroads there were more cars, truck, buses, and planes. As a result, railroads everywhere experienced a reduction in freight and passenger traffic. If this wasn't bad enough railroads like the Erie, Lackawanna, and CNJ got hit hard with high property taxes in Jersey City. This didn't stop the Baltimore and Ohio Railroad in the 1950's from building the world's largest vertical lift bridge over the Arthur Kill. The U.S. Government helped with 90% of the costs for this bridge between Elizabeth and Howland Hook on Staten Island. This bridge is still standing, but isn't used as the railroad tracks are fixed in the "up" position for ship traffic. Bus use increased with the Port Authority's Bus Terminal that opened at 41st Street and 6th Avenue. This nice central location helped bus companies with normal wear and tear as well as gas.

In the early 1950's, the New Jersey Turnpike started to open up in several sections between the George Washington Bridge over the Hudson River and the Delaware Memorial Bridge over the Delaware River. Cars, trucks, and buses were going bridge to bridge and not using the ferryboats.

In 1952 the Pennsylvania Railroad discontinued the use of its Broad Street Station in Philadelphia. On March 31, 1952, the Pennsylvania Railroad discontinued its ferry operation between Philadelphia and Camden. The PRR ferryboat "Haddonfield" made the final crossing at 9:20 p.m. On the Hudson River, the New York Central's West Shore Ferry lost the boat "Catskill" to a fire. By 1952 the CNJ's ferryboats had a form of radar onboard for safety in the fog. New Jersey won its battle with the CNJ over the CRP's earnings in Pennsylvania. As per the courts the State of New Jersey was allowed to tax these earnings of the CNJ.

By April of 1953 the CNJ discontinued passenger service on its "South Branch" between Flemington and Somerville due to a lack of ridership.

June 5, 1953 was the last day for steam passenger service on the Lackawanna Railroad. Train number 1033 with engine number 1137 departed from Hoboken at 5:34 p.m. headed to Dover. After the almost seventy minute run through Hudson, Essex, Union, and Morris Counties there would be no more Lackawanna steam passenger trains ever. Steam freight operations continued for a little while though on the Lackawanna.

During 1954 in New Jersey the Garden State Parkway reached Cape May at the southern tip of the state. With an increase in motor vehicles traffic, a third tube opened up in the Lincoln Tunnel between Weehawken and New York City. By April of 1954 the CNJ discontinued its steam passenger service, but did build a new station in Dunellen. The Hudson and Manhattan Railroad became another victim of other factors like cars as they were now bankrupt and in bad shape. With a reduction in its Pavonia Ferry passenger traffic the Erie Railroad got rid of its boat "Tuxedo."

On March 30, 1955, the Lackawanna stopped its Hoboken to Christopher Street ferry service. As a result the ferryboat "Oswego" was sold off. Hurricane Diane rolled through the area in August of 1955. It dumped more that a dozen inches of rain in about two hours. The Lackawanna had sixty miles of tracks damaged in Pennsylvania which took several weeks to repair. The CNJ also experienced damage over in Pennsylvania as a result of the hurricane. Due to an increase in Parkway and Turnpike traffic, the Pennsylvania Railroad now only one train from New York City direct to Atlantic City.

To make vehicle traffic on the New Jersey Turnpike easier, the Newark Bay Extension Bridge opened up between Newark and Bayonne on March 22, 1956. The Newark Bay Extension Bridge is named for Assemblyman Vincent R. Casciano. He was instrumental in getting it built. By 1956 in Jersey City, the Erie Railroad's Pavonia passenger station was in bad shape and falling apart. Jersey City wanted the Erie to build a new station at the site. The Erie wanted to do away with both the Pavonia Station and the Hudson River ferry service from it. From the Erie's perspective it was simpler to build a station above the Hudson and Manhattan stop a few blocks away. Pavonia's upkeep simply was just not practical. Jersey City even condemned the terminal. After a discussion with the Lackawanna, some of the Erie's commuter trains started using the D L & W Hoboken Terminal.

In 1957 the Erie sold two of its four remaining ferryboats to the Lackawanna. The Erie's "Meadville" and "Youngstown" were renamed "Maplewood" and "Chatham" respectively by the Lackawanna. With only two ferryboats left for Hudson River service, the Erie still wanted to stop it completely. Jersey City put up a fight though against the potential Erie abandonment of the ferry service. Eventually the matter would end up in a Federal Court.

On June 13, 1957, the CNJ's first diesel number 1,000 had its last day of service in the form of a publicity run from Jersey City to Elizabethport. During 1957 Interstate 78 was in the proposal stage.

In April of 1958, the Baltimore and Ohio Railroad discontinued its passenger service to the north of Baltimore. This affected the CNJ in New Jersey as there were no more B & O trains coming into the Communipaw Terminal in Jersey City.

On September 15, 1958, CNJ train number 3314 left Bay Head shortly before 8:30 a.m. on its way to Jersey City. The train picked up passengers along the way as it soon left Elizabethport and started across the Newark Bay Draw Bridge. The consist was made up of one engine, a second engine being pulled to Jersey City, and five passenger coaches. For some reason the engineer disregarded several warning signals that indicated "slow down" as a section of the bridge was completely in the raised position. By the time the engineer noticed one of the vertical lift bridges was in the air and hit the brakes it was too late. The engines and the first two passenger cars plunged through the opening and into the Newark Bay. The third car dangled from the end of the tracks with the last two coaches behind it still on the bridge. Fortunately the first car was empty, but 48 passengers and crew died in this horrible accident.

December 12, 1958 was the last day of operations for the Erie Railroad's Pavonia Ferry Company on the Hudson River. Shortly after 6 p.m. the Erie's ferryboat "Arlington" left Chambers Street in New York City for the Pavonia Terminal. After this last trip to Jersey City it brought an end to more than one hundred years of Erie ferry service on the Hudson

River. By the end of 1958 all of the Erie Railroad's commuter and long distance trains were running to the Lackawanna's Hoboken Terminal. The Lackawanna was having serious financial problems and started to discuss ending all of its suburban passenger operations in New Jersey as of Spring 1959.

Things weren't much better financially for the New York Central's ferry service from Weehawken to New York City. March 24, 1959 was the last day of service for the NYC's Weehawken Ferry (Weehawken to 42nd Street) and West Shore Ferry (Weehawken to Cortland Street). Of course the New York Central now had no need for its West Shore Railroad which was also out of action. Both the railroad and the Weehawken Ferry were victims of the fact that passengers and freight now crossed the Hudson River on the George Washington Bridge or the Holland and Lincoln Tunnels in cars, trucks, and buses. In Weehawken the New York Central had no need to demolish the terminal as it burned in a fire. By December of 1959 the Port Authority of New York and New Jersey was looking at the Great Swamp as a location for a new airport. This plan though only caused residents to join together to fight the proposed airport.

After much discussion between themselves, October 17, 1960 was "merger day" for the Erie and the Lackawanna Railroads. The new Erie Lackawanna RR Company was the result of the Erie absorbing the Lackawanna. From this point on the old DL & W ceased to exist. With more than 3,000 miles of railroad, the Erie Lackawanna could take people from Hoboken to Buffalo, Cleveland, Cincinnati, and Chicago. The merger didn't help things financially in 1960 as the Erie Lackawanna lost slightly more than $7 million.

By 1961 there was no more Pennsylvania Railroad service to Exchange Place in Jersey City. The terminal was abandoned and later demolished. The Hudson and Manhattan Railroad though kept its station at Exchange Place. In fact the current PATH station here still carries the name of Exchange Place. To the north of Exchange Place, the H & M also kept their station near the empty Erie Pavonia Station. The Pavonia Station was later demolished, but the name lives on with the PATH's Pavonia Newport. Along the Delaware River the PRR stopped service on its Belvidere and Delaware Branch from the Trenton area towards Phillipsburg.

On January 24, 1961, the Black River and Western Railroad was incorporated. This railroad started off on the CNJ's old Chester Branch in Morris County. After February 8, 1961, the Lehigh Valley Railroad stopped running its passenger trains across New Jersey. In April of 1961, the Reading Railroad discontinued its "Crusader" that ran between the CNJ Terminal and Philadelphia. The "Crusader" used to leave Jersey City where it followed the CNJ tracks through Elizabeth, Plainfield, and Bound Brook. From here it turned onto the Reading tracks through Hillsborough, Belle Mead, Hopewell, and West Trenton enroute to the Reading Terminal in Philadelphia. In November of 1961 the CNJ assumed control over the Lehigh and New England Railroad in Pennsylvania mostly. By the end of the year the Erie Lackawanna had lost nearly $14 million.

During 1962 the Port Authority of New York and New Jersey assumed control of the defunct Hudson and Manhattan Railroad. The old H & M stations were filthy, the cars were old, railroad ties were rotted, even the wiring was bad. This resulted in the creation of the Port Authority Trans Hudson Corporation or PATH. Everything was cleaned and repaired while new cars were put into service. By now the Port Authority also had control of the George Washington Bridge as well as the Holland and Lincoln Tunnels. Plans were soon in the works for the World Trade Center in Lower Manhattan. Things started to look better for the Erie Lackawanna which only lost about $7 million.

In the southern part of New Jersey, the Pennsylvania-Reading Seashore Lines asked to end its passenger service. This was denied by the ICC. By 1963 the Chesapeake and Ohio Railroad had majority control over the Baltimore and Ohio Railroad's stock. The takeover wasn't official until February 4, 1963.

For the construction of Interstate 80 in New Jersey the old Erie Main Line from the Passaic River to Clifton was removed. It didn't have a negative effect on the Erie Lackawanna as trains were diverted to the old Lackawanna Boonton Branch via Secaucus and South Paterson. Today's New Jersey Transit Main Line is actually a combination of old Erie and Lackawanna trackage.

Prior to the 1960's there was never a bridge between Staten Island and Brooklyn. The U.S. Navy had always blocked a bridge across the New York Bay at this area due to the Brooklyn Navy Yard. When the Brooklyn Navy Yard was no longer in operation, work started on the Verrazzano Narrows Bridge which opened in 1964. The Erie Lackawanna Railroad ended 1964 with a loss on nearly $8.5 million.

By 1965, due to retirements the CNJ only had one ferry boat "Elizabeth" left to take passengers from Communipaw to Liberty Street. To assist "Elizabeth" the CNJ leased "The Narrows" and "The Tides" from New York City. These two boats had just finished up on the discontinued Staten Island to Brooklyn ferry run due to the Verrazzano Bridge. The U.S. Congress authorized the High Speed Ground Transportation Act. This allowed the Pennsylvania to get new high speed electric trains. In May of 1965, the Black River and Western Railroad leased some of the PRR's Flemington Branch from Flemington to Ringoes for excursions. In 1965 the Erie Lackawanna finally had a profit of $3.8 million for the first time since 1958.

In 1966 a boat ran into the CNJ's two northern spans of its four track Newark Bay Drawbridge. The CNJ decided not to bother with repairs and simply used the remaining two tracks over the Newark Bay. November 27, 1966 was the last run of the Erie Lackawanna's "Phoebe Snow" from Hoboken to Buffalo. With all the problems going on, New Jersey finally decided to do something about highways and transportation. The Transportation Act of 1966 created the New Jersey Department of Transportation. This was the first D.O.T. in the United States. The State of New Jersey in 1967 started out by assuming control of the local commuter operations of the CNJ, PRR, Erie Lackawanna, and the Pennsylvania-Reading Seashore Lines.

April 25, 1967 was the last day of ferry service for the CNJ on the Hudson River. The only CNJ ferryboat left was "Elizabeth" which ended out the day with the two leased "The Tides" and "The Narrows." For the first time in the past 306 years there was no ferry service from Communipaw. This left the Erie Lackawanna as the only railroad on the Hudson River with a ferry service. By now the Erie Lackawanna only had two tired ferryboats "Lackawanna" and "Elmira."

In order to preserve passenger service in the Garden State, the Division of Railroad Transportation come up with the Aldene Plan which took effect on April 30, 1967. With this, CNJ and Reading passenger trains would no longer go east past Cranford towards Elizabeth and Jersey City. These trains now switched onto the Lehigh Valley Railroad tracks that came up from Edison, Clark, and Cranford. The passenger trains now left the CNJ Mainline at Aldene Street Junction on the Roselle/Roselle Park border where via the LV they ran through Union and Hillside to Newark's Pennsylvania Railroad Station. From here there was access to New York City via PATH trains. CNJ trains with passengers that came up from the Jersey Shore now switched to the PRR tracks after Perth Amboy enroute to Newark's Pennsylvania Railroad Station. There was for a time a shuttle service from Cranford to Bayonne. With the CNJ's Communipaw Terminal closed, service to it from Bayonne was discontinued. Since there was no more ferry service, the CNJ's Liberty Street Terminal in Lower Manhattan was closed as well. There was still some freight activity in Communipaw with the CNJ and Lehigh Valley though. The Communipaw repair shops soon closed as repairs could be performed in Raritan.

November 22, 1967 was the last day of Hudson River ferryboat service for the Erie Lackawanna. With no ferryboats, Erie Lackawanna commuters now took PATH trains to New York City from underneath the Hoboken Terminal. With more cars on the New York Thruway the New York Central discontinued its "20th Century Limited" in 1967.

After almost 130 ICC meetings during the 1960's, February 1, 1968 was merger day for the Pennsylvania and the New York Central Railroads. The new Penn Central was the result of the greatest merger in U.S. railroad history. One of the problems of the Penn Central was that it was dual headed with top executives in Philadelphia and New York City. The Penn Central owned shares in things like Madison Square Garden, the Rangers, and the Knicks. In Manhattan alone the Penn Central owned almost thirty buildings like Grand Central Station, the Pan Am Building, and the Waldorf Astoria Hotel. The Penn Central had more than 20,000 miles of track in Washington D.C., Canada, and more than fifteen U.S. States. The massive Penn Central had almost 95,000 employees on its payroll.

On June 5, 1968, Senator Robert Kennedy was in Los Angeles's Ambassador Hotel. He had just won the California Democratic Primary for president. Shortly after 12 a.m. Kennedy was shot by Sirhan Sirhan. He later died from his wounds on June 6, 1968. Robert's funeral was held in New York City. Afterwards he was taken to New York's Pennsylvania Station for the trip to Arlington Cemetery in Washington D.C. GG1's 4901 and 4903 led the 21 car funeral train where Kennedy's body rested on a flat car at the end. While RFK's Funeral Train went through Elizabeth, numerous onlookers spilled onto the other tracks. Another train was coming through Elizabeth at the time which ran into the onlookers and killed several people. The Penn Central then shut down all other traffic along the route as Kennedy's four hour trip took eight hours to Washington D.C.

The Penn Central lost millions of dollars in 1968, but that didn't stop the debut of metro liner service from New York City to Washington D.C. With speeds that sometimes reached 120 miles per hour, the Metroliners covered the 226 miles in around three hours. As per the ICC, with its merger the Penn Central had to take in the New Haven Railroad on January 1, 1969. The New Haven Railroad was in bad shape as they lost more than $20 million in 1968.

As the 1970's started, the Erie Lackawanna ceased running long distance trains from Hoboken. With no more mail and express contracts, long distance trains were no longer profitable. In N.J., Erie Lackawanna trains would no longer run past Dover, Netcong, and Port Jervis on its local lines.

On March 16, 1970, the Black River and Western Railroad leased the rest of the trackage from Flemington to Three Bridges at the CNJ Main Line. In the first quarter of 1970 the Penn Central had an income of $5 million a day. On the downside though the Penn Central, with expenses, spent $6 million a day in the same first quarter of 1970. Unable to break even, the Penn Central had a first quarter loss of $102 million in early 1970. This resulted in the Penn Central declaring bankruptcy in June of 1970. At the site of the old ferry terminals in Lower Manhattan work was underway on the World Trade Center. In order to do something to save passenger service in the United States, the U.S. Congress passed the Rail Passenger Service Act. President Nixon signed it into law on October 30, 1970. This act created the National Railroad Passenger Corporation or AMTRAK. The private company was created to merge the nationwide system of passenger railroads. AMTRAK service started on May 1, 1971 as the number 235 "Clocker" left New York's Penn Station just after 12 a.m. for Philadelphia.

In 1972 at just under 1,400 feet high and 110 stories, World Trade Center Tower # 1 was now the tallest building in the world. In New Jersey every major railroad was in bankruptcy. By now with the exception of some Lehigh and Hudson activity and some joint work with the Erie Lackawanna, the CNJ was out of Pennsylvania. Bankruptcy didn't stop the CNJ from introducing its new red and white paint scheme on some of its equipment.

By 1973 the Baltimore and Ohio, the Chesapeake and Ohio, and the Western Maryland Railroads went under the name of The Chessie System. In February of 1973, the Penn Central had a strike that shut down its operations in the Northeastern United States. In 1973 when World Trade Center Tower # 2 at 110 stories went up, it made these the two tallest building in the world. The PATH tracks in Lower Manhattan had been adjusted slightly to provide service to underneath the World Trade Center. In 1974 though the Sears Tower in Chicago eclipsed the World Trade Center as the world's tallest building. During 1974 the Delaware and Raritan Canal was back in the news as New Jersey proclaimed it a state park.

In the Northeastern United States, the Congress allowed for the creation of the Consolidated Rail Corporation or Conrail. Conrail assumed freight and commuter operations of the CNJ, Erie Lackawanna, Reading, Penn Central, L & H, and L.V. Railroads. Conrail took over these bankrupt railroads with poorly maintained tracks, stations, and equipment. Since they were at their prime these railroads declined due to taxation as well as a lack of coal traffic as people now used oil and natural gas. Another problem was that these railroads got hit with high property taxes they never used to pay. People and freight now traveled between cities in planes, cars, and trucks that used new highways that were subsidized by the U.S. Government. All of the tunnel and bridge crossings in the Hudson River area didn't help matters either. The loss of mail contracts on long distance trains led to the railroads simply stopping them. This left money losing commuter operations which only added to the problem. Conrail operated commuter service in New Jersey under a contract from the State. Throughout New Jersey, Conrail operated trains with a mixture of CNJ, Penn Central, Erie Lackawanna, and Reading equipment. On April 1, 1976, AMTRAK purchased much of the Northeast Corridor between Boston and Washington D.C.

On July 17, 1979 the New Jersey Public Transportation Act was signed which created New Jersey Transit. There were other changes in New Jersey as the old CNJ tracks west of High Bridge were abandoned for the construction of Interstate 78. In 1981 direct service from the Reading Terminal in Philadelphia ended to Newark Penn Station. A shuttle service now carried passengers from West Trenton through Belle Mead enroute to Newark Penn Station. This shuttle was named the "Wallsader" for the old "Wall Street" and "Crusader." By 1981 the CSX Corporation was created as a holding company for the Chessie System and the Seaboard Coast Line.

The State of New Jersey passed another act whereby Conrail had to discontinue passenger operations in New Jersey as of December 31, 1982. As of January 1, 1983, New Jersey Transit had full control over buses as well as local passenger trains. New Jersey Transit Rail Operations got started right away with train # 951 that left Hoboken for Dover at 12:30 a.m. By this point due to low ridership the "Wallsader" as well as passenger service to Atlantic City was already discontinued.

NJ Transit inherited locomotives, passenger coaches, and stations that used to belong to the CNJ, Penn Central, Lehigh Valley, PRSL, Erie Lackawanna, and Reading Railroads. What NJT really got though was tired locomotives, 50 year old coaches, and run down stations. NJT slowly began to rebuild the entire system in New Jersey with some new equipment as everything from tracks to stations were refurbished.

In 1984 the old PRR Penn Station in Newark was sold by Amtrak to private persons who in turn leased it to NJ Transit.

Ferry service between New Jersey and Manhattan returned in 1986 when Arthur E. Imperatore bought property on Weehawken's waterfront. His Port Imperial Ferry Company started off with service between Weehawken and Manhattan's 38th Street. After a 33 year absence since the NYC stopped it's ferries, there was once again service between Weehawken and Manhattan.

Things became easier for cars, trucks, and buses to travel straight across New Jersey between the Holland Tunnel and Phillipsburg when the east and west sections of Route 78 linked up in the Watchung Reservation.

During 1987 the Port Imperial Ferry Company expanded its service to Lower Manhattan.

In July of 1987, NJ Transit's $130,000,000 Meadowlands Maintenance Complex or M.M.C. opened in Kearny. With the M.M.C., NJT's equipment could be cleaned, repaired and even completely overhauled under one roof. With this new facility NJT was able to close down the old CNJ diesel shop from 1931 in Elizabeth.

In Hoboken NJ Transit would no longer need the Lackawanna repair shed built back in 1931. In 1988 NJT continued with other improvements as its New Jersey Coast Line from South Amboy to Long Branch was electrified. With this change, electric locomotives headed southbound no longer had to stop at South Amboy for a switch to diesels.

By 1989 the Port Imperial Ferry Company was known as the New York Waterway. It now had a ferry run from New Jersey Transit's Lackawanna Terminal in Hoboken to Lower Manhattan at the foot of the World Trade Center area. With the return of ferry service from Hoboken, people no longer had to rely solely on the PATH trains to access Lower Manhattan.

For the PATH system, its new Exchange Place Station built at a cost of $66 million, was ready in 1989.

In 1989 both Amtrak and NJ Transit brought back service to Atlantic City. At the time Amtrak ran its trains from Philadelphia's 30th St. Station. NJ Transit's service at the time ran from Lindenwold where there was a PATCO connection. Both Amtrak and NJ Transit used the old PRR route across Southern N.J.

During 1994 the N.Y. Waterway brought ferry service back to Exchange Place as its boats began to run between the Colgate Clock and Lower Manhattan. There had been no ferry service from this section of Jersey City since the PRR discontinued its service during the early 1960's. This of course was also the area where the old Paulus Hook Ferry used to depart from way back when.

Due to a problem with low ridership, Amtrak discontinued its Philadelphia to Atlantic City service on April 1, 1995. This left NJ Transit, which now began to run its trains direct to and from Philadelphia's 39th St. Station. On June 7th, 1996, NJ Transit's inaugural Midtown Direct train ran from New Jersey and into New York Penn Station via Amtrak's PRR tunnels under the Hudson River. When Midtown Direct service started three days later for passengers it saved twenty minutes of commuting time. Gladstone, Morristown, and Montclair passengers now had the option of riding directly to 33rd Street in Manhattan via a new connection in Kearny with Amtrak's Northeast Corridor. These riders no longer had to go to the Hoboken Terminal where PATH trains were used to travel to Manhattan's 33rd St. In 1997 Conrail was sold to both the CSX and Norfolk Southern Corporations. On June 1, 1999, both CSX and Norfolk Southern began to operate some of Conrail's lines which included those in New Jersey.

There was 150 mile per hour high speed rail service for the first time in the U.S. with Amtrak's "Acela Express" between Washington D.C. and Boston. The inaugural run with dignitaries ran from Washington D.C. through New Jersey enroute to Boston on November 16, 2000. Acela service for actual passengers began on December 11th along the Northeast Corridor. During its first four weeks 11,000 riders used the new service which produced $1.25 million in revenue for Amtrak. Within just five months some 100,000 passengers took the Acela which brought in $11.9 million in ticket sales. The name Acela is a combination of acceleration and excellence.

Everything was pretty much the same until September 11, 2001. That morning was a typical one as NJ Transit, Amtrak, PATH, and NY Waterway passengers rode from New Jersey into Manhattan. Terrorists were able to hijack American Airlines Flight 11 from Boston to Los Angeles. The terrorists then crashed Flight 11 into the north tower of the World Trade Center at 8:55 a.m. which began to burn. In the meantime, a second group of hijackers took control of United Airlines Flight 175 which was also from Boston to L.A. This hijacked flight slammed into the south tower of the World Trade Center at 9:03 a.m. While both towers burned, a third plane was hijacked by yet another group of hijackers. American Airlines Flight 77 from Washington D.C. to L.A. was flown into the Pentagon at 9:43 a.m. Back in Lower Manhattan, the south tower collapsed completely at 10:05 a.m. About five minutes later a fourth hijacked plane, United Airlines Flight 93 crashed in Somerset County, Pennsylvania. The passengers and crew onboard this plane enroute from Newark Airport to San Francisco fought with the hijackers before the crash. The north tower of the World Trade Center also collapsed at 10:28 a.m. When the two towers collapsed, some 1,600,000 tons of debris came to rest above the PATH station below. It was the first time since the early 1900's (with the exception of floods) that there was no PATH or H & M service to Lower Manhattan. New Jersey residents now had to rely solely on ferryboats in order to access Lower Manhattan. It would take eight months of digging by 3,600 workers daily to remove all the debris after which only the PATH and subway tracks were left at Ground Zero. The PATH station destroyed in the WTC attacks was the first "subway" station in the world to be air conditioned. It will be some time before this PATH service to Lower Manhattan starts up again. In order to restore PATH service to Lower Manhattan it will require millions of dollars although there is no exact figure at the moment.

As part of a $20 billion anti-terrorism package, Congress provided Amtrak with $100 million for safety improvements on the old PRR tunnels underneath both the Hudson and

East Rivers. A plan had to be put on hold after September 11th for a new and third Amtrak/NJ Transit tunnel under the Hudson River.

Prior to Amtrak's creation, railroads like the Erie, CNJ, Lackawanna, PRR, and New York Central always had problems making money on passenger trains. Since Amtrak took over control in the early 1970's, Congress has given it at least $25 billion to help subsidize its 22,000 mile system. The same problems with ridership and revenue that affected the old railroads are still around in 2003 as Amtrak had lost money every year since it began. Of all of Amtrak's stations where its most passengers boarded in 2001, eight of its "top ten" were on the Northeast Corridor between Boston and Washington D.C. Of the top ten stations with the most boardings, three were in New Jersey. Newark, Trenton, and Princeton Junction were fifth, sixth, and ninth respectively. Amtrak lost $1.1 billion in 2001 and Congress gave it $205 million during 2002 to prevent a shutdown of the service.

With its trains, light rail, Newark City Subway, and buses, NJ Transit is the largest statewide system of public transportation in the U.S. Its operating budget for July 2002 through June 2003 was $1.22 billion. While NJT does have a deficit of several billion dollars there have been countless improvements to the system statewide. The $63 million Montclair Connection now allows Boonton Line passengers the ability to switch to Midtown Direct trains in Montclair. Without this project, Boonton Line passengers would have to ride into Hoboken after which the PATH was used to get to Midtown Manhattan. Outside of Hoboken, NJT is spending about $70 million in order to update the Lackawanna's 125 year old Bergen Hill Tunnel. After this tunnel is updated, the Lackawanna's second one built after 1900 will also be repaired. Its older stations are still being refurbished while new ones like the $10.2 million Union (Township) Station have opened. At the other end of N.J., work is currently underway on a new light rail system between Camden and Trenton. A dozen new German-made electric ALP-46 locomotives at a cost of $4.7 million each were just put into service on the Northeast Corridor. These locomotives can pull 12 passenger cars while the older electrics could handle only 9. This will also help with NJT's overcrowding problem since Sept. 11th. There is currently talk underway about bringing back passenger service on Conrail's old CNJ tracks between Lakehurst and Matawan. There might someday soon be a new light rail service between Elizabeth and Cranford on the old abandoned CNJ tracks through the area.

I thought that this was a good spot to end this book although the transportation system in the New Jersey area changes on a daily basis. People still drive cars along the same routes used by the Lenape. If you take the time to look carefully while driving it's easy to still see signs marked with names like the King George Post Road, the Old York Road, or Shunpike. People still cross the Hudson River between New Jersey and Manhattan on newer high speed ferryboats some 400 years after the first informal Dutch ones. People still travel through New Jersey by trains, buses, and cars just as the Lenape, Dutch, and English before. The transportation system in the state has evolved from Indian trails, cart paths, and sail ferries to steamboats, turnpikes, canals and steam railroads. These railroads then went to diesels or electrics, but soon had to compete with cars, trucks, buses, bridges, tunnels, interstate highways, and even airplanes. These same railroads pretty much all went bankrupt, but were "reborn" in the form of Amtrak, Conrail, and NJ Transit. While things are forever changing, everything from the Lenape's Minisink Trail to the Acela Express has a place in the story.

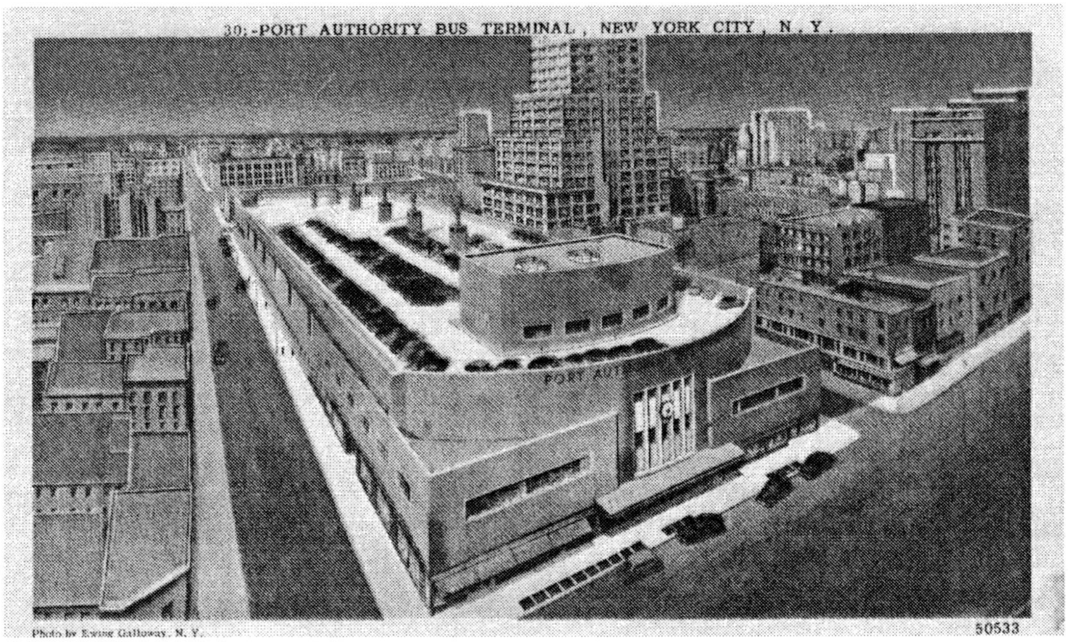
30:-PORT AUTHORITY BUS TERMINAL, NEW YORK CITY, N.Y.
Photo by Ewing Galloway, N. Y.
50533

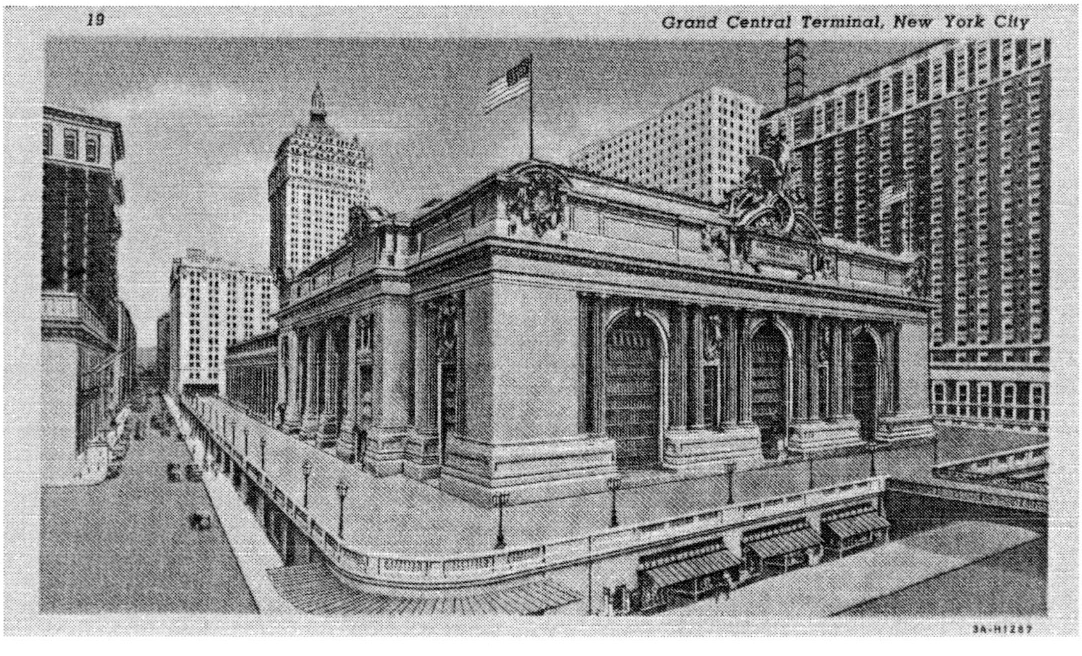
19
Grand Central Terminal, New York City

No
M27667
SERIES C
THE
NEW YORK CENTRAL
Railroad Company.
$ 1000.
REFUNDING AND IMPROVEMENT
MORTGAGE BOND.
PER 5 CENT.
DUE OCT. 1ST 2013.
INTEREST PAYABLE
APRIL 1ST AND OCTOBER 1ST
PRINCIPAL AND INTEREST PAYABLE
IN THE
City of New York.
TRUSTEE'S CERTIFICATE.
This bond is one of the issue of bonds of the series designated therein, described in the within-mentioned indenture.
Guaranty Trust Company of New York,
TRUSTEE,
VICE PRESIDENT,
ASSISTANT SECRETARY.
THE U.S. REVENUE TAX ON THIS BOND HAS BEEN PAID BY STAMPS AFFIXED TO THE MORTGAGE UNDER WHICH IT IS ISSUED,
AND DULY CANCELLED.

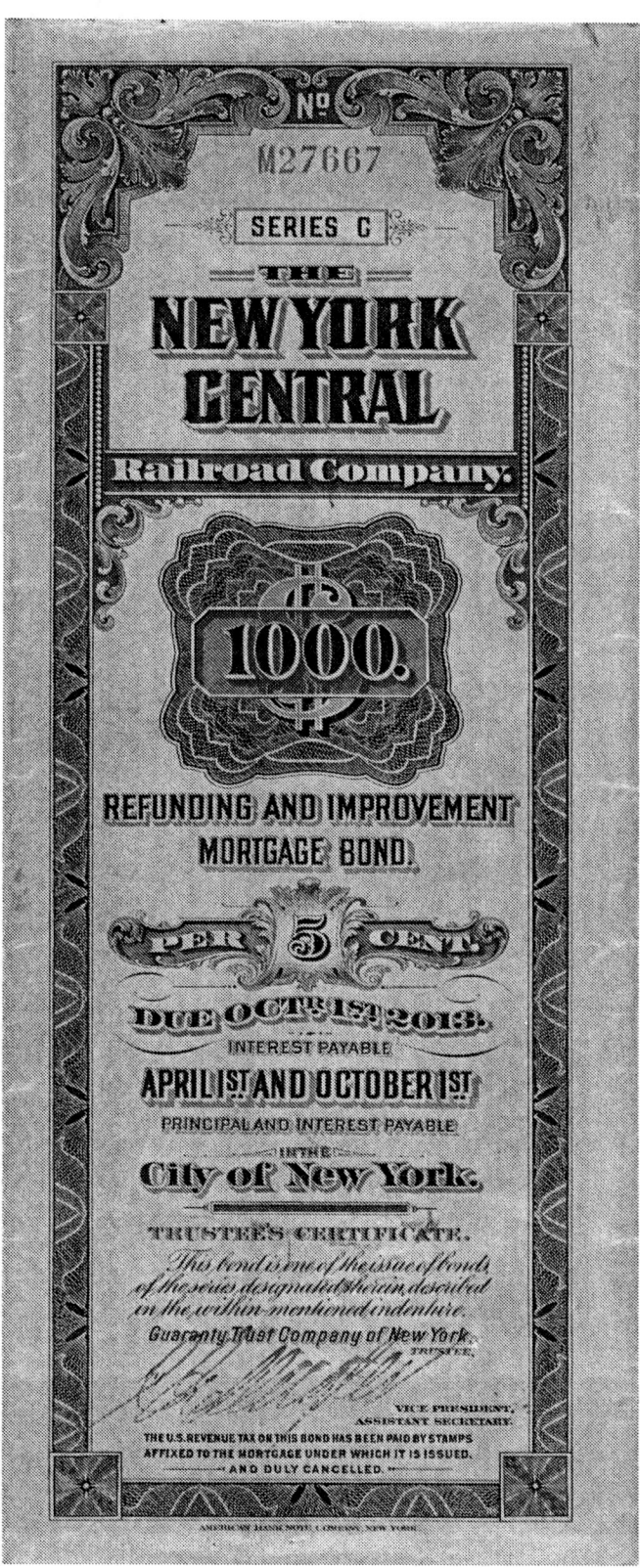

EFFECTIVE SEPTEMBER 30, 1934
CENTRAL RAILROAD
OF NEW JERSEY
THROUGH
TRAINS
N
ALLENTOWN
WILKES-BARRE
SCRANTON
NEW YORK
PHILADELPHIA
W
E
READING
HARRISBURG
ATLANTIC CITY
ASBURY PARK
LAKEWOOD
S
New
Jersey
Central
THE ROUTE OF "THE BLUE COMET"
T. T. 101
(44A)
20M
10-3-34
Order No. 16695

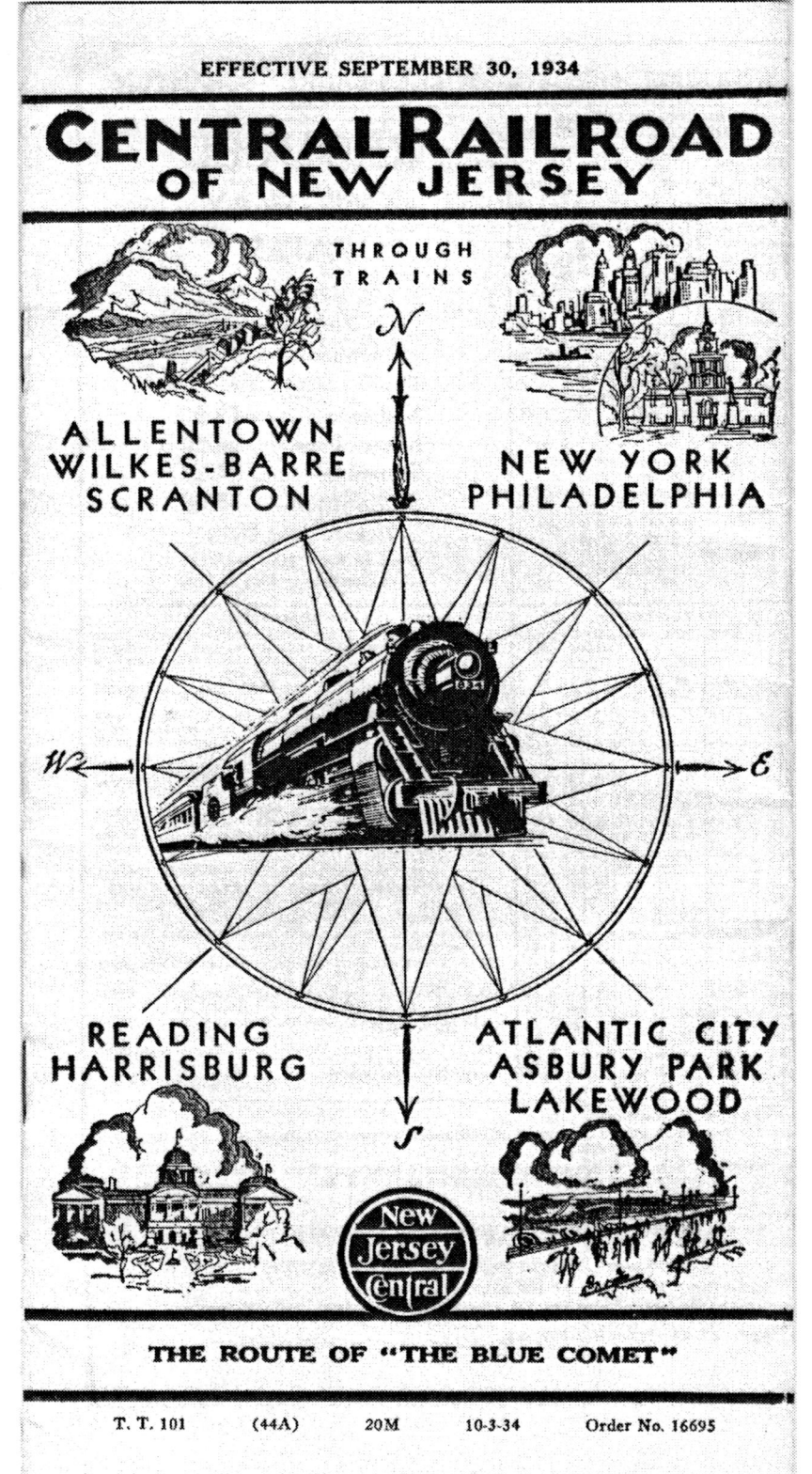

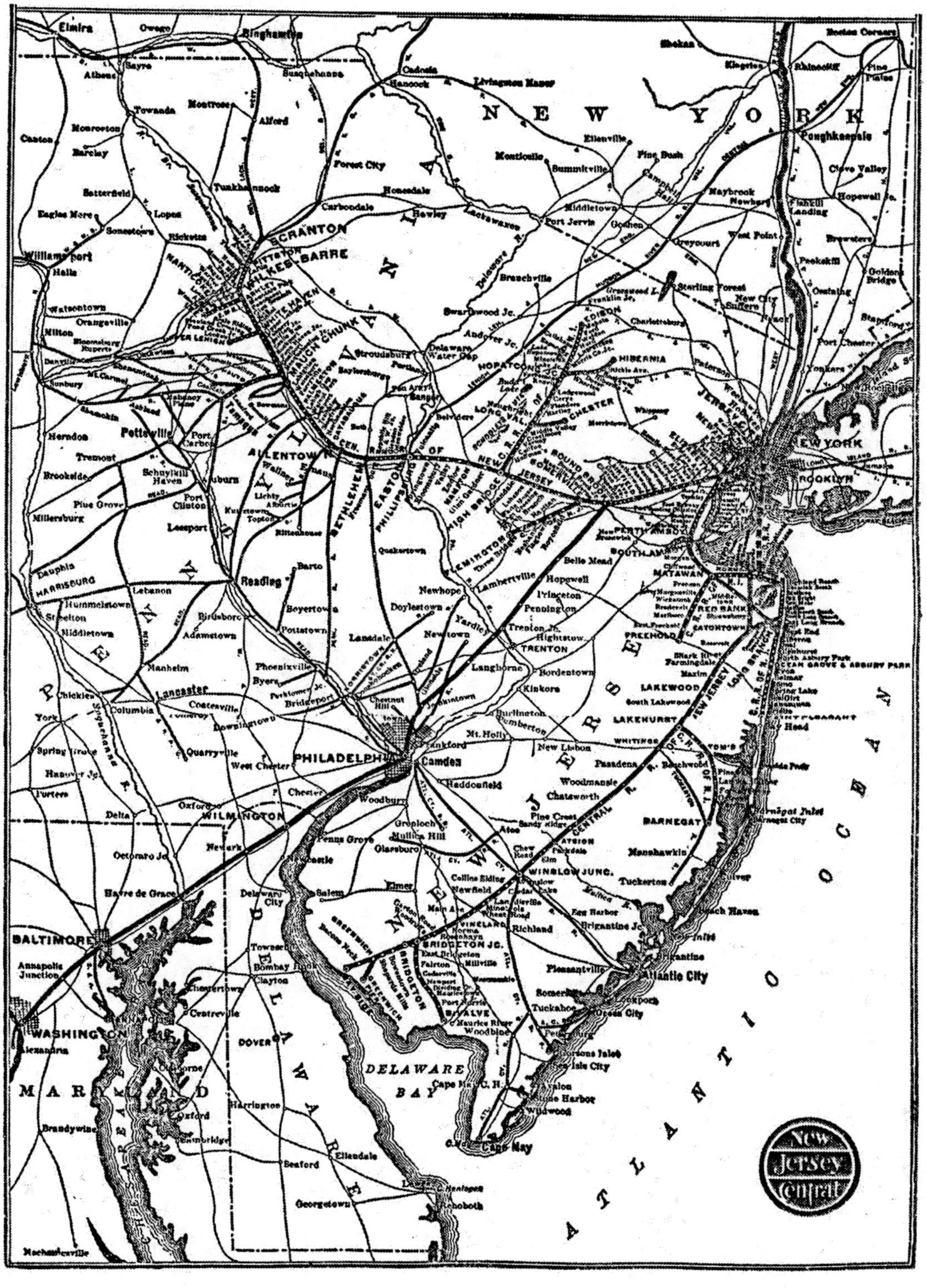
NEW YORK
PENNSYLVANIA
NEW JERSEY
MARYLAND
DELAWARE
ATLANTIC OCEAN
DELAWARE BAY
SCRANTON
WILKES-BARRE
ALLENTOWN
EASTON
BETHLEHEM
PHILLIPSBURG
NEW YORK
BROOKLYN
TRENTON
PHILADELPHIA
Camden
WILMINGTON
BALTIMORE
WASHINGTON
Atlantic City
Cape May
Reading
Harrisburg
Lancaster
Elmira
Binghamton
Poughkeepsie
Lakewood
Lakehurst
Matawan
Red Bank
Bridgeton
Vineland
Winslow Junc.
Barnegat
Tuckerton
Long Branch
Central R. R. of N. J.
New Jersey Central

NEW YORK
ERIE
ERIE RAILROAD
SYSTEM
AND CONNECTIONS

100 SHARES
H490542
100
Shares Without Par Value
Shares Without Par Value
THE NEW YORK CENTRAL RAILROAD COMPANY
This is to Certify that EDDY & CO. **
is the owner of ONE HUNDRED full paid
and non-assessable shares without nominal or par value of the capital stock of The New York Central Railroad Company transferable on the books of the Company in person or by duly authorized attorney upon the surrender of this certificate properly endorsed. This certificate is not valid until countersigned by the transfer agent and registered by the registrar.
Witness the seal of the Company and the signatures of its duly authorized officers this JUN 23 1953
CAPITAL STOCK
THE HANOVER BANK.

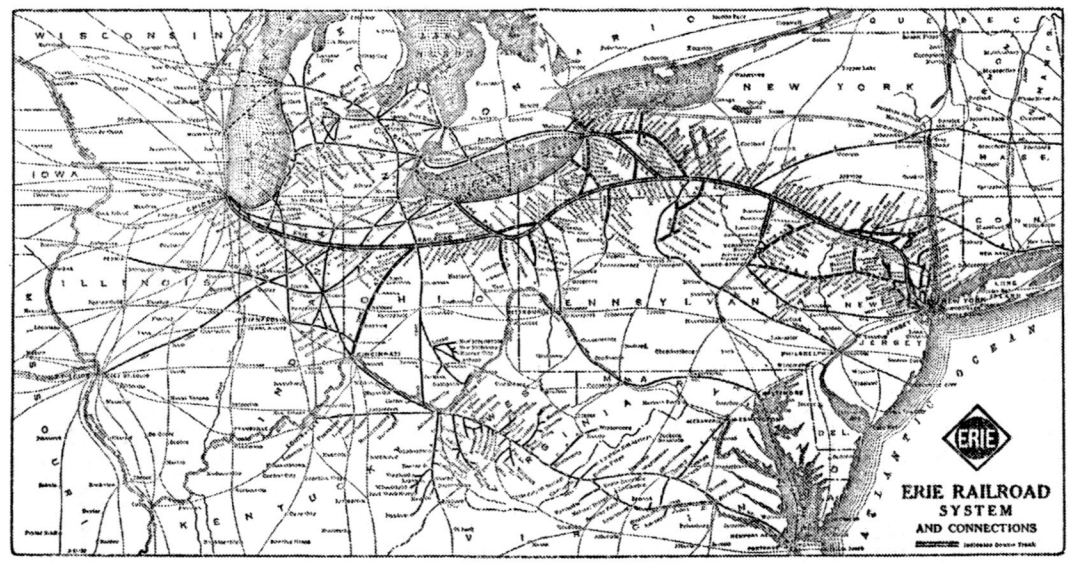

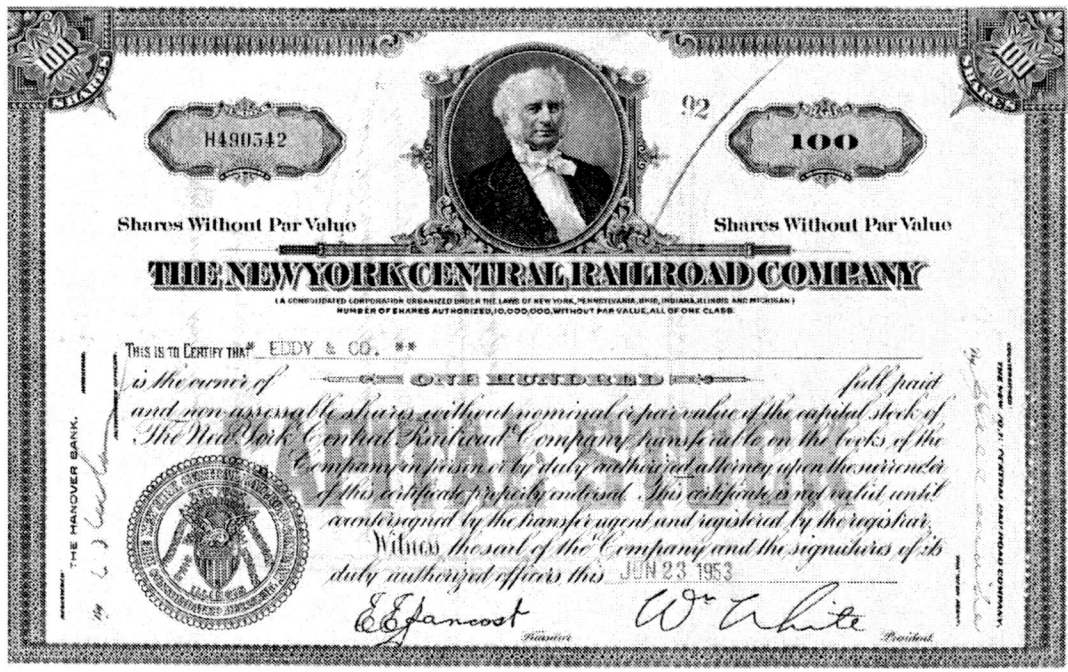

NUMBER
F 730353
SHARES
★10★
THE PENNSYLVANIA RAILROAD COMPANY
This Certifies that SOCIETE DE BANQUE SUISSE is an
entitled to TEN Shares in the
Capital Stock of The Pennsylvania Railroad Company, transferable only in person or by
Attorney on the books of the said Company.
Witness the Seal of the Company and the signatures of the President and Treasurer
Philadelphia, 19th July 1955
SHARES $50 EACH

M
THE PENNSYLVANIA RAILROAD COMPANY
F
Form L-661
H 36553
WEEKLY TICKET (Good only Sunday to Saturday inclusive of week for which issued)
Good for 12 continuous rides in either direction and for the sole use of purchaser whose signature is affixed hereto, and will be forfeited if tendered for any other person. Fares paid in the absence of this ticket will not be refunded. Subject to tariff regulations.
General Passenger Agent
RAHWAY, N. J. and
133
NEWARK, N. J.
NOT GOOD AFTER
SATURDAY
M
2 3 4 5 6 7 8 9 10 11
Conductor will lift for 12th Ride

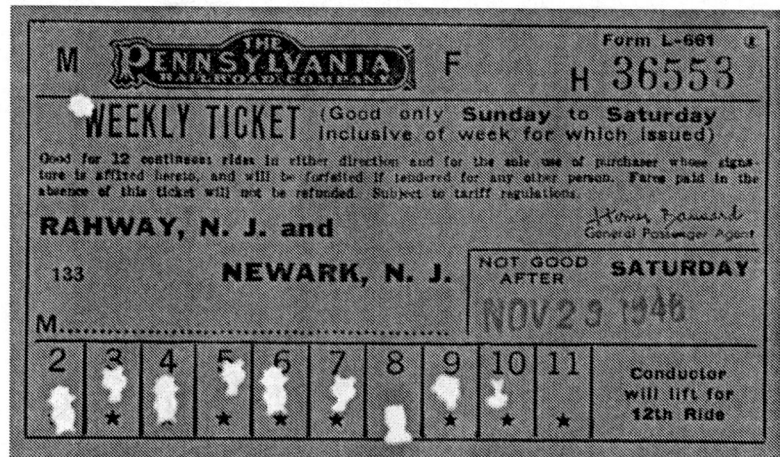

M
THE PENNSYLVANIA RAILROAD COMPANY
F
UNLIMITED-USE MONTHLY COMMUTATION TICKET
Good for unlimited number of rides in either direction, during the period for which issued.
FOR THE SOLE USE OF PURCHASER WHOSE PERSONAL SIGNATURE IS AFFIXED HERETO. This ticket will be forfeited if tendered for any other person. Subject to tariff regulations.
RAHWAY, N. J.
AND
NEWARK, N. J.
NOT GOOD AFTER
11 30
Form LC-115
(133)
4102
1948
1 2 3 4 5 6 7 8 9 10 11 12 13 14 15 16 17 18 19 20 21 22 23 24 25
26 27 28 29 30 31

PENNSYLVANIA RAILROAD

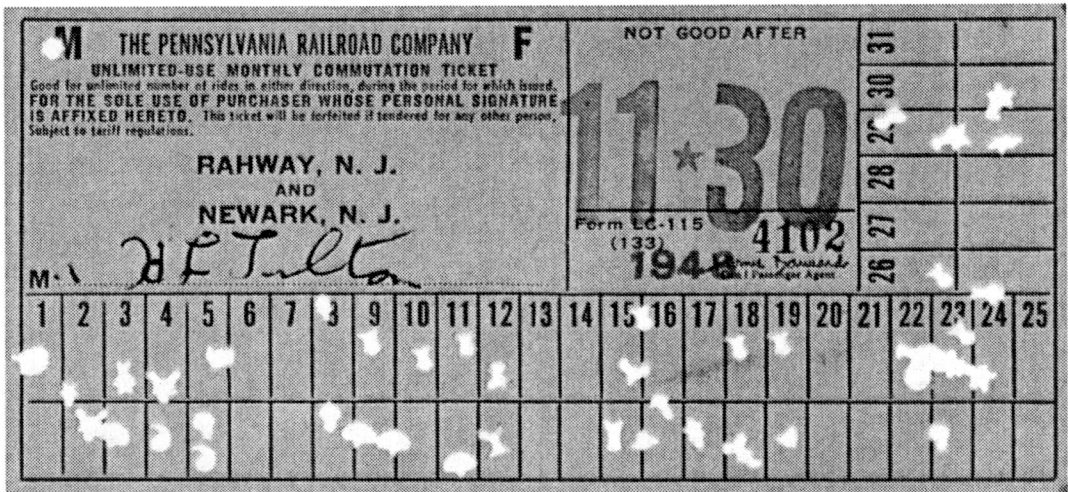

VACATION BOUND?

Travel on Lackawanna's

ALL-NEW LUXURY STREAMLINER

The Phoebe Snow

NEW Observation Tavern-Lounge Car

NEW Easy-Chair Coaches

NEW Spacious Dining Car

NEW Bedroom and Roomette Sleeping Car

Now in 2-Way Daily Service between

NEW YORK, NEWARK, SCRANTON, BINGHAMTON, ELMIRA and BUFFALO

Replete with *new* features, *new* styling and *new* appointments, THE PHOEBE SNOW sets a new high standard in modern travel luxury.

A glimpse of one of THE PHOEBE SNOW coaches reveals a whole new array of comforts and conveniences. Wide vista windows . . . individual reclining seats . . . over-sized luggage racks . . . fluorescent lights . . . circulating ice-water . . . individual vanity tables in the women's lounges . . . and other up-to-the-minute appointments.

For sociability and relaxation, THE PHOEBE SNOW offers a smart new Observation-Lounge Car with deep-cushioned club chairs facing the large picture-windows — and with a separate Tavern section and refreshment bar.

The beautiful and spacious Dining Car of THE PHOEBE SNOW, with its wide panoramic windows, Venetian blinds and colorful drapes, provides a perfect setting for those delicious home-style meals for which the Lackawanna long has been famous.

For overnight travel between New York and Chicago, the westbound PHOEBE SNOW carries a modern, *all-private-room* Sleeping Car, containing 10 roomettes and 6 double bedrooms. Features of these rooms include individual controls for lighting, heating and air-conditioning . . . wardrobe and shoe lockers . . . full-length mirrors . . . and other modern conveniences.

THE PHOEBE SNOW is the latest addition to the fleet of new equipment which Lackawanna is placing in service on mainline trains as part of its vast modernization program.

There's Nothing Lacking on the

Lackawanna Railroad

THE ROUTE OF PHOEBE SNOW

Michael E. Ferlise

REFRESHMENTS

—

Afternoon Tea   Fruit Juice

Assorted Fresh Fruit

Finger Sandwiches   Cookies

Cigars   Cigarettes

Beverages

Gingerale   White Rock

PENNSYLVANIA RAILROAD

Effective 2:01 A.M., October 26, 1958
LACKAWANNA RAILROAD
SUBURBAN TIME TABLES
AND RATES OF FARES
FOR ELECTRIC AND DIESEL-ELECTRIC TRAINS
LACKAWANNA
J. A. CRADDOCK, Superintendent, Hoboken, N. J.
W. H. DOMINICK, Passenger Traffic Manager
140 CEDAR STREET, NEW YORK 6, N. Y.
Lackawanna Railroad

THE LACKAWANNA RAILROAD
IN THE STATE OF
NEW JERSEY
Dingmans Ferry
Sussex
Branchville
Hamburg
Franklin
Ringwood
Lafayette
Branchville Jc.
Newton
Andover
Edison
Delaware Water Gap
Portland
Delaware
Bridgeville
Bangor
Belvidere
Oxford Furnace
Port Murray
Washington
Changewater
Hampton
Martin's Creek
Phillipsburg
High Bridge
Clinton
White House
Pittstown
Milford
Flemington
Hackettstown
Long Valley
Chester
Gladstone
Peapack
Kenvil
Succasunna
Dover
Denville
Mt. Tabor
Morris Plains
Montclair
Morristown
Convent
Madison
Chatham
Paterson
Passaic R.
Hoboken
New York
Staten Island
South Plainfield
Rahway
New Brunswick
Newark
CUT-OFF
LACK
N
E
W
J
E
R
S
E
Y

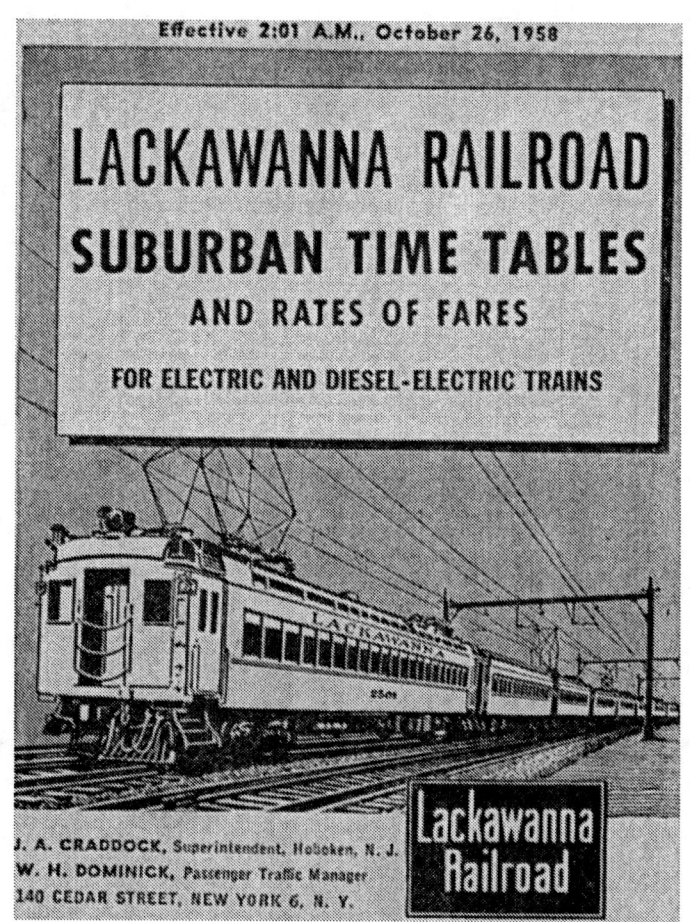

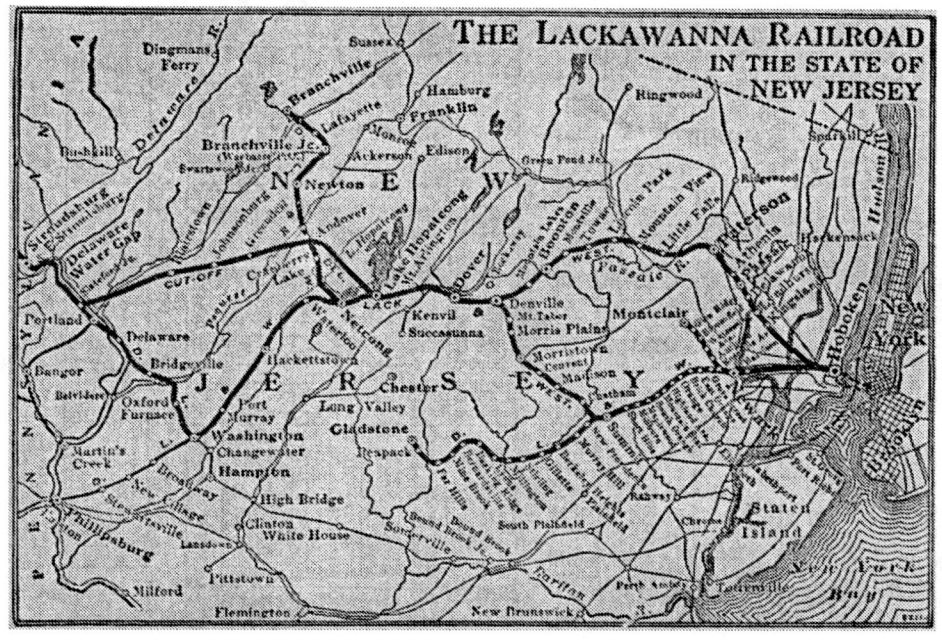

BROADWAY LIMITED

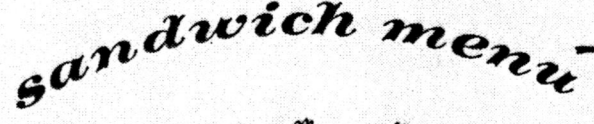

ALL SANDWICHES GARNISHED WITH PICKLE CHIPS AND TWO SLICES OF TOMATO
NO EXTRA CHARGE FOR TOASTED SANDWICHES
ALL SANDWICHES SERVED ON WHITE BREAD
RYE OR WHOLE WHEAT WILL BE SUBSTITUTED ON REQUEST

Cold Roast Beef....2.35

Open Faced Chopped Steak with Melted Cheese on Toast...1.75

Triple Decker Club...2.35

Ham and Cheese (*American or Swiss Cheese*), Lettuce...1.45

Open Faced Sliced Tomato, Egg and Anchovy...1.50

Cold Turkey with Lettuce & Mayonnaise...1.85

Sliced Cold Chicken and Ham with Lettuce...2.10

Swiss Cheese, Sliced Egg, Lettuce, Tomato...1.45

Imported Sardine...1.60

Ham with Lettuce...1.10

RUSSIAN OR MAYONNAISE DRESSING SERVED ON REQUEST

20-1-67

PENNSYLVANIA RAILROAD

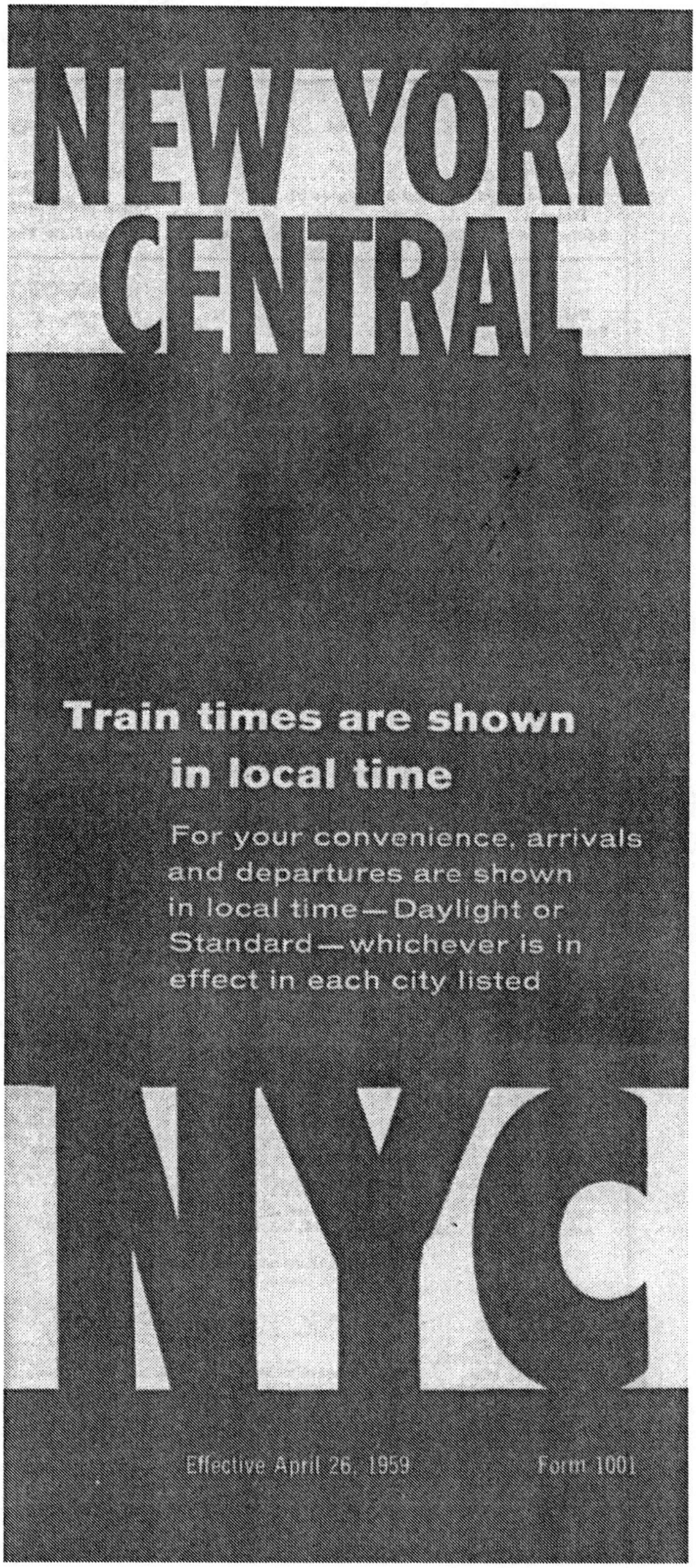
NEW YORK
CENTRAL
Train times are shown
in local time
For your convenience, arrivals
and departures are shown
in local time—Daylight or
Standard—whichever is in
effect in each city listed
NYC
Effective April 26, 1959
Form 1001

WISCONSIN
IOWA
ILLINOIS
MISSOURI
KENTUCKY
PENNSYLVANIA
NEW YORK
NEW YORK
Central

THE DELAWAR LACKAWANNA
AND WESTEN RAILROAD
AND THROUGCONNECTIONS
LAKE ONTRIO
LAKE SUPERIOR
OHIO
KENTUCKY
VACATION LAND
LACKAWANNA
NEW
JERSEY
M.D.
NEW YORK CITY

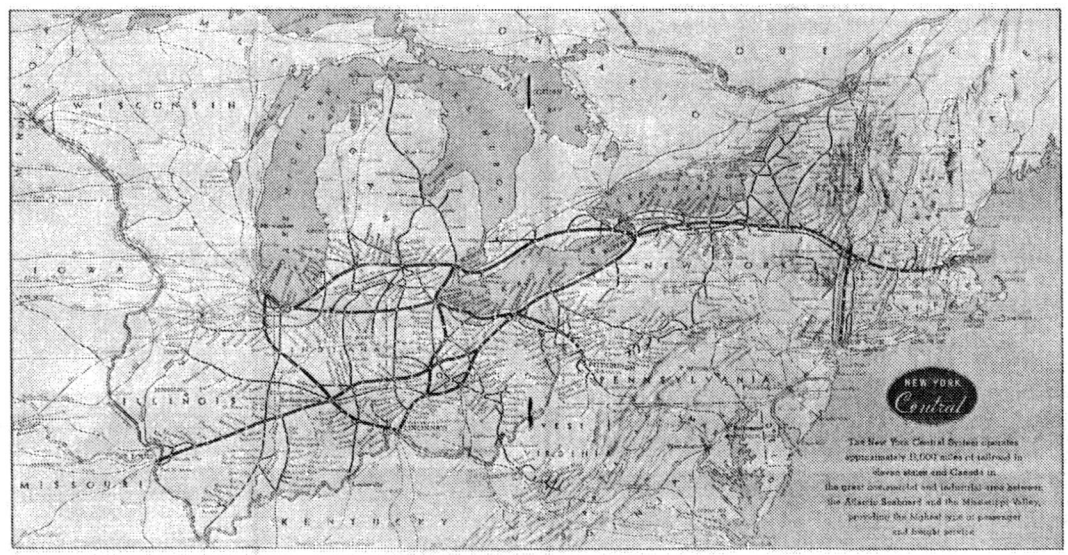

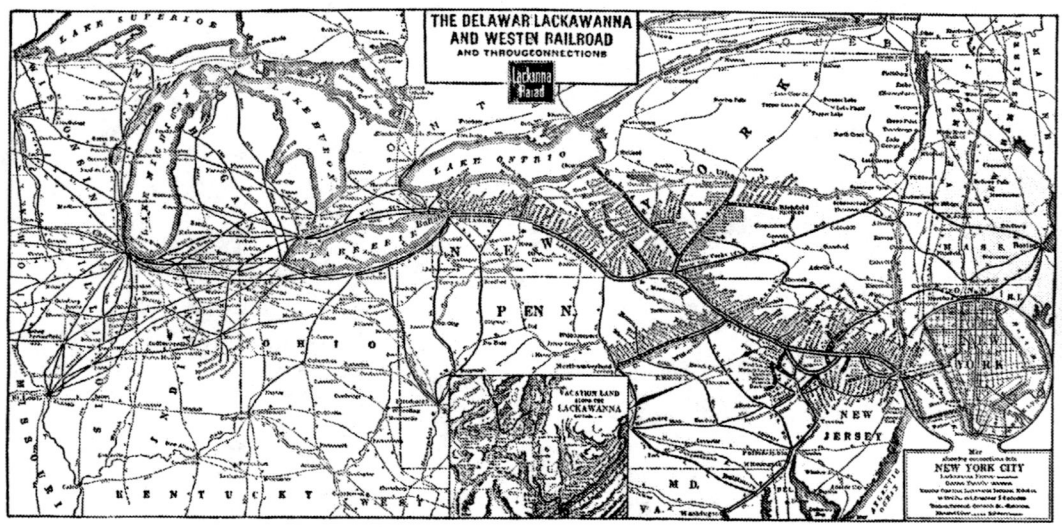

NEW YORK
Philadelphia
Wilmington Baltimore
WASHINGTON

Pennsylvania Railroad

TIME TABLE

Eastern Standard Time

Michael E. Ferlise

Pennsylvania Railroad

TIME TABLE

Eastern Standard Time

See more...
the safe, easy,
fun-way,
by train!

EFFECTIVE OCTOBER 30, 1966

NEW YORK
Philadelphia
Wilmington Baltimore
WASHINGTON
Pennsylvania Railroad
TIME TABLE
Eastern Daylight Time

Take The
PENNSY
To The Fair
the fast,
thrifty,
fun-
way!

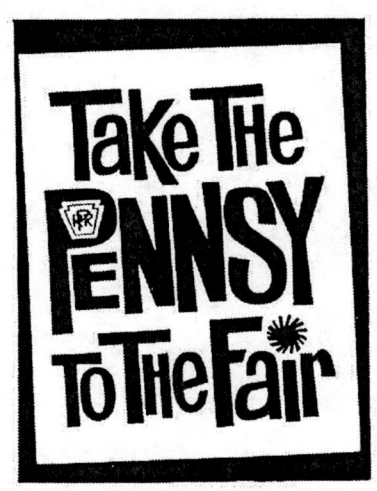

NEW YORK
Philadelphia
Wilmington Baltimore
WASHINGTON
Pennsylvania Railroad
TIME TABLE
Eastern Daylight Time
SHOWTIME IN NEW YORK
New York TheaTour Package includes Broadway shows, best hotels and sightseeing. Plans for 2 to 6 day visit. You name the shows. We'll go after the tickets! For complete information ask your Pennsy Ticket Agent about New York TheaTours.
DISCOVER AMERICA
See more . . . the safe, easy, fun-way, by train!

NEW YORK
Philadelphia
Wilmington Baltimore
WASHINGTON

Pennsylvania Railroad

TIME TABLE

Local Time

HOTEL
HARRINGTON

11th and E Sts., N.W. Washington, D.C.

MIDWAY BETWEEN THE CAPITOL AND THE WHITE HOUSE

Sample Rooms
Cafeteria
Singles from $9.75
Doubles from $11.00
In the Heart of the Business District

R. V. BRYCE
Managing Director
Phone NAtional 8-8140

300 ROOMS **COMPLETELY AIR CONDITIONED**

No. C 5014
SERIES A PREFERRED STOCK (5%)
SERIES A PREFERRED STOCK (5%)
ERIE-LACKAWANNA RAILROAD COMPANY
This is to Certify that
HARRY E. HAMILTON & MARGARET E HAMILTON JT TEN WROS
is the owner of
FIFTY
FULLY PAID AND NON-ASSESSABLE SHARES OF THE PAR VALUE OF $100 EACH OF THE SERIES A PREFERRED STOCK (5%)
MORGAN GUARANTY TRUST COMPANY OF NEW YORK
THE FIRST NATIONAL CITY BANK OF NEW YORK
NOV 16 1962

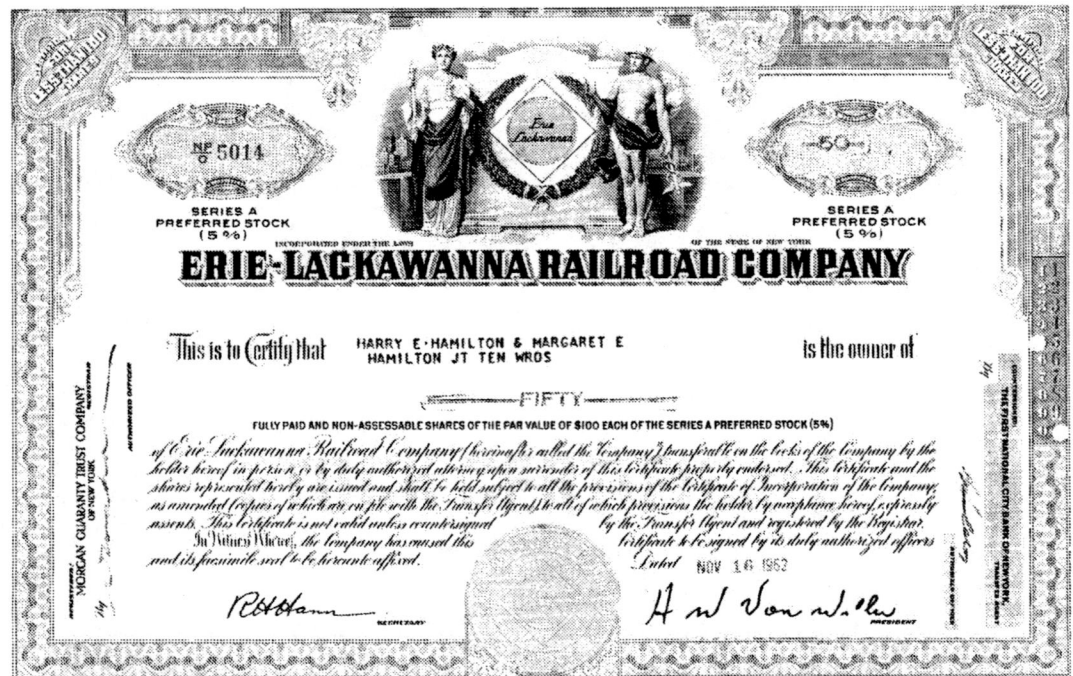

Food and Refreshment Services Provided on

The 20th Century Limited

Located just behind the rear sleepercoach, the mid-train lounge is yours to enjoy. The waiter assigned to this section of the double-unit dining car will be glad to serve your favorite beverage.

In the dining area, the COACH GRILL features a complete dinner for $2.95 (or a steak dinner for only $3.25), as well as sandwiches and other a la carte items.

For those who prefer more formal dining, THE CENTURY ROOM offers a luxurious service. Gentlemen patronizing this room will please wear jackets.

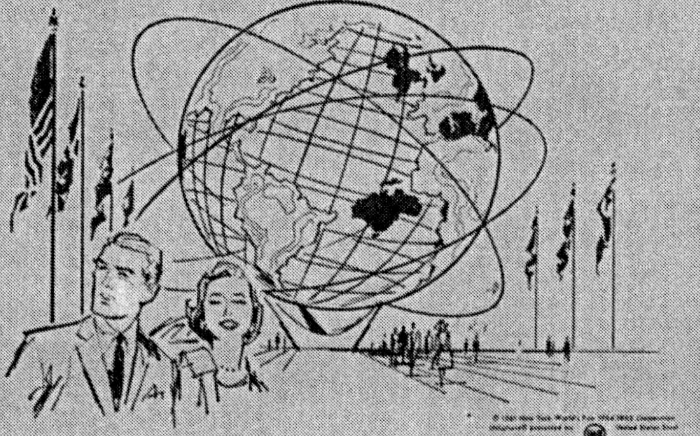

New York World's Fair 1964

Make plans now to go the easiest way imaginable . . . on the Pennsy!

It's only 12 min. from PRR's Penn Station to the Fair's Main Gateway via Long Island Rail Road

only 50c!

IT'S A NEVER-TO-BE-FORGOTTEN EXPERIENCE—a visit to the New York World's Fair. The vast range of exhibits seem to span every conceivable subject, from a Hong Kong garden to expositions on man's daring plans to journey forth among the stars.

In addition to exhibits that present the industrial, scientific, cultural, and spiritual heritage of our world (and an astonishing glimpse of the unfolding tomorrow) there are also the joys of the moment: Exotic restaurants, sports contests, theatrical performances, and a vast lake amusement area that's skirted by an elevated monorail.

And remember, the easiest way to get there is on the Pennsylvania Railroad.

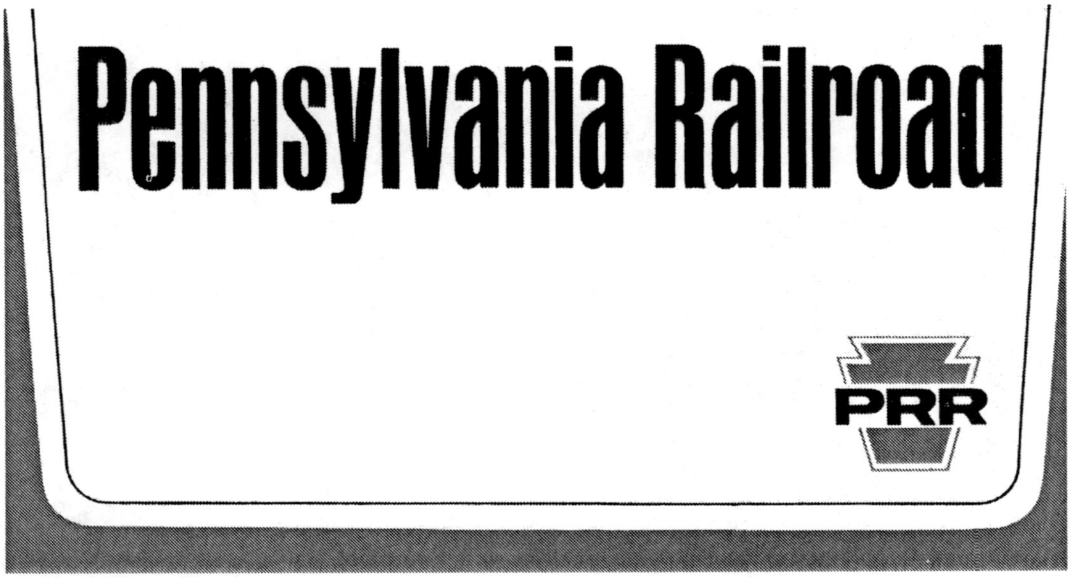

Michael E. Ferlise

Pennsylvania Railroad

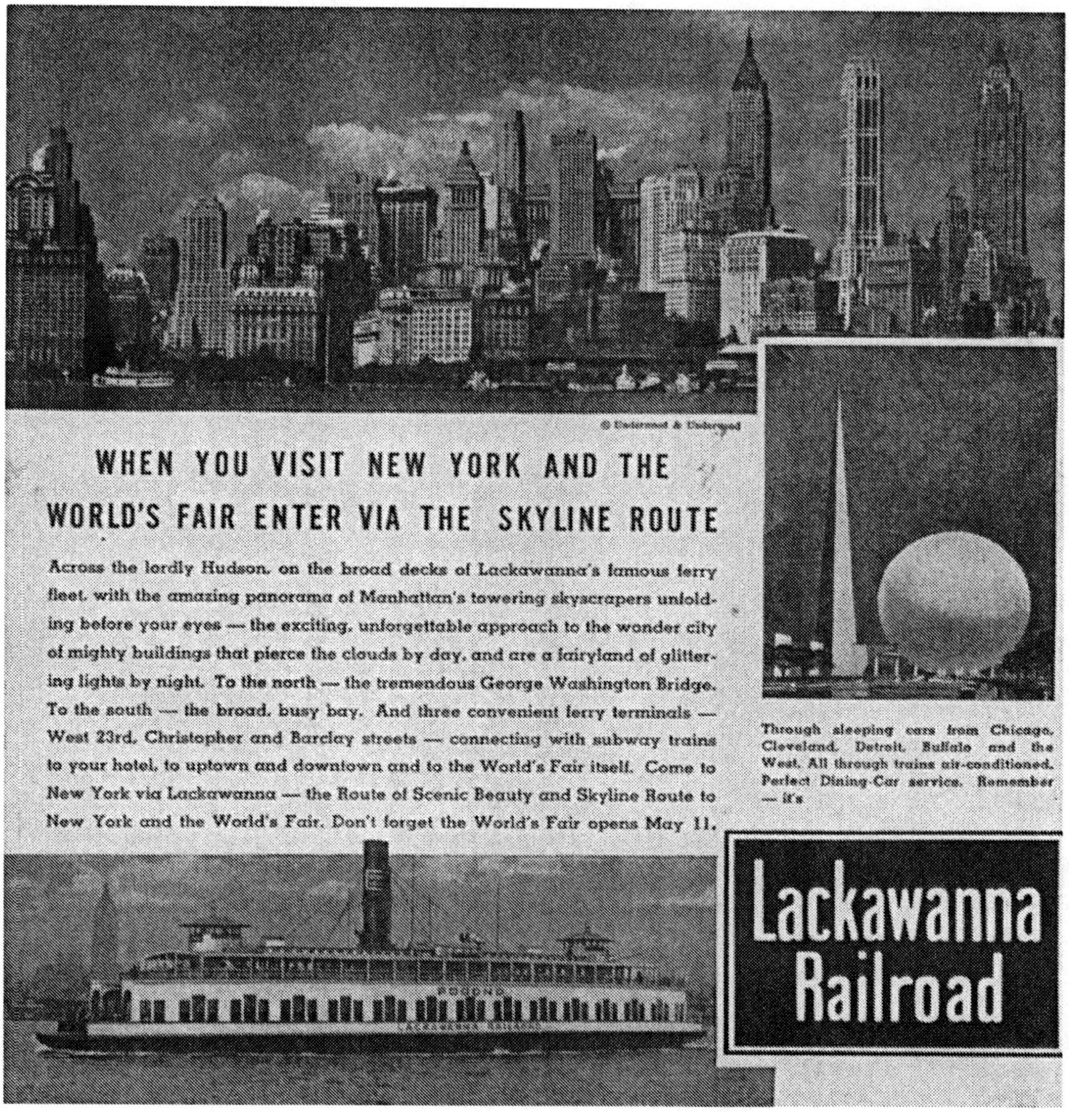
© Underwood & Underwood
WHEN YOU VISIT NEW YORK AND THE WORLD'S FAIR ENTER VIA THE SKYLINE ROUTE
Across the lordly Hudson, on the broad decks of Lackawanna's famous ferry fleet, with the amazing panorama of Manhattan's towering skyscrapers unfolding before your eyes — the exciting, unforgettable approach to the wonder city of mighty buildings that pierce the clouds by day, and are a fairyland of glittering lights by night. To the north — the tremendous George Washington Bridge. To the south — the broad, busy bay. And three convenient ferry terminals — West 23rd, Christopher and Barclay streets — connecting with subway trains to your hotel, to uptown and downtown and to the World's Fair itself. Come to New York via Lackawanna — the Route of Scenic Beauty and Skyline Route to New York and the World's Fair. Don't forget the World's Fair opens May 11.
Through sleeping cars from Chicago, Cleveland, Detroit, Buffalo and the West. All through trains air-conditioned. Perfect Dining-Car service. Remember — it's
Lackawanna Railroad

Next time your husband goes to New York or Chicago he'll probably do something he shouldn't.

He'll get into a tizzy.

All that rushing about. Zipping out at the speed of sound. Zipping back. Airport traffic. Trays on the knee. Cramped space. It's enough to drive a husband psycho.

All of which could have been avoided if he'd taken the Broadway Limited.

The Broadway Limited doesn't go at the speed of sound. It goes at the speed of a train. It <u>is</u> a train, in fact.

It takes a whole night to get there. But that's not its only advantage.

For one, your husband will be comfortable. We've solved the legroom problem by eliminating the other legs. All rooms are private and come in six sizes. Useful for sleeping, relaxing, working and contemplation of the countryside.

For another, he'll have a real choice of real food. Served on real plates on real tables.

Two club cars will give him an opportunity to meet other businessmen. And time to discuss important matters.

Of course, he'll be away from you a little longer. But he'll be much nicer when he comes back.

On second thought, why not go along with him for the ride? At half fare.

The Broadway Limited between New York and Chicago

NEW YORK CENTRAL SYSTEM
Twentieth Century Limited

VALET SERVICE

Clothing Sponged and Pressed
(Apply to Porter)

Suit	$1.25
Overcoat	1.25
Coat	.75
Trousers	.50
Vest	.25
Lady's Skirt (Plain)	1.00
Lady's Skirt (Pleated)	1.25
Lady's Coat	1.25
Lady's Dress	1.25

NOTICE!

TO OUR PASSENGERS DESTINED FOR POINTS IN CANADA AND MICHIGAN:

A diner-lounge car is assigned to the Empire State Express from New York to Buffalo. This car features a choice of hot meals as well as a variety of a la carte items and refreshments.

Beyond Buffalo, a parlor-buffet-lounge car is operated. Snacks and sandwiches are served in this car.

NEW YORK CENTRAL SYSTEM

ROAD TO THE FUTURE

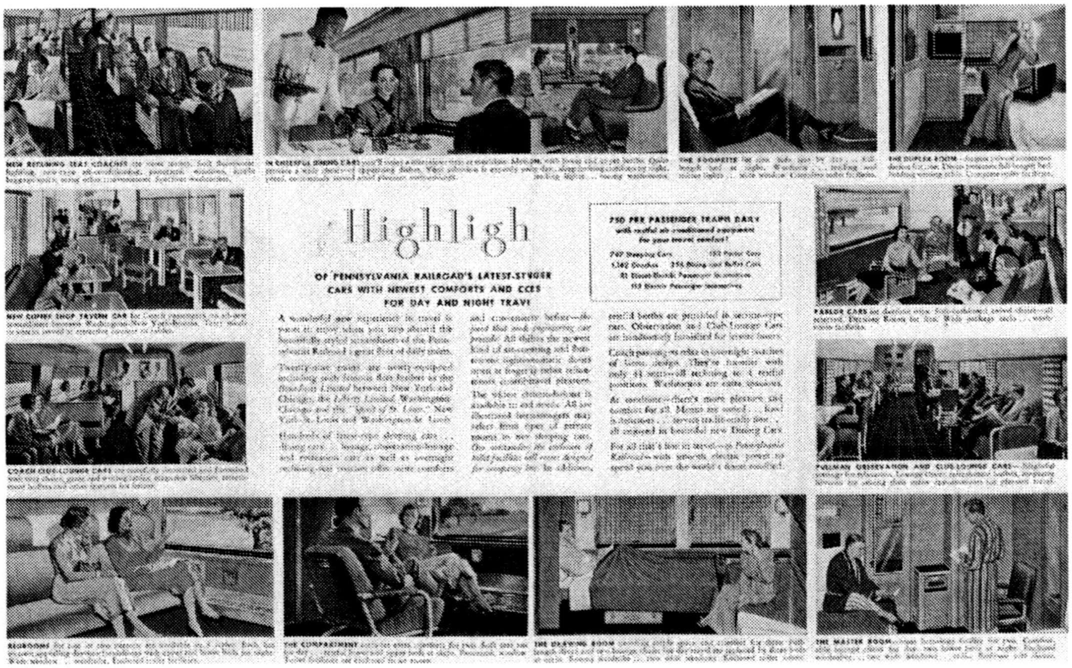
Highligh
OF PENNSYLVANIA RAILROAD'S
CARS WITH NEWEST COMFORTS AND
FOR DAY AND NIGHT

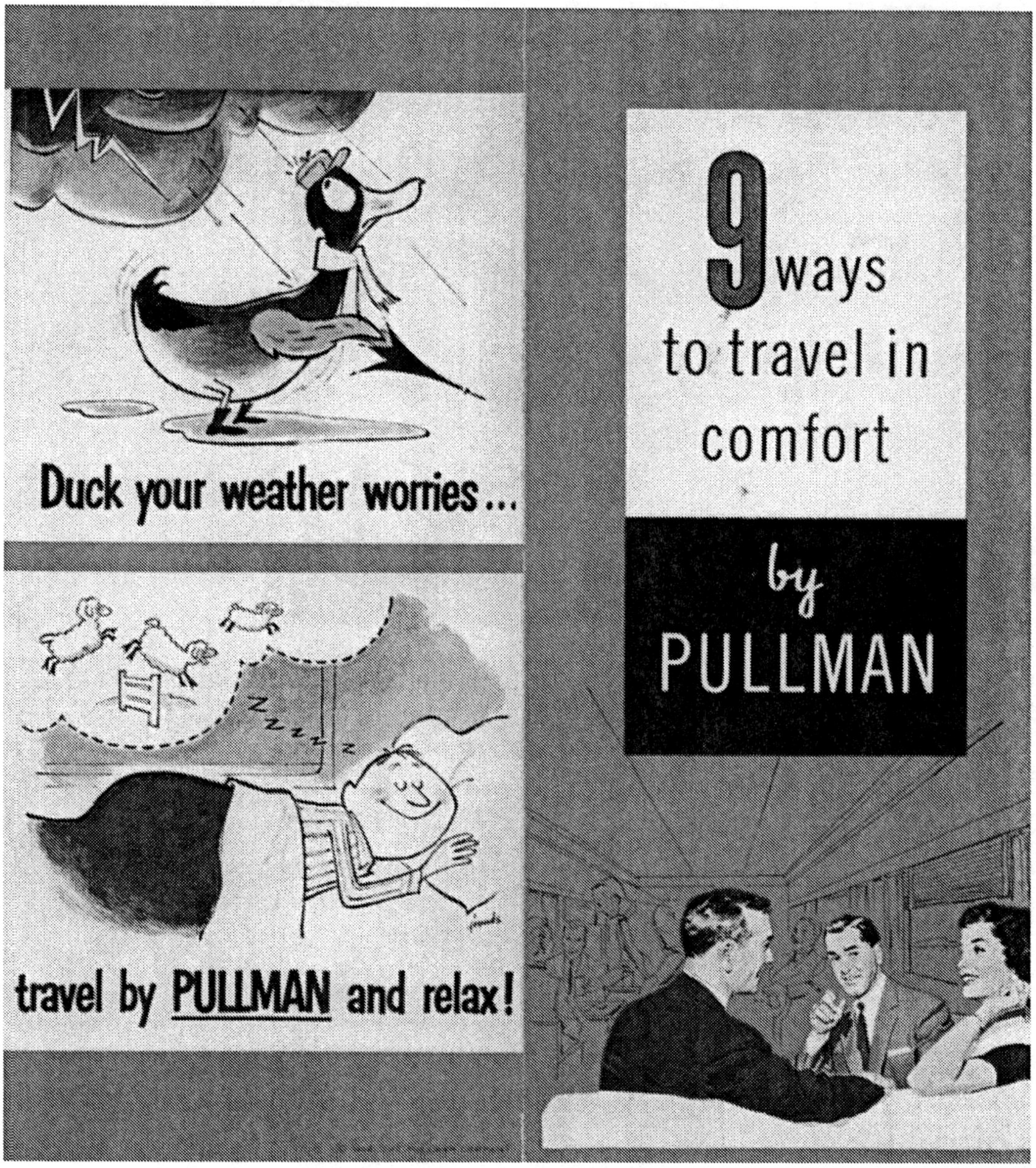
Duck your weather worries...
travel by PULLMAN and relax!
9 ways
to travel in
comfort
by
PULLMAN

HERE ARE NINE OF THE COMFORTABLE PULLMAN ACCOMMODATIONS:

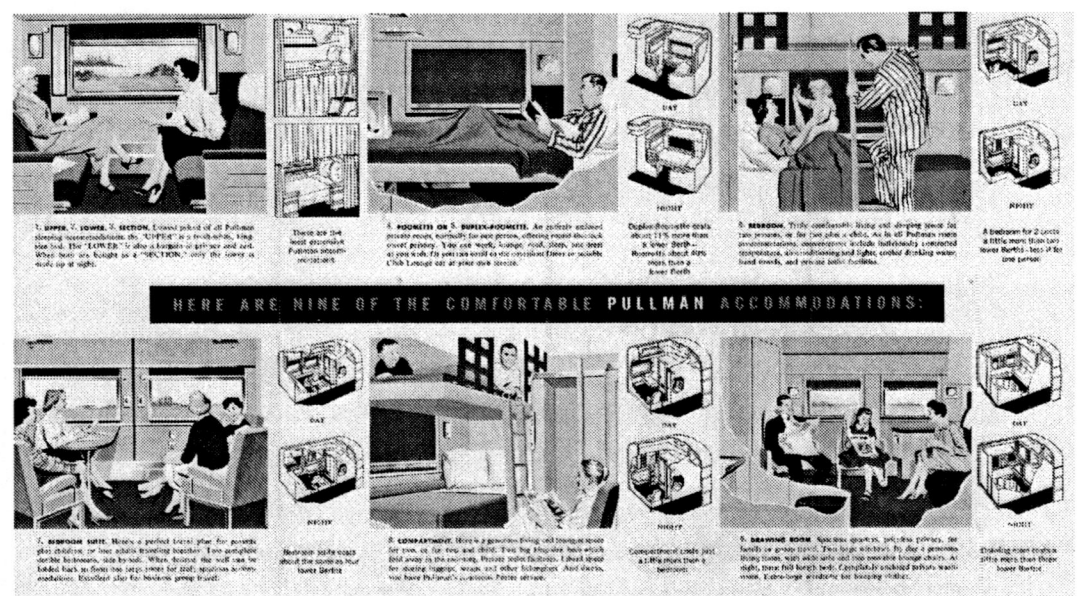

THE NEW HIGH-SPEED CORRIDOR TRAIN
Comfortable, quiet and safe at 160 mph
THE Budd COMPANY

Ultra-modern and luxurious, parlor car interiors feature the ultimate in passenger comfort and service. Easy chairs, in-seat dining, soft lights and carpets are just a few of the parlor car comforts and conveniences.

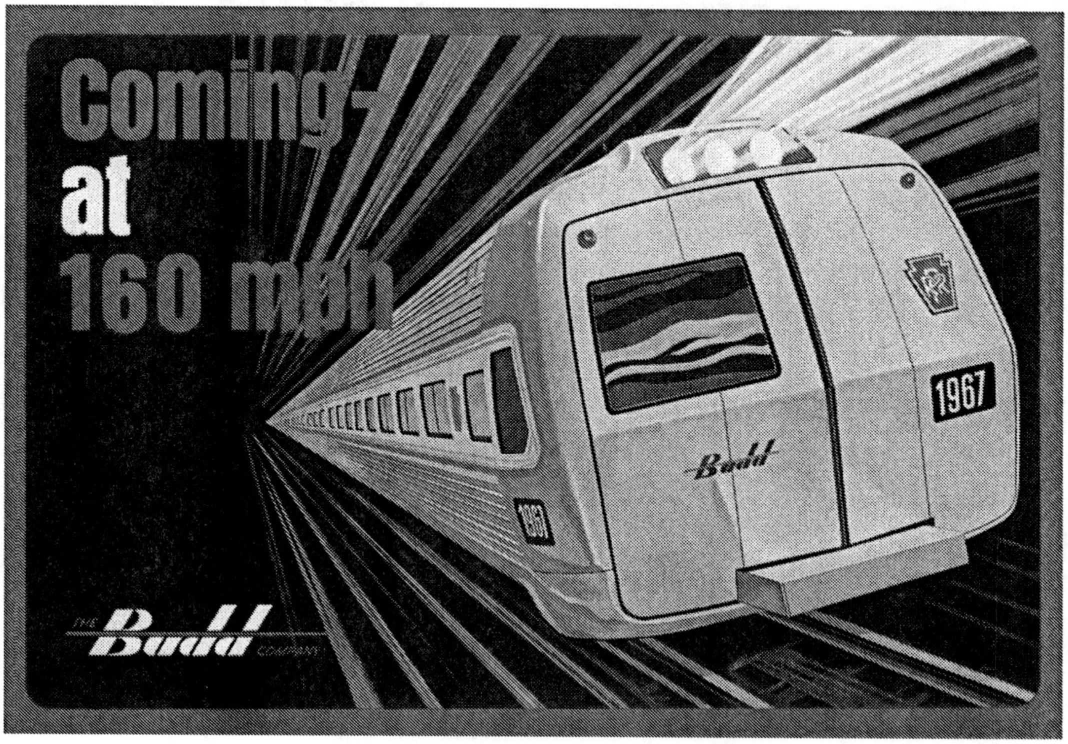
Coming -
at
160 mph
1967
Budd
1967
THE Budd COMPANY

EFFECTIVE 2.01 A.M.
APRIL 24, 1966

ERIE
LACKAWANNA
time table

the Friendly Service Route

BETWEEN
**NEW YORK · THE POCONOS · SCRANTON · BINGHAMTON · ELMIRA
BUFFALO · JAMESTOWN · YOUNGSTOWN · CLEVELAND · AKRON · CHICAGO**

ERIE LACKAWANNA RAILROAD

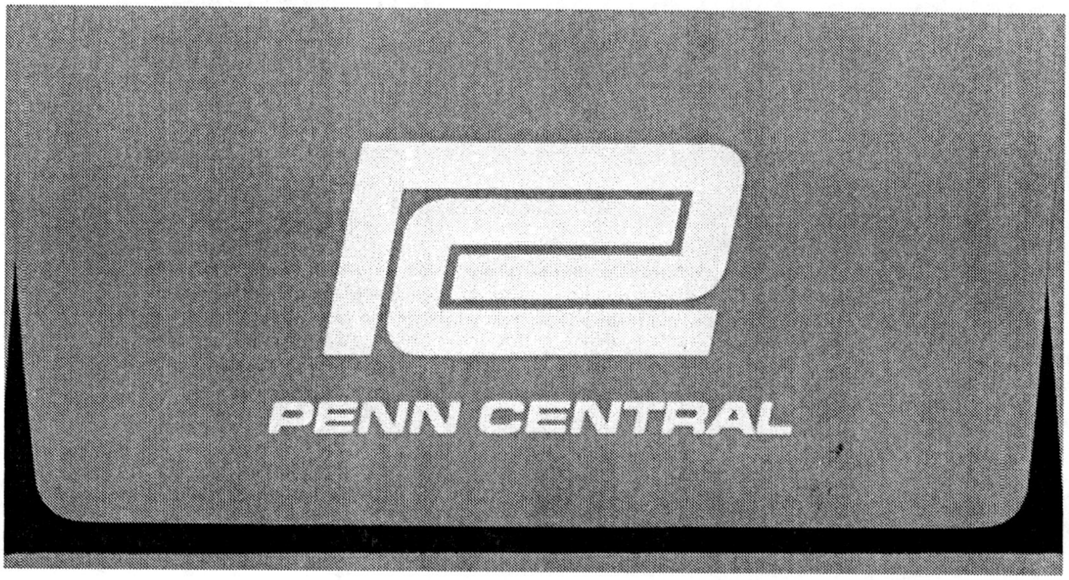
PENN CENTRAL

EMPIRE SERVICE

An attendant has been assigned to this train, with the following items for sale:

Orange Juice .25   Tomato Juice .25

Sliced Ham Sandwich .60

American Cheese Sandwich .55

Danish Pastry .25

Potato Chips .15   Peanuts .10

Coffee .20   Milk .20

Alcoholic Beverages, Soft Drinks, etc.

Scotch, Bourbon, Canadian
or Blended Whiskey 1.00
*(served with club soda or ginger ale
at no extra charge)*

Manhattan, Martini or Vodka Martini 1.00
(served "on the rocks" style)

Vodka and Tonic or Gin and Tonic 1.00

Beer (12 oz. can) .55   Ale (12 oz. can) .60

Soft Drinks (12 oz. can) .35

PENN CENTRAL

Effective October 26, 1969
PENN CENTRAL
EAST WEST TIMETABLE
Effective October 26, 1969
PENN CENTRAL
EAST WEST TIMETABLE
MONTREAL
TORONTO
SYRACUSE
BUFFALO
ALBANY
BOSTON
DETROIT
CHICAGO
TOLEDO
FORT WAYNE
CLEVELAND
NEW YORK
LOGANSPORT
COLUMBUS
HARRISBURG
INDIANAPOLIS
PITTSBURGH
PHILADELPHIA
BALTIMORE
WASHINGTON
CINCINNATI
ST. LOUIS
LOUISVILLE
N
W
E
S

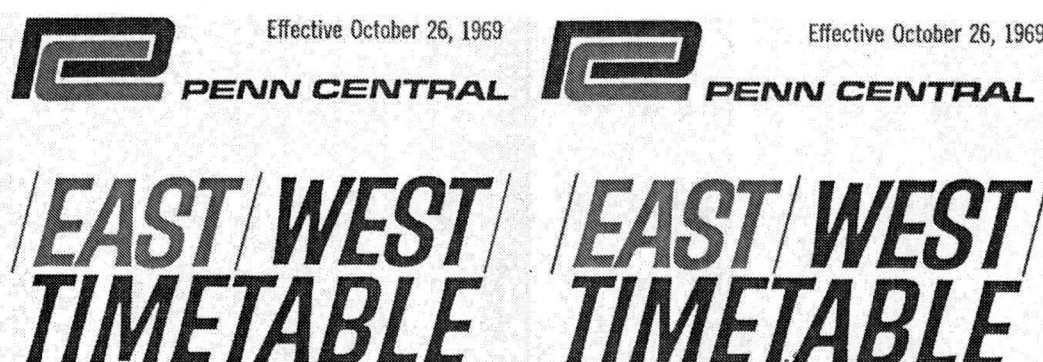

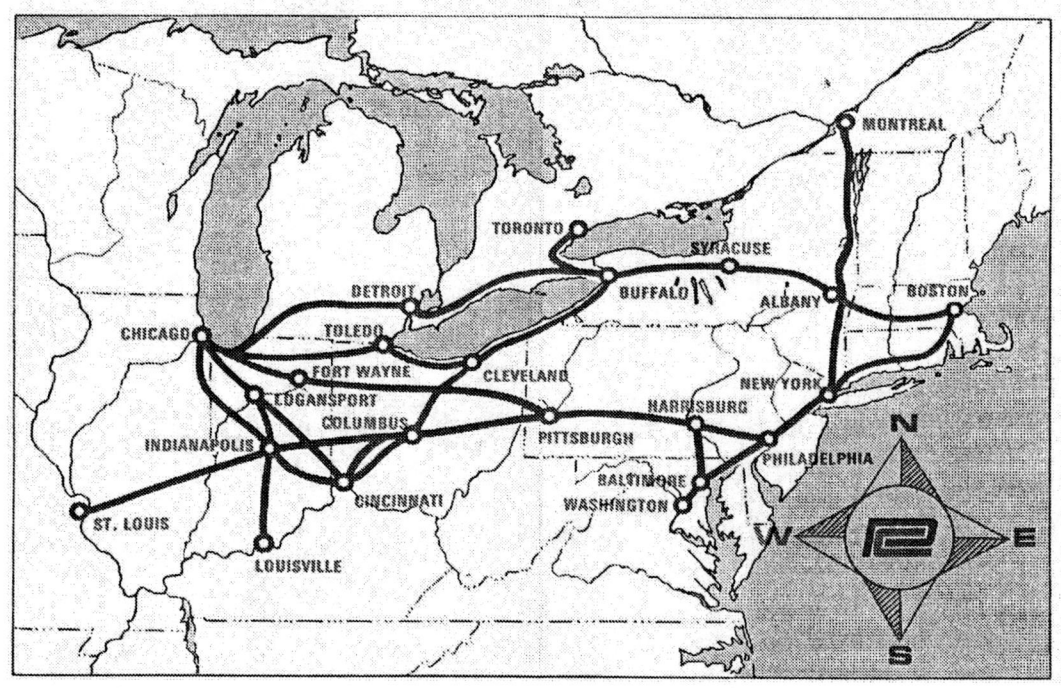

TIMETABLE

The Metroliners

NEW YORK
NEWARK • TRENTON
PHILADELPHIA
WILMINGTON • BALTIMORE
WASHINGTON

Effective February 10, 1969

	2001 DAILY	2003 DAILY
	AM	PM
NEW YORK Lv	8:30	4:15
NEWARK .... "	c 8:44	c 4:29
TRENTON .... "	9:18	5:03
PHILADELPHIA ...... " Penn Central Station—30th St.	9:46	5:31
WILMINGTON .... "	10:10	5:55
BALTIMORE .... "	10:57	6:42
WASHINGTON ....Ar	11:29 AM	7:14 PM

	2002 DAILY	2000 DAILY
	AM	PM
WASHINGTON Lv	8:20	3:55
BALTIMORE .... "	8:52	4:27
WILMINGTON .... "	9:37	5:12
PHILADELPHIA ...... " Penn Central Station—30th St.	10:00	5:35
TRENTON .... "	10:29	6:04
NEWARK ....Ar	d 11:06	d 6:41
NEW YORK ....Ar	11:19 AM	6:54 PM

c Stops only to receive passengers
d Stops only to discharge passengers

Trenton does not sell tickets to Newark.
Newark does not sell tickets to Trenton.

Trains listed above are subject to change or cancellation without notice.

Building Better Transit for Tomorrow

PATH passengers travelling to and from lower Manhattan soon will be using the ultra-modern rail transit terminal now nearing completion within the foundations of The World Trade Center. Located just west of the existing 61-year-old Hudson Terminal, which it will replace, the PATH World Trade Center Terminal is scheduled to be completed in mid-1971.

The World Trade Center, being built by The Port of New York Authority and to be completed in stages between 1970 and 1973, features two 110-story tower buildings devoted to international commerce and other governmental activities. Construction of the new PATH terminal, an integral part of the project, has moved ahead in conjunction with World Trade Center building contracts. PATH service to the existing Hudson Terminal is being maintained while the work goes on.

Longer and wider platforms will permit longer trains and provide increased passenger comfort.

The Penn Central
ground shuttle:

New York NEWARK TRENTON

Philadelphia

WILMINGTON   BALTIMORE

Washington

Effective Date: May 17, 1970

*Including
The Metroliners*

Amtrak

New York NEWARK TRENTON

Philadelphia

WILMINGTON-BALTIMORE-CAPITAL BELTWAY

Washington

Effective Date: June 7, 1971

The intercity trains shown herein are
operated by the Penn Central Transportation Company under contract for the
NATIONAL RAILROAD PASSENGER COR-
PORATION.

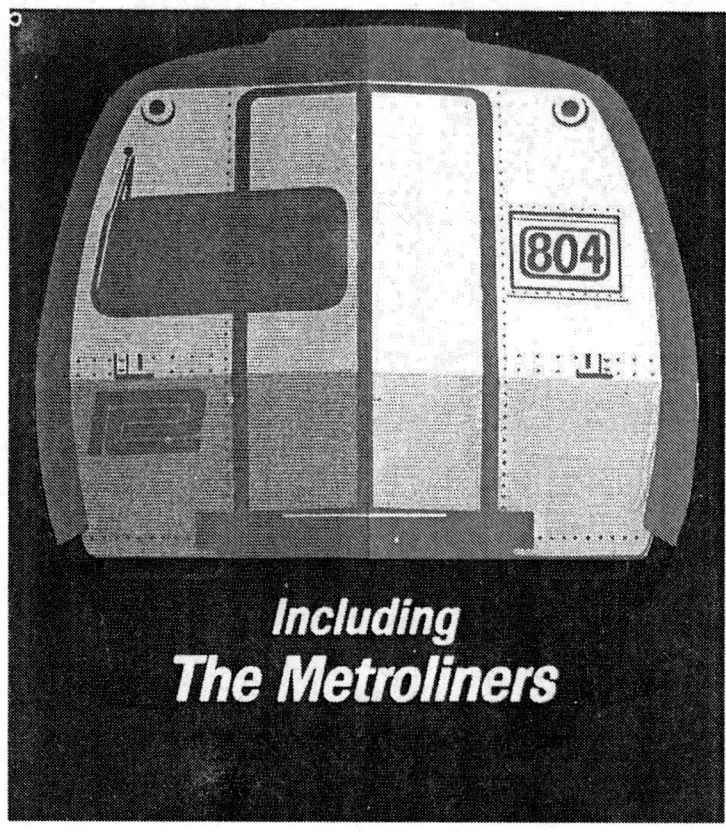

Including
The Metroliners

22
WEEK ENDING: JUNE 5, 1971
22

Erie Lackawanna Railway Company
WEEKLY COMMUTATION TICKET
Good for unlimited rides during calendar week shown between Hoboken and
BASKING RIDGE
FOR THE EXCLUSIVE USE OF PURCHASER WHOSE SIGNATURE MUST BE AFFIXED BELOW
INSERT IN SEAT CLIP
INSERT IN SEAT CLIP
M..
INFORMATION ON REVERSE SIDE
IT IS NECESSARY TO DISPLAY THIS TICKET IN SEAT CLIP FOR ENTIRE JOURNEY
TAKE TICKET WITH YOU WHEN YOU LEAVE TRAIN
Form WC
20
R.H. Taylor

22
WEEK ENDING: JUNE 5, 1971
22

Amtrak
Amtrak
829

PASSENGER'S NAME
DESTINATION
DEPARTURE TIME
CAR NUMBER SEAT NUMBER
GATE NUMBER

Amtrak

National Railroad Passenger Corporation

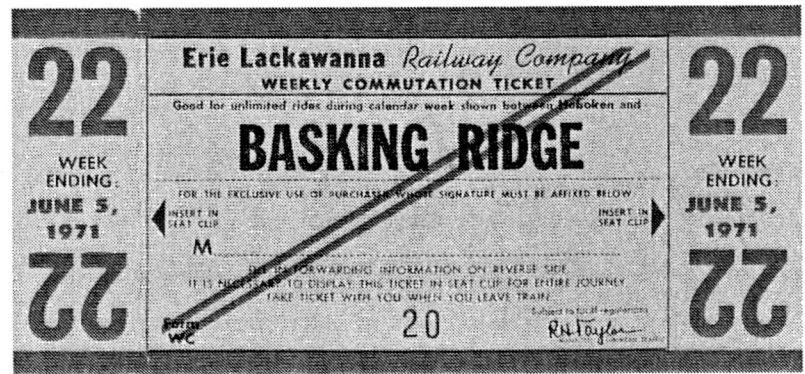

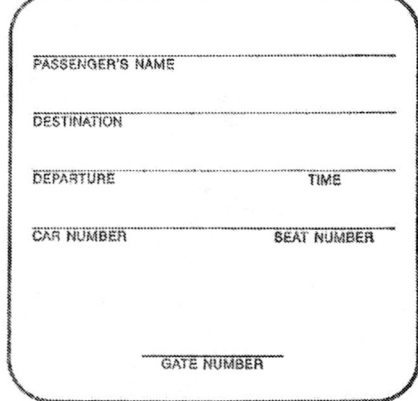

NEW YORK & LONG BRANCH RAILROAD

TIME TABLE NO. 370

In Effect

Sunday, October 29, 1972
at 0301 HOURS

Eastern Standard Time

FOR THE GOVERNMENT OF EMPLOYES ONLY

C. H. ALLEN Vice President and Gen. Mgr.	G. R. FULLER General Superintendent
J. A. CONNELLY Director of Passenger Operations	D. N. NELSON Superintendent

SAFETY ALWAYS
Make this railroad the safest on which to work and travel.

NEW YORK & LONG BRANCH RAILROAD

TIME TABLE NO. 373

In Effect
Sunday, October 27, 1974
at 0301 HOURS

Eastern Standard Time

FOR THE GOVERNMENT OF EMPLOYES ONLY

G. R. FULLER	S. J. GULA
General Manager	Superintendent

B. C. STAMETS
Manager, Passenger Operations

SAFETY ALWAYS
Make this railroad the safest
on which to work and travel.

Here is Jersey Central's first train, consisting of a locomotive, a wood car and one coach. The locomotive is the "Eagle," built by Baldwin at Philadelphia in 1838. It pulled the first train to Plainfield January 1, 1839.

This Spring, The Central Railroad Company of New Jersey celebrates its 125th year of continuous service under the same name.

Its predecessor companies go back some 143 years to the Elizabethtown and Somerville Railway Co., which was incorporated in 1831. CNJ is one of the oldest railroads in the United States and its name aptly describes its mission—to serve the people of the State of New Jersey.

Despite its small size, CNJ's history has been one of progress and many firsts in the railroad industry. In 1872 it was the first railroad to furnish regulation uniforms for passenger conductors and trainmen. In 1893 it operated the first automatic semaphore signal in the United States. In 1925 it became the first railroad to acquire and operate a diesel electric locomotive. It was the first railroad to use television as an industrial application at its coal piers in Jersey City. The railroad's bridge across Newark Bay is one and two-fifths miles long and believed to be the longest railroad drawbridge of its type in the world.

More recently, CNJ built the largest piggyback container terminal in the Port Newark complex for the handling of marine and domestic piggyback and container shipments. It established many through routes with other railroads to provide high speed service to important points. As you read this time table, there are new passenger operations to Phillipsburg and a new high speed piggyback train to Chicago operating in conjunction with the Erie Lackawanna.

CNJ will continue to dedicate itself to the people of New Jersey to provide the kind of passenger and freight service that they need and deserve. We have attempted to make this time table a little more attractive and easier for you to read, and at the same time tell you some of the events that have made the CNJ the oldest railroad in the United States operating under the same name.

The railroad appreciates your patronage and looks forward to serving you for the next 125 years.

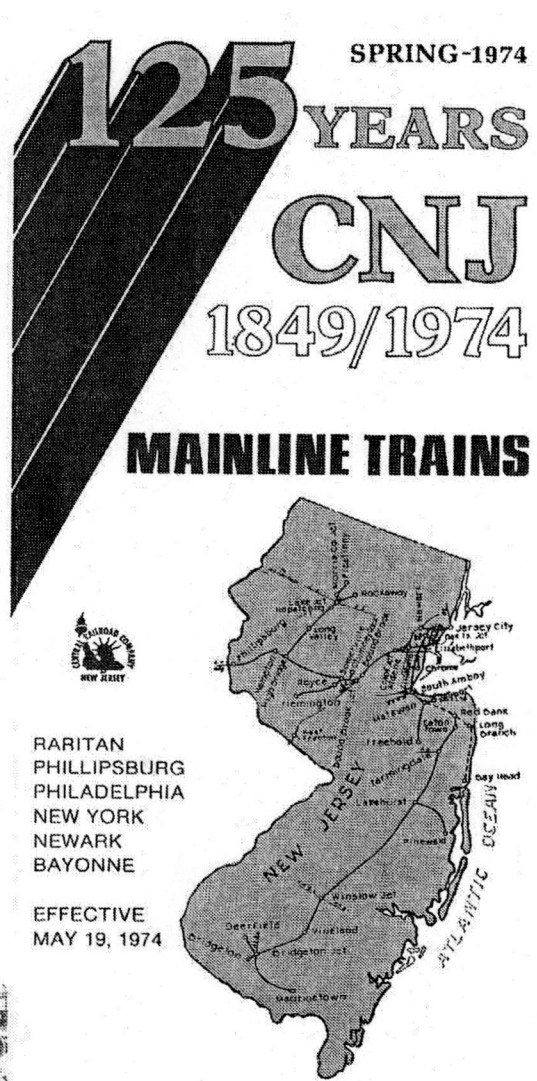

SPRING-1974

125 YEARS CNJ 1849/1974

MAINLINE TRAINS

Jersey City
South Amboy
Red Bank
Long Branch
Bay Head
NEW JERSEY
Vineland
Winslow Jct
Bridgeton Jct
ATLANTIC OCEAN

RARITAN
PHILLIPSBURG
PHILADELPHIA
NEW YORK
NEWARK
BAYONNE

EFFECTIVE
MAY 19, 1974

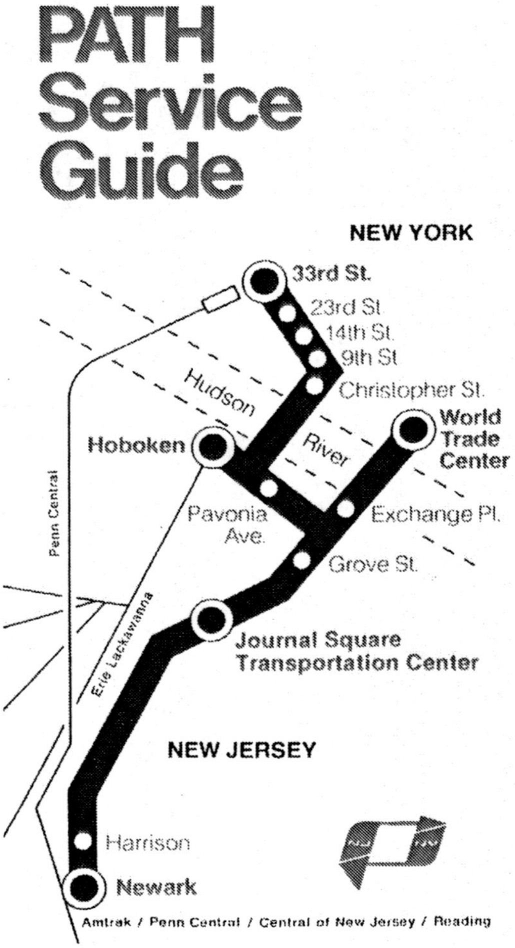
PATH
Service
Guide
NEW YORK
33rd St.
23rd St
14th St.
9th St
Christopher St.
Hudson
River
World
Trade
Center
Hoboken
Pavonia
Ave.
Exchange Pl.
Grove St.
Penn Central
Erie Lackawanna
Journal Square
Transportation Center
NEW JERSEY
Harrison
Newark
Amtrak / Penn Central / Central of New Jersey / Reading

TRENTON
NEW BRUNSWICK
NEW YORK
AND INTERMEDIATE POINTS
TIMETABLE EFFECTIVE APRIL 29, 1979

N.J.D.O.T. Commuter Rail Service

- New York
- Newark
- Elizabeth
- Linden
- Rahway
- Metro Park (Iselin)
- Metuchen
- Edison
- New Brunswick
- Princeton Junction
- Trenton

Operated by Conrail Under Contract

With the

Department of Transportation

State of New Jersey

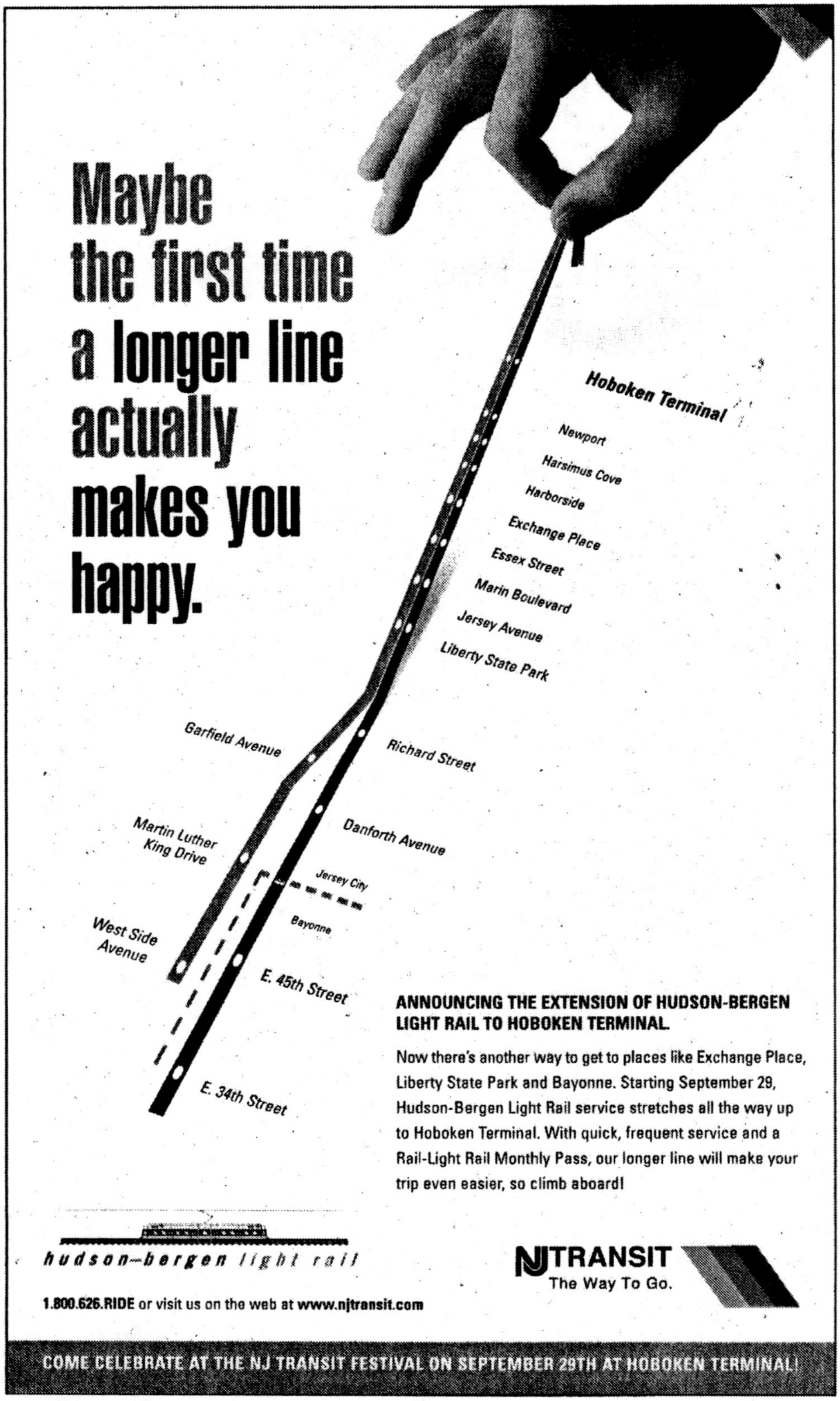
Maybe the first time a longer line actually makes you happy.
Hoboken Terminal
Newport
Harsimus Cove
Harborside
Exchange Place
Essex Street
Marin Boulevard
Jersey Avenue
Liberty State Park
Garfield Avenue
Richard Street
Martin Luther King Drive
Danforth Avenue
Jersey City
Bayonne
West Side Avenue
E. 45th Street
E. 34th Street
ANNOUNCING THE EXTENSION OF HUDSON-BERGEN LIGHT RAIL TO HOBOKEN TERMINAL.
Now there's another way to get to places like Exchange Place, Liberty State Park and Bayonne. Starting September 29, Hudson-Bergen Light Rail service stretches all the way up to Hoboken Terminal. With quick, frequent service and a Rail-Light Rail Monthly Pass, our longer line will make your trip even easier, so climb aboard!
hudson-bergen light rail
NJTRANSIT
The Way To Go.
1.800.626.RIDE or visit us on the web at www.njtransit.com
COME CELEBRATE AT THE NJ TRANSIT FESTIVAL ON SEPTEMBER 29TH AT HOBOKEN TERMINAL!

Amtrak® Northeast Rail System
Quebec
VIA to Gaspe and Halifax
VIA to Winnipeg, Edmonton and Vancouver
Ottawa
VIA Rail Canada
MONTREAL
St. Lambert
St. Albans
Burlington-Essex Junction
Waterbury-Stowe
Montpelier-Barre
Randolph
Rutland
White River Junction
Windsor-Mt. Ascutney
Old Orchard Beach
Portland
Saco
Wells
Dover
Durham
Exeter
Haverhill
BOSTON
Framingham
Route 128
Providence
Kingston
Westerly
Mystic
New London
Old Saybrook
New Haven
Hartford
Foxwoods Casino
Claremont
Bellows Falls
Brattleboro
Amherst
Springfield
Worcester
Fair Haven
Killington/Okemo
Rouses Point
Plattsburgh
Port Kent
Westport
Lake Placid
Port Henry
Ticonderoga
Whitehall
Fort Edward-Glens Falls
Saratoga Springs
Rome
Utica
Amsterdam
Schenectady
Albany-Rensselaer
Pittsfield
Hudson
Rhinecliff
Poughkeepsie
Croton-Harmon
Yonkers
NEW YORK
Newark
Newark Intl. Airport
Metropark
LaGuardia Airport
JFK Airport
New Brunswick
Princeton Junction
Trenton
Cornwells Heights
North Philadelphia
PHILADELPHIA
N.J. TRANSIT
Atlantic City
Kingston
TORONTO
Kitchener
Stratford
Oakville
Aldershot
London
Grimsby
St. Catharines
Niagara Falls
Port Huron
Windsor
BUFFALO
Rochester
Syracuse
Dunkirk
Fredonia
Jamestown
Erie
CLEVELAND
To Chicago
Huntingdon
Tyrone
Altoona
Greensburg
Harrisburg
PITTSBURGH
Johnstown
Latrobe
Lewistown
Wilmington
BALTIMORE
Newark
Aberdeen
BWI Airport
New Carrollton
Cumberland
Harpers Ferry
Dulles Airport
Alexandria
Warrenton
WASHINGTON, D.C.
Huntington
Charleston
Shenandoah National Park
Charlottesville
To Chicago
Woodbridge
Quantico
Fredericksburg
Ashland
Richmond
Williamsburg
Newport News
Norfolk
Virginia Beach
White Sulphur Springs
Lynchburg
Petersburg
To Atlanta and New Orleans
To Florida
New York
• New Rochelle
• Stamford
• Bridgeport
• New Haven
• Wallingford
• Meriden
• Berlin
• Hartford
• Windsor
• Windsor Locks
Springfield
Philadelphia
• Ardmore
• Paoli
• Exton
• Downingtown
• Coatesville
• Parkesburg
• Lancaster
• Mount Joy
• Elizabethtown
• Middletown
Harrisburg
LEGEND
Amtrak Train Routes Shown in this Timetable
Amtrak Train Routes Shown in the National Timetable (not all stations are shown on this map)
Amtrak/VIA Rail Canada Routes Joint Through Service
Connecting Thruway Motorcoach or Local Bus Services
Connecting Rail Services
Amtrak Vacations Destinations
For Information and Reservations
1-800-USA-RAIL
(For U.S. and Canada Only. International Inquirers Should Call Their Local Amtrak International Sales Representative.)
www.amtrak.com

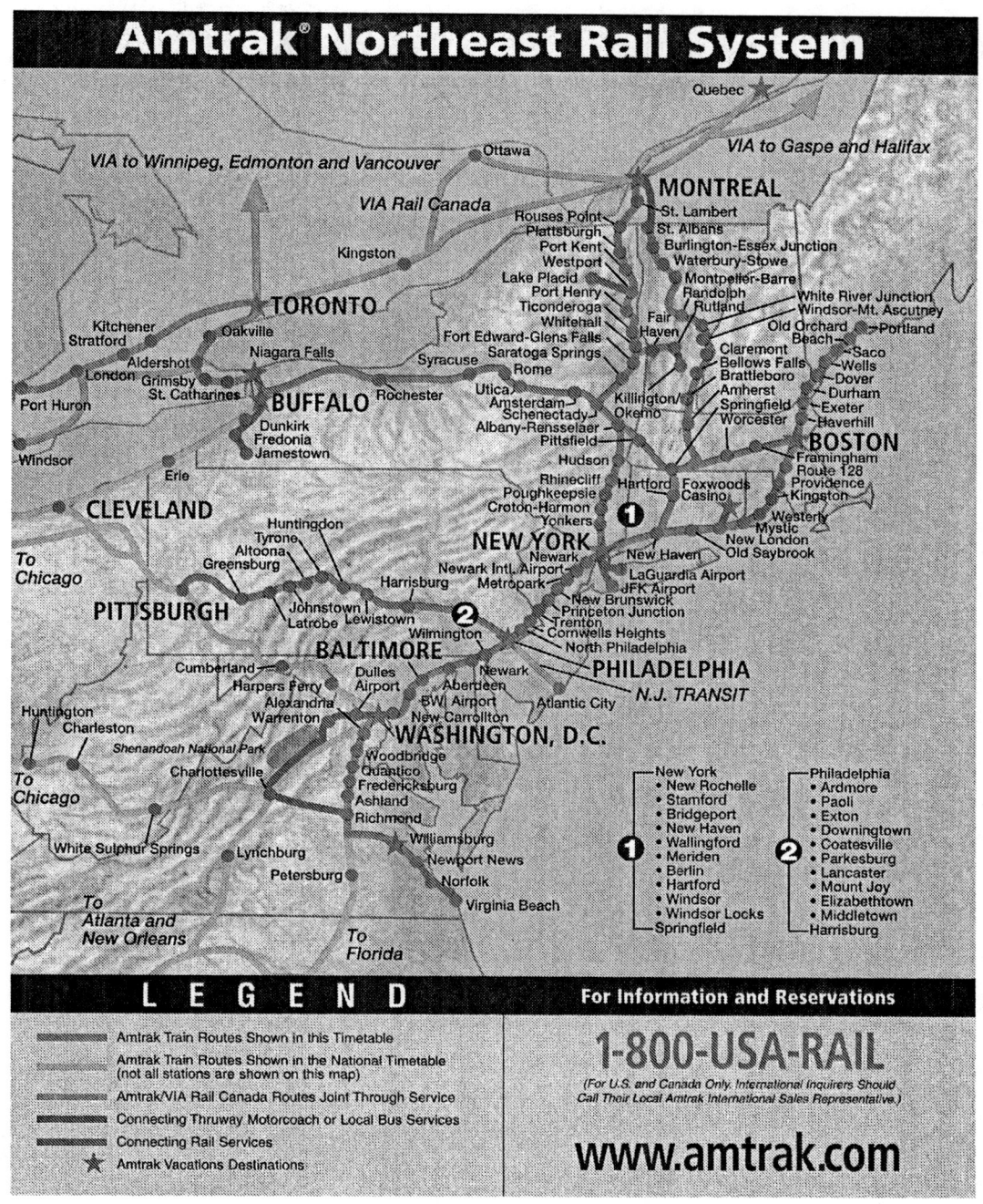

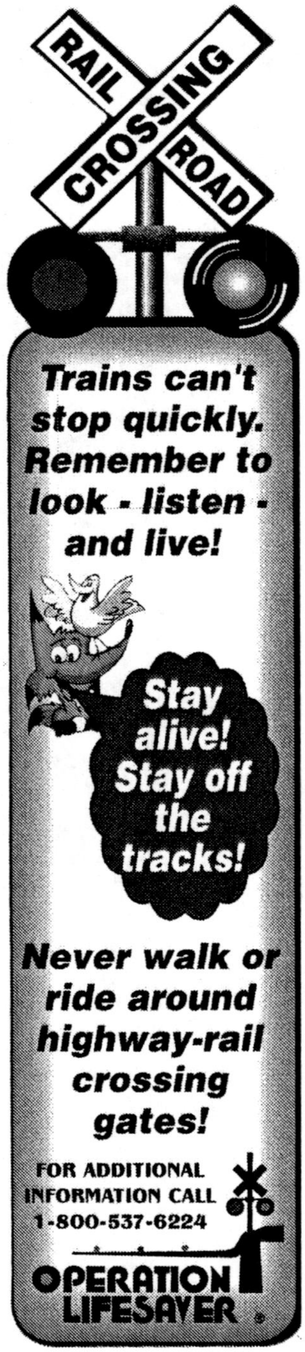
RAIL
CROSSING
ROAD
Trains can't stop quickly. Remember to look - listen - and live!
Stay alive! Stay off the tracks!
Never walk or ride around highway-rail crossing gates!
FOR ADDITIONAL INFORMATION CALL 1-800-537-6224
OPERATION LIFESAVER

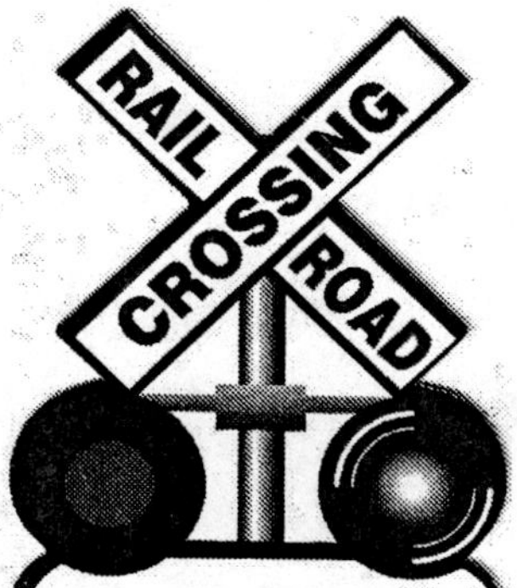
RAIL
ROAD
CROSSING

STAY OFF!
STAY AWAY!
STAY ALIVE!

TRACK FACTS

Fact #1: You can not judge the distance and speed of an oncoming train.

Fact #2: Railroad tracks, trestles, bridges and railroad yards are private property.

Fact #3: A train can appear on any track at any time.

Fact #4: Climbing between railcars is a deadly game.

Fact #5: Items thrown at a train or placed on the tracks can injure, bystanders or you..

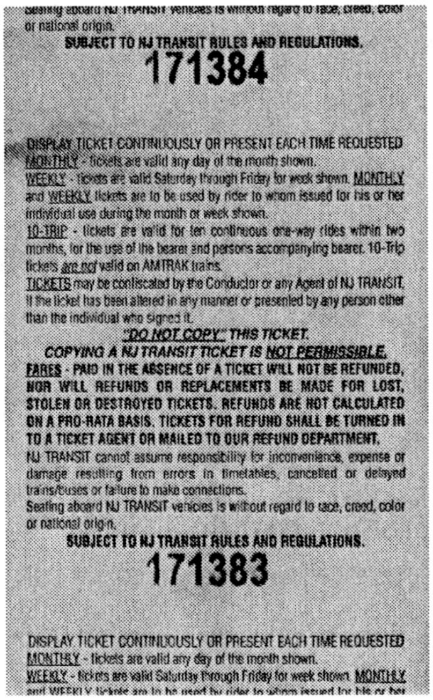

Seating aboard NJ TRANSIT vehicles is without regard to race, creed, color or national origin.
SUBJECT TO NJ TRANSIT RULES AND REGULATIONS.

171384

DISPLAY TICKET CONTINUOUSLY OR PRESENT EACH TIME REQUESTED
MONTHLY - tickets are valid any day of the month shown.
WEEKLY - tickets are valid Saturday through Friday for week shown. MONTHLY
and WEEKLY tickets are to be used by rider to whom issued for his or her
individual use during the month or week shown.
10-TRIP - tickets are valid for ten continuous one-way rides within two
months, for the use of the bearer and persons accompanying bearer. 10-Trip
tickets are not valid on AMTRAK trains.
TICKETS may be confiscated by the Conductor or any Agent of NJ TRANSIT,
if the ticket has been altered in any manner or presented by any person other
than the individual who signed it.
"DO NOT COPY" THIS TICKET.
COPYING A NJ TRANSIT TICKET IS NOT PERMISSIBLE.
FARES - PAID IN THE ABSENCE OF A TICKET WILL NOT BE REFUNDED,
NOR WILL REFUNDS OR REPLACEMENTS BE MADE FOR LOST,
STOLEN OR DESTROYED TICKETS. REFUNDS ARE NOT CALCULATED
ON A PRO-RATA BASIS. TICKETS FOR REFUND SHALL BE TURNED IN
TO A TICKET AGENT OR MAILED TO OUR REFUND DEPARTMENT.
NJ TRANSIT cannot assume responsibility for inconvenience, expense or
damage resulting from errors in timetables, cancelled or delayed
trains/buses or failure to make connections.
Seating aboard NJ TRANSIT vehicles is without regard to race, creed, color
or national origin.
SUBJECT TO NJ TRANSIT RULES AND REGULATIONS.

171383

DISPLAY TICKET CONTINUOUSLY OR PRESENT EACH TIME REQUESTED
MONTHLY - tickets are valid any day of the month shown.
WEEKLY - tickets are valid Saturday through Friday for week shown. MONTHLY
and WEEKLY tickets are to be used by rider to whom issued for his or her

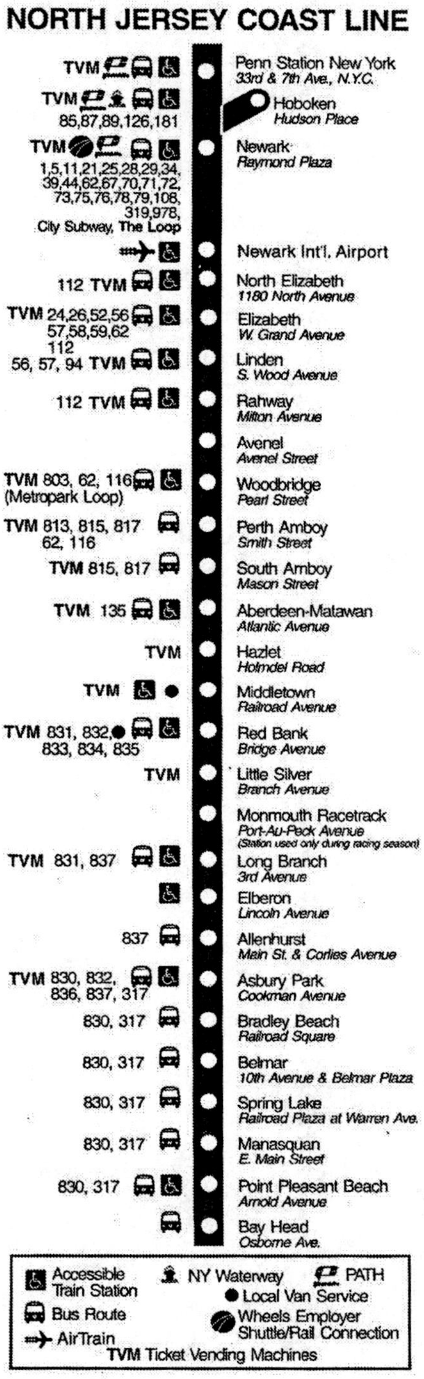

NORTH JERSEY COAST LINE

	Station	
TVM 🚆📱🚌♿	Penn Station New York	*33rd & 7th Ave., N.Y.C.*
TVM 🚆📱🚌♿ 85,87,89,126,181	Hoboken	*Hudson Place*
TVM 🚆📱🚌♿ 1,5,11,21,25,28,29,34, 39,44,62,67,70,71,72, 73,75,76,78,79,106, 319,978, City Subway, The Loop	Newark	*Raymond Plaza*
✈♿	Newark Int'l. Airport	
112 TVM 🚌♿	North Elizabeth	*1180 North Avenue*
TVM 24,26,52,56 🚌♿ 57,58,59,62 112	Elizabeth	*W. Grand Avenue*
56, 57, 94 TVM 🚌♿	Linden	*S. Wood Avenue*
112 TVM 🚌♿	Rahway	*Milton Avenue*
	Avenel	*Avenel Street*
TVM 803, 62, 116 🚌♿ (Metropark Loop)	Woodbridge	*Pearl Street*
TVM 813, 815, 817 🚌 62, 116	Perth Amboy	*Smith Street*
TVM 815, 817 🚌	South Amboy	*Mason Street*
TVM 135 🚌♿	Aberdeen-Matawan	*Atlantic Avenue*
TVM	Hazlet	*Holmdel Road*
TVM ♿●	Middletown	*Railroad Avenue*
TVM 831, 832,● 🚌♿ 833, 834, 835	Red Bank	*Bridge Avenue*
TVM	Little Silver	*Branch Avenue*
	Monmouth Racetrack	*Port-Au-Peck Avenue* *(Station used only during racing season)*
TVM 831, 837 🚌♿	Long Branch	*3rd Avenue*
♿	Elberon	*Lincoln Avenue*
837 🚌	Allenhurst	*Main St. & Corlies Avenue*
TVM 830, 832, ♿ 836, 837, 317	Asbury Park	*Cookman Avenue*
830, 317 🚌	Bradley Beach	*Railroad Square*
830, 317 🚌	Belmar	*10th Avenue & Belmar Plaza*
830, 317 🚌	Spring Lake	*Railroad Plaza at Warren Ave.*
830, 317 🚌	Manasquan	*E. Main Street*
830, 317 🚌♿	Point Pleasant Beach	*Arnold Avenue*
🚌	Bay Head	*Osborne Ave.*

♿ Accessible Train Station	🚢 NY Waterway	📱 PATH
🚌 Bus Route	● Local Van Service	
✈ AirTrain	🌐 Wheels Employer Shuttle/Rail Connection	
TVM Ticket Vending Machines		

NJ TRANSIT
NORTH JERSEY COAST LINE

Effective: June 16, 2002

BAY HEAD, POINT PLEASANT BEACH, BELMAR, LONG BRANCH, ABERDEEN-MATAWAN, NEWARK INTERNATIONAL AIRPORT, NEWARK, HOBOKEN, NEW YORK and intermediate points

✈ AIRTRAIN

NJ TRANSIT
The Way To Go.
www.njtransit.com

Michael E. Ferlise

NORTHEAST CORRIDOR LINE

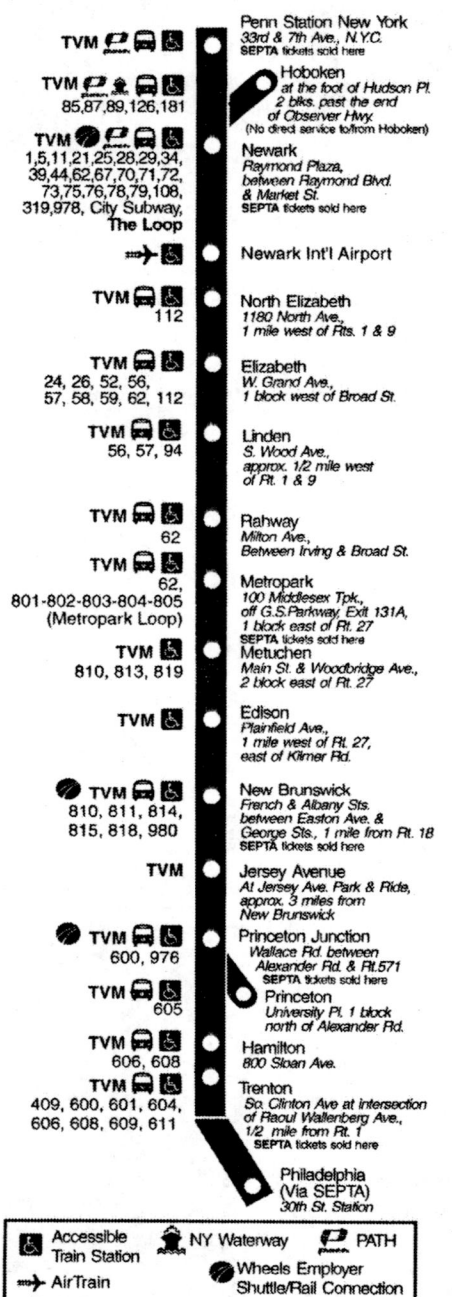

	Station	Location
TVM 🅿 🚌 ♿	**Penn Station New York**	33rd & 7th Ave., N.Y.C. SEPTA tickets sold here
TVM 🅿 🚶 🚌 ♿ 85,87,89,126,181	**Hoboken**	at the foot of Hudson Pl. 2 blks. past the end of Observer Hwy. (No direct service to/from Hoboken)
TVM 🌐 🅿 🚌 ♿ 1,5,11,21,25,28,29,34, 39,44,62,67,70,71,72, 73,75,76,78,79,108, 319,978, City Subway, **The Loop**	**Newark**	Raymond Plaza, between Raymond Blvd. & Market St. SEPTA tickets sold here
✈ ♿	**Newark Int'l Airport**	
TVM 🚌 ♿ 112	**North Elizabeth**	1180 North Ave., 1 mile west of Rts. 1 & 9
TVM 🚌 ♿ 24, 26, 52, 56, 57, 58, 59, 62, 112	**Elizabeth**	W. Grand Ave., 1 block west of Broad St.
TVM 🚌 ♿ 56, 57, 94	**Linden**	S. Wood Ave., approx. 1/2 mile west of Rt. 1 & 9
TVM 🚌 ♿ 62	**Rahway**	Milton Ave., Between Irving & Broad St.
TVM 🚌 ♿ 62, 801-802-803-804-805 (Metropark Loop)	**Metropark**	100 Middlesex Tpk., off G.S.Parkway, Exit 131A, 1 block east of Rt. 27 SEPTA tickets sold here
TVM ♿ 810, 813, 819	**Metuchen**	Main St. & Woodbridge Ave., 2 block east of Rt. 27
TVM ♿	**Edison**	Plainfield Ave., 1 mile west of Rt. 27, east of Kilmer Rd.
🌑 TVM 🚌 ♿ 810, 811, 814, 815, 818, 980	**New Brunswick**	French & Albany Sts. between Easton Ave. & George Sts., 1 mile from Rt. 18 SEPTA tickets sold here
TVM	**Jersey Avenue**	At Jersey Ave. Park & Ride, approx. 3 miles from New Brunswick
🌑 TVM 🚌 ♿ 600, 976	**Princeton Junction**	Wallace Rd. between Alexander Rd. & Rt.571 SEPTA tickets sold here
TVM 🚌 ♿ 605	**Princeton**	University Pl. 1 block north of Alexander Rd.
TVM 🚌 ♿ 606, 608	**Hamilton**	800 Sloan Ave.
TVM 🚌 ♿ 409, 600, 601, 604, 606, 608, 609, 611	**Trenton**	So. Clinton Ave at intersection of Raoul Wallenberg Ave., 1/2 mile from Rt. 1 SEPTA tickets sold here
	Philadelphia (Via SEPTA)	30th St. Station

♿ **Accessible Train Station**	🌑 NY Waterway	🅿 **PATH**
✈ **AirTrain**	🌑 Wheels Employer Shuttle/Rail Connection	
🚌 **Bus Route**	**TVM** Ticket Vending Machines	

NJ TRANSIT
NORTHEAST CORRIDOR LINE

Effective: August 3, 2002

TRENTON, PRINCETON JUNCTION, NEW BRUNSWICK, METUCHEN, METROPARK, ELIZABETH, NEWARK INTERNATIONAL AIRPORT, NEWARK, NEW YORK and intermediate points

CONNECTING PATH SERVICE TO JERSEY CITY AND NEW YORK

AIRTRAIN

NJ TRANSIT
The Way To Go.

www.njtransit.com

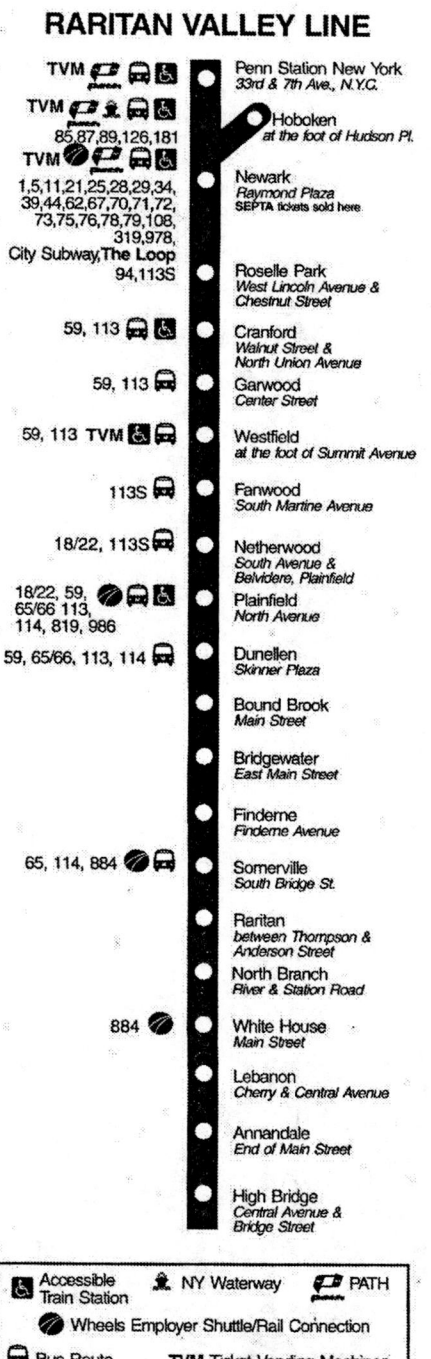

RARITAN VALLEY LINE

	Station
TVM 🚆🚌♿	**Penn Station New York** *33rd & 7th Ave., N.Y.C.*
TVM 🚆🚶🚌♿ 85,87,89,126,181	**Hoboken** *at the foot of Hudson Pl.*
TVM 🚆🚌♿ 1,5,11,21,25,28,29,34, 39,44,62,67,70,71,72, 73,75,76,78,79,108, 319,978, City Subway, The Loop	**Newark** *Raymond Plaza* SEPTA tickets sold here
94,113S	**Roselle Park** *West Lincoln Avenue & Chestnut Street*
59, 113 🚌♿	**Cranford** *Walnut Street & North Union Avenue*
59, 113 🚌	**Garwood** *Center Street*
59, 113 TVM ♿🚌	**Westfield** *at the foot of Summit Avenue*
113S 🚌	**Fanwood** *South Martine Avenue*
18/22, 113S 🚌	**Netherwood** *South Avenue & Belvidere, Plainfield*
18/22, 59, 🚌♿ 65/66 113, 114, 819, 986	**Plainfield** *North Avenue*
59, 65/66, 113, 114 🚌	**Dunellen** *Skinner Plaza*
	Bound Brook *Main Street*
	Bridgewater *East Main Street*
	Finderne *Finderne Avenue*
65, 114, 884 🚌	**Somerville** *South Bridge St.*
	Raritan *between Thompson & Anderson Street*
	North Branch *River & Station Road*
884	**White House** *Main Street*
	Lebanon *Cherry & Central Avenue*
	Annandale *End of Main Street*
	High Bridge *Central Avenue & Bridge Street*

♿ Accessible Train Station   🚶 NY Waterway   🚆 PATH
🌀 Wheels Employer Shuttle/Rail Connection
🚌 Bus Route   **TVM** Ticket Vending Machines

NJ TRANSIT
RARITAN VALLEY LINE

Effective: August 3, 2002

HIGH BRIDGE, RARITAN, SOMERVILLE, PLAINFIELD WESTFIELD, NEWARK, NEW YORK and intermediate points

CONNECTING PATH AND FERRY SERVICE TO NEW YORK

NJ TRANSIT The Way To Go.
www.njtransit.com

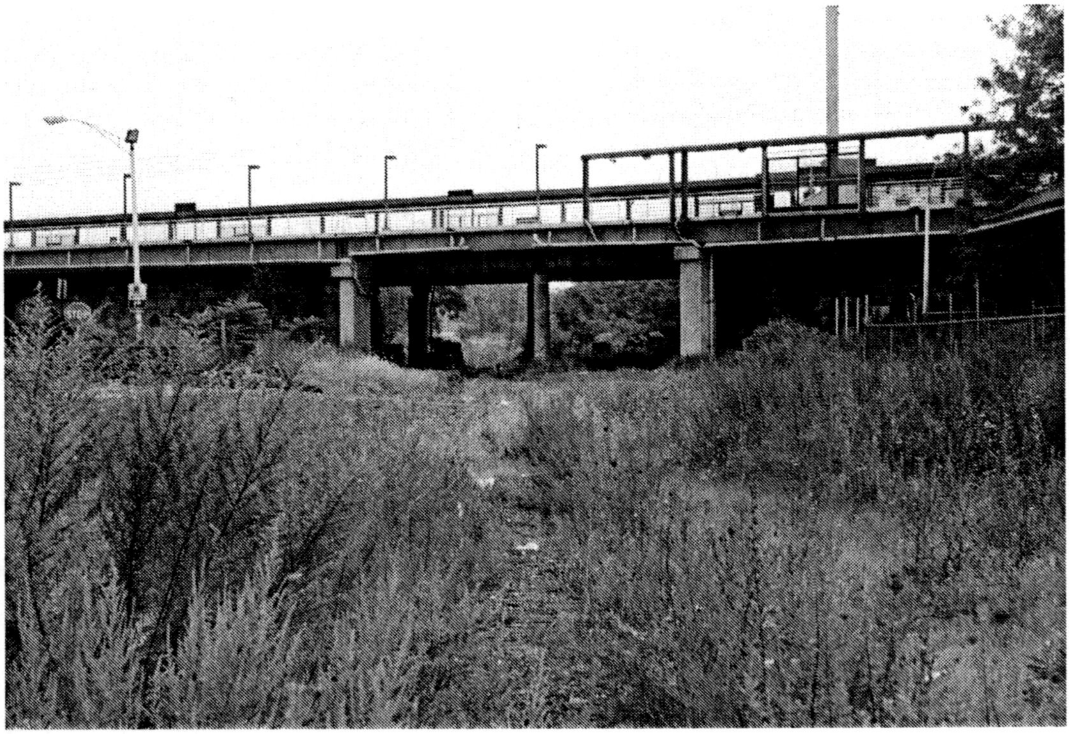

Old CRRNJ Mainline
In Elizabeth towards Bayonne

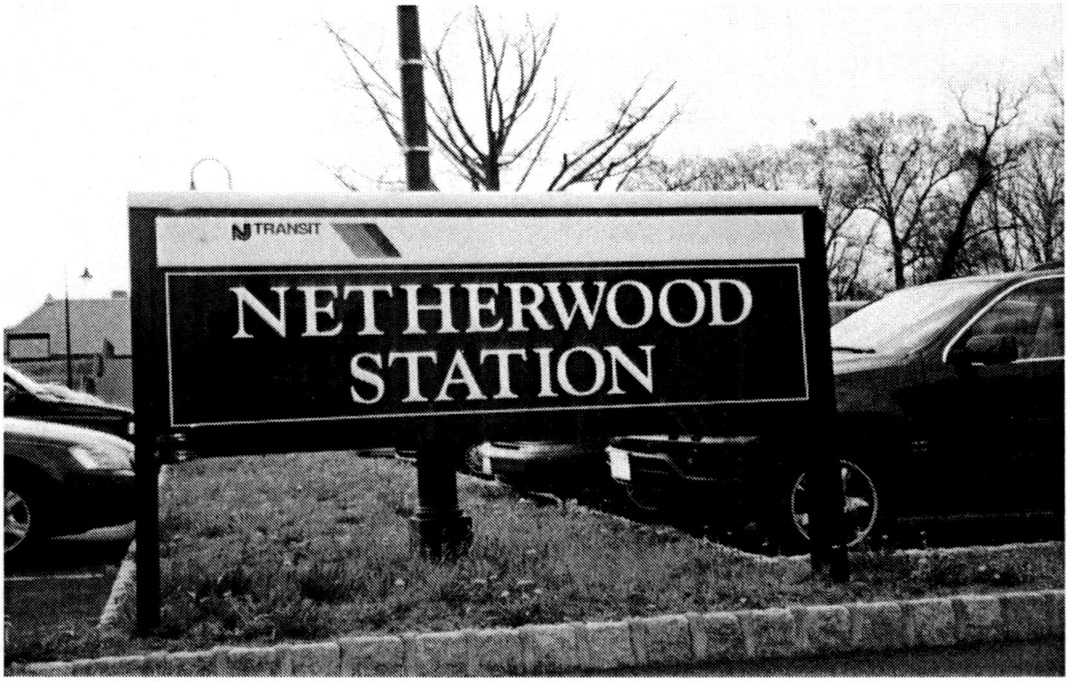
NJ TRANSIT
NETHERWOOD
STATION

Plainfield

The Old Rahway Valley RR...

Old Ice Water Fountain
Lackawanna terminal Hoboken

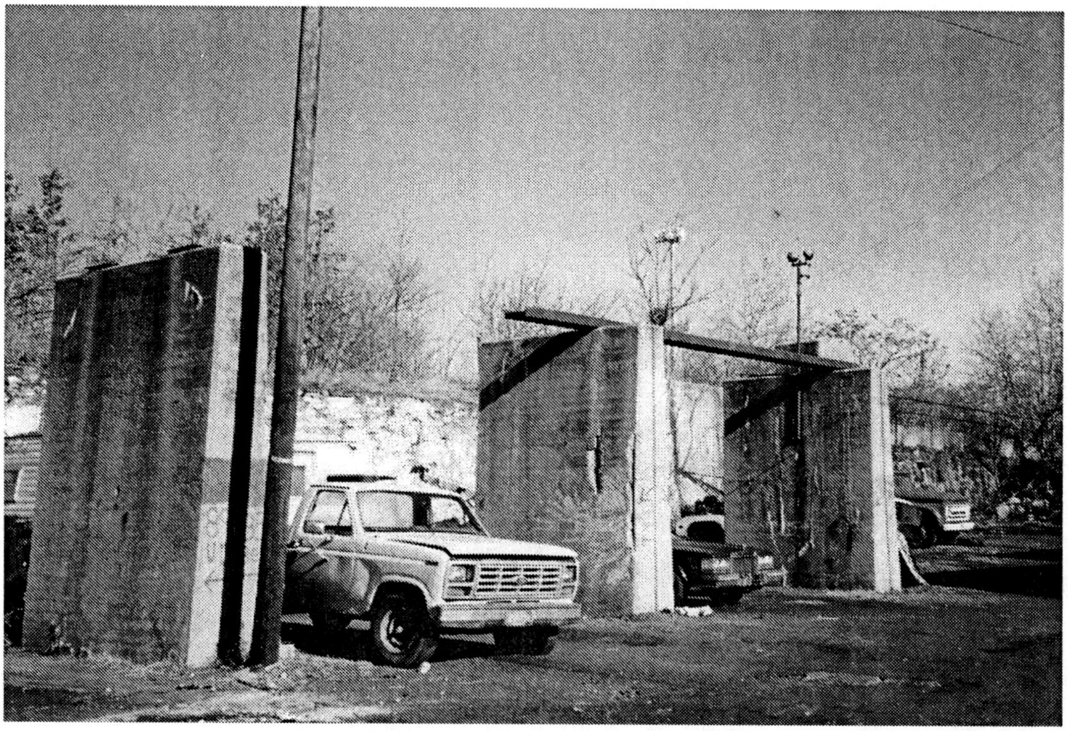

Old CRRNJ Coal Ramp - Elizabeth

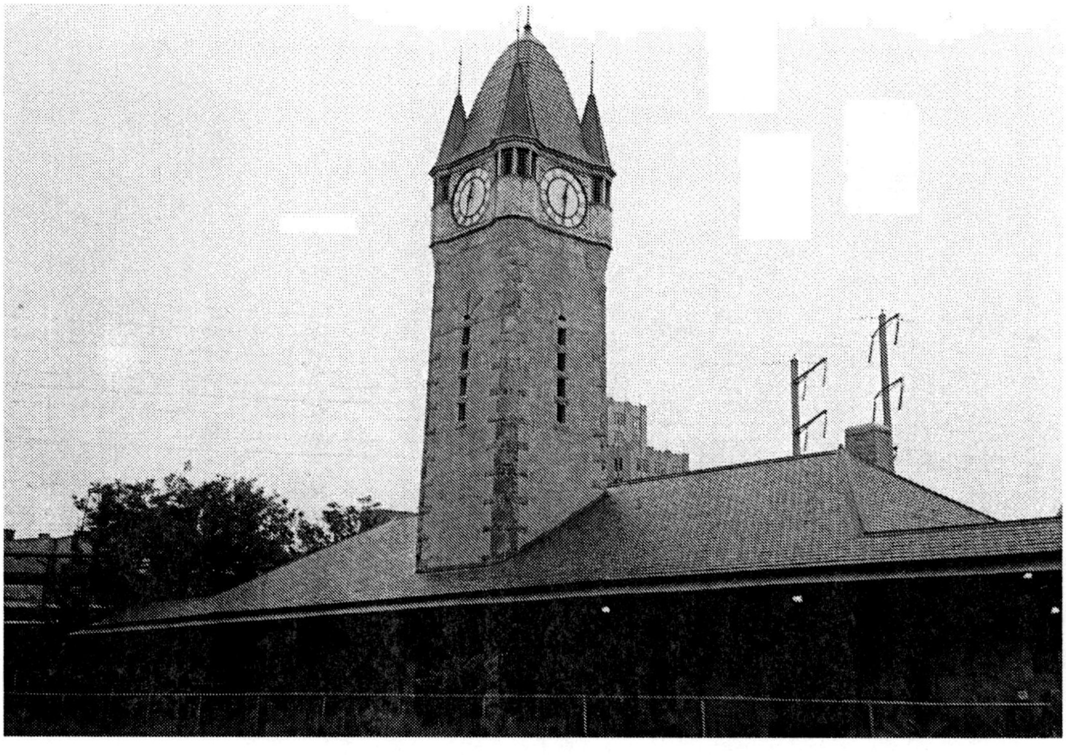

Old CRRNJ Station - Elizabeth

Old Jersey Central Logo - Plainfield

Abandoned CRRNJ 4 track Mainline Elizabeth

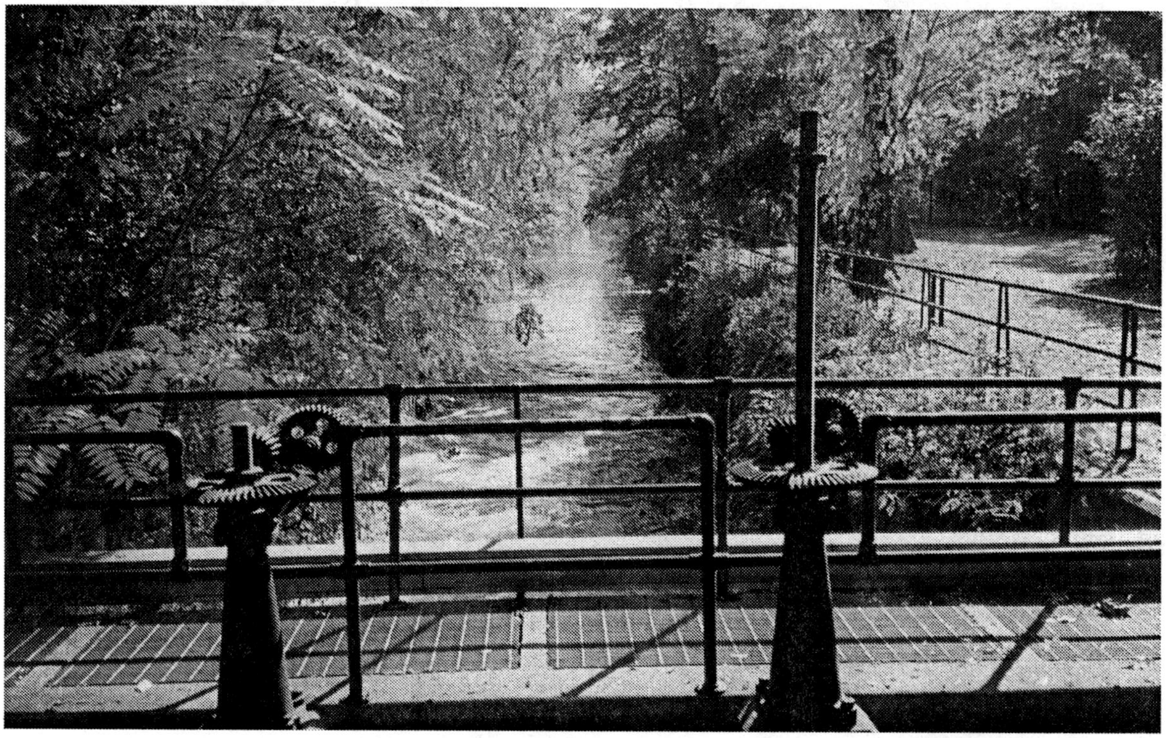

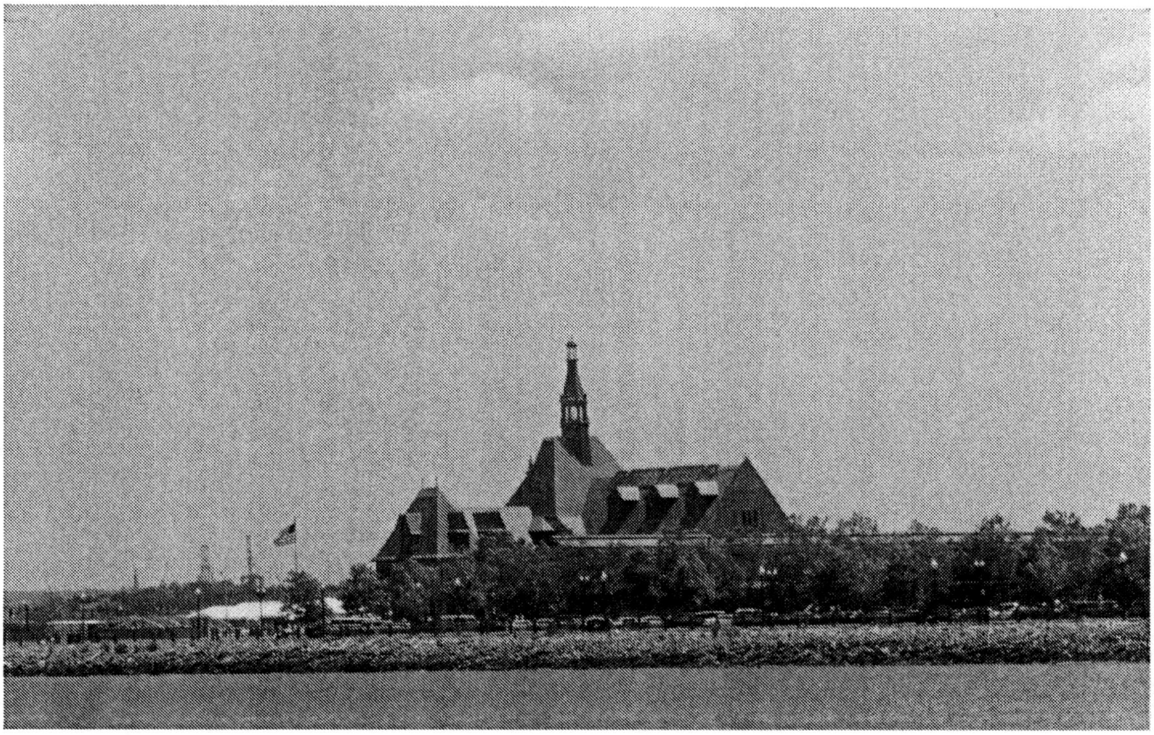

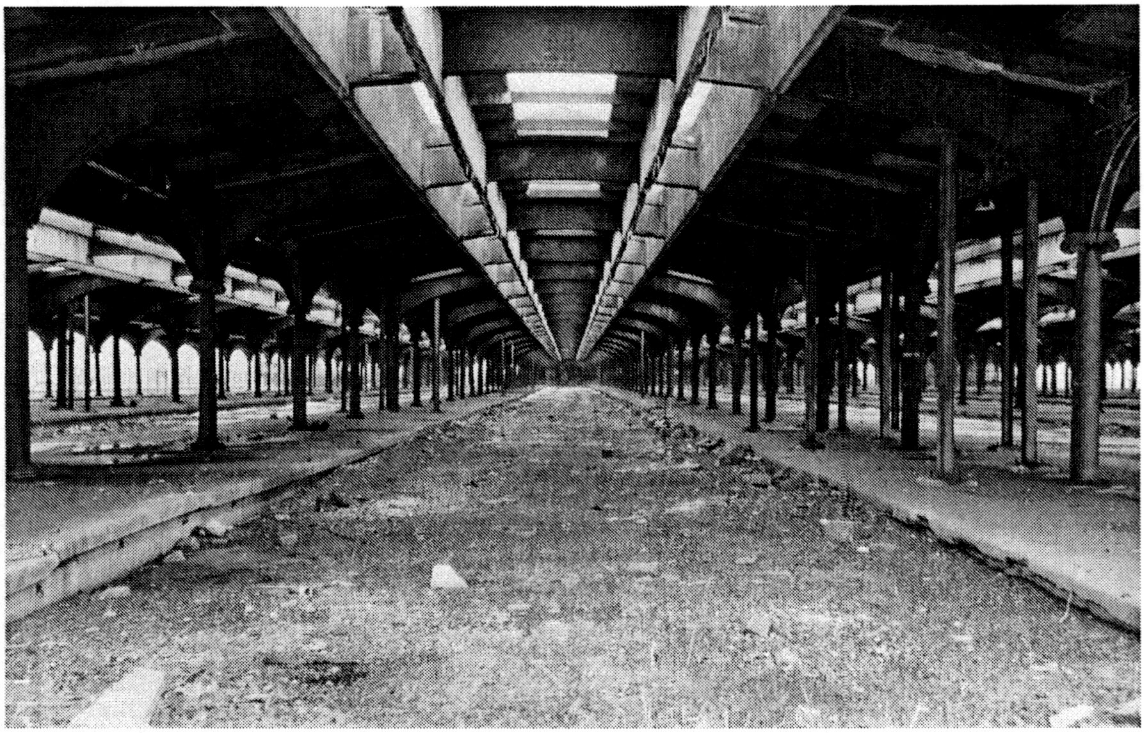

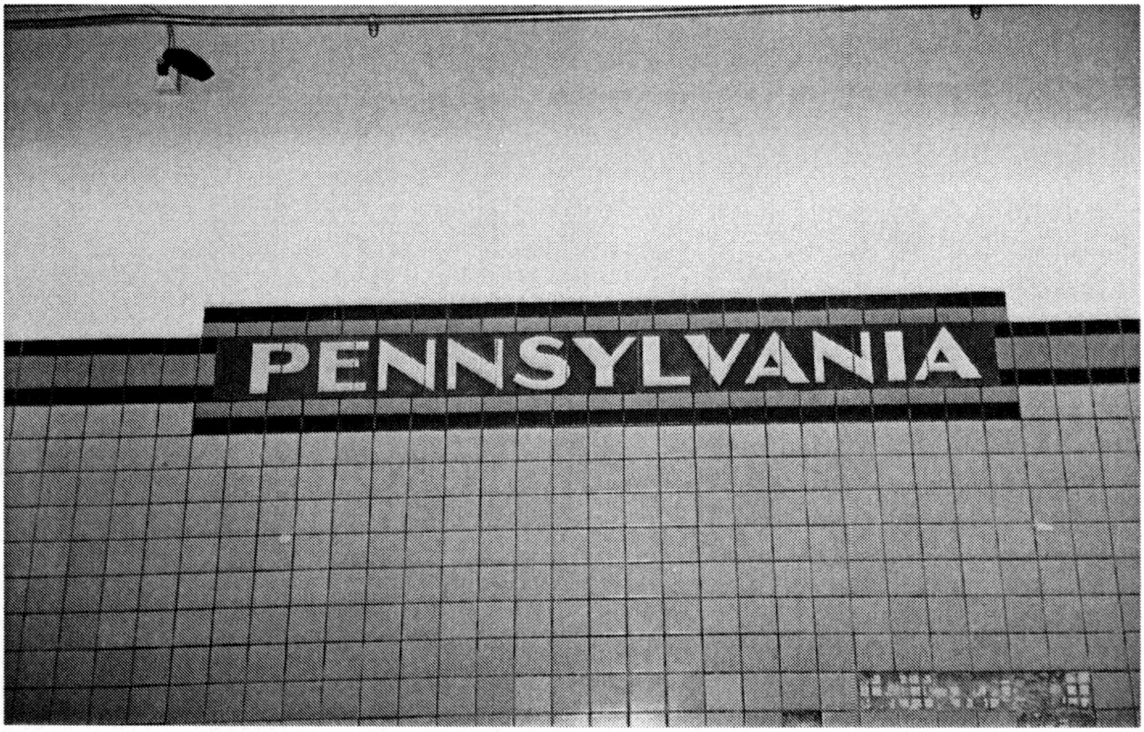
PENNSYLVANIA

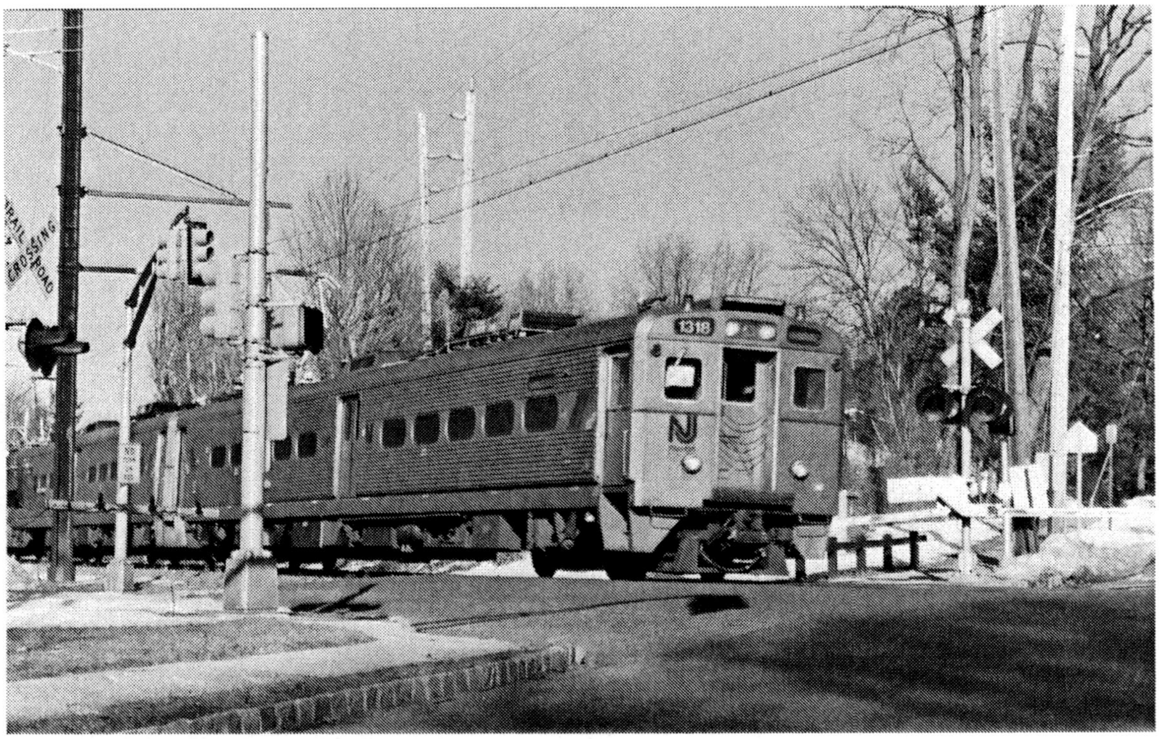
1318

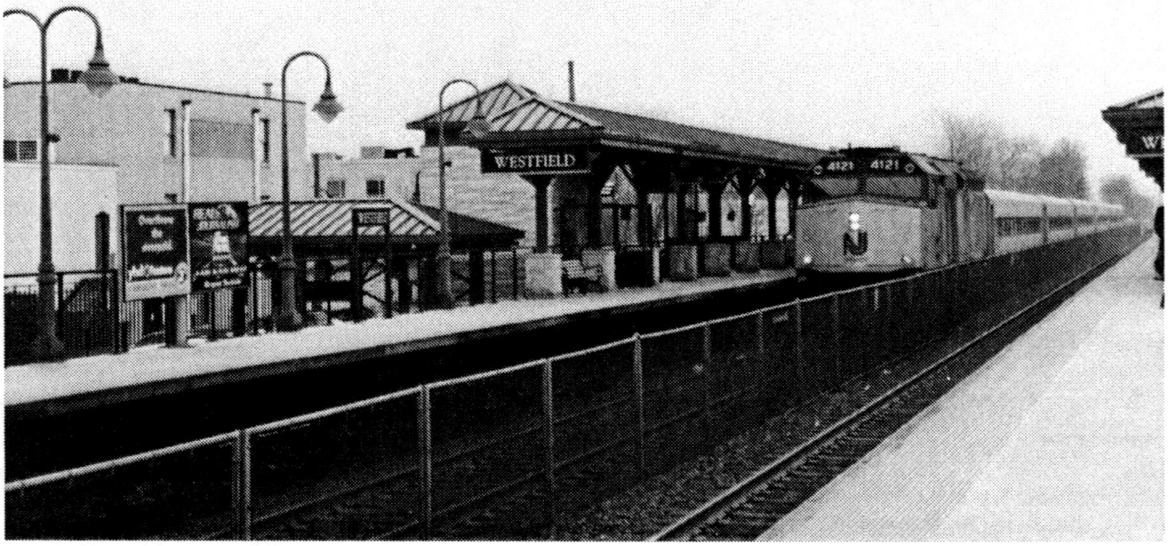
WESTFIELD
4121 4121

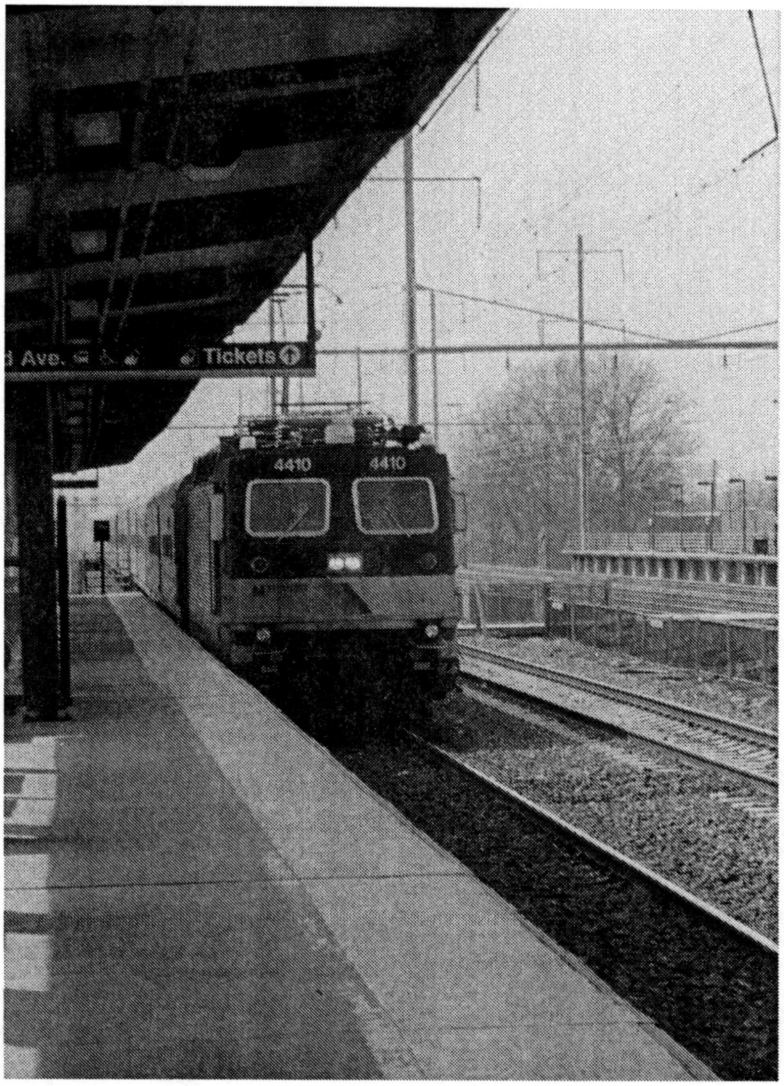
Tickets
4410
4410

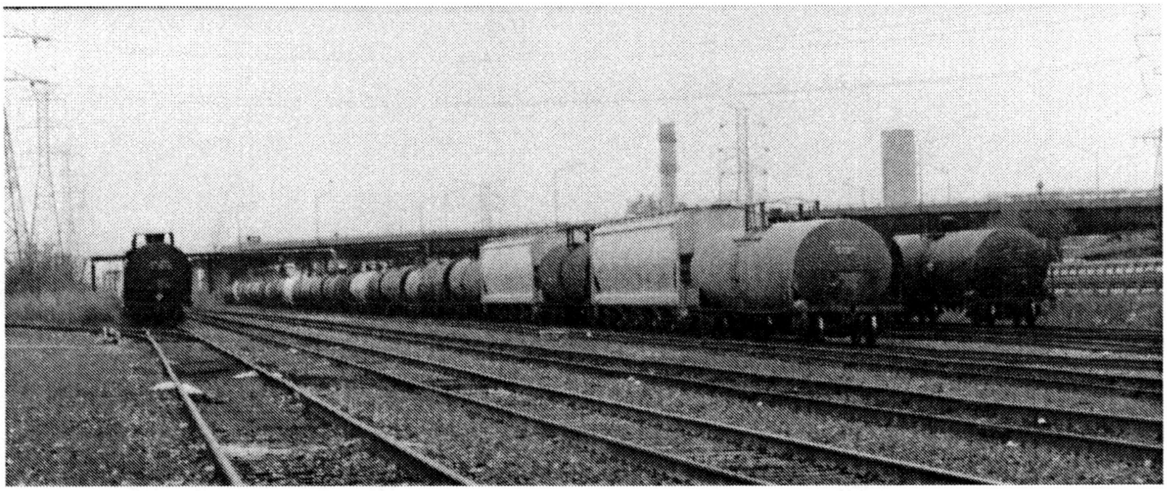

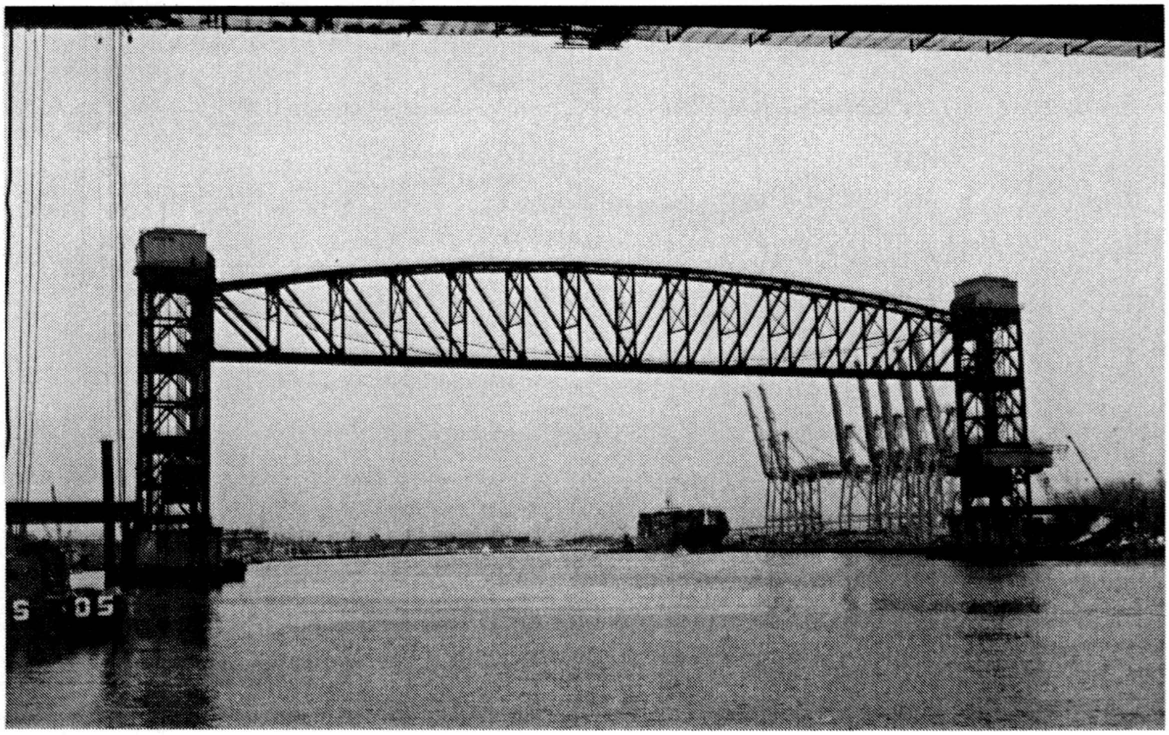
S 05

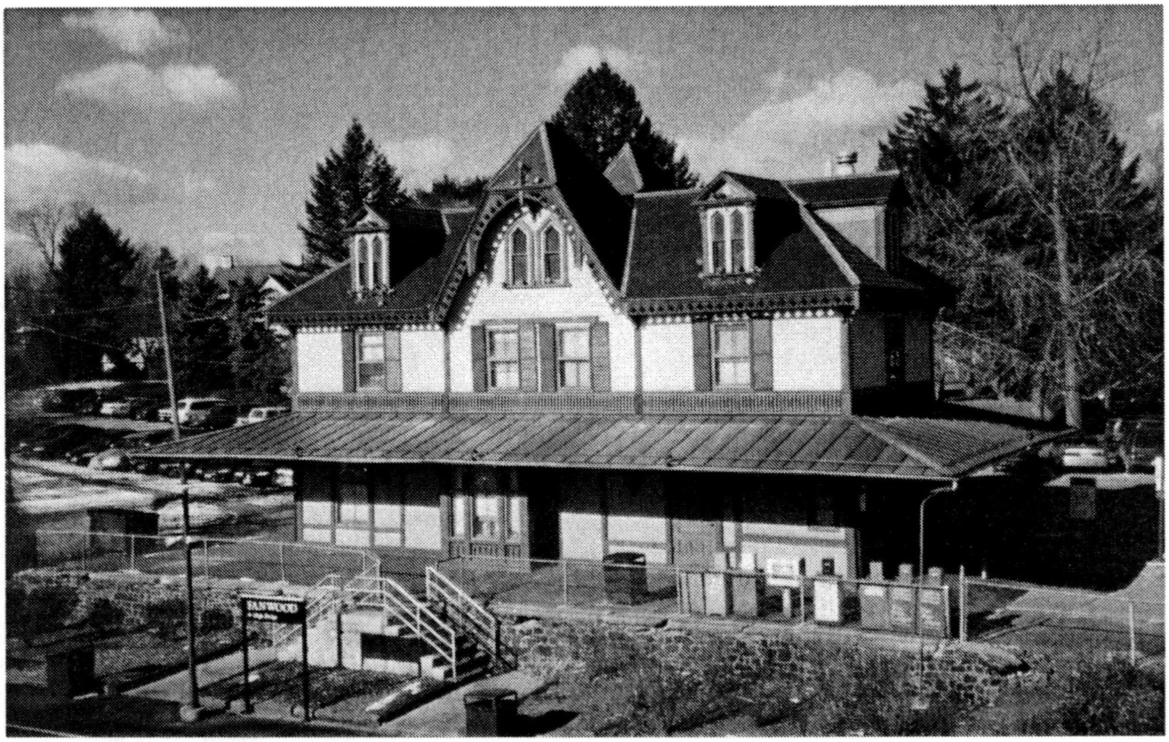

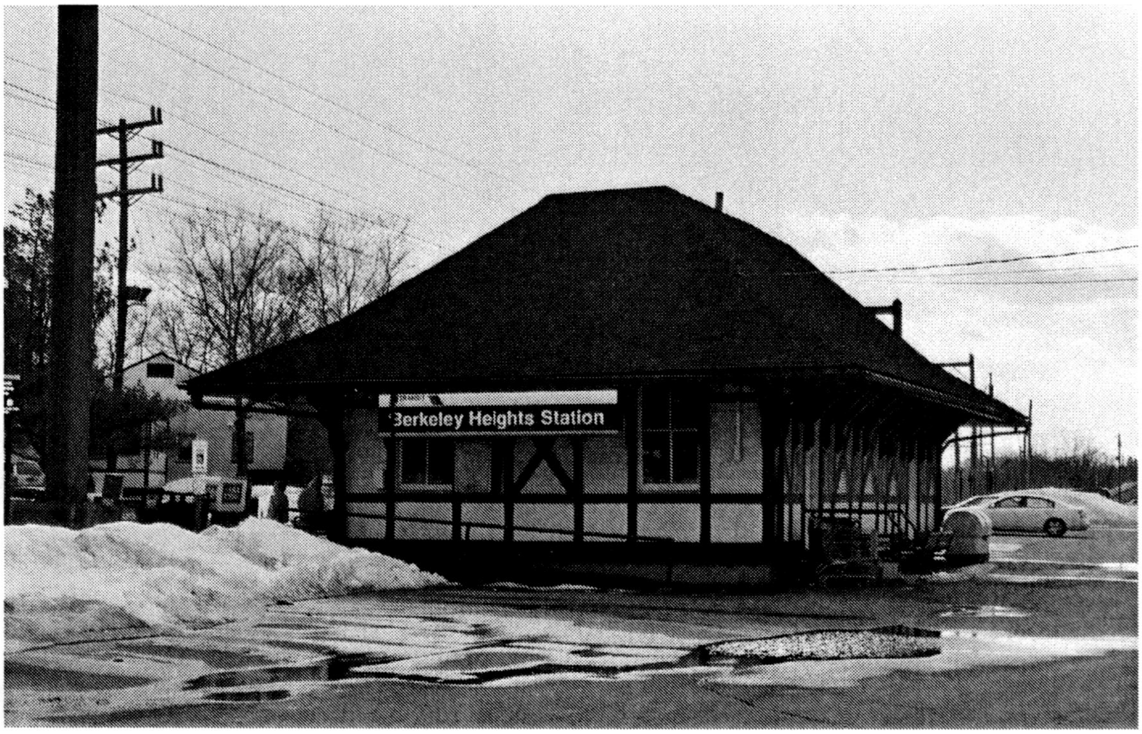
Berkeley Heights Station

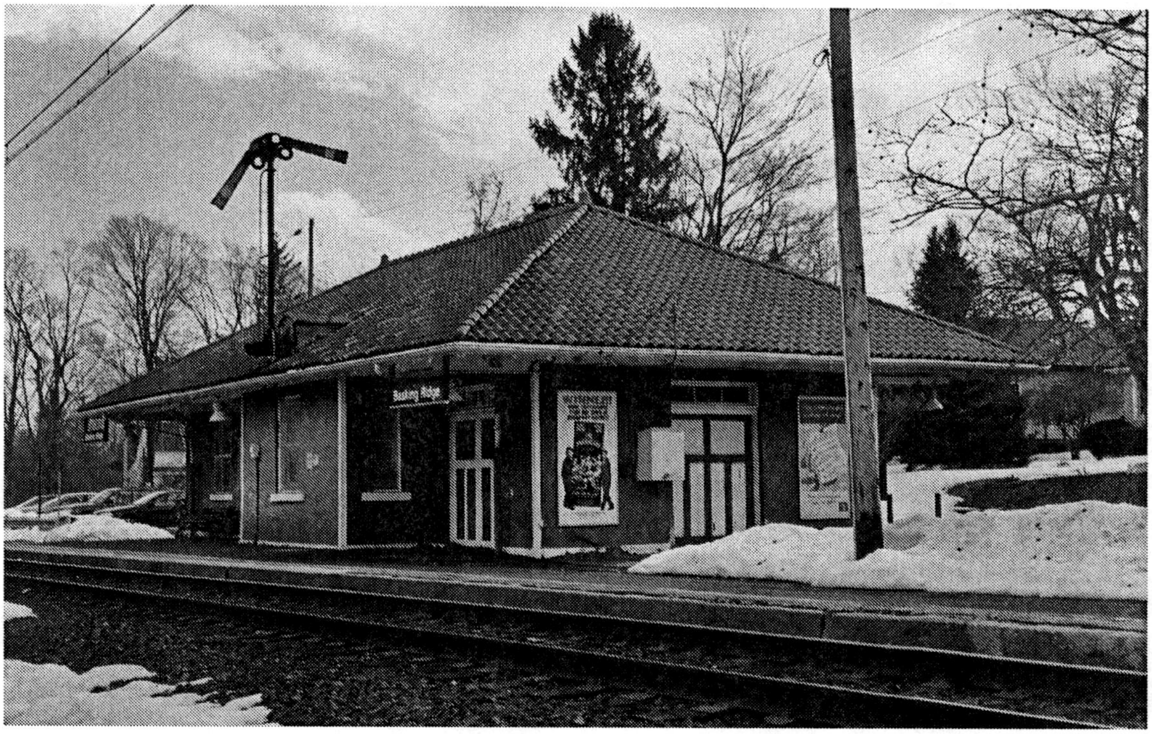
Basking Ridge

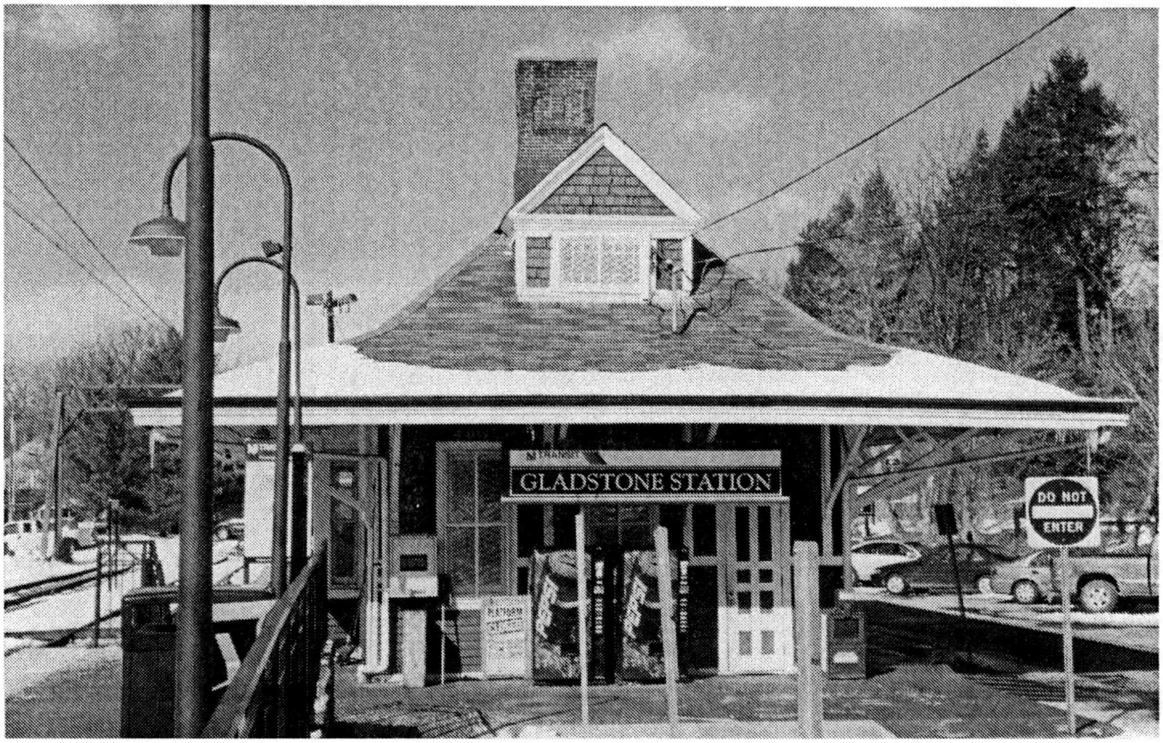
GLADSTONE STATION
DO NOT
ENTER

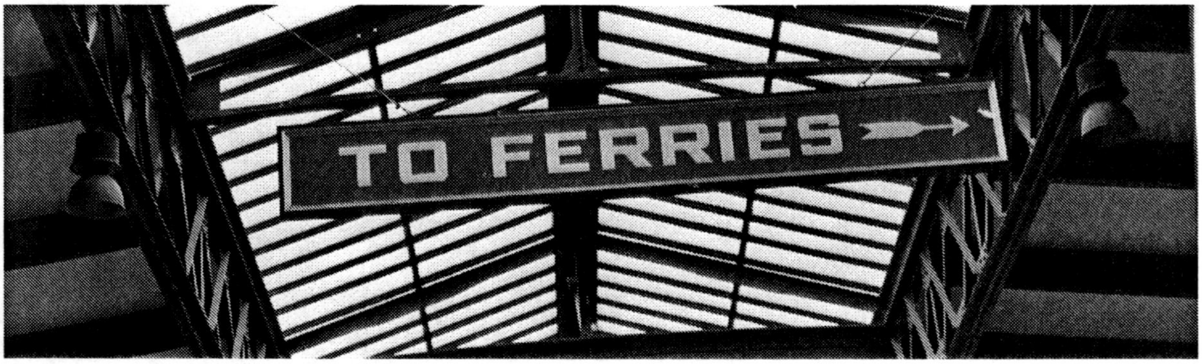
TO FERRIES

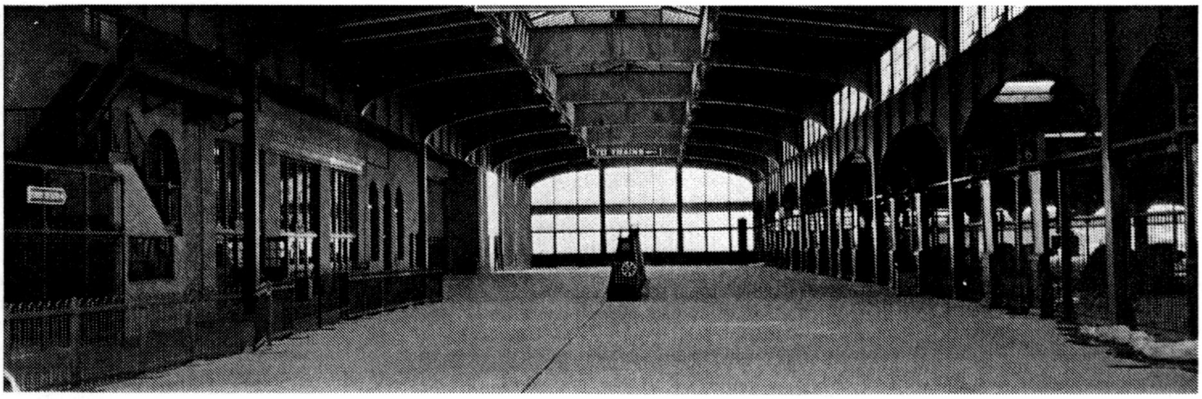

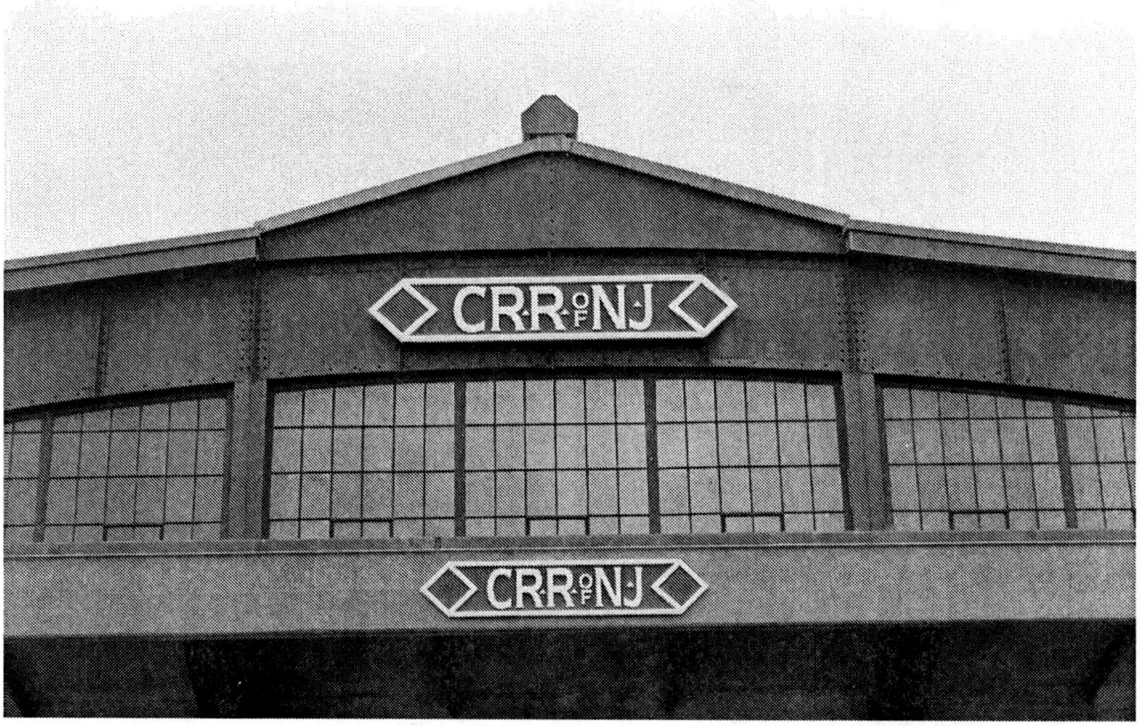
CRR OF NJ
CRR OF NJ

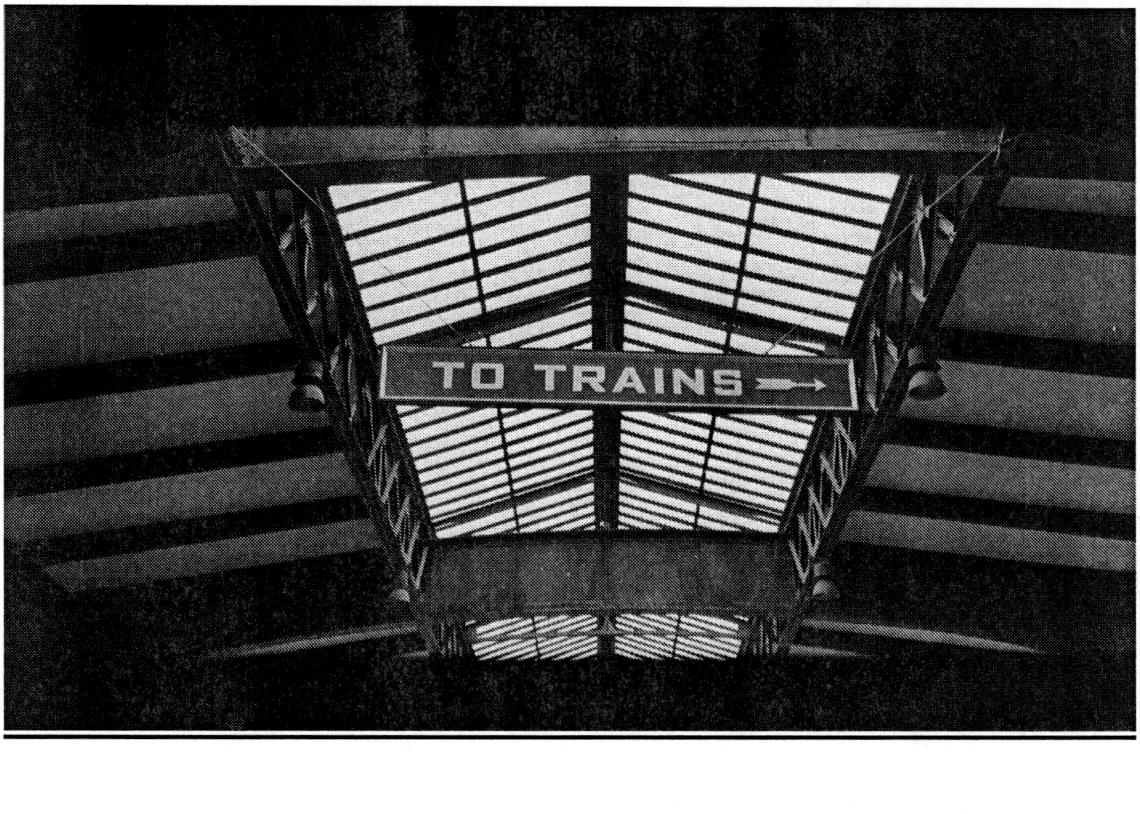
TO TRAINS

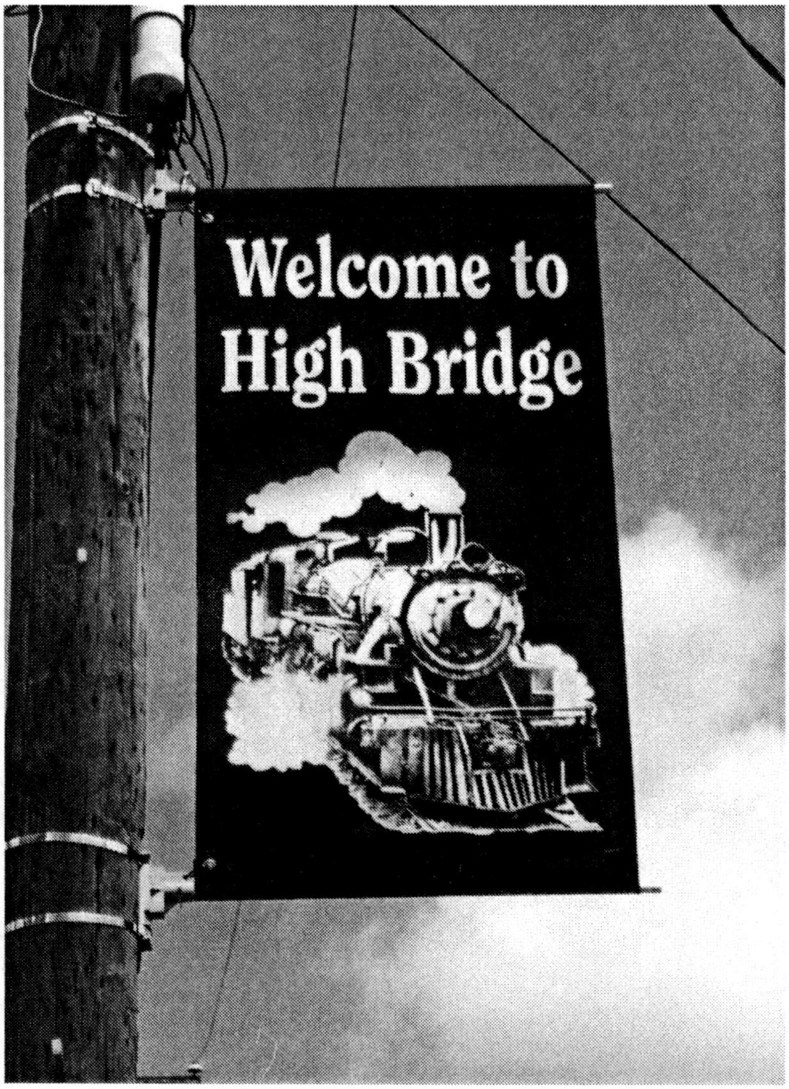
Welcome to
High Bridge

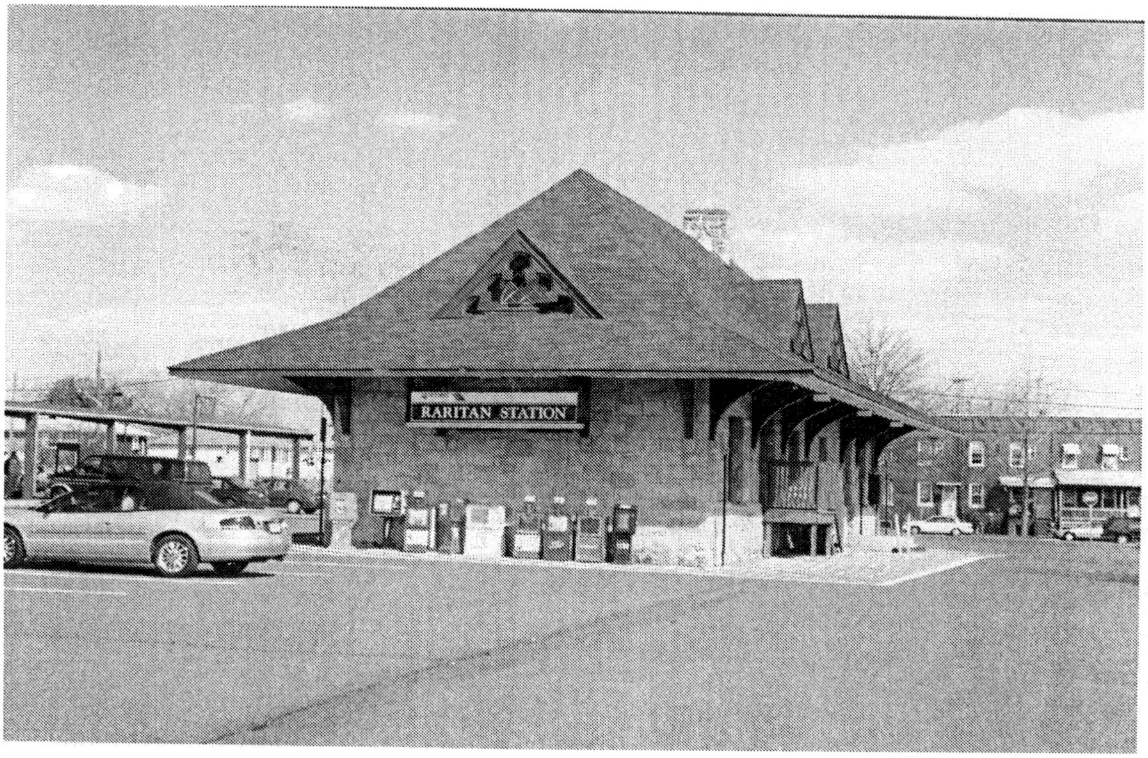
RARITAN STATION

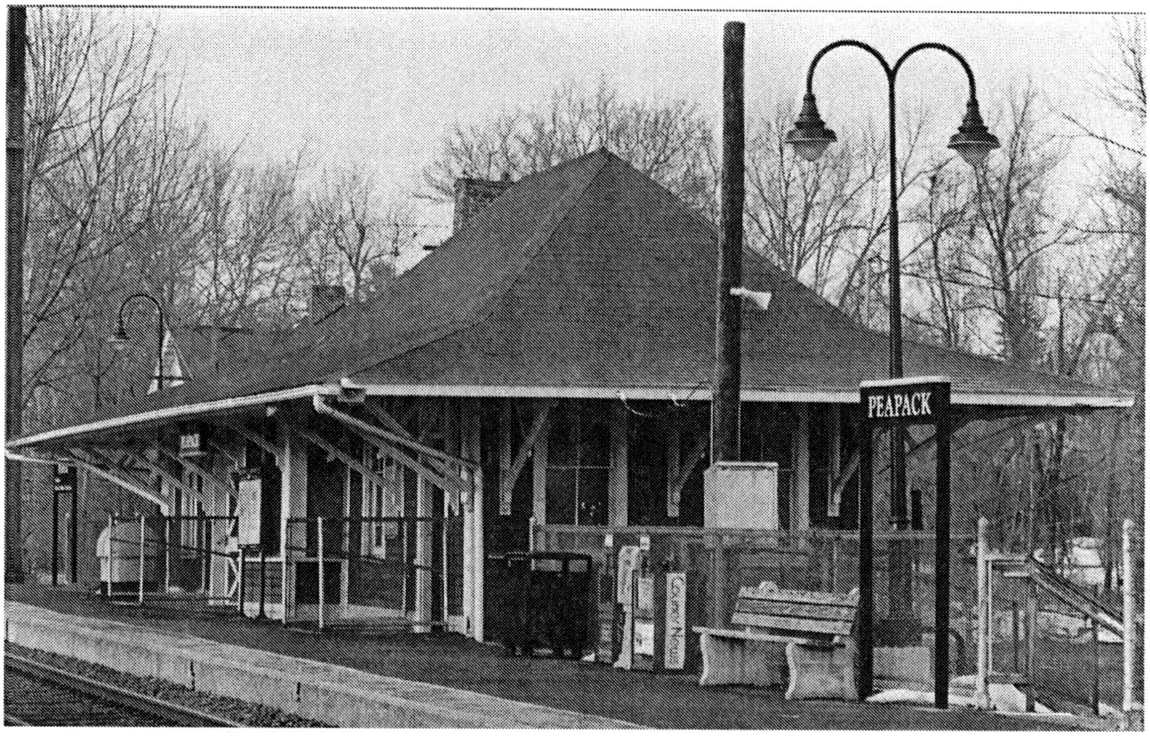
PEAPACK

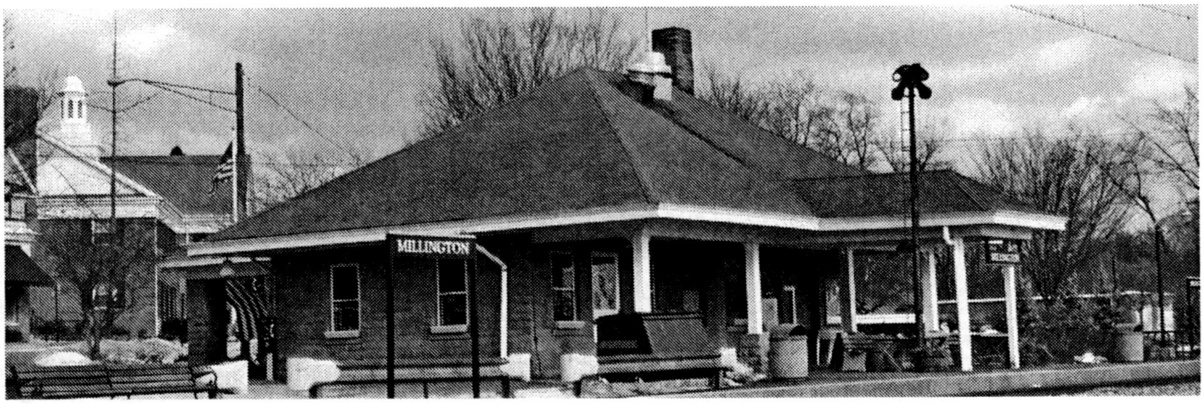
MILLINGTON

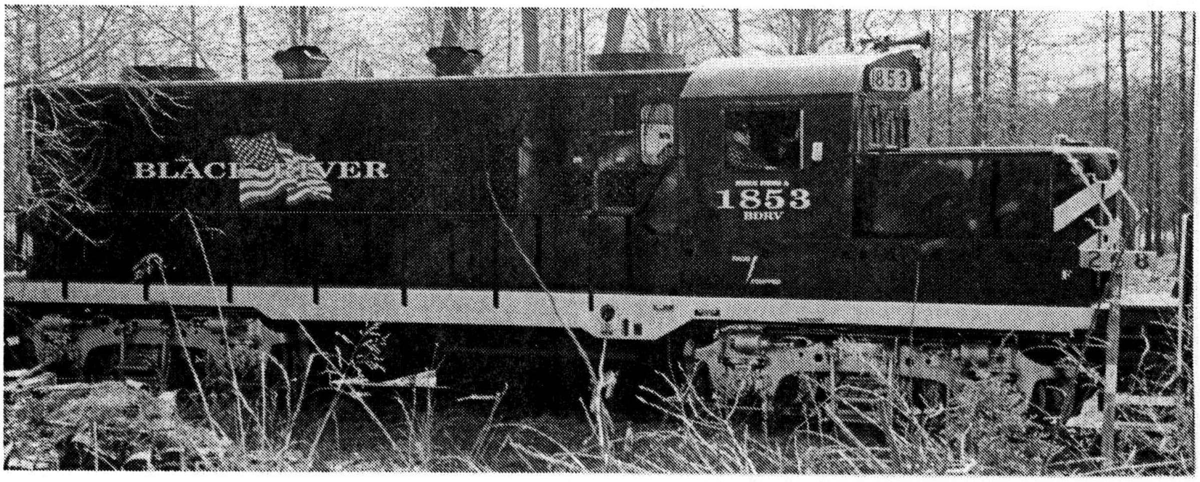
1853
BDRV

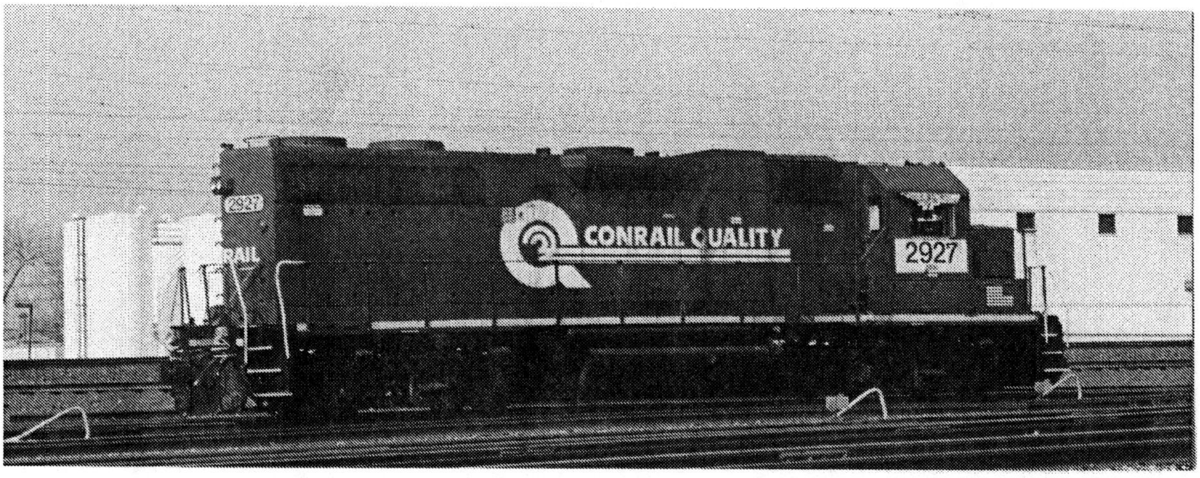
CONRAIL QUALITY
2927

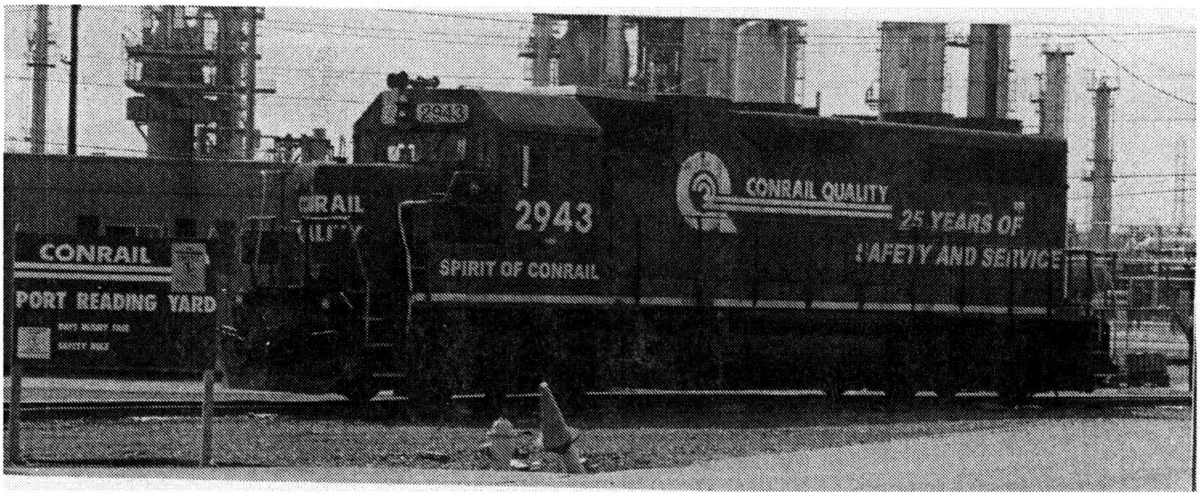
CONRAIL
PORT READING YARD
2943
SPIRIT OF CONRAIL
CONRAIL QUALITY
25 YEARS OF

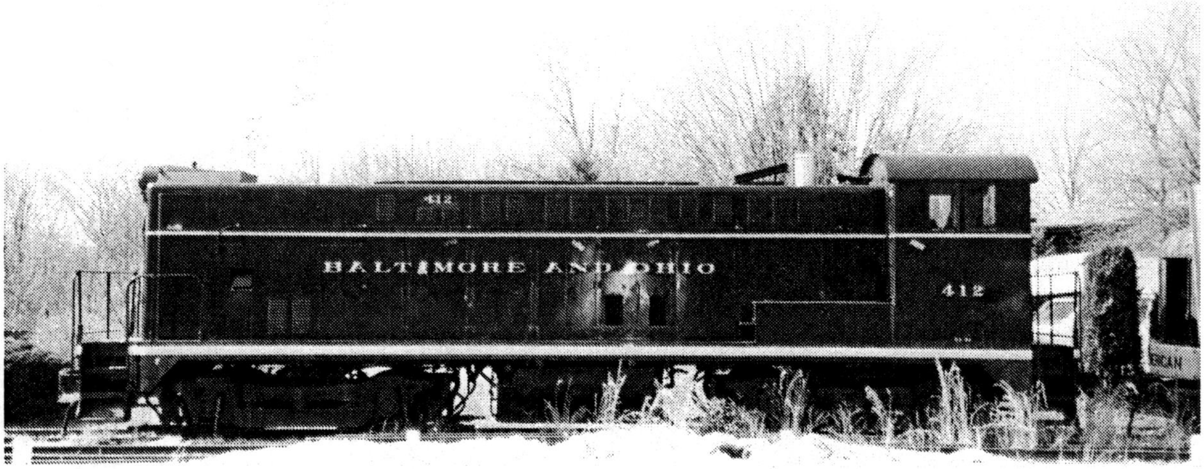
BALTIMORE AND OHIO
412

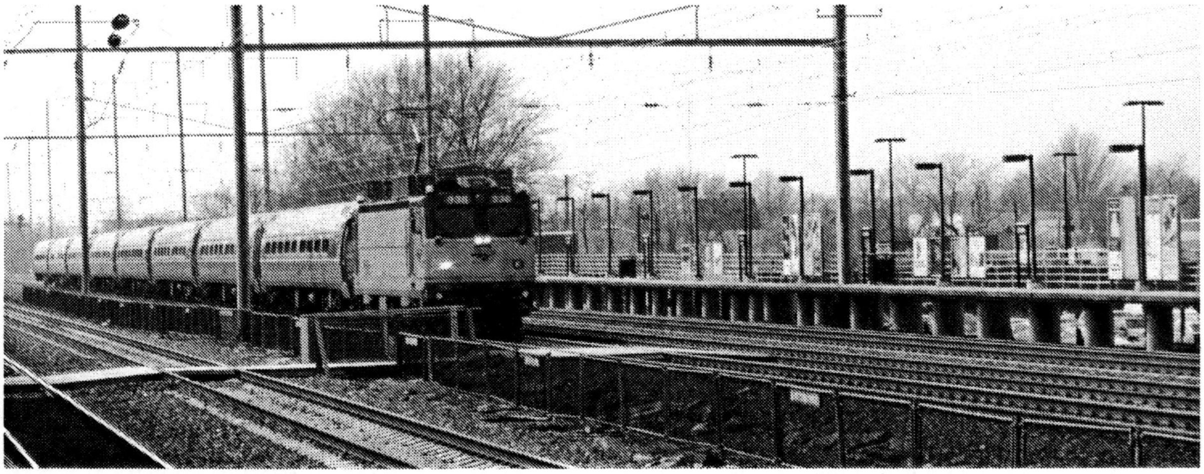

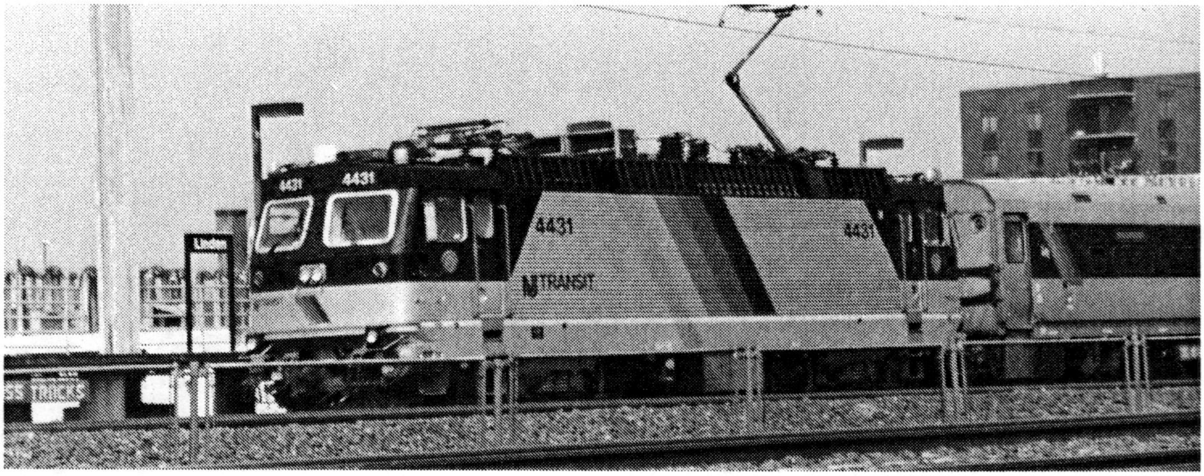
4431
TRANSIT
TRACKS

BIBLIOGRAPHY

Alden, John R. A History of the American Revolution. New York: Alfred A. Knopf Inc., 1969.

Anderson, Elaine. The Central Railroad of New Jersey's First 100 Years. Easton, PA: Center for Canal History and Technology, 1984.

Angle, Paul M. A Pictorial History of the Civil War Years. New York: Nelson Doubleday, Inc., 1967.

Aquilina, Charles L., Richard T. Koles, and Jean-Rae Turner. Elizabethtown and Union County: A Pictorial History. Norfolk, VA: The Donning Company, 1982.

Armstrong, Harry, and Tom Wilk. New Jersey Firsts: The Famous, Infamous, and Quirky of the Garden State. Philadelphia, PA: Camino Books Inc., 1999.

Bernet, Gerald E. Jersey Central Diesels. Halifax, PA: Withers Publishing, 1990.

Bill, Alfred Hoyt. New Jersey and the Revolutionary War. Princeton, N.J.: D. Van Nostrand Company Inc., 1964.

Bishop, Gordon. Gems of New Jersey. Englewood Cliffs, N.J.: Prentice Hall, Inc., 1985.

Bossler, Craig T. CNJ/LV Color Guide to Freight and Passenger Equipment. Edison, N.J.: Morning Sun Books Inc., 1994.

Braeman, John. The Road to Independence: A Documents History of the Cause of the American Revolution 1763-1776. New York: GP Putnam and Sons, 1963.

Brennan, William J. Jersey Central Lines in Color. Edison, N.J.: Morning Sun Books, Inc., 1991.

Brennan, William J. Jersey Central Lines in Color: Vol. 2. Edison, N.J.: Morning Sun Books, Inc., 1993.

Casey, Robert J., and W.A.S. Douglas. The Lackawanna Story: The First Hundred Years of the Delaware Lackawanna and Western RR. New York: McGraw-Hill Book Company, Inc., 1951.

Carleton, Paul. The Jersey Central Story. Dunnellon, Florida: D. Carleton Railbooks, 1992.

Carleton, Paul. The Hudson and Manhattan RR Revisited. Dunnellon, Florida: D. Carleton Books, 1990.

Cawley, James and Margaret. Along the Old York Road. Rahway, N.J.: Quinn and Bolden Company, Inc., 1965.

Cawley, James and Margaret. Exploring the Little Rivers of New Jersey. New Brunswick, N.J.: Rutgers University Press, 1961.

Clarke, Clorinda. The American Revolution 1775-83: A British View. New York: McGraw Hill Book Company, 1967.

Baxter, Raymond J., and Arthur G. Adams. Railroad Ferries of the Hudson and Stories of a deckhand. New York: Fordham University Press, 1999.

Clements, John. New Jersey Facts: A Comprehensive Look at New Jersey Today County by County. Dallas, TX.: Clements Research II, Inc., 1988.

Coates, Wes. 50th Anniversary 1931-1981 Suburban Electrification: Delaware, Lackawanna and Western RR. Jersey Central Chapter of the National Railway Historical Society, 1981.

Cunningham, John T. Newark. Newark, N.J.: Newark Historical Society, 1988.

Cunningham, John T. This is New Jersey. 3rd ed. New Brunswick, N.J.: Rutgers University Press, 1991.

Cunningham, John T. New Jersey: A Mirror on America. Florham Park, N.J.: Afton Publishing Company, 1976.

Cunningham, John T. Chatham: At the Crossing of the Fishawack. Chatham, N.J.: Chatham Historical Society, 1967.

Cunningham, John T. The New Jersey Sampler: Historic Tales of Old New Jersey. Upper Montclair, N.J.: The New Jersey Almanac Inc., 1964.

Donovan, Frank. Mr. Jeffersons Declaration: The Story Behind the Declaration of Independence. New York: Dodd, Mead and Company, 1968.

Daughen, Joseph R., and Peter Binzen. The Wreck of the Penn Central. New York: A Signet Book Published by the New American Library, 1971.

Della Penna, Craig P. 24 Great Rail-Trails of NJ: The Essential Outdoor Guide to the Garden State's Best Multi-Use Recreational Trails Built on Abandoned RR Grades. Amherst, Mass.: New England Cartographics, 1999.

Dorfinger, Don. Phoebe Snow: The Lady and the Train. Bernardsville, N.J.: Hill Press, 1979.

Dutcher, David C.G. A Concise History of the American Revolution. Eastern National 1999

Dwyer, William M. The Day is Ours: An Inside View of the Battles of Trenton and Princeton: November 1776-Jan 1977. New Brunswick, N.J.: Rutgers University Press, 1983.

Fast, Howard. The Crossing. Newark, N.J.: N.J. Historical Society, 1984.

Feirstein, Sanna. Naming New York: Manhattan Places and How They Got Their Names. New York: NY University Press, 2001.

Fleming, Thomas J. 1776 Year of Illusions. New York: W.W. Norton and Company, 1975.

Fleming, Thomas J. New Jersey: A History. New York: W.W. Norton and Company, 1984.

French, Kenneth. Railroads of Hoboken and Jersey City. Charleston, S.C.: Arcadia Publishing, 2002.

Hakim, Joy. A History of US From Colonies to Country 1710-1791. New York: Oxford University Press, 1993.

Hallahan, William H. The Day the American Revolution Began: 19 April 1775. New York: Harper Collins Publishers Inc., 2001.

Hansen, Harry. The Boston Massacre: An Episode of Dissent and Violence. New York: Hastings House, 1970.

Henderson, John. Jersey City Westbound. Flushing, N.Y.: H and M Productions.

Henderson, John. Gotham Turnstiles: A Visual Depiction of Rapid Transit in the New York Metropolitan Area From 1958-1968. Flushing, N.Y.: H and M Productions.

Hutton, Ann Hawkes. George Washington Crossed Here Christmas Night 1776. Philadelphia, PA.: Dorentz and Company, Inc., 1948.

Jacobs, Timothy. The History of the Baltimore and Ohio: America's First Railroad. New York: Crescent Books, 1989.

Jensen, USNR Lt. Oliver. Carrier War. New York: Pocket Books Inc., 1945.

Johnson, Curt. Battles of the American Revolution. New York; Bonanza Books, 1984.

Ketchum, Richard M. The Winter Soldiers. Garden City, NY: Doubleday Company, Inc., 1973.

Klein, Aaron E. The History of the New York Central System. Bonanza Books, 1985.

Komelski, Peter L. 26 Miles to Jersey City. Flanders, N.J.: Railroad Avenue Enterprises, Inc., 1983.

Lloyd Jr., Gordon. and Louis A. Marre. Conrail Motive Power Review: Vol 1 the First Ten Years 1976-1986. Glendale, California: Interurban Press, 1992.

Macken, Lynda Lee. Haunted Places in NJ: Ghosts of the Garden State. Forked River, N.J.: Black Cat Press, 2001.

McCloy, James F., and Ray Miller Jr. The Jersey Devil. Wallingford, PA.: The Middle Atlantic Press.

McCormick, Richard P. New Jersey From Colony to State 1609-1789. Cedar Grove, N.J.: Rae Publishing Company, 1981.

Nemeth, Tom, and Homer Hill. The Gladstone Branch: Affectionately Known as the P & D (Passaic and Delaware). Bernardsville, N.J.: Hill Press, 1978.

New Jersey Bell Telephone Company. Tales of NJ. 1963.

Pearsall, Ronald. Kings and Queens: A History of British Monarchy. New York: Todtri Productions Limited, 1996.

Pennisi, Bob. The Northeast Railroad Scene Vol. 4. the Erie Lackawanna: A Brief Look Before Conrail. Flanders, N.J.: Railroad Avenue Enterprises, 1979.

Pierce, Harry H. Railroads of NY: A Study in Govt Aid 1826-1875. Harvard, Mass.: Harvard University Press, 1953.

Robinson, Walter F., PHD. Old Bergen Township (Now Hudson County): In the American Revolution. Bayonne, N.J.: Bayonne Bicentennial Committee, 1978.

Rosenbaum, Joel, and Tom Gallo. Iron Horses Across the Garden State: New York to Philadelphia By Rail. Piscataway, N.J.: Rail Pace Publications, 1985.

Rosenbaum, Joel, and Tom Gallo. NJ Transit Rail Operations. Piscataway, N.J.: Railpace Company, Inc., 1996.

Rubel, David. America's War for Independence: A Concise Illustrated History of the American Revolution. New York: Silver Moon Press/Agincourt Press, 1992.

Sarapin, Janice Kohl. Old Burial Grounds of New Jersey: A Guide. New Brunswick, N.J.: Rutgers University Press, 1994.

Scleicher, William A., and Susan J. Winter. Somerset County: Crossroads of American Revolution. Charleston, S.C.: Arcadia Publishing, 1999.

Scull, Theodore W. Hobokens Lackawanna Terminal. New York: Quadrant Press, 1987.

Scull, Theodore W. The Staten Island Ferry. New York: Quadrant Press, 1982

Society of Colonial Wars in the State of New Jersey. Historic Roadsides in New Jersey. Philadelphia, PA: Press of Innes and Sons, 1928

Smith, Samuel Stelle. The Battle of Trenton. Monmouth Beach, N.J.: Phillip Freneau Press, 1965.

Stockton, Frank R. Stories of New Jersey. New Brunswick, N.J.: Rutgers University Press, 1961.

Sweetland, David R. Lackawanna Railroad in Color. Edison, N.J.: Morning Sun Books, Inc., 1990.

Thayer, Theodore. Colonial and Revolutionary Morris County. Morristown, N.J.: Compton Press Inc., 1975.

Tunis, Edwin. The Tavern at the Ferry. New York. Thomas Y. Crowell Company, 1973.

Michael E. Ferlise

Viet, Richard F. Old Canals of New Jersey: A Historical Geography. Little Falls, N.J.: NJ Geographical Press, 1963.

Yeats, Lauren Pancurak. Linden NJ. Dover, N.H.: Arcadia Publishing, 1997.

Zimmerman, Karl R. Erie Lackawanna East. New York: Quadrant Press, 1975.

Additionally, the following websites were referenced:

Amtrak: http://www.amtrak.com
Battleship New Jersey: http://www.battleship-newjersey.com
Bayonne: http://www.bayonnenj.org
Conrail: http://www.conrail.com
Long Hill: http://www.longhillnj.org
Morristown and Erie Railway Inc: http://www.merail.com
Morrisville: http://www.mv.org
New Jersey Transit: http://www.njtransit.com
Plainfield: http://www.plainfield.com
PSE & G: http://www.pseg.com
Robert R. Livingston: http://www.factmonster.com
September 11, 2001: http://cnn.com
Sussex County: http://www.gate.net
Yardley: http://www.livingplaces.com

Michael E. Ferlise

Newspapers that were referenced:

The Star Ledger

Periodicals that were referenced:

Gomez, John K., "Industrial Strength: Travels Through The Hudson and Manhattan Powerhouse." Weird NJ, Bloomfield, N.J.; Volume # 15, October 2000.

Moran, Mark, "The History, and the Mysteries of Blairsden." Weird NJ, Bloomfield, N.J.; Volume # 12, May 1999.

Michael E. Ferlise

About the Author

Michael E. Ferlise was born in 1971 and grew up in New Providence, New Jersey. He is a 1994 graduate from Kean College with a B.A. in Political Science. Michael has been employed as a New Jersey State Parole Officer assigned to Union County since 1997. He currently lives Basking Ridge.

Printed in the United States
16028LVS00001B/177-216